English in the Southern United States

The English of the southern United States is possibly the most studied regional variety of any language because of its rich internal diversity, its distinctiveness among regional varieties in the United States, its significance as a marker of regional identity, and the general folkloric appeal of southern culture. However, most if not all books about Southern American English have been directed almost exclusively toward scholars already working in the field. This volume, written by a team of experts many of whom are internationally known, provides a broad overview of the foundations of, and current research on, language variation in the southern United States designed to invite new inquiry and inquirers. It explores historical and cultural elements, iconic contemporary features, and current changes in progress. Central themes, issues, and topics of scholarly investigation and debate figure prominently throughout the volume. The extensive bibliography at the end of the book will facilitate continued research.

STEPHEN J. NAGLE is Professor of English at Coastal Carolina University. He is the author of *Inferential Change and Syntactic Modality in English* (1989), editor of a monograph on political changes in eastern Europe (1992), and the author or co-author of articles on English historical syntax, auxiliary verbs in southern English, and teaching English as a second language.

SARA L. SANDERS is Professor of English at Coastal Carolina University. She is the author or co-author of articles related to language use, language learning, and language diversity. She was the compositor of the *Linguistic Atlas of the Middle and South Atlantic States* (*LAMSAS*) for three years.

English in the Southern United States

STUDIES IN ENGLISH LANGUAGE

The aim of this series is to provide a framework for original work on the English language. All are based securely on empirical research, and represent theoretical and descriptive contributions to our knowledge of national varieties of English, both written and spoken. The series will cover a broad range of topics in English grammar, vocabulary, discourse, and pragmatics, and is aimed at an international readership.

Already published

Christian Mair
Infinitival complement clauses in English: a study of syntax in discourse

Charles F. Meyer
Apposition in contemporary English

Jan Firbas
Functional sentence perspective in written and spoken communication

Izchak M. Schlesinger
Cognitive space and linguistic case

Katie Wales
Personal pronouns in present-day English

Laura Wright
The development of standard English, 1300–1800: theories, descriptions, conflicts

Charles F. Meyer
English corpus linguistics: theory and practice

English in the Southern United States

Edited by

STEPHEN J. NAGLE
Coastal Carolina University

and

SARA L. SANDERS
Coastal Carolina University

CAMBRIDGE
UNIVERSITY PRESS

CAMBRIDGE UNIVERSITY PRESS
Cambridge, New York, Melbourne, Madrid, Cape Town, Singapore, São Paulo

Cambridge University Press
The Edinburgh Building, Cambridge CB2 8RU, UK

Published in the United States of America by Cambridge University Press, New York

www.cambridge.org
Information on this title: www.cambridge.org/9780521822640

First published 2003
Third printing 2006

A catalogue record for this publication is available from the British Library

Library of Congress Cataloguing in Publication data

English in the southern United States/edited by Stephen J. Nagle and Sara L. Sanders.
    p.   cm. – (Studies in English language)
Includes bibliographical references and index.
ISBN 0 521 82264 5
    1. English language – Southern States.   2. English language – Southern States – Foreign
elements–African.   3. English language–Social aspects–Southern States.   4. African Americans–
Southern States – Languages.   5. English language – Variation – Southern States.   6. English
language – Dialects – Southern States.   7. African languages – Influence on English.   8. Black
English – Southern States.   9. Americanisms – Southern States.   I. Nagle, Stephen J., 1948–
II. Sanders, Sara L.   III. Series.

PE2922 .E54 2003
427′.975 – dc21   2002073585

ISBN 978-0-521-82264-0 hardback

Transferred to digital printing 2008

This book is dedicated to
Michael Montgomery,
a linguist's linguist and a true southern gentleman,
whose work continues to shape the course of the
study of Southern English

Contents

Notes on the contributors	*page* xi	
Acknowledgments	xiv	
	Introduction	1
1	The origins of Southern American English JOHN ALGEO	6
2	Shakespeare in the coves and hollows? Toward a history of Southern English EDGAR SCHNEIDER	17
3	Eight grammatical features of southern United States speech present in early modern London prison narratives LAURA WRIGHT	36
4	The shared ancestry of African-American and American-White Southern Englishes: some speculations dictated by history SALIKOKO MUFWENE	64
5	The complex grammatical history of African-American and white vernaculars in the South PATRICIA CUKOR-AVILA	82
6	Grammatical features of southern speech: *yall*, *might could*, and *fixin to* CYNTHIA BERNSTEIN	106
7	Sounding southern: a look at the phonology of English in the South GEORGE DORRILL	119

8   Vowel shifting in the southern states   126
    CRAWFORD FEAGIN

9   Enclave dialect communities in the South   141
    WALT WOLFRAM

10 Urbanization and the evolution of Southern American
    English   159
    JAN TILLERY AND GUY BAILEY

11 The Englishes of southern Louisiana   173
    CONNIE EBLE

12 Features and uses of southern style   189
    BARBARA JOHNSTONE

    References   208
    Index   233

Notes on the contributors

John Algeo is Professor Emeritus at the University of Georgia. He is the author, co-author, or editor of several books including the third, fourth, and fifth editions of *The Origins and Development of the English Language* (with Thomas Pyles) and volume 6 of the *Cambridge History of the English Language*. He has been a Fulbright Research Fellow and a Guggenheim Fellow at the University of London and was Editor of *American Speech* for ten years. He is a Past-President of the American Dialect Society.

Guy Bailey is Provost and Vice President for Academic Affairs at the University of Texas – San Antonio. He is the author, co-author, or co-editor of nine books and monographs, including *African-American English: Structure, History and Use* (1998, with Salikoko S. Mufwene, John R. Rickford, and John Baugh) and has been author or co-author of over sixty journal articles on African-American Vernacular English, Southern English, creole Englishes, sociolinguistics, and dialectology

Cynthia Goldin Bernstein is Professor of English at the University of Memphis. She is the author of articles in *American Speech, Journal of English Linguistics, SECOL Review*, editor or co-editor of three books including *Language Variety in the South Revisited* (1997, with Thomas Nunnally and Robin Sabino) and *Windows on Southern Speech* (in progress). Her articles and book chapters cover both linguistic and literary topics.

Patricia Cukor-Avila is Associate Professor of English at the University of North Texas. She is co-editor of *The Emergence of Black English: Texts and Commentary* (1991, with Guy Bailey and Natalie Maynor). In addition to her articles on sociolinguistics, she has written articles and given conference presentations on bilingualism and language acquisition.

George T. Dorrill is Associate Professor of English at Southeastern Louisiana University. He is the author of *Black and White Speech in the Southern United States: Evidence from the Linguistic Atlas of the Middle and South Atlantic States* (1987) and of several articles on the phonology of southern speech. He is a former assistant editor of the *Linguistic Atlas of the Middle and South Atlantic States* and is co-author of articles during the early stages (1970s) of compilation and publication of fieldwork for that project.

Connie Eble is Professor of English at the University of North Carolina – Chapel Hill and has been Editor of *American Speech*, quarterly journal of the American Dialect Society since 1996. She published *Slang and Sociability: In-Group Language Among College Students* (1996) and is the leading authority on college slang in the United States.

Crawford Feagin was mostly recently Visiting Professor at the University of Zurich and was a Fulbright Professor at the University of Klagenfurt (Austria). She is the co-editor or author of five books including *Towards a Social Science of Language: I Variation and Change in Language* and *II: Social Interaction and Discourse Structure* (1996, 1997, with Gregory Guy, Deborah Schiffrin, and John Baugh), and *Development and Diversity: Linguistic Variation across Time and Space* (1990, with Jerold A. Edmondson and Peter Mühlhaüsler).

Barbara Johnstone is Professor of English and Rhetoric at Carnegie Mellon University. She works at the interdisciplinary intersection of discourse analysis, sociolinguistics, and critical theory and is the author of five books including *Qualitative Methods in Sociolinguistics* (2000), *The Linguistic Individual* (1996), and *Stories, Community, and Place* (1990). She is also the author of a book on Arabic discourse and has written numerous research articles and book chapters about narrative, repetition, self-expression and regional variation.

Salikoko S. Mufwene is Professor of Linguistics at the University of Chicago. He has held visiting professorships at the Université de Lyon III, the University of the West Indies, the National University of Singapore, and Harvard University. He is the author of *The Ecology of Language Evolution* (2001), co-author of *Creolization of Language and Culture* (2001, with Robert Chaudenson – main author); and editor of *Africanisms in Afro-American Language* (1993), *Topics in African Linguistics* (1993, with Lioba Moshi); and *African-American English: Structure, History, and Use* (1998, with John R. Rickford, Guy Bailey, and John Baugh).

Edgar W. Schneider is Professor of English Linguistics at the University of Regensburg, Germany, after previous appointments in Bamberg, Georgia, and Berlin. He has written and edited several books (including *American Earlier Black English*, 1989; *Introduction to Quantitative Analysis of Linguistic Survey Data*, 1996; *Focus on the USA*, 1996; *Englishes Around the World*, 1997; *Degrees of Restructuring in Creole Languages*, 2000) and has published widely on the dialectology, sociolinguistics, history, semantics, and varieties of English.

Jan Tillery is Associate Professor of English at the University of Texas – San Antonio. She is the author or co-author of articles on southern speech and the methodology of sociolinguistics including "The nationalization of a southernism" (2000, with Guy Bailey, *Journal of English Linguistics*) and "The Rutledge effect: the impact of interviewers of survey results in linguistics" (1999, with Guy Bailey, *American Speech*).

Walt Wolfram is William C. Friday Distinguished Professor at North Carolina State University. He has pioneered research on a wide range of American vernacular dialects, including many southern varieties, and has authored or co-authored sixteen books including *American English: Dialects and Variation* (1998), *Language Variation in School and Community (1999)*, and a seminal descriptive linguistic book on African-American Vernacular English: *A Sociolinguistic Description of Detroit Negro Speech (1969)*. He is the author of over two hundred articles on a broad range of sociolinguistic topics.

Laura Wright is Lecturer in English Language at the University of Cambridge, and works on the history of English from documentary sources, particularly the history of the London dialect. In 2000 she published an edited volume (*The Development of Standard English 1300–1800: Theories, Descriptions, Conflicts*) reopening the question of how standard English came about. Most recently Wright has been transcribing sixteenth-century testimonies from London's Bridewell, from whence speakers were transported to Virginia and the Caribbean plantations, and eighteenth-century documents from the island of St. Helena, which contain testimonies from both the white employees of the East India Company who lived there, and their black slaves.

Acknowledgments

The editors gratefully acknowledge Coastal Carolina University's support of this project through the Thomas W. and Robin W. Edwards College of Humanities and Fine Arts, especially the encouragement and resources of Charles Joyner, director of the Waccamaw Center for Cultural and Historical Studies. We also appreciate the able and willing assistance of Geoffrey Parsons, Patricia Bennett, and Lori Ard in the University's Office of International Programs, whose friendship, expertise, and technology eased our way in producing a final, edited version of this manuscript.

We are indebted to the Southeastern Conference on Linguistics (SECOL), which has provided and continues to provide a fertile ground for the exploration of all aspects of Southern English. The idea for this volume emerged during discussions at a SECOL conference; all of the people involved in the writing and editing of this book have contributed significantly to that organization and have gained much from its conferences and publications. Special thanks to SECOL members Thomas Nunnally, Greta Little, and Connie Eble who provided advice in the early stages of this project.

It has been a pleasure to work with Katharina Brett, Senior Commissioning Editor in Language and Linguistics at Cambridge University Press. She is remarkably effective and efficient, and this volume has profited from her suggestions and keen insights.

Above all, we'd like to thank the authors for their enthusiastic response to the invitation to write a chapter for this book, for their carefully considered contributions, and for their invaluable and timely editorial advice at each stage of the process. It has truly been a privilege to be in partnership with this fine group of linguists, scholars, and writers.

Introduction

The English of the southern United States may be the most studied regional variety of any language. Though there has been no comprehensive bibliography on the topic since Michael Montgomery and James McMillan's (1989) admirable annotated compilation with over 3,500 entries, it is safe to say that the number of articles, monographs, and books on Southern English approaches or exceeds 4,000, with no abatement in sight. What is the allure of this variety of English? Perhaps its rich internal diversity, perhaps its distinctiveness among regional varieties in the United States, perhaps the folkloric appeal of southern culture in general. Whatever attracts so many to Southern English, Michael Montgomery stands in the vanguard of the myriad scholars who have explored the language and culture of the South. Michael is the quintessential linguist. As author, collaborator, corpus linguist, editor, field researcher, lexicographer, mentor, writer and recipient of grants, he has set a standard for leadership and achievement as a scholar. References in the ensuing chapters to over thirty of his works are not for honorific purposes; his imprint is found in virtually every research area within the study of Southern English.

Inspired by Michael Montgomery's life and work, the authors and editors of *English in the Southern United States* have undertaken the challenge of creating a volume to capture the past and present of Southern English, to bring our field of research to an even broader community, and to serve as a small platform for launching future research in southern studies. We have endeavored to enrich the climate of ongoing and future inquiry by exploring central themes, issues, and topics in the study of Southern English. Throughout the volume, previous and new data on iconic linguistic features and cultural origins of this diverse regional variety are investigated. Finally, an extensive bibliography provides an additional resource to facilitate further research. Since this is, then, both an up-to-date scholarly text and an introduction (and invitation) to the field, we have organized the contributions in chapters which stand independently but are also arranged in a sequence that might prove useful for instructional purposes.

John Algeo opens the volume with an outline of the principal cultural elements of the linguistic heredity of the southern United States. He first, however,

cautions the reader that concepts such as *language*, *family*, and *descent* are useful but limited metaphors, noting that "a language is not a thing," but rather
"a general abstract system (*langue*) embracing many such abstract systems
(*paroles*) that overlap in major ways" and that "Southern American English is not
a thing or a single entity." Thus, "no Hadrian's Wall divides Southern American
English from Midland American English." He then examines "multiple lines of
descent" in the linguistic heredity of the South, most prominently the "English
core," the "Scots-Irish stratum" and the "African stratum." Finally he explores
the notion of "choice" in the development and evolution of a language variety, from maintaining earlier forms to borrowing through language contact, to
outright innovation.

In chapter 2, Edgar Schneider follows in the spirit of Algeo's metaphorical
view of *language* and related terms, stating that it is "presumptuous to talk of
'Southern English' as a putatively homogeneous entity in itself." His title
"Shakespeare in the coves and hollows? . . . " evokes the pop-culture folk notion
that vernacular Southern English is essentially archaic and Elizabethan.
Schneider embarks on a detailed look at several iconic features of southern speech
in order to determine how archaic or innovative this variety actually is. Using his
own research and extensively incorporating the work of others, he acknowledges
that there is "some limited continuity of forms derived from British dialects,"
but he concurs with Bailey (1997b) that many of the oft-noted features of today's
Southern English have developed or rapidly increased in usage since the middle
to late nineteenth century.

In chapter 3, Laura Wright reinforces Algeo's suggestion of an English core
source for southern speech. There has been considerable investigation of and
focus on Scots-Irish elements in southern vernacular in the past fifteen years as
well, and many have postulated creole sources for various features of African-
American and, to a lesser degree, southern white vernaculars. Using data from
London court and prison archives, Wright's research finds Early Modern English
vernacular predecessors of some hallmark grammatical features of current
Southern vernacular, some of which have been previously attributed primarily to external influences, such as West African creole or Scots-Irish, for example
a+verb+*ing* (as in *he was a making water against the wall*). Another interesting
example is her citations of some potential antecedents of adverbial *liketa* (as in
I liketa died = "nearly"), which is sometimes viewed as a new form. As she notes,
the earlier uses of *like to* (*liketa*) are not semantically and syntactically identical
with current usage in the South, but her data suggest the potential for historical
transmission. She concludes her chapter by examining how her investigated features have advanced and declined in usage and have assumed new sociolinguistic
and ethnic identities, becoming "indexical of social properties such as region,
class, and race."

Continuing the explorations of linguistic and cultural ancestry, Salikoko
Mufwene in chapter 4 examines various positions on the sociohistorical relationship between African-American Vernacular English and the vernacular English

of southern whites, a sometimes contentious topic of debate over the last three decades. While acknowledging limited creole influence on the speech of the South, he discounts the notion of an early discrete creole-influenced African-American vernacular interacting with a similarly discrete early white koiné. He proposes alternatively that the numerous commonalities between the two vernaculars "can be explained primarily by their common, coextensive histories of over 200 years during which their speakers interacted regularly with each other," while many of their differences "can be attributed to the divergence that resulted from the widespread institutionalization of segregation in the late nineteenth century."

Patricia Cukor-Avila examines in chapter 5 characteristic grammatical features of African-American Vernacular English (AAVE) and Southern White Vernacular English (SWVE) investigated in previous research, and incorporates new data from recorded interviews with African Americans and whites between 1907 and 1982 in an ongoing ethnolinguistic study of rural Texas speech. Comparing the results of this research with other studies, she maintains that the relationship between grammars of the vernacular speech of African Americans and whites is one of both shared and unique features that have changed over time, reflecting historical periods in which the respective populations have been in closer or more distant social proximity. She notes that "because both vernaculars are changing over time as reflexes of their sociohistorical context, making generalizations about the relationship between AAVE and SWVE grammars is difficult at best." Her chapter nonetheless captures important generalizations about similarities and divergent features within these varieties.

In chapter 6 Cynthia Bernstein examines three core grammatical features of southern speech evident to the linguist and the non-linguist alike: pronominal *yall*, modal auxiliary combinations such as *might could*, and inchoative *fixin to* (= "about to"), with considerable attention to the body of relevant research. She chooses these three features since "their use is spread widely among regional and social dialects in the South," and they "are not associated with one particular variety of Southern English." Her discussion of *yall* ranges from theories of its origin to its several linguistic functions. She selects *might could* as a canonical example of the "double modal" or "multiple modal" auxiliaries common in the southern United States (and found to varying degrees in northern British English and Scots vernaculars as well) and examines their history, meaning, structure, and use. Her discussion of *fixin to* (*I was just fixin to leave*) centers on evidence for its grammaticalization as a "quasi-modal." Finally, to put these features in the broader grammatical context of Southern English, she revisits Wolfram and Schilling-Estes' (1998) outline of its principal grammatical traits.

Chapters 7 and 8 deal exclusively with phonology. George Dorrill, noting Michael Montgomery's (1989a) statement that "the South is the most distinct speech region in the United States," points to the difficulty in identifying a set of phonological features that delimit southern speech, even with the salience of phonology to the identity of Southern English. He ascribes this difficulty to

4 Stephen J. Nagle and Sara L. Sanders

extensive regional and sociolinguistic variation as well as continuing phonological evolution and innovation. Nonetheless, his survey of early and more recent dialectal investigations and specific phonological features recurrent in them establishes a core repertoire of sounds of the South. Crawford Feagin then elaborately examines research on perhaps the most widespread of ongoing current southern phonological innovations: the "Southern Shift" first identified by William Labov and his colleagues three decades ago. Feagin compares and contrasts findings of the major studies, by herself and others, on this fascinating change in progress and argues that "the combination of vowel shifting and diphthongization [in the South] results in an extremely complex phonology," distinguishing this region from the rest of the country. She also maintains that ongoing contact between southern and non-southern varieties "suggests a coming homogenization and consolidation in the South." Southern phonology will nonetheless remain distinctive (though perhaps less so than previously) since other regions are undergoing their own phonological evolution.

In chapter 9, Walt Wolfram explores the nature of dialect enclaves, areas in which "a speech community has been historically disconnected from the wider socio-spatial, dominant population groups in the region." Four such enclaves in the South are selected for this study, each of which has been investigated separately by Wolfram and his colleagues from the mid 1970s to the present. His purpose here is not so much to elucidate comprehensively various linguistic features of each of the enclave communities (though many of these features are discussed), but rather to "understand the kinds of general sociolinguistic principles that might account for their dialect maintenance and development." Similarly to Schneider's (in this volume) and Bailey's (1997b) emphasis on innovation in the South, he stresses that enclave dialects are not to be seen as insular repositories of "traditional dialect features." Instead, there is no rule: the Chesapeake Bay dialect "seems to be intensifying among younger speakers" in the face of increased external exposure, while the Outer Banks dialect of North Carolina seems to be waning. Thus, in looking at language varieties "it is necessary to recognize the unique social and linguistic circumstances that characterize each speech community and their effect on language change and maintenance within that community."

While many of the chapters in this volume discuss conservative and innovative forms in varieties of Southern English, Jan Tillery and Guy Bailey in chapter 10 focus almost exclusively on linguistic innovation in the South. Presenting evidence from a variety of research projects of their own, oftentimes with various colleagues, and from other research studies, they compile a formidable body of support for the claim of Bailey (1997b) that innovation, not conservatism as is often suggested in the popular culture, is responsible for the distinctiveness of southern speech. Indeed, they state, Southern English "is not a conservative dialect bound to its past, but rather a dynamic, innovative variety that has experienced rapid, fundamental change over the last century and a quarter," much of whose change "coincides with two major periods of urbanization . . . and with the dialect contact that resulted from urbanization."

Connie Eble in chapter 11 leads the reader into the world of Louisiana English, exotic (along with its Louisiana French counterparts) in the popular culture and a target of considerable linguistic research as well. Although dialects of French have received more scholarly attention than have their English neighbors, she notes that "the Englishes that developed in the formerly French-speaking regions of Louisiana offer patterns of dialect variation almost as difficult to distinguish as do French varieties." Grounding her discussion in the historical setting of French and English in Louisiana, Eble presents central features of Cajun English and New Orleans English and flavors her discussion with references to popular handbooks, pamphlets, and glossaries (some electronic). It becomes apparent in her blend of linguistic research and pop-culture treatments how closely language is linked to social and regional identity in Louisiana.

Barbara Johnstone closes the volume with a portrait of southern speech in discourse, that is, "southern style." From politeness, to conditional syntax and indirectness ("negative politeness"), to verbal artistry in oratory and everyday discourse, to story telling/narrative, she analyzes rhetorical foundations of southern speech. She then looks at how these strategies are put to use. Her chapter concludes with a detailed discussion of the importance of work still to be done since "some southerners continue to orient to and use language differently from people elsewhere, and some people from elsewhere continue to draw on stereotyped notions of what southern speech means as they evaluate and interact with southerners and the South." Will features of southern style accommodate to increased contact with other varieties or will southern style persist and evolve as a response to maintain "localness" in the face of outside forces?

It will surely be fascinating – to the cultural anthropologist, the historian, the linguist, the sociologist, and anyone else who as profession or avocation watches the evolution of communities – to follow the future paths of English in the southern United States, a region where for so many people speech is at the core of their southern identity. The authors and editors invite and encourage new exploration and new explorers of Southern English, and we thank Michael Montgomery for bringing us to this task.

1   The origins of Southern American English

JOHN ALGEO

1   Introduction

The origins of Southern American English can be found on the islands off the shore of the Netherlands and in northern Germany and southern Denmark (where English speakers dwelled before they crossed the channel to invade the British Isles) or, to go back a bit further, on grassy plains somewhere in mid Eurasia (where the Proto-Indo-European-speaking peoples had their Urheimat) and, even before that, perhaps in the Great Rift Valley of East Africa (where *Homo sapiens* may have originated). That is, Southern American English has the same origins as all other dialects of English, all Indo-European languages, and maybe all human languages.

To be sure, such answers to the question "What are the origins of Southern American English?" go deeper into origins than the question normally asks for. But it is important to keep in mind that, when we talk about the "origins" of anything, our talk is always relative to other things and times. To ask about the "origins" of a speechway like Southern presumes that it popped into existence at some point as a departure from another speechway.

But all language is always changing, so every *état de langue* is at every moment a departure from what it used to be. Southern did not depart from "general" American, much less early Modern English or Proto-Germanic or Proto-Indo-European or Proto-Human. Like the galaxies of the cosmos, all languages are flying apart from one another, and there is no center. To compare language to the expanding universe is, however, a metaphor, and we need to be wary of metaphor.

2   Metaphors of origin

Most talk about languages and their history – like talk about everything else – uses metaphor. Much of our discourse is necessarily metaphorical. Metaphor can be enlightening, but it also "darkeneth counsel by words without knowledge" when we forget its limitations. We discuss the history of languages with metaphors that have severe limitations, and the only practical way to deal with those limitations is to be aware of them.

With languages, a pervasive metaphor is reification, by which we treat an abstraction as though it were a physical thing. A language is not a thing; it has no shape, weight, size, or color. A language is a personal abstract system in the mind, brain, tongue, and ears of each user. Or, more accurately, a language is a general abstract system (*langue*) embracing many such personal abstract systems (*paroles*) that overlap one another in major ways.

Each personal system is constantly changing throughout the lifetime of its user; and consequently each general system is constantly changing as well. The reality is an ever adapting, fluctuating, fuzzy, messy pattern of behavior more or less shared by a great many persons at any one time, whose history we try to relate as though it were instead a thing with a clear outline and identity, like a pyramid or a canyon.

Southern American English is not a thing or a single entity. Lee Pederson (2001) has analyzed what is here called "Southern" into eighteen subvarieties on four hierarchical levels:

Southern
   Coastal
      Atlantic
      Gulf
   Interior
      Piedmont
      Gulf Plains
         eastern
         central
         western
   Delta
      upper
         Arkansas River basin
         Yazoo River basin
         Red River basin
      lower
         Atchafalaya River basin
         Lower Mississippi River basin
South Midland
   highlands
      eastern: Virginia, Kentucky, east Tennessee, Georgia Blue Ridge
      central: middle Tennessee, upper Alabama Cumberlands
      western: Missouri and Arkansas Ozarks
   piney woods
      Georgia and Alabama wire grass
      Florida and Alabama sand hills and pine flats
      Mississippi and Louisiana piney woods
      east Texas pine flats   (Pederson 2001)

Each of these subvarieties (which could be further subdivided right down to the momentary existence of their speakers' idiolects) has its own characteristic features of phonology, vocabulary, and grammar; and each of those characteristics has its own origin and history. When we look at language systems in this way, we catch a glimpse of the Buddhist principle of *anatman*, namely that nothing has a separate, whole identity. Does an abstraction have an origin in the way a thing does?

Another metaphor of language history is that of the "family." We talk of "relatedness," "sister languages," "descent," "parent languages," and so on. Such metaphors not only reify languages, but they also treat them as personal entities with a life span, distinct boundaries separating them, and clearly definable relationships with one another. Languages are not persons that spawn one another, but a system that alters so much over time that we find it useful to define boundaries between its stages and to give distinct names to the stages we have defined.

A closely related metaphor is that of the language tree, which is useful on a gross level but cannot easily diagram some important language connections. For example, languages not only develop out of one another, but also affect one another in various other ways. In a typical language tree diagram, English is shown to be a development of the West Germanic branch of Proto-Germanic. But Latin has been a major influence on English vocabulary, either directly or through French, by both its native Italic word-stock and its borrowings from Greek. Moreover, French and Norse have significantly affected English grammar. And over the course of time, a variety of causes have radically changed the typological structure of English from dominantly inflectional to dominantly isolating. None of that is shown by a tree diagram, which treats each language system as though it were an independent and stabile entity.

But that's not the way a language is. The boundaries, both diachronic and synchronic, between one speechway and another are, to a considerable extent, arbitrary. No Hadrian's Wall divides Southern American English from Midland American English, or early Modern English from late Modern. One speechway flows into another, chronologically, spatially, socially, and in every other way. It is for our convenience and our interest that we create the divisions we draw between speechways.

For geographical, historical, cultural, and other reasons, we recognize a regional dialect of English in America we call "Southern." That dialect has some features of lexis and grammar that, in their sum, are different from the sum of contrasting features in other dialects. It is therefore reasonable to ask about the origins of those features and their sum. And that, in fact, is what we mean when we ask, "What are the origins of Southern American English?" But in answering that question, we need to keep in mind that Southern American English is not a thing with clearly defined boundaries, but is instead a generalized pattern of a large number of personal abstract mental systems and associated behavior that are ill defined and ever changing.

We cannot escape metaphors in talking about language origins. But we can be aware of them, and we can vary them. One variation is to think of the origins of a language as comparable to the origins of a human personality, the product of heredity, environment, and choice.

3   The heredity of Southern American English

The heredity of Southern American English involves neither two parents, as the family metaphor suggests, nor a single ancestor, as the language tree depicts. It includes multiple lines of descent.

3.1   The English core

The first origins of Southern American English are in the initial colonial settlement by British immigrants. The first permanent English-speaking settlement in America was in Jamestown, Virginia, in 1607, so American English began with Southern. The colony never thrived, partly because its land was marshy and thus unhealthful and partly because its leading settlers were of an English class unaccustomed to the rigors of pioneering, so it was more of a curtain-raiser than a first act. Yet Jamestown is notable as the place where the economically important crop of tobacco was first cultivated, the first African slaves were imported, and the first representative government was established. All of those features were to be characteristic of the American South, and the last one of America as a whole.

The first settlers of the American colonies had a variety of origins (Bailyn 1986a,b). David Hackett Fischer (whose views on cultural continuity have not gone unchallenged) has proposed a colonial settlement of America from Britain in four major waves, of which that occurring in 1642–75 brought immigrants from southern and western England, consisting principally of gentry and their servants. The early settlement of the American South was therefore unlike that of most of the other early colonies, where the immigrants were preponderantly middle or independent working class. The early period of the Virginia settlement coincided with the English Civil War and Puritan Commonwealth, when younger sons, whose traditional careers in the army or clergy were closed to them by the Puritan government of England, flocked to the New World to seek their fortunes. Yet by far the bulk of the early Virginia settlers were indentured servants: rural, male, and illiterate. The "ancestral connection to southern and southwestern England" has accordingly been called "the Cavalier myth of the Old Dominion's origin" (Montgomery 2001: 110).

Fischer (1989: 256–64), citing a variety of studies, attributes practically all Virginia linguistic characteristics to the dialects of the south and west of England. Moreover, because of the gentry's associations with the motherland, a firmer connection was maintained with England than was the case in other colonies, so linguistic influence was also maintained. For example, [r]-dropping in America, probably introduced from England during the colonial period, is most widespread in the coastal South, where it is typical of the regional speech. Elsewhere in the United States it is confined to smaller areas centered on major port cities (Boston and New York). The rest of the coastal South (the Carolinas and Georgia), having been settled from Virginia or on land at one time associated with the Virginia colony, shares the characteristic.

3.2   The Scots-Irish stratum

But Southern American English is not derived solely from one wave of settlement. Another wave identified by Fischer (1989) lasted longer than any of the others (1717–75) and consisted of more immigrants, especially from northern England, Scotland, and northern Ireland (the Scots-Irish). They came in family groups in search of economic improvement. They came to all the colonies, but settled notably the Appalachian region of the western South. Their immigration was part, albeit the major part, of a more general Celtic cultural migration.

Michael Montgomery, who has spent a decade in pursuing the "transatlantic comparison of English and Scots in Scotland and Ulster on the one hand with English in America (especially in the American South and Appalachia) on the other" (2001: 117), has traced the overall history of the Scots-Irish migration and summarized the scholarly study of it in his chapter in *The Cambridge History of the English Language*. He cites (2001: 89) Stephen Thernstrom (1980) as identifying five British linguistic profiles in addition to English proper: "Lowland Scottish, Highland Scottish, Irish, Scots-Irish (Protestants from Ulster mainly of Lowland Scottish background), and Welsh." The largest and most influential of these groups during the early period, however, were the Scots-Irish, who settled the inland South (Montgomery 2001: 91):

> In America the great majority of Scotch-Irish landed in Delaware or Penn-sylvania and soon headed to frontier areas, reaching the interior of Virginia in the 1730s and the Carolinas in the 1750s. They and their descendants settled and were culturally dominant in much of the interior or upper south – the Carolinas, Georgia, Tennessee, and Kentucky – within two generations.

Various linguistic features, such as the Southern double modals (*might could, might would*; cf. Bernstein in this volume), have been traced to Scots-Irish influence, but the principal domain of that influence was vocabulary (Montgomery 2001: 127):

> Comparisons of Appalachian or Upper South vocabulary (as labeled by *DARE*) with Ulster and Scottish works reveal more extensive connections: *airish* "chilly, cool," *back* "to endorse a document, letter," *back-set* "a setback or reversal (in health)," *bad man* "the devil," *barefooted* "undiluted," *beal* "suppurate, fester," *biddable* "obedient, docile," *bonny-clabber* "curdled sour milk," *brickle* "brittle," *cadgy* "lively, aroused," *chancy*

"doubtful, dangerous," *contrary* "to oppose, vex, anger," *creel* "to twist, wrench, give way," *discomfit* "to inconvenience," *fireboard* "mantel," *hippin* "diaper," *ill* "bad-tempered," *let on* "to pretend," *muley* "hornless cow," *nicker* "whinny," *poor* "scrawny," *swan* or *swanny* "to swear," and *take up* "begin" . . . One of the more intriguing Ulster contributions is *cracker* "white Southerner."

3.3   The African stratum

Although the English origins of Southern American speech can be traced primarily to, first, a coastal population consisting primarily of lower-class indentured servants plus a minority of upper-class (or upwardly aspiring middle-class) persons and, second, an interior Scots-Irish population, the formative influences on Southern American English were not limited to British colonists. Another important factor was the language of the African slave population. Dutch slave traders introduced African slavery to America in 1619, and by the time the trade was abolished in 1807, some 400,000 Africans had been forcibly settled in America. The height of the trade was in the eighteenth century, when slaves were needed to staff the plantation economy of tobacco, rice, and cotton cultivation.

In addition to the field hands, whose services made the southern plantation economy possible, other slaves were house servants, who lived in intimate relationship with their masters, often serving as nurses for the white family's children, and skilled craftsmen. It was through the latter two groups that the language of African slaves became an important influence on Southern English.

The African stratum is a contributing factor to the existence of a number of social or ethnic varieties spoken by African Americans within the southern area and elsewhere. Those varieties range from the Gullah Creole spoken on the islands off the coast of South Carolina and Georgia to various nonstandard varieties of African-American Vernacular English (AAVE), as well as varieties of standard American English embellished with features from the nonstandard varieties and spoken by both blacks and whites. Various features from African-American English, including elements of the African stratum, have entered standard English, and are continuing to do so. The scope of the African-American varieties and their characteristics have been surveyed by Salikoko Mufwene (2001a), who has also done much primary research in documenting and analyzing them (cf. also Mufwene's chapter in this volume).

The question of the origins of African-American English is a debated and contentious one, often intertwined with other social and political questions. Two extreme positions are, on the one hand, that African American is a development of the nonstandard regional and social usage of early English settlers with minor contributions from African languages; or, on the other hand, that African American is in origin a separate creole language – an African system into which English words have been inserted – that has imperfectly but increasingly assimilated to the norm of standard English.

It is possible that the disagreement about the origins of African-American English is a product of invalid assumptions about the coherence and consistency of language varieties. Perhaps the reality is a number of different patterns of development, moving in different ways, within the generalization we call "African-American English." If so, the problem is the way we have asked the question. What is clear is that African-American English, whatever its origin, and the African stratum, whatever its role in forming African-American English, have influenced Southern American English and English generally.

African influence is readily apparent in the vocabulary, although precise origins are often difficult to identify. Examples are *gumbo, voodoo* (both through Louisiana French), *banjo, buckra* "boss" or derogatory for "white man," *cooter* "turtle," *goober* (and its synonyms *pinder* and *goober pea*), and *okra*. There is a temptation to ascribe many other terms to African sources if they are associated especially with the African-American population and possible African etyma can be located for them (such as *boogie-woogie*) and, regrettably, even if they are not so associated and their actual origin has been well-established outside Africa (such as *OK*).

Other terms whose ultimate origins are unknown have also come into general southern and general American use from the African-American community, for example, *to bad-mouth* and much of the vocabulary of popular music, including *jazz, dig, hip, jive,* and *rap* (Cassidy and Hall 2001). There are fewer indications of the general extension of African-American pronunciations or grammatical forms. Thus Ronald Butters (2001: 330) observes, "Though most Americans today are aware of the AAVE [African-American Vernacular English] invariant *be* and are likely even to use it when imitating AAVE, it has not spread into other varieties of American English."

3.4   The Amerindian and Polynesian strata

When the first English-speaking settlers arrived in America, they found the land already inhabited by the Amerindian population, consisting of many groups diverse in culture and language. It has been estimated that when Europeans first arrived, the land area of the present United States was populated by speakers of 350 to 500 languages, of which some 200 still survive (Romaine 2001: 154–5).

The Amerindian contribution was almost entirely lexical, especially terms for New World fauna, such as *raccoon*; flora, such as *persimmon*; artifacts, such as *moccasin* and *tomahawk*; place names, such as *Shenandoah*; and other cultural referents, such as *pone* (as in *corn pone*), all from Virginia Algonquian languages. Hawaiian has contributed terms like *aloha, lei, hula,* and *ukulele*.

3.5   Other immigrant strata

Large numbers of settlers came to America also from other countries and linguistic areas. Prominent among them were Chinese, Danes, Dutch, Finns, French,

Germans, Italians, Japanese, Jews, Portuguese, Russians and other Slavs, Scandinavians, Spaniards, and Swiss. Those ethnic groups settled mainly outside the South, and so their influence was for the most part directly on or through other regional dialects.

4   The environment of Southern American English

Robert Frost observed, "The land was ours before we were the land's." A language cannot but be affected by the environment in which it is used. Speakers settle in a place, and then the place affects their speech. Whatever the origins of particular southern features in British dialects or non-English languages, it is clear that a new amalgam grew up in America, of which a formative influence was the new environment – that is, whatever was around the speakers to be spoken of.

American speech generally and southern speech specifically were often commented upon favorably by British visitors to the colonies (as quoted by Boorstin 1958: 274): "The Planters, and even the Native Negroes generally talk good English without Idiom or Tone." The impression of "good English" and uniform accent "without Idiom or Tone" is perhaps due to the fact that the colonists as a whole were of more uniform background than the population of the British Isles, but also that communication among the colonies was relatively abundant. That communication, easier and more frequent than contact with the motherland, created a sense of connectedness and of belonging to each other and to the land.

Not all Britons, however, were equally pleased with what they heard in the colonies. One such, Francis Moore (writing in 1735), observed that "the town of Savannah . . . stands upon the flat of a hill, the bank of the river (which they in barbarous English call a bluff) is steep and about forty-five foot perpendicular" (cited by Mathews 1931: 13). English rivers generally do not have steep banks, and therefore the English had no need for a term to designate them. The American colonists did have such a need and met it by adapting a nautical adjective meaning "presenting a broad flattened [or] a bold and almost perpendicular front" (*OED*) to use as a noun. Another such topographical term in the southern Appalachians is *bald* "a mountain whose summit is bare of forest," also shifted from adjective to noun, to denote a feature of the landscape for which no other term was available.

The adapted uses of *bluff* and *bald* illustrate the effect of environment on Southern American English (or for that matter on all American varieties). The colonists had to talk about things they had not encountered in the motherland. For some such things, they borrowed words from other languages, Amerindian or other immigrant languages; for others, they coined new words out of their own native resources, so *bluff* and *bald* changed their parts of speech and meanings.

Words did not have to shift their part of speech to shift their meaning in America. A well-known example of a shift in meaning only is *corn*, meaning "grain" such as wheat, oats, barley, rye, etc. in Britain, but "Indian corn, maize" in America, where the colonists learned from the Amerindian population to use the latter as a chief foodstuff. That shift was not specifically southern, but a similar shift in *plantation* is. The original sense of that word was "an act of planting"; its early use in America was "a settlement, colony"; but by the beginning of the eighteenth century it had developed what is today its most usual sense: "An estate or farm, esp. in a tropical or subtropical country, on which cotton, tobacco, sugar-cane, coffee, or other crops are cultivated, formerly chiefly by servile labour" (as the *OED* puts it). The growth of the plantation system in the South provided the environment to promote a semantic shift in the term.

The environment about which we talk is constantly changing, so new experiences continually present themselves and call for a linguistic response. An example is the popularity of soft drinks, which have a considerable history, involving some notable contributors. Jan Baptist Helmont (1580–1644), the Belgian "father of biochemistry," identified carbon dioxide as the product of fermenting grape juice and coined the term *gas* for such states of matter as distinct from atmospheric air. In the late seventeenth century, lemonade was being marketed in Paris and the naturally effervescent water of some European springs was sold for its therapeutic value.

Robert Boyle, one of the founders of the Royal Society, in 1685 proposed "the imitation of natural medicinal waters by chymical and other artificial wayes." Nearly a century later, Joseph Priestley, famed for his work with oxygen and English grammar, in 1772 demonstrated a practical way to carbonate water with a pump, and for this, Priestley has been dubbed "the father of the soft drink industry." Shortly thereafter Antoine Lavoisier repeated the demonstration in Paris. By the end of the eighteenth century, artificially carbonated water was being sold in England by an apothecary and in Switzerland by Jacob Schweppe, a jeweler. The initial use of the water was medicinal. By the middle of the nineteenth century, a variety of flavorings were being added to the carbonated water, but it was not until 1886, when Coca-Cola was invented by an Atlanta, Georgia, pharmacist and flavored with extracts from the kola nut that the soft drink industry came into its own.

Terms for the drink have evolved as well. The oldest appears to be *soda water* (1802), followed by *pop* (1812, for the sound produced when a bottle is opened), *soda* in *soda bottle* (1824 by Lord Bryon), *soda pop* (1863 by Walt Whitman), and *soft drink* (1880). It is perhaps noteworthy that the generic term used by *Merriam Webster's Collegiate Dictionary*, tenth edition, in definitions of related words is *soda pop*; that used by the *OED* is variably *soda water* or the descriptive terms "effervescing beverage" and "soft drink." The last has no lexical entry in the *OED*, but is exemplified only in syntactic combinations of the adjective *soft* "of beverages, nonalcoholic" (labeled by the *OED* as "orig. dial. and U.S."). *Soft drink* is, however, the lemma used by the *Encyclopaedia Britannica* and is perhaps the most widely used generic.

With the advent of Coca-Cola in 1886 (the term is attested from 1887), a new phase in the commercial history of soft drinks began, and one especially connected with the South. The Georgia-originated drink spawned imitators, notably the North Carolina Pepsi-Cola in 1903. The short form *Coke* (1909) was followed by *Pepsi* (trademark registration in 1915 claiming use since 1911). The generic use of *cola* is attested from 1920. But the particularly southern use is of *coca-cola* (often pronounced [ˌkokˈolə]) or *coke* as a generic for any soft drink, usually though not necessarily a carbonated one. The syncopated pronunciation is attested from 1919 for the trade name, and the generic use of both full and short forms from about 1960 (Cassidy and Hall's *DARE* s.v. *coca-cola*).

5   Choice in Southern American English

Sometimes, faced with variety in English use, Americans have chosen a particular option for reasons that are unknown. A general example is American *fall* versus British *autumn*. *Fall* as a season name is attested in English, earliest in the phrase *fall of the leaf*, from the sixteenth century, but is possibly much older and has become the most usual term for the season in American English. *Autumn* is a fourteenth-century loanword from Old French and is now the most usual term in Britain, but is largely restricted to formal contexts in America. Why the choice should have gone in different directions on either side of the Atlantic is not clear.

A more specifically southern example is the nonstandard pronoun *hit* for standard English *it*. The form with aspiration is, of course, original, going back to the Old English third-person-neuter personal pronoun *hit*. Forms with and without aspiration are found in various early Germanic languages, but the dominant form in early English was the aspirated *hit*. In the early thirteenth century, the unaspirated form began to appear, along with a further elided '*t*, both perhaps due to lack of stress, the tendency being to elide [h] at the beginning of unstressed syllables as well as unstressed vowels. The aspirated *hit* disappeared from standard use after the early Modern period (the *OED*'s last example of its use is by Queen Elizabeth I), but it survived in nonstandard dialect, as in Southern American English, as Frederic Cassidy and Joan Hall's *Dictionary of American Regional English* (1985-) shows. Why it did so is unclear, the "colonial lag" hypothesis being a label of dubious appropriateness, not an explanation (Montgomery 2001).

Some individual features in all varieties of American English, including Southern, can be traced to various sources: variable features in earlier standard English, dialectal varieties of English in the British Isles, aboriginal languages in America, other immigrant languages, later borrowings from abroad, and American innovations in response to the environment of the New World. But some features that distinguish Southern American English (or indeed any variety) have no clear motivation or explanation. Why do Americans tend to say *fall* rather than *autumn*? Why do some Southerners say *hit* rather than *it*? They simply use one of the available options, but why they use that option rather than another is unexplained. It's just the way it is.

The three published volumes of Cassidy and Hall's *Dictionary of American Regional English* (1985-), covering the vocabulary from A to O (omicron not yet omega), contain some 4,500 words labeled "Inland South," "South," "South Atlantic," "Southeast," or "South Midland," plus others labeled for individual states and areas like "Appalachians." To answer adequately the question posed by the title of this chapter, we would need to consider at least the history of all those words, as well as those to come in the range of N to Z, with respect to their phonology, morphology, and syntax. It is a daunting task. But the labors of scholars like Michael Montgomery, others cited here, and many others unnamed, make it possible.

2 Shakespeare in the coves and hollows: Toward a history of Southern English

EDGAR W. SCHNEIDER

1 Introduction

Within the United States of America, the South clearly is a region which is distinct in many ways – historically, culturally, and also linguistically. The dialect spoken in the southern United States differs from the type of American English spoken elsewhere; it is a variety which most Americans can identify, and towards which strong attitudes prevail, as Preston (1996) has shown. Much has been written about Southern English (cf. the monumental bibliography by McMillan and Montgomery 1989, and recent collections such as Montgomery and Bailey 1986 and Bernstein, Nunnally, and Sabino 1997), and with Lee Pederson's *Linguistic Atlas of the Gulf States* an extremely rich documentation is available that will keep analysts busy for decades to come (cf. Montgomery's thorough and competent discussion of this source, 1993a). In contrast, relatively little is known about the historical roots and the evolution of this dialect. Some general assumptions and statements have been brought forward, but to a considerable extent these have remained unsupported by linguistic documentation: a history of Southern English remains to be written. In fact, this state of affairs is by no means typical only of Southern English; as Montgomery (1996b) points out, virtually no serious, text-based research has been carried out on colonial American English in general. Montgomery's own work contributed more than any other to a remedy for this situation, for instance by defining necessary methodological steps and standards for comparisons between potentially related language varieties (1989b, 1997b), by working out exemplary analyses with great care (e.g. 1989b, 1997b), and by pointing out and documenting the enormous potential of archival sources such as early letters (cf. Montgomery, Fuller, and DeMarse 1993; Schneider and Montgomery 2001).

The present chapter is intended to document what information on the diachrony of Southern English is available at this point, and to contribute some facts and considerations toward such a history. Essentially, in its three main sections I will be surveying the kinds of sources, some old and some new, that have been employed in the quest for uncovering facts about earlier Southern English;

I will investigate how much can be attributed to British English roots; and I will be presenting a novel source of information on early nineteenth-century southern dialect, the "Southern Plantation Overseers' Corpus," a joint project by Michael Montgomery and this author.

Methodologically and theoretically, this approach ties in with several other research projects and initiatives that have attempted to learn about the history and evolution of nonstandard varieties and dialects in the last decades. For instance, in creole studies, much energy has been devoted to the unearthing and documentation of earlier stages of certain creole languages with the aim of contributing towards an understanding of creole genesis (cf. Rickford 1987b on Guyanese Creole; D'Costa and Lalla 1989 on Jamaican Creole; Arends 1995 on Sranan, and many others). With respect to dialects of English, Michael Montgomery (e.g. 1989b, 1997b) has carried out important work on the roots of Appalachian English; and Elizabeth Gordon at the University of Canterbury and her collaborators have pursued a fascinating project on the "Origins of New Zealand English" (ONZE; e.g. Gordon 1998). All of these research activities have had to face essentially the same fundamental problem: the limited amount and the questionable quality of sources of earlier nonstandard speech that have come down to us. Typically, dialect utterances of earlier times were not considered worthy of preservation by outside observers, and dialect speakers themselves usually were not literate, so it is only in exceptional instances that dialect was written down and that such records have been preserved. Finding such sources is one important task; assessing their reliability and validity is another (Schneider 2001). However, the energy that linguists have devoted to such work recently shows that these attempts have been regarded as fruitful and valuable research initiatives.

There are essentially two types of motivations and goals that have driven this line of research. One is strictly linguistic in character; it is understood nowadays that if we want to understand language change and evolution, we need to look at language variation and change in its natural context, in early vernaculars, not (or not primarily) in the standard records which have been preserved in considerably larger numbers. By their very nature, standard records fail to document the intricacies of small-scale variation patterns and changes in everyday linguistic behavior that reflect principles of language change most naturally. The second motivation is a sociocultural one; the provenance of any cultural system, including a dialect, is a source of identity and frequently dignity to the human beings who represent this particular culture. In many contexts, to know where we have come from is to know who we are. This applies to Southern English as well; in the light of the stigma that is frequently associated with this dialect, especially outside of the area, it is important to recognize that within the South stereotypes prevail according to which Southern English represents a retention of "Shakespearian English" or "Elizabethan English" – a belief which attributes historical dignity to an otherwise stigmatized aspect of one's own culture and behavior.

2   Southern English and its history: some facts and some gaps in knowledge

Before looking at historical aspects in the narrow sense, it will be necessary to briefly survey some essential facts and definitions concerning the nature, the uniformity, and the origins of Southern English.

In a sense, it is even presumptuous to talk of "Southern English" as a putatively homogeneous linguistic entity in itself (cf. Dorrill in this volume). Certainly the region as a whole is marked by a few common historical and cultural traits. The South is typically understood as the region south of the Mason and Dixon line, consisting of the states of the old Confederacy which seceded from the Union over the issue of slavery and subsequently lost the Civil War. This implies that the Old South was marked by facts like a largely rural economy and the presence of large numbers of people of African descent, originally brought to the region forcibly as slaves. On the other hand, there is obviously also a great deal of cultural variability within the South; after all, it is an enormously large region, covering about a dozen states and an area of more than half a million square miles with a population of over fifty million people. Thus, to some extent the notions of both "the South" and "Southern English" entail a certain degree of abstraction, an emphasis on shared characteristics rather than features and details which vary from one state or area to another. Still, this abstraction is justified by a common understanding of "the South" as a largely uniform region. Linguistically, there is a set of "features of Southern English" which are considered characteristic of the region in general, notwithstanding local details of all kinds, including aspects of pronunciation like the "southern drawl" or the "*pin/pen*-merger" (cf. Dorrill in this volume), elements of grammar like the ubiquitous second-person-plural pronoun *y'all* (cf. Bernstein in this volume), and a set of typical vocabulary items. In abstracting from local detail and discussing Southern English in general, I will adopt this tradition of emphasizing the region's homogeneity at the expense of its local heterogeneity.

It should be noted, however, that I will be concerned with Southern English as spoken by white people, not African Americans. It is clear and undisputed that African-American Vernacular English (AAVE) is closely related to and presumably a daughter variety of Southern English, but it underwent considerable changes with the migration of large numbers of African Americans to northern cities and the resulting urbanization and, to some extent, ghettoization early in the twentieth century. As is well known, an extensive linguistic discussion on AAVE has been going on, and hundreds of articles and books have been written on this topic (cf. most recently Mufwene et al. 1998; Lanehart 2001; and Cukor-Avila in this volume). However, this is a separate issue, simply not the topic of the present paper.

Even when operating under the "homogeneity assumption" outlined earlier, it will be necessary to point out the most important division of Southern English into its two major branches, associated with the cultural division into the "Lower South" and the "Upper South" (cf. Schneider 1998). The Lower South and its dialect are associated with the stereotypical plantation culture of the cotton belt along the coastal plains, stretching from the tidewater of Virginia to the bottom lands of Texas. In contrast, north of the "fall line," the line where the flat bottomlands start to rise to the interior hills and mountains, the Piedmont and mountain area of the interior is known as the Upper South, most typically associated with the Appalachian and to some extent also Ozark regions and the "hillbilly" stereotype. There are differences in the economic bases and the population structures of earlier days between the two regions. The soils of the Lower South permitted large-scale cotton and tobacco plantations, which led to a relatively strong presence of African Americans. On the other hand, the hills and mountains of the interior supported small-scale farming, lumbering, and mining, and thus the conditions of life resulted in a relatively limited presence of people of African descent. This difference also reflects an important historical distinction, as the two variants of southern culture were embodied by different settler streams. The population of the Lower South essentially descends from early settlers from southern parts of England, while the settlers of the interior came a little later and tended to come from northern England and, especially, Scotland and Northern Ireland known as the "Scots-Irish" in the US (cf. Algeo in this volume). To some extent, therefore, dialect differences between Lower and Upper southern varieties have been interpreted as retentions of differences between southern and northern dialects in England.

Until recently, relatively little was really known on the history and the early stages of Southern English. Of course, there has always been the persistent folk mythology mentioned earlier, embodied prototypically in statements such as this:

> The correspondence and writings of Queen Elizabeth I and such men as Sir Walter Raleigh, Marlowe, Dryden, Bacon and even Shakespeare are sprinkled with words and expressions which today are commonplace in remote regions of North Carolina. You hear the Queen's English in the coves and hollows of the Blue Ridge and Great Smoky mountains and on the windswept Outer Banks where time moves more leisurely. (*A Dictionary of the Queen's English* n.d.: Preface, unpaginated)

Of course, this is nothing but folk mythology – Southern English did branch off of varieties of British English in the early Modern English period, which in turn is commonly associated with Shakespeare and Queen Elizabeth, but there is no justification for the belief that this stage of the language should have been retained in an unmodified form. This persistent folk belief can be regarded as a popular variant of an attitude which has also prevailed among dialectologists and scholars writing on Southern English: the idea that the dialect has been shaped largely by "colonial lag" (Marckwardt 1958: 59–80), the preservation of archaic features of British dialectal provenance. This position is most closely associated with the name of Hans Kurath, the founding father of American dialectology, who in a series of articles (1928, 1964, 1968, 1970, 1972) has attempted to trace

British dialectal sources of American dialect features, including those of Southern English. This is also the spirit that informed the only book-length investigation so far of the relationship between British dialects and southern dialect, remarkably a study that is almost seventy years old (Brooks 1935). It was partly the lack of serious historical documentation and investigation that has helped maintain this position even in the light of the absence of positive evidence. McDavid attributed this lack of interest in the dialect and its diachronic documentation to "the inability of the genteel tradition of southern humanistic studies to focus seriously on everyday speech" (1967: 118) – thus, this retentionist assumption has gone largely unchallenged for decades.

Recently, however, a radical alternative was proposed by Bailey (1997b). Essentially, Bailey's claim is that Southern English was shaped not by retentions of British dialect features but rather by late nineteenth-century innovations, that is, linguistic developments of the post-Civil War, "Reconstruction" period, when Southerners used distinct dialect features to express their regional identity threatened by the presence of large numbers of "Yankees." Thus, Southern English is assumed to be not centuries but rather less than 150 years old. Clearly, this claim can be regarded as provocative, and it is likely to spark further investigation of this issue. To this end it is important to see what evidence is available for historical analyses.

3   Sources, old and new

This section surveys a variety of sources that have been and can be employed in investigating historical stages of Southern English. They are quite different in character, and thus indicative of the possibilities and limitations that condition and constrain diachronic dialect investigations. Some of these sources have been available for a while, and in a few cases their diachronic potential has only recently been developed; others have been discovered recently and still await further exploration. It goes without saying that such a listing will need to be suggestive and cannot claim to be exhaustive.

As is well known and documented (e.g. Davis 1983), American dialect geography, spearheaded by Kurath, Raven McDavid and, most recently, Bill Kretzschmar and Lee Pederson, has resulted in a series of regional linguistic atlases which have been used mostly to investigate regional dialect differences and the location of dialect boundaries. However, it has been the traditional goal of dialect geography to document long-standing, i.e. historically older, linguistic forms in dialects and to make their interpretation possible in the light of sound changes and their evolution from historical stages of the language. In the southern states, fieldwork began in the 1930s for *LAMSAS*, the *Linguistic Atlas of the Middle and South Atlantic States* (Kretzschmar et al. 1994), and extended until the 1970s with Pederson's *Linguistic Atlas of the Gulf States* (*LAGS*, Pederson et al. 1986–92). These projects sampled informants of all age groups, so that we have records of speakers who were in their eighties and nineties in the 1930s as well as of people who were young in the 1970s. Under the assumption of the "apparent time construct" (Bailey et al. 1991) that different generations of speakers may be taken to represent different stages in the development of a language variety and that the speech of an individual is shaped decidedly during one's childhood and adolescence, this data set provides diachronic evidence of Southern English extending over one and a half centuries, with data for speakers born in the 1840s providing a window into the past. Bailey (1997b) developed this ingenious strategy of diachronic investigation (and expanded it with data from another source to be discussed below). He categorized informants from these projects by birth decades and thus tabulated frequency changes of the users of select linguistic forms. Figure 2.1, from Bailey (1997b: 256), provides powerful illustration of this strategy. It documents the percentage of speakers out of those born in a given interval whose speech record displays the merger of mid-high short front vowels before nasals, one characteristic feature of present-day southern dialect. Interestingly enough, Bailey shows that early nineteenth-century records display this phenomenon only marginally; it is only during the late nineteenth and early twentieth century that a consistent frequency increase, in line with his historical interpretation, can be documented. This is one piece of strong evidence supportive of his claim of a post-Civil War genesis of what is now perceived as southern dialect, and it convincingly documents the strong potential of linguistic atlas records for diachronic investigations.

Ideally, of course, we would like to have direct written records of the speech forms of earlier days that we are interested in; but for sociocultural reasons such records are available only to a limited extent, and they need to be evaluated carefully (Montgomery 1999: 21–7; Schneider 2001). Clearly, plenty of such records still exist in archives, although the rarity of records written in dialect makes archival search a time-consuming and difficult procedure. I would like to discuss and present two such sources, a study that has turned out to be most successful and a collection that looks promising.

To the best of my knowledge, Eliason's *Tarheel Talk* (1956) is the only book-length investigation and documentation of earlier southern dialect, based upon historical records and archival sources. Eliason surveyed a wide range of manuscript sources and old records and screened them for traces of vernacular language, including legal papers, bills and occupational records, plantation books and overseers' reports, church records, children's and students' writings, diaries, and so on. His book provides a rich documentation and a systematic presentation of linguistic variants found in these sources, representative of dialect spoken in North Carolina before 1860. In the present context it is most interesting to note that he says there are "plentiful" records which "reflect colloquial usage" (Eliason 1956: 27) of the old days – clearly there should be room and material for Ph.D. or other research projects along these lines in other states as well.

Another diachronically promising source, largely unused so far in linguistic contexts except for small-scale investigations by Guy Bailey and some of his associates, is the collection of *Tennessee Civil War Veterans Questionnaires*

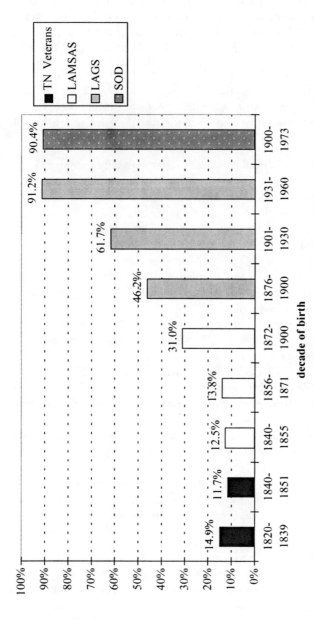

Figure 2.1 Spread of the *pin/pen* merger in apparent time: project informants by date of birth (from Bailey 1997b: 256)

(Elliott and Moxley 1985). This collection goes back to local historians early in the twentieth century who had the idea of collecting and preserving authentic recollections of the Civil War by those who had experienced it. Between 1915 and 1922 they sent out questionnaires to veterans of the Civil War in the state of Tennessee, asking them to submit their written responses. The questionnaire consisted of some forty questions, including, for example, the following:

(FORM NO. 1)
The chief purpose of the following questions is to bring out facts that will be of service in writing a true history of the Old South. Such a history has not yet been written. By answering these questions you will make a valuable contribution to the history of your State.

1. State your full name and present Post Office address:
2. State your age now:
3. In what State and county were you born?:
4. In what State and county were you living when you enlisted in the service of the Confederacy, or of the Federal Government?:
5. What was your occupation before the war?:
6. What was the occupation of your father?:
7. If you owned land or other property at the opening of the war, state what kind of property you owned, and state the value of your property as near as you can:
8. Did you or your parents own slaves? If so, how many?:
9. If your parents owned land, state about how many acres:
10. State as near as you can the value of all the property owned by your parents, including land, when the war opened:
11. What kind of house did your parents occupy? State whether it was a log house or frame house or built of other materials, and state the number of rooms it had:
12. As a boy and young man, state what kind of work you did. If you worked on a farm, state to what extent you plowed, worked with a hoe, and did other kinds of similar work:
13. State clearly what kind of work your father did, and what the duties of your mother were. State all the kinds of work done in the house as well as you can remember – that is, cooking, spinning, weaving, etc.
14. Did your parents keep any servants? If so, how many?

Obviously, the project was a timely and exceptionally successful one. A very large number of Civil War veterans were highly motivated to share their war and lifetime experiences even despite their limited literacy, a fact which provides for the high degree of linguistic authenticity and usefulness of these records for the purpose of dialect investigation. More than 1,600 responses were returned, and later the entire collection was published in an unedited form, thus preserving the linguistic authenticity of the records. Here is a selection from a sample response, illustrative of the kind of material that this collection provides (Elliott and Moxley 1985: 341–2):

1. G.R. Boles, Sparta Tenn.
2. 72 (73?)
3. Fentress co., Tenn.
4. White co., Tenn.
5. I was on the farm with my father plowing, howing, reeping, mowing . . .
6. a farmer and raising of cattle and hoges
7. i had some hoges an cattle worth a bout five hundred dollar and when the federal army tok it all so i was left with oute anney thing
8. no slaves
9. 150 acres
10. a boute 2 thousand dollar
11. partley loge and fraime hade 5 rooms
12. i don all kinds of farm work from the ho handle to the handle of the mowing _ [sic] and the handle of a pitch fork
13. my father don farm work my mother she had her cotan and flax she spunn and wove cloth she had her flax whell and spun flax thread and made _ [sic] clothes and all kinds of clothes
14. no servants

It should be obvious, due to its nature, that this collection should be also of interest for linguistic investigations, providing a rare but extensive documentation of a variety of Southern English which is presumably characteristic of mid-nineteenth-century speech. Clearly, limitations apply, as with all written records, but the amount and character of these materials should allow for interesting investigations (as its use by Bailey in the analysis reproduced in figure 2.1 indicates). The veterans represent all social strata, so historical sociolinguistic investigations of class differences should be possible (on the other hand, as all respondents are male and white, variability for gender and ethnicity cannot be investigated in this data set). While many individual answers are relatively brief, frequently consisting only of one word or just a few words without full syntactic embedding, there are a couple of questions (for instance those about battle experiences) that also provide for paragraph-length fluent text. Certain phenomena clearly cannot be studied on the basis of this material (for instance, obviously there are no questions at all); on the other hand, we get a reasonable documentation of vocabulary items in certain word fields, some pronunciation phenomena, and some nonstandard morphology. The above selection, for example, illustrates a few features of southern dialect, including two instances of zero plural in the word *dollar* after numerals, the past-tense form *don*, and left-dislocation syntax in *my mother she had*; whether certain spelling deviations allow for phonetic interpretation is a considerably more knotty question that could only be answered in a broader analysis and with great reluctance.

Another obvious but problematic source of earlier dialect forms is literary dialect, either dialect literature in itself or the representation of dialect utterances by individuals in novels or other works of art from earlier days. It is well known that for linguistic investigations literary dialect tends to be a problematic and unreliable source. We cannot tell how familiar an author was with the dialect he or she rendered in the mouth of a literary character, and the quality of such representations is known to be uneven (Ives 1971). Research has shown that literary dialect tends to overrepresent a small number of stereotypical features but in many cases fails to record other dialect phenomena of which a writer or a speech community may be unaware; and there is also a strong tendency to portray variable linguistic features as used categorically, thus misrepresenting frequency distributions of formal variants. Still, the study by Ellis (1994) is a fine example of how, given the necessary care and reluctance, literary dialect can be made use of in analyzing earlier language variation. Ellis investigated subject–verb concord in southern literature from the early nineteenth century, and he succeeded in providing reliable documentation of the "northern concord rule," a complex quantitative distribution of the verbal -s ending dependent upon the formal realization of the subject (see below, section 5; cf. Montgomery 1997b).

Finally, a promising "window into the past" of a regional dialect can be found in the phenomenon of a speech island, a community that was cut off from the majority of practitioners of its culture and speech forms by some historical accident. Isolated from later developments in the mainstream community and presumably leaning toward the retention of patterns from what are perceived as the good old days, the speech of such a community is likely to be characteristic of an earlier stage of that of the mainstream group. For Southern English, such a speech-island community exists in a city appropriately named *Americana* in southern Brazil, founded after the loss of the Civil War by emigrants from the South who were not willing to stay in the South under northern dominance. Almost one and a half centuries later the descendents of these Southerners still speak English in an all-Portuguese environment (although the young generation is now giving up this ancestral language), and their dialect has been analyzed as a retention of mid-nineteenth-century Southern English uninfluenced by later developments (Medeiros 1982; Montgomery and Melo 1990; Bailey and Smith 1992). In general, these investigations have provided interesting results on the state of Southern English at the time of the Civil War. The Americana speakers display some of the features commonly associated with Southern English, like r-lessness, the retention of the sound /j/ in the pronunciation of words like *tune*, *duke*, or *new*, and the pronoun *y'all*, while for others there is only very little and doubtful documentation (for example, for the monophthongization of /ai/, and, in line with Bailey's results presented in figure 2.1 above, the merger of *pin* and *pen*) or no traces at all (which applies to the southern drawl and the use of double modals; cf. Bernstein in this volume for an overview of double modals).

4   British roots?

Obviously, it should be possible to test the conventional, retentionist hypothesis, the belief that Southern English dialect largely consists of British dialectal forms preserved in the southern United States, by simply looking for southern speech forms in records of British English dialect. Strangely enough, until recently the only systematic attempt at such a comparison was Brooks' study of 1935, based upon very doubtful written sources (Southern English, for instance, was taken to be represented by Harris' *Uncle Remus Stories*, i.e. a literary dialect of African-American English). Despite obvious methodological limitations, Brooks' results are interesting; he claims that many of the features of Southern English derive from southwestern British dialects. At the time of Brooks' investigation, dialect atlases both in Britain and in America were just being initiated, and it was only decades later that a more reliable comparison based upon systematic sets of linguistic atlas records became possible. Schneider (forthcoming) carries out such a systematic comparison. I screened dialect project data (such as the *Linguistic Atlas of England* and the *Survey of English Dialects*, or various dialect dictionaries) for the presence of forms considered to be characteristic of Southern English in British dialects. Clearly, such a comparison is also not without problems, as all it is able to establish are formal correspondences, which is not the same as proof of direct transmission (cf. Montgomery 1989b for a thorough discussion of the methodological questions entailed in such a procedure). Still, this comparison is at least a serious beginning, and it does provide some interesting results. This section summarizes the main findings of Schneider (forthcoming); for further details and closer considerations of the methodological questions involved, the original source should be consulted. I will discuss, in turn, correspondences on the levels of phonology, morphology, and vocabulary.

Table 2.1 shows the results of the comparison of phonological features. The rows of this table list characteristic pronunciation features of Southern English (briefly identified as phonetic processes, in some cases employing the lexical categories established by Wells 1982). For five regions of England, subdivided further into thirteen subregions, the columns show whether and where the *Linguistic Atlas of England* (Orton et al. 1978) and the *Survey of English Dialects* (Orton et al. 1962–71) show documentation of the same phenomenon, occurring relatively systematically or at least weakly and marginally. For some southern pronunciation patterns, possible sources in England can be identified; for others this is not the case at all. None of the British English regions qualify as strong donor regions. Relatively speaking, the southwest and, less so, the southeast of England show more correspondences than most of the other regions; but, in general, the number of matches remains relatively low, even more so if varying distributional constraints are taken into consideration.

With respect to morphology, two types of forms can be distinguished. It is well known that throughout the English-speaking world inflectional morphology and grammar tend to be socially marked rather than regionally distinctive; thus,

Table 2.1 *Possible British source regions for pronunciation features of Southern American English*

	North		West Central			East Central		South western			Eastern		
	Nhb	Low N	Lan	Stf	sYks	Lei	Lin	wSW	nSW	eSW	cenE	East	SouthE
drawl: offglide short Vs													
drawl: long nuclei										(+)			
ɪ > ɛ /_N				X				X				X	X
ɛ > ɪ /_N			(+)		(+)								
/aɪ/ > monophthongal								X	(+)	X		X	X
/aɪ/ > /ɔɪ/								(+)	X	X			
FACE: monophthong		(+)	X	X	X		X	X					
FACE: inglide		X	X	X								(+)	
GOAT: monophthong		(+)						X	X	(+)			
GOAT: inglide		(+)										(+)	
GOAT: /ʌ/ onset											(+)	(+)	
HOUSE: [æu] / [ɛu]						X	(+)	X			X	X	X
HOUSE: [əu]/[ʌu]				X				X	X				
FLEECE: inglide		(+)											
THOUGHT: upglide								X	X	X		X	
/ʊ/ in roof													
GOOSE: fronting													
GOOSE: inglide													
KIT: umlaut / shading						X							
FOOT: fronting								(+)					
laxing of tense Vs													
[-r] in yellow etc.									X	X			X
[-r] in straw etc.									X	(+)			
vocalization of /-l/													X
sum total	—	1 (4)	2 (1)	4	1 (1)	2	1 (1)	7 (2)	6 (1)	4 (3)	1 (1)	4 (3)	5

Regional division after Trudgill (1990: 33); source: *LAE* (Orton et al. 1978)
X = feature documented   (+) = feature weakly / partly documented

there is a relatively large set of forms which are found in a great many regions and cannot be regarded as characteristic of any particular region. These include: multiple negation; uses of the form *ain't*; *them* as a demonstrative; some aspects of verbal concord, like the very widespread lack of an inflectional ending in the third singular with negatives (as in *he don't*), less so in positive contexts (as in *what make*) and, conversely, an -*s* ending appended to non-third-singular subjects (*I says*); non-standard copula forms like non-concord *is* or finite *be;* uninflected noun genitives; and many more. All of these forms can be found in descriptions of the grammar of Southern English as well, and some may occur more frequently in the South than in other regions. On the other hand, they all occur in a great many, sometimes most other English-speaking regions as well, and therefore they cannot be considered as distinctive or characteristic of Southern English exclusively in any way. As possible diagnostics of transatlantic dialect transmission in individual instances these forms simply fail to qualify, although in a broader sense, of course, they provide some support for the assumption that Southern English (but not Southern English exclusively) can be traced back to British dialect forms.

Secondly, there is a set of morphological and syntactic forms which are considered hallmarks of Southern English, including the pronoun *y'all*, the use of double modals like *might could* (Montgomery 1998), the use of perfective *done*, counterfactual *liketa*, and others (cf. Bernstein in this volume). Results of searches for these forms in British dialects are all similarly futile. In not a single instance can a strong case be built for direct transmission, and none of these features can be identified in British English dialects in the same forms and uses (but cf. Wright in this volume for additional evidence on possible sources of *liketa*). Of course, there are formal similarities which could be argued for as evidence of linguistic relatedness. For instance, the pronoun *y'all* is not found at all anywhere in Britain, but other distinct second-plural pronouns, such as *youse*, are, and of course so are occasional chance co-occurrences of the words *you* and *all*. The case of the origin of double modals is a complex one, on which much has been written in recent years. Double modals do occur in Scotland, but the lexical forms found there are not the same as the ones in the American South, and for various reasons it is difficult to build a case for direct transmission. Thus, it has been argued that the mechanism of double modal formation comprises both shared inheritance and independent development (Montgomery and Nagle 1993; cf. Fennell and Butters 1996). Similarly, for perfective *done* formal input in Scottish dialect in the form of a three-verb cluster "*is/has+done+*past participle" can be identified (Schneider 1983a), but on the other hand this pattern is quite different from southern uses of *done*, so at the very least some formal input must have undergone drastic modifications. In fact, this statement characterizes the question of the formal input to southern morphology in general. Certainly there may have been distant formal sources from which southern features may have developed in the long run, but the characteristically Southern English uses and patterns are all unique to the South, undocumented in Britain and thus innovations of southern dialect.

Finally, for a lexical comparison a list of eighty-nine items of Southern English words and expressions was compiled, and these were looked for in English dialect dictionaries and dialect atlases. It turned out that the words could be categorized on the basis of three types of relationships.

Firstly, there was evidence for direct transmission: twenty-three words (or 26 percent of the entire set) are used in the same way in some dialect of British English as in Southern English. These include the following as examples:

> *bray* "sound made by horse"
> *chitt(er)lin(g)s* "hog intestines"
> *disremember* "forget"
> *has(s)let* "liver and lungs"
> *mulligrubs* "fit of bad humor"

Secondly, an additional nineteen words (21 percent) are also related to British dialect words, but they have been modified in some way: either the meaning has changed slightly, or the form of the word is not quite identical. Here are a few examples of such modifications:

> SAmE *battercakes* "pancakes" – *to batter* "to stir up with a fork or spoon as in making pancakes" (Westmoreland)
> *corn house* "corn crib" – *to house* "store crops," *to house corn* "get it under cover" (var. counties)
> *drop* "plant (a crop)" – ~ "to plant potatoes" (Cheshire), "to sow seeds at intervals" (Devon)
> *lightwood* "kindling" – *lighting wood* (Sussex)
> *lumber room* "store room" – *lumber attic* (Scotland)
> *pulley bone* "wishbone"– *pulling bone* (Shropshire)
> *turn (of wood)* "armload" – *turn* "double quantity of anything, as much as can be done / fetched with one return" (Sussex, Hampshire, Isle of Wight, Cornwall)

There remains a third category which comprises more than half of all words of my Southern English corpus (forty-seven words, 53 percent) for which no possible source in any British dialect record could be detected. In other words, more than half of all the distinctly southern lexical items are innovations of Southern English and have not been inherited from British dialects, as far as we can tell.

5   The Southern Plantation Overseers' Corpus

The Southern Plantation Overseers' Corpus (SPOC) is another source and research tool that promises to provide new insights into the nature of early southern dialect. It is the product of a joint research effort of the present author and Michael Montgomery of the University of South Carolina (cf. Schneider and

Table 2.2 *SPOC, Sample corpus from the Carolinas*

Collection	Writer	Dates	State	No. letters	No. words
Ball	Hugh McCauly	1814–16	SC	12	4,605
Ruffin	William Meadow	1827–33	NC	20	5,737
Ruffin	Alexander Carter	1851–7	NC	96	22,298
Yancey	J. C. Doyal	1858	NC	12	5,153

Note: The Ball Papers are deposited in the South Caroliniana Library, University of South Carolina; the other three collections are housed in the Southern Historical Collection, University of North Carolina at Chapel Hill.

Montgomery 2001). SPOC is a computer-readable electronic text collection of letters written by overseers on southern plantations in the first half of the nineteenth century. Montgomery has collected these letters from historical archives throughout the South; Schneider has turned them into an electronic corpus. Plantation overseers had to report to absentee owners of the plantation on a regular basis, usually once a month, so in these letters they describe the business of running the plantation and the routine events like planting, the state of the crops, the weather, diseases among slaves, and so on. What is interesting is that the overseers usually had but limited education, so this is an informal, relatively personal text type which comes as close as reasonably possible to nonstandard speech patterns of the period. There is good reason to assume that the letters were hand-written by the overseers themselves, and that they can be regarded as representative of their speech. An impression of the nature of this material can be gained from a few letters reproduced in Schneider and Montgomery (2001: 404–7) and from a listing of features to be found in the texts given there.

The entire SPOC consists of 536 letters by fifty different writers, and it comprises about 155,000 words; the time span covered stretches from 1794 to 1876. We are beginning to analyze select features in this corpus. The analyses below,[1] however, build upon a sample corpus from the Carolinas only, an earlier selection of 140 letters by four different writers comprising a little under a third of the entire corpus. The composition of this sample corpus is detailed in table 2.2.

In a sense, the SPOC can be used for two different purposes: to study internal variation within this stylistically and sociolinguistically circumscribed corpus, and to put the findings in perspective as a stage in the diachronic evolution of Southern English. The following paragraphs and table are meant to illustrate these uses.

Table 2.3 illustrates a system-internal analysis of variability in a feature which for various reasons is of interest in this context: the so-called "subject type constraint," also known as the "northern concord rule." This is a somewhat peculiar rule found in several dialects of English. It predicts that the presence or absence of a verbal suffix in the finite predicate depends not only upon the grammatical

Table 2.3 *The subject-type constraint in the third plural and singular (SPOC sample corpus)*

Suffix	3rd-person plural			3rd-person singular		
	Total	N____	Pro____	Total	N____	Pro____
-s	96	92	4	754	583	171
	(60.8%)	(83.6%)	(8.3%)	(96.2%)	(97.3%)	(92.4%)
-Ø	62	18	44	30	16	14
	(38.2%)	(16.4%)	(91.7%)	(3.8%)	(2.7%)	(7.6%)
sum	158	110	48	784	599	185

Significance levels (chi-square test):
3rd. pl.: highly sig. at p < .001 (χ^2=76.35, 1 df)
3rd. sing.: sig. at p < 0.01 (χ^2=7.93, 1 df)

category of person (as it does in Standard English) but also upon the formal realization of the subject, especially in the third-person plural. There is a high probability for a verbal -s suffix (or, correspondingly, the form *is* as the realization of the copula) to occur if the subject is realized by a full lexical noun phrase, while, conversely, no marking tends to be found after a pronominal subject (i.e. usually *they*). This is a rule known to operate in northern dialects of English and in Scots as well as in Appalachian English in the US. Interestingly enough, Montgomery, Fuller, and DeMarse (1993) documented it in mid-nineteenth-century African-American English, though no trace of it has been found in present-day AAVE. Thus, the question is when and how this fairly complex grammatical rule was transmitted from British to American dialects (cf. Montgomery 1997b).

The evidence of the SPOC, shown in table 2.3, is of interest in this context because it provides strong documentation for the regular presence of this rule in earlier Southern English, thus establishing an important connecting point in the transatlantic transmission of this pattern. The effect of this rule is shown to be extremely strong in the third-person plural; with full noun phrase subjects, 83.6 percent of all verbs are inflected, while after the pronoun *they* only 8.3 percent have an -s ending, and 91.7 percent of the predicates are uninflected. This is a distribution which, according to significance testing by means of the chi-square test, is not a chance product with less than .1 percent error margin. In addition, statistically significant documentation (with a 1 percent confidence level) can also be provided for the same constraint to operate in the third-person singular, where it is obviously weaker and has not been documented to the same extent in related varieties. In this context, the tendency to add a third-singular -s ending, as in standard English, is strongly predominant, but after pronoun subjects as many as 7.6 percent of all predicates are uninflected, as against only 2.7 percent of the predicates after full-noun phrases. Thus, the SPOC documents this pattern to have been more widespread, both regionally and structurally, than has been previously suspected, and it shows earlier Southern English to have been a pivotal point in the transmission of English, especially northern English dialectal features, to the US.

Another obvious use of the SPOC is the testing of a diachronic hypothesis as to the origins of Southern English, following Bailey's claim (1997b). If Bailey is right, then those features which he believes originated only after the Civil War should not show up in the SPOC; on the other hand, those features which he believes are older should be found in the corpus. This line of thinking is pursued in Schneider and Montgomery (2001: 397–8), where the SPOC is screened for occurrences of ten grammatical features of earlier Southern English listed and dated by Bailey (1997b). The results show that out of four features which Bailey claims to have been in regular use before 1875 three are documented in the early nineteenth-century southern corpus (preverbal *a-*, the use of a verbal *-s* suffix after nominal plural forms, and perfective *done*). Conversely, the six features which he categorizes as younger in nature are not observed in this data set. While these are preliminary findings, which in some cases will have to be supplemented by closer analyses of the exact conditions governing the structural behavior of certain forms, the evidence drawn from the overseers' corpus provides some confirmation for Bailey's far-reaching claim as to the origins of Southern English.

6   Conclusion

It is apparent from the research cited in this chapter and others in this volume that historical dialectology and historical sociolinguistics are vibrant subfields of linguistics these days, with new methods and new sources promising further insights into the nature of earlier language varieties and of language evolution processes in general. In a sense, this also involves a plea to do more archival research and to uncover additional sources, a method pioneered by Michael Montgomery in recent years. Interdisciplinary collaboration with historians and archivists has turned out to be fruitful for this particular branch of linguistics.

In conclusion, I would like to summarize some preliminary findings with respect to the nature of earlier Southern English, and I would like to make a proposition which results from these findings and resolves some of the apparent paradoxes encountered in the description of Southern English and its earlier phases.

Two general statements appear to be justified on the emergence of Southern English and its relationship with input dialects from Great Britain:

- While it is clear that forms of Southern English go back to British dialectal input, the evidence at hand clearly constrains the importance that can be attributed to this original input. Claims that Southern English is essentially a retention of older British dialectal forms simply cannot be upheld. On all the levels of language organization that I looked at – phonology, morphology, and grammar – I found essentially the same fundamental result: while there is some limited continuity of forms derived from British dialects, there is also a great deal of internal dynamics to be observed, which has substantially altered and modified this input; and there is strong evidence for much innovation in the emergence of southern dialect. Substantial parts of it cannot be accounted for as the transmission of English dialectal input. The situation is best grasped by a notion suggested by Gordon and Trudgill (1999), that of "embryonic" features; such features were inherited from colonial input and did exist marginally in earlier forms of the language, but it is more important and more characteristic to observe that in a new context these input forms have developed their full creative potential and have resulted in new and substantially modified linguistic elements and structures.

• This is in line with the assumption that a very dynamic evolution of southern dialect occurred in the Reconstruction period after the Civil War. With Bailey (1997b), it appears that many of the features associated with Southern English nowadays developed in that period; so, in a sense, substantial parts of Southern English are relatively recent innovations.[2]

Obviously, there is a difference involved between two slightly different concepts of Southern English: an older, essentially rural dialect which is represented in older and traditional sources (including literary texts) on the one hand, and a set of forms that sociolinguists find to be characteristic of present-day southern speakers on the other. Adopting a distinction proposed by Trudgill for English dialects, who distinguishes "traditional" from "modern dialects" (1990), I suggest that it makes sense to introduce a similar distinction between two prototypical types of Southern English, to be called "Traditional Southern" versus "New Southern." Traditional southern dialect is associated with the antebellum, rural plantation culture of the Old South and its related value system. Linguistically, it is marked by r- lessness, /j/ retention, the use of intrusive /r/, a fairly frequent use of the verbal -s suffix in all grammatical persons, and the use of a preverbal a- onset before verbal -ing forms. In contrast, New Southern can be regarded as the product of late nineteenth-century and early twentieth-century developments which are also embodied in the sociocultural catchphrase of the "New South," associated, amongst other things, with urbanization, industrialization, in-migration, and a characterization of the region as the "sunbelt" of the United States. Linguistically, New Southern is expressed by the increasing use of rhoticity among the young, the loss of /j/ before /u/, the monophthongization of /ai/ in certain phonetic environments, the merger of /ɪ/ and /ɛ/ before nasals as in pin and pen, the southern drawl, the use of the pronoun y'all, and idiomatic expressions like fixin' to (cf. Berstein in this volume). New Southern is found predominantly among the young and among urban dwellers, and it illustrates the fact that dialects and linguistic expressions are always in flux, reflecting changes in the perception of one's own identities.

Notes

1. Tables 2.2 and 2.3 are reproduced from Schneider and Montgomery (2001).
2. Incidentally, recent work by Kautzsch (2002, originally a University of Regensburg Ph.D. dissertation), based upon a broad comparative analysis of empirical sources, shows a similar diachronic assessment to apply to the emergence of African-American English as well.

3 Eight grammatical features of southern United States speech present in early modern London prison narratives

LAURA WRIGHT

1 Introduction

This chapter compares selected grammatical features found in southern United States speech with those found in an archive of early modern prisoners' narratives, the MS Minutes of the Court of Governors of the Royal Hospitals of Bridewell and Bethlem, viewable on microfilm in the Guildhall Library, London. The purpose of the exercise is to provide data for the very earliest states of Southern United States English, as many of the vagrants and petty criminals who passed through the court were transported to the new colony in Virginia. The speech that each transportee brought with him or her to the New World may very soon have been modified as they were deprived of their usual speech community and surrounded by speakers from elsewhere. However, vagrants and criminals kept on arriving from the London courts. The first prisoner to be sentenced to transportation by the Court of Bridewell was on 2 October 1607 (the Jamestown colony was founded on 13 May 1607), and prisoners continued to be transported officially into the 1640s, and unofficially thereafter, due to the lucrative illegal practice of "spiriting" or kidnapping. And other London courts continued transporting people into the 1700s.[1]

Many people were sentenced to go to Virginia, but although the Court Recorders were meticulous about recording names and dates in the Court Minute Books, destinations were frequently merely "beyond sea" or "to a plantation." It is certain that more Londoners were sent to Virginia from Bridewell than are explicitly stated as such in the Minutes. The Bridewell Court Recorder wrote down the name, date, and the offence of the person sentenced. They were sometimes convicted of crime, but frequently the main reason for transportation was vagrancy. The Virginia Company needed English people to go and settle the foundering new colony (which nearly failed altogether), and London's homeless poor were to be its hapless new working populace. The governors of the hospital and their deputies had powers to apprehend vagrants:

ye may take into the said house all such suspect persons as shall be presented
unto you as lewd and idle; ye may also examine and punish the same according to your discretions . . . Ye have also authority to visit taverns, alehouses,
dicing-houses, bowling-alleys, tennis-plays, and all other suspect places
and houses of evil resort within the city of London and the suburbs of the
same, and within the shire of Middlesex; and not only to enter into the said
houses and places, but also to apprehend, commit to ward, and punish at
your discretions, as well the landlords or tenants of such houses as have any
such lewd persons resorting unto them, whether they be men or women . . .
(*Charity Commissioners' Report* 1557 [1837]: 391, modernized spelling)

Wright (forthcoming a) summarizes the role of the Corporation of the City of
London in peopling the new Virginia Colony, and lists the names of the earliest
transportees from Bridewell, 1607–24 (forthcoming a: Appendix A).

2   The language of the MS Minutes of the Court of Governors of the Royal Hospitals of Bridewell and Bethlem

The advantage of using the language of the Minutes of the Court of Governors
of the Royal Hospitals of Bridewell and Bethlem as a point of comparison is
that the language of the compeers of the prisoners are recorded; the archive
tells us (insofar as written language can) what basilectal London English was
like at the point of departure. Nearly four hundred years has passed since the
first prisoner was transported in 1607, and American speakers have subsequently
interacted with incomers from other places, so the constructions found in the
Bridewell Court Minute Books cannot be identical with present-day American
speech. With all due caution, this chapter posits the likelihood of selected features
having their origin in the speech of transported London prisoners. I say "with
all due caution," because each feature needs to be looked at individually in the
light of its subsequent history. It is entirely possible for a feature to have been
introduced to the American South by transported Londoners, but then to have
fallen out of use in the southern states, only to be reintroduced by speakers from
elsewhere at a later date. And although it is not easy to prove, many of the features
discussed here may have been retained in southern United States speech precisely
because they map on to features existing in other languages or other dialects (see,
for example, possessive zero and third-person-singular zero below). As Holm
says with regard to present-day southern United States features that may be
derived both from an Early Modern English source and from a West African
creole source: "the convergence of both is more often a satisfactory explanation,
not because it is a tactic to placate everyone, but simply because it reflects what
is known about the way languages mix" (Holm 1991: 233–4). What can be stated
with a certain amount of confidence is that the transported Londoners' speech
patterns would have formed part of the mix of the emerging Virginia dialect –
and probably greatly influenced its basilect.

The database consists of c.150,000 words transcribed from the Bridewell Court Minute Books, which, it should be noted, is a small fraction of what remains to be transcribed. It is heavily weighted towards the decades from 1559–1600, because the principle of selection was transcription of cases containing speech-based features – usually, use of the first and second persons. The Court Recorders of the late sixteenth century took down much of the Early Modern English spoken by the examinants and witnesses,[2] and entries are fulsome. However, by 1600 they had begun to write in a far more elliptical style, merely giving the bare outline of a case, and hence the seventeenth-century records contain far less useful data.

3   Selected features present in the Bridewell Court Minute Books which are found in similar constructions in present-day southern United States speech

The illustrations that follow will be discussed in the following order: firstly a brief note about a feature's history and presence in present-day southern United States speech, and then quotations from the Bridewell Court Minute Books demonstrating how that feature, or one like it, was used "at the point of departure." This phrase is to be interpreted loosely. By the early 1600s the Bridewell Court Minute Books had become terse and hence there are fewer examples of the grammatical variants discussed here, so if a feature is present in the period 1559–1607, then it has been included as relevant to the matter in hand. In the following extracts, material given in italics has been expanded from the medieval abbreviation and suspension system, which was still in use.

3.1   Invariant be

Invariant *be* is one of the most discussed features of African-American Vernacular English, and forms one of its characteristic features (Wolfram and Schilling-Estes 1998: 171). Labov (1998: 120) says "The particle *be* is the most frequent and the most salient of the AA elements in AAVE." AAVE non-finite *be* carries no tense information and can appear in any temporal context, although it frequently co-occurs with verbs referring to present situations, as it often has a habitual aspect. Labov (1998: 122) notes that AAVE *be* has developed a "steady-state," durative, "indicating a higher state of reality than normally predicated" aspect in recent years.

There are two kinds of invariant *be* to be found in the Court Minute Books: plural indicative *be*, and subjunctive *be*, both singular and plural.

3.1.1 Plural indicative be. The default plural indicative form of the verb *to be* in Early Modern London English was *are*, as in present-day Standard English. However, northern *are* only entered London English during the Middle English period, and plural *be* remained the more common variant (Lass 1992: 141) until around 1500. Many sixteenth-century writers used both *be* and *are*. In Nevalainen and Raumolin-Brunberg's (1996: 67) corpus of letters written in the period

1590–1620, *are* has not yet gone to completion and plural *be* is present as a minority variant in each category studied. Lass (1999: 176) reports a survey of the Epistle and glosses to Spenser's *Shepheardes Calendar* of 1597, in which he found *be* and *are* in a ratio of about 2 to 1, with *be* preponderating in negations, subordinate clauses, and after *there*. Plural indicative *be* occurs in the Bridewell Court Minute Books in passages of reported narrative, and it probably indicates that some individuals still had old-fashioned southern plural *be* in their idiolects, whilst other Londoners had adopted the newer form, *are*. It does not occur in the pattern *be*+verb+*ing*, which Bailey (1993) has identified as a post-1944 phenomenon in Texan speech.

I have only come across plural indicative *be* in the Court Minute Books in entries for the years 1575–7 (interestingly, the same point in time when verbal *-s* makes its first appearance in this archive, although it was in use in London far earlier, see section 3.2.2 below).

(1)   fo. 220v, 21 December 1575
       & againe the saide M^r ffarmo^r Did vse most comonlie in the Somm*er* to go to his naked bedd, then if my M^r weare not in the waie my M^{rs} wolde be suer to go vppe to him, But the mayde at that tyme wolde saie that manie tymes there **be** those that sitt at the Dore whist their wifes Do make them cockoldes, & so did my M^r./ This that I haue nowe declared is the truthe
       (aspect: habitual) (speaker: Mrs. Ragland's maid)

(2)   fo. 21, 26 June 1576
       Also he saieth that many prentices came to M^{rs} breme And he knoweth one of them whose name is John Cossarte about the further ende of chepe side or watlingestrete And he saieth that ther **be** very many in chepe side that Do kepe Mrs Breame
       (aspect: durative) (speaker: Richarde Rolles, servant to Jane Trosse. Plural *are* also features in Rolles' narrative)

(3)   fo. 22v, 26 June 1576
       Mrs Breame saieth that will*i*am Mekens in fetter lane is a bawde and his wiffe also And Dothe knowe the wemen that **be** lewde almost all And Dothe carry them to strangers And he is abell to tell of all sor*tes* of men & wemen that **be** lewde
       (aspect: durative, non-punctual) (speaker: Mrs. Breame, prostitute. Plural *are* also features in Mrs. Breame's narrative)

(4)   fo. 23, 26 June 1576
       And he is a whoremonger And kepeth Elizabeth Cowp*er* and others and his wiffe knoweth it & also she plaieth the harlott And he knoweth it And they kepe the dore one for another while they **be** naught And yf any prevy serche come ther house must not be serched
       (aspect: habitual) (speaker: Mrs. Breame, prostitute. Plural *are* also features in Mrs. Breame's narrative)

(5)   fo. 117v, 21 December 1576
       More he knoweth two wemen wch be comon bawdes that promysed to
       bringe in goldsmythes wyfe of chepe syde to one of my Lord of Oxfordes
       men to the Dolphyn in the backesyde of olde ffyshestreat
       (aspect: durative) (speaker: Henry Boyer)

(6)   fo. 130, 130v, 23 December 1576
       he resortes to the same horse head in S^t katheryn wth the same Edwardes
       many tymes to whores that be kept there There is in white crosse streate
       one m^r Crosse kepes ijo Daughters y^t be whores very many straungers
       resortes thither . . .
       (aspect: durative) (speaker: Melcher Pelche, pimp. Plural *are* also features
       in Pelche's narrative)

(7)   fo. 250, 22 October 1577
       He saieth that ther be other that came and will declare more of his lewde
       delynge when tyme doth sarve
       (aspect: ?) (speaker: Henry Boyer)

The examples given here constitute most of the tokens of plural *be* to be found
in the database. The cases from which these examples are taken are all extremely
long, which might have something to do with why they have not been standardized to *are*. The witnesses and examinants Mrs. Ragland's maid, Richarde Rolles,
Mrs. Breame, and Melcher Pelche also had plural *are* as a majority variant in their
testimonies, and it may be conjectured that over these lengthy testimonies the
Court Recorder let the occasional plural *be* slip through without emending it to the
recently standardized *are*. If this conjecture is correct, the transportees would
have had plural *be* as a variant in their speech, but by the point of departure
it seemed to carry unfavorable social connotations for the written medium
(such as being too colloquial, vulgar or old-fashioned). It looks as though before
dropping out of speech altogether, plural *be* functioned as a durative aspect marker
in Early Modern London English. Obviously the evidence of just five informants
is insufficient data, but as plural *be* was on its last legs in the City at the point of
departure it rarely shows up in writing: people who were sufficiently educated
to know how to write preferred *are*. So these five informants provide us with a
window onto late plural *be* that we would not normally be able to detect.

3.1.2 Subjunctive be. For a full discussion of the subjunctive mood see Wright
(2001). By and large, in the Bridewell Court Minute Books the subjunctive is
triggered by *until, if, whether, although, and*, etc.

(8)   fo. 222v, 6 October 1575
       the Hospitalitie of the saide John & Jane, wch allureth and entyceth many
       yonge men to their vtter ruyne & decay, not onelie in expendinge & con-
       sumynge their goodes & good name, but also entisinge them to suche incon-
       venienses that are & be abhomynable & detestable before the face of god
       (Court Recorder's summary of a written statement by ffowlke Mounslowe)

(9)   fo. 110, 19 December 1576
She sayeth that watwood*es* cheife brokinge is to bringe wemen he will go
to the ffeild*es* amonge those wemen that are Dryinge clothes & will trye
them by gevinge a quarte of wyne or som*e* other thinge whether they be
for hym and yf they be he poynt*es* them tyme & place for the purpose

(10)   fo. 150v, 9 January 1576
She answered I am fered I shalbe wth childe whie said Robsons wyfe that
w[ch] one man getteth another spoyleth It is better for a woma*n* to be kept by
ij° or iij men then by one And yf thou be wth childe I can make yt a litter
of whelpes I can fetche a yerke[3] oute of Riders garden that will Doo yt

(11)   fo. 246, 10 October 1577
And this exa*min*ant saieth that they beinge thus in the rome eu*er*ye man soe
wth his woman Grenewood tolde this exa*min*ant that she might ther see that
euerye man had ther chosen his frende And it was fallen out that she must
be frende to him the said Grenewoode but saied Grenewood althoughe
they be mynded to doe it here yet I will not haue my sin*n*e knowen to them
but I will come home to you whervpon she tolde him wher she dwelt that
he might come to her

(12)   fo. 281, 21 January 1577
Then wises wiffe saied her husbande was a very raskall and a vagabonde
and a knave what shall I make my frende my foe that hath done soe moche
for me and bestowed soe moche monye and Jewell*es* on me I will never
confesse it And[4] I be racked

(13)   fo. 327, 16 July 1578
John Evans a roge taken wanderinge in the stretes by *willia*[m] witchens
constable in S[t] Dunstons in theaste[5] and haueinge about him divers false
pasport*es* conterfet wherof he can giue noe accompte but one he confesseth
he caused to be conterfeyted by a scoller of Oxfforde his name he knoweth
not he gaue him twoe pott*es* of bere for his wrytinge of it, he is setto labor
till he be whipped at a cart*es* arse[6] by my L*ord* maiors order but after-
wardes the xix[th] of Julye 1578 in presens of M[r] Winche M[r] Warfeilde
and M[r] Clerke as my L*ord* Maio[r] required he was here whipped and
d*eliver*ed

(14)   fo. 62, Saturday 8 August 1618
Gillian Richardson brought in by Constable Ashe in Blackfryars for ron-
ninge from her m[r]: who hath taken money to Carry her to Virginia is by
order of Court kept here vntill her m[r]: be ready to goe att the Charg*es* of
the p*a*rishon*er*s

(15)   fo. 41v, Saturday 15 September 1627
Daniell Banes from Dep*uty* Steward an appr*e*ntice for Virginia runaway to
stay till dep*uty* Steward sonne be here the next weeke

(16)   fo. 84v, 22 August 1628
       Ro: Parks by Ma^rshall ffitch v*agrant* boy saith he should goe to Virginia to
       be sent to his M^r to see **if** it **be** true

(17)   fo. 130, 5 June 1629
       James Tomlinson by M^r Tr*easur*er for being disorderly in the night time
       and drunke to worke **till** the Marchant who he saith would send him and
       his wife to St *Christ*ofers **be** sent for

(18)   fo. 100v, 18 January 1636 (i.e. 1637)
       . . . the Cou^{rt} **thinke fitt that** a bill of Indictm*en*^{t} **be** pr*efer*ed likewise
       ag*ains*^{t} him for breaking out of the Pesthouse when he was sent out of this
       hospitall having then a plague sore vpon him & is to be kept here at worke
       till Sessions

This is just a brief selection from the many instances of subjunctive *be* in the
Court Minute Books. The Early Modern English distribution of subjunctive and
plural *be* is not identical to present-day invariant *be* in AAVE, but it gives us some
idea of the original input. In particular, the Early Modern subjunctive triggers
whether, so, if, until, unless, although, etc., may still play a role in present-day
Southern White Vernacular English. Feagin (1979: 251–5) noticed that a sixty-
one-year-old, female, white, rural informant with only eight years of schooling
used invariant *be* as follows:

   (i)   I put her up till I be sure
   (ii)   It caught up with you after you be here a little bit
   (iii) After you be there so long, you're ready to get up and go again!
   (iv)   Or if I be out there, I'll . . .
   (v)   You hope she calls you, you don't be here
   (vi)   It's a wonder they don't be sick

When read from an Early Modern perspective, these extracts look like examples
of subjunctive *be* (similarly, several of Bailey and Bassett's [1986: 172–3] SWVE
extracts conform to Early Modern usage).

   To summarize: some transportees probably had plural indicative *be* as a variant
in their speech at the point of departure, and on the evidence of the few examples
given here, it would seem that plural indicative *be* may perhaps have had a durative
aspect. Most speakers would have had subjunctive *be*, both plural and singular,
in clauses governed by *whether, so, if, until, unless, although*, etc., and this may
still be present in some Southerners' idiolects – but it does not account for all
southern usages of invariant *be*.

3.2   *Third-person present-tense indicative singular zero*

At the point of departure there were three ways of marking third-person present-
tense indicative singular verbs, *-s*, *-th*, and zero. *-th* was the default, *-s* was the

incoming form, and zero is only found occasionally in the indicative, although it was the default in the subjunctive mood.[7] Until recently it has been assumed that -*th* was just a conservative written convention by the early 1600s, and that Londoners actually said -*s* (see Lass 1999: 162–6 for a discussion). However, Nevalainen and Raumolin-Brunberg (2000) have reopened this question by surveying a corpus of Early Modern letters, and conclude (2000: 238) "Variation is . . . clearly in evidence in the verbal suffix in the spoken registers of Londoners even in the middle of the seventeenth century." It now seems probable that the transportees had all three methods of marking the third-person present-tense indicative singular in their speech when they settled in Virginia (cf. Wright 2001, forthcoming b). By and large, zero was used to mark the present-tense subjunctive mood, but -*s* was also used for this purpose, so -*s* and zero overlapped.

In present-day southern United States speech, the third-person-singular present tense is marked with both -*s* and zero (see Cukor-Avila [1997b: 296] for a summary). AAVE speakers and SWVE speakers both use the zero morpheme to mark this slot, but in differing amounts, with some AAVE speakers presently using it far more frequently than SWVE speakers.[8] It has been argued that the southern United States third-person-singular present-tense zero suffix goes back to a creole system which is typically uninflected, as are several West African languages. It has also been noted that specific British dialects, notably East Anglian, are -*s* deleting (see Schneider 1982: 20–1 for a summary). The Bridewell data show that the earliest transportees had third-person zero in their present-tense system, but that it was only sporadic in the indicative mood. However, zero was the older form in the third-person subjunctive, and at the point of departure this zero was in the process of being ousted by the incoming -*s* suffix. Both zero and -*s* were used to mark the subjunctive, and this state of overlapping variation was carried to Virginia in the early 1600s.

3.2.1 Singular -th. -*th* is the default form in the Bridewell Court Minute Books well into the seventeenth century, although -*s* had been in use in London writing since the late 1300s (Lass 1999: 138).

(19) fo. 168, Saturday 29 February 1619
      Margaret Withering James Luellyn brought in by the Const*able* Bishops-
      gate Luellyn **saieth** he is by trade a pickadella[9] maker but **liueth**
      suspitiously in ffrench Alley is kept at Worke / withering for a V*agrant*
      is kept for Virginia

3.2.2 Singular -s. The incoming third-person present-tense singular indicative mood form was -*s*. It is found in London writing from the late fourteenth century, and some London writers used it frequently in the fifteenth century (such as Lydgate), and others hardly at all (such as Caxton) (Lass 1999: 139). -*s* continued to alternate with -*th* for the best part of three hundred years before ousting -*th* altogether. In the Bridewell Court Minute Books, -s first enters in the mid 1570s and then disappears from use, only to reappear a few decades later. Even when -s reappears, -th also continued to be used side-by-side well into the first half of the seventeenth century in this archive.

(20)   fo. 63, 14 September 1576
       She **saieth** there is one Phillip & one Melchior that are comen carriers of men & women to Norris house at the ship at temple barre & she **saies** that Jane Ridley and Marie Creake is able to tell you of great matters & very many if she be well ex*amined*

(21)   fo. 21v, Wednesday 26 March 1605
       William Rodes brought in for y^t he would haue mischeved his father; hauing locte himself into a chamber where his father being a very olde man lay sicke; he **saith** he is married and his wief **maketh** bone lace and he himself **sell**es Inke & sometyme broomes kepte to be sent for a soldier

(22)   fo. 41v, Wednesday 3 July 1605
       Mary Strange by warrant from Sr Stephen Some for one that **vseth** to gett into mens howses vnder the Collo^r of kindlinge of stick*es* and by that meanes **steales** and **fylches** all she cann com*e* by: ordred to be ponished & deliu*e*red *on* bond for hir good behaviou^r

(23)   fo. 137, Saturday 14 August 1619
       Thomas Beckwith Charles Benson sent in from the Marshall by the Court in Redcrosstreete Beckwth **sayeth** hee **dwelleth** wth one Tony that **Maketh** Bushes[10] for Tavernes who **dwelles** att Clarkenwell both v*a*g*rants* are p*o*nish*ed* & del*ivere*d . . . John Rosse sent in by Sr Thomas Bennett his warra*n*^{t} the *ser*vant of one Thomas Browne ffruiterer who **carryeth** outward & neu*er* **geves** his M^r accompte thereof an vncivill & vnrully fellowe, his Mr **Testefies** that hee was dronke when hee was taken, is powled p*o*nish*ed* & vppon his submission d*elivere*d to his M^r:./ Raphe Anderson brought in from the Marshall by Const*able* Bromsgraue in Carter lane for a v*a*g*rant* **sayeth** hee is a Broomeman & **dwelles** in kent M^r ffraunc*es* Anderson **hath** vndertaken to see him sent home wherevppon hee is d*elivere*d

3.2.3 Subjunctive singular zero. The older way inherited from Old English of marking the subjunctive was with a zero suffix. For a discussion of the subjunctive mood in Early Modern English see Wright (2001: 243–5).[11] Early Modern English had the kinds of subjunctive triggers with which we are still familiar today, albeit in formal language, such as the concessive subjunctive (expressing a kind of challenge or defiance), as in (30) "shee is to bee warned that shee take Course hee wander noe more"; and the hortatory subjunctive (expressing an exhortation and command), as in (33) "It is ordered that M^r. Tr*easu*rer doe pay" (cf. Mustanoja 1960: 455). But in Early Modern English, several other conditional and concessive links were followed by the subjunctive mood, which nowadays take the indicative (conditional links are when the action in the main clause depends upon the fulfilment of the condition in the subordinate clause, as in (31) "yf the said Walker lye here onelie for the busines betweene his M^r & him, That then his M^r take his Course in Lawe against him"; concessive links are when the main clause is in an adversative relation to the subordinate clause, as in (25) "Althoughe she be accused by manye yet she denyeth all" (cf. Rissanen 1999: 307–8)). Those illustrated here are clauses governed by *as* (24), *although* (25), *whether* (26), *so that* (27), *unless* (28), *until* (29), *if* (31), *so as* (32).

(24) fo. 167, 20 August 1575
      And there they bothe swore in the presence of the saide Hi*ll* Howso*n* & hills wiffe **as** god **Judge** there sowles they did not se one a nother that night

(25) fo. 259v, 11 December 1577
      Dorothie Wise wiffe of Thomas wise beinge exa*min*ed of her lewde liffe ffor that ther hath bene gret complante made of her aswell by James Marcadye as other **Althoughe** she **be** accused by manye yet she denyeth all / she is setto spinninge wth the matrone she sayeth at last that her husbande kept one Cokes wiffe of Braynforde Elizabeth Cowp*er* Marget Goldesmyth, Joane Merrill and others and vsed ther bodies

(26) fo. 312v, 27 May 1578
      Agnes ffrenche beinge chardged by m^r Babham wth the Judgement*es* of god And asked whether her former exa*min*aci*on*s be trwe or not and **whether** she **haue** saied any thinge for feare or favor she sayeth that it is all merelye trwe

(27) fo. 21v, Wednesday 24 May 1598
      So allwayes **that** the said Gregorye ffountaine **do** well and honestlye beare and demeane himself towards the said parishioners and Churchwardens and the gouernors of the said Hospitall

(28) fo. 42, Saturday 25 April 1618
      the hempman testefyed that he refused to worke, wherevpon this Courte appointed he should be sett in the Stock*es*, and haue no meate **vnles** he **doe** worke

(29) fo. 135, Saturday 31 July 1619
      John Ashford brought in by warra*n*^{t} from Sr John Leman for a Com*m*on drunckard offringe to stabbe men in the streete & bee the death of them, in his dronkennesse is kepte att worke **vntill** hee **find** suretyes for his better behavio^r

(30) fo. 143v, Saturday 18 September 1619
      Henry Killocke brought in by the Marshall & Consta*ble* Milkstreete formerly sent to his Mother of good sufficiency in Barbican & nowe againe taken is sent to his Mother, and shee is to bee **warned that** shee **take** Course hee **wander** noe more

(31)   fo. 184v, Saturday 5 May 1620
It is ordered that Phillip Walker shalbee *delivered* to the m*a*rshall to carry him to Mr Recorder, and to lett his wife knowe, that **yf** the said Walker **lye** here onelie for the busines betweene his M^r & him, That **then** his M^r **take** his Course in Lawe against him

(32)   fo. 337v, Saturday 28 June 1623
Ordered the sonne of Eli*z* Briggs shall haue a suite of Clothes given him, **soe as** his father in lawe **come** and **vndertake** that hee shall no more bee chargeable, or troblesome to this hospitall

(33)   fo. 292v, 17 August 1632
It is **ordered that** M^r. Tr*easu*rer **doe pay** to M^r. Drake in Chepside for sending a boy to Virginia

3.2.4 Variation between indicative and subjunctive suffixes. However, many subjunctives were also marked by -*s*, so that there was considerable overlap between -*s* and zero, and modal verbs were used as a variant. Compare *if* in (31) which triggers a zero suffix, with *if* in (34), where the verb carries an indicative -*s* suffix; and *till* in (36) and (37) which is followed by both a modal verb and a subjunctive verb.

(34)   fo. 167v, 20 August 1575
. . . But there came in Diu*ers* wome*n* as witnesses, wch do saie that his wiffe liveth a very eve*ll* lyffe wth him, and the saide Joha*n* Hathe saide to hir mother, Come out, and **yf** he **beates** yo*u* he **beates** yo*u*, he is ordered to be detayned p*r*iso*n*er

(35)   fo. 183, Saturday 29 April 1620
John Paul brought in by Warra*n*^{t} from Sr John Leman d*e*live*r*ed to goe to Bohemia hee was taken dronck and abused the wife of Mr Bright vinten*er*, in his dronkennesse, but his po*nishment* spared **in regard** hee **goes** for a soldier

(36)   fo. 271v, 23 March 1631 (ie 1632?)
Hamey a moore by M*r* Tr*easu*rer va*grant* blackmore[12] who hath bene here before is to worke **till** he **may be sent** beyond Seas into his owne Countrey/ Edward Grave Edward Barton by Marshall ffitch Grave was lately sent away hence and bound app*r*entice to Capt*ain* Royden to goe to the Barbathoes who is run from him therfore the Capt. to returne xl^s. he had with him backe againe to worke./ Barton hath bene burnt in the hand who was now taken attempting to open a dore with an instrum*en*^{t} or key in the locke in the tyme of devine service on sonday last va*grant* p*er*son po*nished* and to remayne here **till** he **find** suerties for his good behavio^r

(37)   fo. 290v, 3 August 1632
Suzan Kendall Anne Thomas by Const*able* Jackson Bushopsgate were both taken by the watch Kendall will goe to Virginia to worke **till** she **may be**

sent away./ Thomas for a suspicious person saith she is with child but doth not soe appeare she is to worke here till her mother vndertake for her departure out of towne

3.2.5 Indicative singular zero. This is one of the indexical features of present-day AAVE (see Wolfram 1991: 108; Wolfram and Schilling-Estes 1998: 171, 341), although it is also present in SWVE too. Feagin (1979: 189–90) found that third-person present-tense indicative singular zero occurred 2.7 percent of the time (23/844) in the speech of her southern urban working-class white informants, and 4 percent of the time (9/225) in the speech of her southern rural white informants. This is as compared to Labov's finding of 64 percent (699/1089) in the speech of black teenage gang members in Harlem. Third-person-singular present-tense indicative zeros are not frequent in the Bridewell Court Minute Books, but they do occasionally occur, and have been noted in other Early Modern English writings (see Wright 2001: 250–2; Visser 1963–73: paragraph 840).

(38) fo. 23, 23v, 26 June 1576
      She saieth that Mrs Esgriges said that yf m^r Recorder medle wth her she would stop his mouthe/ She saieth that Sineor deprosper the Italian **Do** kepe Elizabeth Cowper and paid xs a weke for it

(39) fo. 125v, 28 December 1576
      He sayeth the same ffrenchman is a bawde & a pander[13] and **declare** many thinges of dyuers men & wemen

3.2.6 The historic present. The historic present, described in Fischer (1992: 242–5) as first encountered in Late Middle English, is the use of the non-past in a past-time narrative context. Rissanen (1999: 226–7) calls it "the vividly reporting present." It is usually thought to have imparted a colloquial flavor to the narrative (as in present-day English), but may have had aspectual connotations as well. As (40) shows, it was present in the speech of the transportees at the point of departure, and adds another function to the zero, -s, and -th suffixes:

(40) fo. 220v, 21 December 1575
      I did see my m^{rs} make hir selfe vnredie standinge in the chamber windowe nexte to m^r ffarmo^{rs} chamber, & when she was all vnlaced she **goeth** into m^r ffarmo^{rs} chamber, & I did steale vppe the stayres, to se what she wolde do there goinge in that order, & so I **see** hir come to the hether side of m^r ffarmo^{rs} bedd

Although the distribution of third-person-singular zero in Early Modern London English is different from that of present-day AAVE and SWVE, (19)–(40) demonstrate that not only was third-person-singular present-tense zero present at the point of departure, but that -s, -th, and zero had overlapping functional loads, with zero used as a minority variant in the indicative singular, and -s used as an incoming variant in the subjunctive.

3.3   Third-person present-tense indicative plural -s and the they-*constraint*

Plural verbal *-s* is attested in the nineteenth-century in the southern United States (Bailey 1997b: 267), and it is widespread in British dialects. At the point of departure the default third-person-plural indicative and subjunctive marker was zero, but the transportees also had *-th* and *-s* as alternative variants (see Schendl [1996, 2000]; Wright [forthcoming b] for a discussion).

3.3.1 Plural zero. Zero was the default way of expressing the third-person-plural present tense in Early Modern London English. It stems from the Middle English Midland paradigm, whereby the third-person indicative present-tense plural was marked with both *-en* and *-s*. Over time, the /n/ was lost, and the remaining *-e* suffix went through a period of being variably pronounced until finally it was lost altogether. Lass (1999: 162–3) notes that plural zero took quite a long time to get established; late sixteenth-century writing typically shows the kind of variation seen in (41)–(54).

3.3.2 Plural -th. -th is the next most common plural variant, and often follows a dummy subject. It is a relict of the Middle English southern paradigm, which used *-th* to mark both the third-person indicative present-tense singular and plural (Lass 1999: 162).

(41)   fo. 126v, 11 May 1575
       Thomas Noble and Homfrey Russhel*l*, dwellinge in shorditche **hathe** geve*n* their wordes

(42)   fo. 165, 13 August 1575
       Richarde Hil*l* came to this courte and complayned that diu*ers* suspected p*er*sons **hathe** resorted to the howse of Jo*h*n Holgate

(43)   fo. 67v, 22 September 1576
       Also he saith that there is one Edehall lienge at one Thomas Ayland*es* house in Goldinge lane and there **resortith** Dyvers Prentic*es* thither & to Ayland*es* daughter vnder collo[r] of Mariage

(44)   fo. 119, 2 January 1576
       He sayeth that the same Pudsey & R & w[m] Chase **hath** bene at all the Bawdes howses aboute London at blacke Luces at Stales and all the rest as they confessed them selves

(45)   fo. 119v, 2 January 1576
       He sayeth that John Byllyard is aqu*a*unted wth very many younge men in Londo*n* and also he is a pandar & Carryer of them to Lewde howses & to the Company of lewde & naughtie wemen who he is very well acquaynted wth all he knoweth all the Bawdes howses & all the Comon hores and many younge men that **vseth** them

(46) fo. 121v, 2 January 1576
He sayeth that Webbe Ellyott & Jones **doth** go together & would often saye to Shawe he had no good stuffe they could go to other howses & fynde better

(47) fo. 329v, Saturday 10 May 1623
ffrauncis Reynold by warran^t from Sr Tho*mas* Bennett to bee kepte in safetie because shee attempted two seuerall times to cast her selfe away into the Thames ouer the Iron pikes att the drawe bridge shee is wth childe and is kepte vntill her husband and his M^r may bee spoken wth wch m^r Cooke & Mr Watson **pr**omis**e**th to **p**er**f**orme

3.3.3 Plural -s. *-s* is the incoming form at this date, and it was used as a minority plural variant, as in present-day London English. It is a relict of the Middle English Midland paradigm, whereby the third-person indicative present-tense singular was marked with *-th* and *-s*, and the plural with *-en* and *-s* (Lass 1999: 162–3). Over time, *-en* reduced to zero and became the standard form, but *-s* is retained widely in nonstandard dialects. Plural *-s*, present in many nonstandard dialects, has been viewed as hypercorrection of an underlying creole by AAVE speakers (see Cukor-Avila 1997b: 296). Feagin (1979: 190–6), amongst others, has shown this to be erroneous; the Bridewell data supports her argument.

(48) fo. 124v, 28 December 1576
Melcher Pelse sayeth that John Thom*a*s and his wyfe are bawdes they **Dwell** in Seathinge lane very many marryners & other Englishe men Lewdly **Resort***es* thither

(49) fo. 125v, 28 December 1576
& there is a ffrenche ma*n* that vseth to bringe her to and froo and he lyveth by her the ffolkes of the howse **knowes** hym to be a very bawde/ He sayeth the same ffrenchman is a bawde & a pander and Declare many thinges of Dyu*ers* men & weme*n* He sayeth that m^{res} whaley in longe lane is a bawde and hath naughtie wemen in her howse and many men **resorte** thither from the bowlinge Alley and she sendeth for whores for them

(50) fo. 161, 23 January 1576
Roase fflower sayeth that a frowe^{14} one [blank – LCW] a s*er*uinge mans wyfe hard by her kepeth a bawdy howse there at the mynories her whores are Dutche weme*n* and **goeth** wth Bracelett*es* of golde and many m*er*chant*es* **resort***es* thither m*a*rgarett m^{res} kendall*es* mayde nowe lyinge wth m^r Evans at temple barre laye at the ffrowes & paide vj^s a weike for her bourde

Note that the examples all come from the testimonies of the very detailed cases of 1575 and 1576 transcribed so far. After 1600 the cases became terser, and minority variants became more standardized in this archive. The plural variants of zero, *-s*, and *-th* persisted into the seventeenth and eighteenth centuries. The

-*s* plural appears considerably later than the -*s* singular, the first known London example being 1515, but it then became very common in London writing as a minority variant of zero (Lass 1999: 165–6).

3.3.4 The they-*constraint*. For some speakers in early modern London there was a proximity constraint on third-person-plural present-tense indicative marking. For such speakers, verbs with a noun phrase subject or null subject were marked by -*s* or -*th*; but if the pronoun *they* was adjacent to the verb, then the verb was marked by zero, as in (51) *they go, and commeth*; (52) *there resorteth, they lye*; (53) *they haue, & hathe*, (54) *Makyn Easte and wise sayeth, They saye*. In Wright (forthcoming b) I label this the *they*-constraint, because the pronoun *they* has an effect on the adjacent verb. Previous scholars have used a plethora of labels for this phenomenon, such as the "personal pronoun rule," "the northern paradigm," "the NP/PRO constraint," the "northern present-tense rule," "the subject type constraint and proximity to subject constraint," "the northern subject rule" (see Wright forthcoming b for attributions). My purpose in adding to this confusion is to focus on the effect of the pronoun *they* rather than its regional origin (which was northern Britain), as by the point of departure the *they*-constraint had travelled well beyond its original heartland. The *they*-constraint is found sporadically in early modern London writing and is occasionally present in the Bridewell Court Minute Books. It is found in present-day southern United States speech, where it was greatly reinforced in the later seventeenth and eighteenth centuries by Scots-Irish settlers, who had far higher ratios (see Montgomery 1997b, 1996b: 222–9).

(51)   fo. 35, <> May 1574 (the date is missing, but is between the 5th and the 11th) This dotterells howse hathe two or three wenches that **vseth** there dalie And **is** there occupied wth sarving men and othere and at nighte they **go** to bed in an othere place And **commeth** againe in the mornynge And so **is** there continewally abused as the saide Dorcas saythe

(52)   fo. 122v, 30 April 1575
John hanckocke *alias* Jacke of the kitchi*n* saithe there **resorteth** to the howse of willi*a*m Cooke in kentishe strete, ffraunces Cole, & Thomas Cole his Brother, & also one Thomas Smithe, who be very Theves, . . . And also that none of those **haue** M[rs] & that they **lye** there contynuallie

(53)   fo. 167, 20 August 1575
And that whe*n* the said Jo*h*n hathe come to the Dore they **haue** go*n* in-together & locked the dore, and went in and satte in by the fyer & **hathe** plaied at cardes

(54)   fo. 105, 17 December 1576
Makyn Easte and wise **sayeth** that m*a*rshall carryed his owne wyfe to Acerbo velutelloes howse at Newington **They saye** he is a bawde to his owne wyfe

To summarize: third-person-plural -*s*, -*th* were minority variants in Early Modern English, and plural -*s* continues to be present in southern United States speech. The *they*-constraint was introduced to the New World by the transportees and is still present in southern United States speech, where its continuing presence may be accounted for by the later incursion of Ulster Scots speakers.

3.4 Possessive constructions

In Early Modern English, both the -*s* genitive and the *of* genitive were used pretty much as in present-day Standard English. The -*s* genitive was favored in informal and personal texts, and if the head had a human referent, or had other postmodifying elements (see Rissanen 1999: 201–4; Raumolin-Brunberg 1991: 201). There were also two other ways of marking possessive relationships. The pronoun *his* or *her* could be inserted between the head noun and the object (Barber 1976: 200–1). This practice goes back to Old English, but by the Early Modern period, *his* is mostly found with personal names ending in -*s*, and *her* with female personal names. Also, certain classes of Old English nouns did not add a genitive -*s* suffix, which explains compounds such as *ladybird* ("my lady's bird") and *mother tongue* ("your mother's tongue") (Fischer 1992: 225).

3.4.1 Possessive -s. This was and is the default way of marking possession.

(55) fo. 329, 329v, 7 June 1578
      Mr Neames did knowe of Smithes and Bates frendes entisement*es* and threating*es* to this exami*n*ant and he councelled her not to be ruled by Smyth nor Bates frendes sayeinge that if she did denye that wch she had deposed beinge troth As she saied it was he wolde forsake her and leave her of

3.4.2 The double-marked possessive. In Early Modern English the possessive relationship was sometimes doubly marked, as in *a friend of my sister's* (see Rissanen 1999: 203). In (57) the likely interpretation is that the possessive is doubly marked, and that there was one poor fellow who owned one suit of clothes, rather than several poor fellows owned one suit of clothes between them:

(56) fo. 241–241v, 26 September 1577
      the said Boyer also saieth that by meanes of A gentleman **of my lorde of Oxffordes** wch he came acquaynted wth at wo^rcesto^r house whoe desired verye earnestlye to mete wth m^rs Howe

(57) fo. 150, Saturday 30 October 1619
      Richard Ballard brought in by the Marshall & Constable ffysher Smythfield for a notorious pilferinge va*grant* that stole away a sute of clothes **of the poore fellowes** that sweepeth the Yards is po*ll*ed & de*live*red by passe and a shert and shoes to him given

3.4.3 Insertion of his *and* her. See (23) "Sr Thomas Bennett his warra*n*^{t}" and (82) "his m^r his howse" for examples with *his*.

(58)   fo. 93 Saturday 15 January 1618

Martha Owen ffraunc*es* Lawrence brought in by warra*n*^{t} from Sr Tho*mas* Bennett, Owen was abortivelie deliu*e*red of a liquid lumpe in the said **Lawrence her house,** begotten (as she sayeth) by John Kinge shoemaker, wch Lawrence did see, and cast into the house of Office.[15] Owen is by order of Court p*o*nished & d*e*liv*e*red and Lawrence is d*e*liv*e*red by Sr Thomas Bennett*es* direcc*i*on signified by m^r Perie

3.4.4 The zero-marked possessive. The zero-marked possessive was still present in the late 1500s and early 1600s in London speech; nowadays it is found predominantly in black speech (see Mufwene 1998: 74–5), including Liberian Settler English (see Singler 1991: 267), and is considered to be one of the features indexical of AAVE (see Wolfram 1971: 146; 1991: 108; Wolfram and Schilling-Estes 1998: 171). Holm (1991: 241) notes an example in the Ex-Slave Recordings: *the white folk kitchen.* Some linguists have claimed that this is an African substrate feature, because several of the original West African languages that the early slaves would have spoken didn't mark possession by inflexional morphology but by word order alone (Schneider 1982: 30). This might help explain why black speakers have retained this seventeenth-century feature to a greater degree than in other Englishes. The zero-marked possessive is present in the Ex-Slave Narratives, but only at a low degree of 9.3 percent (35/377) (Schneider 1982: 30), which could indicate that this is a feature that has been revivified by a process of exaptation (see section 4), to become indexical of present-day African–American Vernacular English.

(59)   fo. 276, 13 January 1577

She sayeth that wrey had thuse of her bodye ones at **widoe Goldwell house** hard by thabby in westm*inster* wch was wthin iij dayes after her last delyverye w^{ch} **Goldwell wiffe** is a bawde and kepeth ill resorte in her house

(60)   fo. 312v, 27 May 1578

And she sayeth that the said Barlowe is bawde to his wiffe and knoweth it and mett full yesternight wth a yonge man on his staires cominge downe and saied nothinge to him wch man had then abused his wiffe as Barlowe well knewe besids ther was **the said Barlowe owne brother** then ther also that night

(61)   fo. 28v, Saturday 14 February 1617

Robert Bowers brought in from M^r dep*uty* Hickman, a fellowe that will not be ruled by his freind*es*, he is by order of Court kept att **his father Charges** to be sent to Virginia

Thus, possessive zero was a variant at the point of departure and its presence in AAVE is not an innovation as such. Early Modern English was characterized by variation, which the process of standardization has greatly reduced. What *is* an innovation is the way in which black speakers have preferred the zero variant and use it in higher ratios than other speakers do.

3.5   *liketa*

In present-day southern United States varieties, *liketa* (*have*) + verb + -*ed* has the semantic property of *almost, just about, nearly*; as in *I liketa had a heart attack* (see Feagin 1979: 174–82, 344, Appendix B; Bailey 1997b: 259; Bernstein in this volume). "*Liketa* occurs in both positive and negative sentences, but not in questions and commands. It may co-occur with the intensifier *just*; it always occurs in the past." "The meaning of *liketa* is 'almost'; it occurs before the main verb, generally in violent contexts" (Feagin 1979: 178, 184). Wolfram and Schilling-Estes (1998: 335) note that it is counterfactual, in that it signals an impending event that did not, in fact, occur. *Liketa* has had an interesting social trajectory in that it is first attested in Early Modern English, became regarded as part of the standard register and was used by writers such as Shakespeare, Ben Jonson, Samuel Johnson, Steele, Defoe, Swift, Fielding, George Washington, and Dickens, but then for some reason became regarded as vulgar at some point in the nineteenth century. The *Oxford English Dictionary* finds it rather difficult to classify, with entries spread across two headwords, and includes no British quotations later than the 1800s, only ones which it labels as "Now *vulgar* and *dial.* (*U.S.*)." Feagin's 1979 detailed study of white informants in Anniston, Alabama, showed that there was a slight tendency for *liketa* to be used more by women and girls than by men and boys; that there was greater, though not exclusive, working-class usage; and for the complement to be either literally or metaphorically dire: consider her informants' quotations "My daddy liketa kill me one time with a ham string!," "You liketa run me over, didn't you!" (said by a filling-station owner). Tillery and Bailey (2001) note that "the *Dictionary of American Regional English* (*DARE*) documents *liketa* as early as 1808 in Virginia, 1845 in Georgia, and 1886 in the southern Appalachians"; Feagin (1979: 183) found earlier instances in George Washington's writings of 1753 and 1784. Bailey and Ross (1988: 206) present a quotation from a captain's ship's log from 1692: "we . . . had *like to* have taken the third." I have located the following *like to* + verb constructions in the Bridewell archive:

(62)   fo. 125, 28 December 1576
   Hunma*n* & his wiffe at the George in Shorte Southwarke in An Alley by the walnott tree are bawdes & doo kepe whores contynually for suche as come she her selfe & others goeth abroade Hunma*ne* laye wth a queane[16] that kepes a vittelinge howse hard by hym and was **like to** Ryde in Southwarke for yt she kept vitlinge in his sello[r]

(63)   fo. 215v, 8 May 1577

...he was a thick sett man wth verye stompe gret leg*ges* and gret guttey fellowe full sett/ And he had some reasonable store of grey heares in his bearde and his heade And **like to** be an awncyent[17] cytizen Mrs Higgens said it was a contre gentleman but it was not so like for he had no sworde nor rapio^r nor dagger nor apparell like a contre man

(64)   fo. 84, Saturday 18 January 1605

Thomas Olliver sent in by Constable Hick*es* of Ludgate, for An incestious[18] Begger, and a Co*m*en follower of Coaches; & had **like to** haue puld a gentlewoman out of a Coache; ponished & deliu*er*ed on sureties for his good behauior hereafter

These are not quite the same as present-day United States southern usages in that syntactically the Bridewell instances are (62) *was like to* + base form, (63) *like to* + base form, (64) *like to have* + verb + *-ed*. In present-day American usage only the third, *like to* (*have*) + verb + *-ed* occurs, and it is only (64) which is unambiguously semantically like present-day American usage. However, two of the three display the dire or violent complement noticed by Feagin (1979: 181), and two of the three signal an impending event that did not in fact occur.

There are several quotations in the *Oxford English Dictionary* under *like* adv. and *like* v.[2] which seem to be relevant to the southern United States sense: *OED like* adv. 9. a. "That may reasonably be expected *to* (do, etc.), likely *to*"; cf. 1592 Shakespeare "my graue is like to be my wedding bed" (*Romeo and Juliet* I.v.187) which might fit the first Bridewell quotation, if "and was like to Ryde in Southwarke for yt" is understood to mean "and she or he was likely to ride in Southwark for it." But consider *OED like* adv. 9. b.:

> (Now colloq. or dial.) Apparently on the point of. Sometimes (?by anaco-luthon) with ellipsis of the vb. substantive, so that *like* becomes = "was (or were) like" (now chiefly *U.S. colloq.*). Also in confused use, *had like to* (for *was like to*), chiefly with perf. inf: = "had come near to, narrowly missed (-ing)."

The first four quotations given under *like* adv. 9. b. are:

> "c.1560 Wriothesley *Chron.* (1875) II. 135 Wherefore that plee would not serve, and so [they] had like to haue had judgment without triall." (compare "wherefore that plea would not serve, and so they almost had judgement without trial")
> "1565 J. Sparke in *Hawkins' Voy.* (1878) 26 Which had like to haue turned us to great displeasure." (compare "which had almost turned us to great displeasure")
> "1586 A. Day *Eng. Secretary* II. (1625) 80 That he had like to have knockt his head against the gallowes" (compare "that he had almost knocked his head against the gallows")

"1600 Shakespeare *As You Like It* V.iv.48 I haue had foure quarrels, and like to haue fought one." (compare "I have had four quarrels, and almost fought one")

Was like to is an earlier form, meaning "apparently on the point of." To be whipped whilst riding at cart's arse, or at cart's tail, was a common punishment for bawdry (see also (13); n. 6.). Although in present-day Standard English null-subject slots are assumed to be referring to the most recently mentioned subject, this was not always the case in Early Modern English writing. I suggest that in (62) the *like to* clause should be interpreted as belonging to the subordinate clause, rather than as a co-ordinated main clause, and the ellipted relative pronoun is *who/that*, giving the meaning that the prostitute who kept the victualling house had previously narrowly escaped punishment for prostitution.

OED like v.[2] 2. b. is where southern United States *liketa* is to be found. The definition is as follows:

> To look like or be near *to* doing (something) or *to* being treated (in a specified manner). Now *vulgar* and *dial.* (*U.S.*), chiefly in compound tenses, *had* (rarely *were*) *liked to*, or (dial.) *am* (*is*, etc.) *liken* (for *liking*) *to*, etc.

The first quotation is from 1426. All of *OED*'s quotations except for one are of the construction "*like to have* + verb + *-ed*," and all have a dire or violent complement.

In (63), the man under discussion is described as either "he was likely to be an ancient citizen," or, "he was almost an ancient citizen." Both interpretations seem possible. There is nothing, so far as I can discover, essentially imminently dire about being described as "awncyent" in early modern London. (64) is the only context in which the sense *almost, nearly, just about* is unambiguous, the syntax is *like to have* + verb + *-ed*, and the complement is violent. We may conclude that *liketa* as used in present-day United States southern speech was present in the speech of the early settlers from London, but that it had a greater range semantically and syntactically, which has since become restricted.

3.6   Zero-subject relative pronouns

Zero in subject position was common in Middle English writing (Fischer 1992: 306–7), and is common in sixteenth-century texts, both formal and informal. In Early Modern English the zero subject is most common in *there is/there are* constructions (Rissanen 1999: 298), as in the Bridewell quotations below. Zero-subject relative pronouns are found in present-day speech in the southern United States, and also in present-day London English (cf. Schneider 1982: 36; Mufwene 1998: 77 for AAVE; Wolfram and Schilling-Estes 1996: 110 for Okracoke speech; Wolfram and Schilling-Estes 1998: 343 for general southern usage). Martin and Wolfram (1998: 32) notice that in present-day AAVE the zero subject is also "particularly prominent with existential sentences such as *There's/It's a teacher brought some food for the party.*" Montgomery (1991: 185–7) analysed subject-relative pronoun deletion in the Ex-Slave Recordings (as in *she got a daughter ^ stay out here in the country*) and found that subject zero forms were much more likely to have human head nouns than non-human ones, just as in the Bridewell examples given below.[19] Subject pronoun deletion is one of those features which only became stigmatized by the prescriptivist grammarians, and is preserved in many non-standard dialects.

(65) fo. 105, 26 March 1575
she Answered, that Thomas saide his vnckle & his Aunt wolde not live longe, & then he was suer of his Land*es* & goodes, and also **there was a woma*n* ^ ha<d> tolde him,** that his Aunte wolde not live longe

(66) fo. 22v, 26 June 1576
And **ther is a gentlewoman ^ lyeth nowe in his house** in a damoske govne whose name is Jane

(67) fo. 249v, 22 October 1577
He saieth that about a yere and more agone he had a mayde whose name is Godlye and **ther was a stranger ^ had thuse of her bodye** in m^r Harden the p*ar*son of Islingdons studye this Megge ffollantyne tolde him

(68) fo. 279v, 21 January 1577
One night **ther was ij strangers gent*lemen* ^ came** to East*es* and one lay wth Marie Dornelley thother wth this exa*mi*n*a*t the gent*leman* gaue ether of them to East xs and to Marie and this exa*mi*n*a*t vs apeice/ wherof East had xijd a peice besides

(69) fo. 226, 10 June 1577
He harde William Bartlet saye that **Millsent Porte^r sent A l*ette*re to John Bentley ^ compared him to the Jellyfloer**[20] and the bay tree and her to the marygolde And desyred that the seede of the bay tree might haue good successe wch laye hid full close

(70) fo. 66, Wednesday 23 October 1605
John Thorpe aforesaid beinge exa*mi*ned vtterly denieth, that hee eu*er* had the vse of her bodie: And saith, at that time hee was driueinge those Oxen to the feild, **there was another Butchers boie ^ went wth him:** It is ordered, that hee shalbee kept for sureties to discharge the Cittie of the childe

Although this feature looks as though it shares properties of deletion found in creoles, zero relative pronouns in subject position have a long history and are widespread in nonstandard dialects.

3.7 Nonstandard preterits

During the Middle English period (from around 1066 to around 1500) three major developments took place in the strong verb system: there was a reduction in the number of vowel grades per verb (compare *ride* ~ *rode* ~ *ridden*); "hybridization" or mixing of forms from more than one class in the conjugation; and strong verbs conjugated as though they were weak (Lass 1992: 131–3). It is the latter two processes which concern us here, as standardization has since determined which verbs are strong and which are weak in present-day Standard English, but other dialects have preserved some of the multiplicity that prevailed in Middle English. For a discussion of nonstandard past-tense and past-participle forms in present-day southern United States speech, see McDavid (1998), Pederson (1983: 133). Schneider (1982: 23–5) analyzed the nonstandard preterits and past participles used in the Slave Narrative Collection compiled by the Federal Writers' Project in the mid 1930s, and details how almost all of the nonstandard verb forms shown there are widespread in other nonstandard British and American dialects. In particular, he notes that *see* was used as a preterit form (1982: 24), as it was in early modern London (see (75)).

3.7.1 Simplex forms

(71) fo. 143v–144v, 2 January 1576
… And there vpon I **rysse** from the table and asked of her and she strayte wayes graunted me my most ffylthye desyer but I did not deale wth her … And then ffreema*n* and John Hayward & I **ridd** together when we came A most there And soe when we came thither ffreema*n* had agreed wth the ffolkes of the howse that we should lye all together in one Chamber and so we did

(72) fo. 61v, 7 September 1576
he came acquaynted wth her for that he lent her husbond money & her husbond had then a sute in thelde hall/ wherein he **holpe** her husbond

(73) fo. 10v, Saturday 26 January 1604
And then the said Elizabeth willed this Exa*m*ina*n*t to write certen libelling verses wch the said Elizabeth would tell this Exa*m*ina*n*t by word of mowth (wch he did) and for want of Incke **writt** them first wth black leade and afterward*es* wth Incke wch the said Eliz: lost

(74) fo. 42, Saturday 25 April 1618
Richard Robert*es* one that hath violentlie and wth force kept the possession of the house late Harrisons, and two padlock*es* beinge **hanged** vpon the dores, he **brake** through the walls, and threatneth that he will keepe the house in despight of governme*n*^t

(75) fo. 50, Saturday 20 June 1618
they both p*ar*ted from Gibbs his house, and he went about his busines and that about x a Clocke **he see** her standinge att the Rayles againe, and then

went in and acquainted m^r Johnson therof and from that time afterward*es*
he see her no more, till they mett att the Justices

(76)   fo. 127v, Saturday 19 June 1619
William Smyth brought in by warr*an*^{t} from Sr Thomas Middleton for a
vagr*an*^{t} who beinge shipped for Virginia **runne** away & tooke wth him
divers thing*es* belongeinge to others, is kepte

(77)   fo. 258v, 20 January 1631 (i.e. 1632)
by order of Sessions **holden** the 13th of Ja*n* 1631

Lass (1999: 166–75) discusses the extraordinary amount of variation present in
the Early Modern English verb. He identifies three main evolutionary pathways
for strong verbs, and a fourth combination form:

- Historically expected vowel grades: *write ~ wrote ~ have written*
- Historical participle or past plural vowel generalised to both the past and past
  participle: *write ~ writ ~ have writ*
- Historical past singular vowel generalized to both the past and past participle:
  write ~ wrote ~ have wrote
- A combination of all three: *write ~ writ ~ have wrote*

Apart from this generalization, each verb has its own history, and much of the early
modern innovation has been undone in later times (Lass 1999: 168). Especially,
alternants became fixed by the eighteenth-century prescriptive grammarians,
such as Dr. Johnson (1999: 169), and so standardized speech has lost them,
whereas nonstandard dialects have preserved many.

3.7.2 Double-marked forms. Double-marked forms are not common in the
Bridewell Court Minute Books but they do occur occasionally. They have been
noted in present-day Okracoke speech, e.g. *she had came here* (Wolfram and
Schilling-Estes 1996: 110; 1998: 332) and Texas speech e.g. *me an' the manager
had became good friends* (Bailey 1993: 296).

(78)   fo. 47v, 14 July 1576
she saieth That Tringe Goffes wief doth knowe that he kept her & was
many tymes wth them when they mett & when they **had dranck** togither
Tring goffes wief wold leve them together in the chamber for the nonnce
& goe her waie

(79)   fo. 247, 10 October 1577
she saieth that Horspoll*es* wiffe did knowe for what purpose she and the
stranger was ther./ she saieth that Horsepoll*es* wiffe asked wher she laye
that she might send for her when anye bodye **did came** she saieth that the
same Horsepoll*es* wiffe is a bawde.

Nonstandard preterits are another feature which has been ascribed to hypercorrection on the part of AAVE speakers due to an underlying creole, but as

noted by Schneider (1982) and demonstrated here, they are simply a feature of nonstandard English.

3.8   a+*verb*+ing

The construction *to be a-doing* was at its height between 1500 and 1700 (Mustanoja 1960: 587). It goes back to a combination of the preposition *on* + the verbal noun ending in *-ing*, and during the seventeenth century is found in formal and educated writing, but it became nonstandard during the course of the eighteenth century (Rissanen: 1999: 217). Schneider (1982: 28) notes that *a*+verb+*ing* is well attested in both American and British dialects, and Wolfram and Schilling-Estes (1998: 334) single out Appalachian speech as particularly prone. Feagin (1979: 100–19) presents a study of *a*+verb+*ing* in SWVE. *a*- largely sits before verbs beginning with a consonant, and the preferred environment is after a final consonant on the end of the preceding word. The prefix does not seem to carry much meaning other than perhaps intensity, and often follows verbs of sensory perception such as *see, hear*. It is most likely to be fixed to verbs of action.

(80)   fo. 66v, 25 September 1574
        Item the ffirste acquantaunc That I had of Lawrence Holden was by goinge to his howse wth some of my ffellowes & wth stockye a **drincking**

(81)   fo. 118, 27 April 1575
        M^r yonge Alledged that he had a litle boye, who had a skalde hed, & that boye begged for him & gott muche monnye by him, & in thende the boye was taken from him to be healed in Sainte Barthelmewes, & yet he after that gott the same boye againe & sente him a **begginge** againe as he did before

(82)   fo. 141, 2 January 1576
        The said Edward for that he by his owne confessyon Doth saye he hath lefte his m^r his howse in the nighte & come oute of the wyndow & left yt open & went a **Dawncesinge** all nighte & Deceaved his m^r of his monye hath here correccion

(83)   fo. 104, 15 February 1636 (i.e. 1637)
        Mary Williams alias Parie Hester Clements sent in by Constable Parker farringdon w^thout Willia^ms for seizing on Mr Nicholls the Beadle when he was a **making** water again^st the wall in a very vnseemely manner is a common nightwalker and an old Customer ponished Clements was taken in her company in the night Willia^m ffoure is willing to take her to verginea set by for that purpose & he to give securitie to transport her

This feature has been identified as being of creole origin because the prefix has been compared to preverbal aspectual markers in creole Englishes (cf. Feagin 1979: 100–19).[21] Although the feature itself is simply a historic form, it has had an up-and-down social trajectory, in common with, for example, glide insertion (*cyan* for *can*) and [ð]-fronting (*bovver* for *bother*), which also used to be socially acceptable London forms during the eighteenth century, but which then came to be considered vulgar. It is tempting to see *a*+verb+*ing*'s survival in AAVE as being reinforced by the aforementioned aspectual marking found in creoles, but it is hard to see what, if any, aspectual connotations *a*+verb+*ing* actually has or has had, and *a*+verb+*ing* is and has always been spoken by southern whites, too.

4   Summary

The eight Early Modern English features considered here all have present-day reflexes in the southern United States. The current view of the relationship of AAVE to SWVE is that the two have been diverging in recent decades (see, for example, Labov's [1998: 123] comments on the work of Bailey and Rickford). It seems as though certain minority variants which entered the southern United States with the first Early Modern English speakers remained in use as variants in southern idiolects for many generations, and then in the speech of later generations, some of these became indexical of social properties such as region, class and race.

- In the case of invariant *be*, traditional usage (which is not yet fully understood) has recently developed into a new construction which is indexical of region, age, class, and perhaps race (see Bailey [1993] *be*+verb-*ing*). Historic plural indicative *be* has expanded its function into the singular and become preponderant in AAVE. Subjunctive *be* may still be present in older rural SWVE, but this needs further investigation.
- In the case of third-person-singular zero, which was very much a minority variant at the point of departure, usage ratios have increased and the newly preponderant zero has taken on the sociolinguistic property of race marker. Similarly, possessive zero seems to have become indexical of AAVE, now being used in greater ratios than it was historically.
- In the case of third-person-plural -*s*, *liketa*, *a*+verb+*ing*, nonstandard preterits, and zero-subject relative pronouns, usage has remained more or less stable. Because standardization has had little influence on vernacular speech, these features have come to connote southernness and perhaps working-class affiliation.
- The *they*-constraint is now in decline, and being, it seems, below the threshold of perception is unlikely to have carried any sociolinguistic encoding.

It is probably no accident that the features considered here marked by zero suffixes (third-person-singular zero, the zero-marked possessive and invariant *be*) map onto features found in creole Englishes, and have become indexical of AAVE.

The emphasis throughout this chapter has been on reporting the amount of variation[22] present at the point of departure for the eight features considered here. These are summarized in table 3.1.

Table 3.1 *List of variants for eight Early Modern English features found in the Bridewell Court Minute Books*

Feature	Variant
invariant *be*	plural indicative *be*
	subjunctive *be*
third-person-singular	*-th*
	-s indicative
	-s subjunctive
	zero indicative
	zero subjunctive
third-person-plural	*-th*
	-s
	zero
possessive marker	*-s, of*
	double-marked genitives
	zero-marked genitives
	his/her insertion
liketa	synonyms such as *nearly*
zero-subject relative pronouns	*who, which, that*
non-standard preterits	standard preterits
a+verb+*ing*	verb+*ing*

Natural language is full of variation, which, from a historical perspective, can be viewed as incoming variants, variants in a stable state, and outgoing variants. It is common for incoming and outgoing forms to exist side by side for centuries, until one dies out altogether. Once variants lose their function (as, for example, happened with third-person-singular zero, which used to mark the subjunctive mood), they then become available for some other kind of function, such as a marker of social grouping. This is known as the process of exaptation (Lass 1990; Wright 2001: 237, 254). Lass's (1990: 91) five-step schema for exaptation is as follows:

Step 1. A feature has a grammatical function (e.g. in Old English, third-person zero marks the subjunctive)

Step 2. The grammatical feature is lost (e.g. with the general loss of inflectional suffixes in Middle English, zero is no longer contrastive and hence cannot "mark" anything)

Step 3. The grammatical feature is now junk

Step 4. Adapt or die – the feature either dies out, or becomes redeployed for some other purpose (e.g. centuries later, third-person zero becomes preferred by AAVE speakers)

Step 5. Result (e.g. third-person zero is now an indexical marker of AAVE in many US communities)

Variants can expand or retract, or take on a new lease of life by changing their function. The eight features considered here may stem originally from Early Modern English, but their existence over the last four hundred years has been shaped considerably by the other systems with which southern United States speakers have come into contact (notably Ulster Scots speakers, and the descendants of West African speakers). The social context in which speakers lived determined to what extent their speech was open to external influence, be it in rural isolation in the Appalachians, or in social segregation on a plantation. A historical perspective such as has been provided here can present, in a crude kind of way, how variants entered the system, but in order to understand the current distribution, patterns of historical speaker interaction[23] need to be identified.

Notes

1. The Royal Hospital Court of Bridewell and Bethlem was not the only London court to sentence people to transportation. See, for example, Wareing (2000), which analyzes data from the Middlesex Sessions Papers 1645–1718, recording the transporting of offenders to the New World from the Middlesex courts.
2. For a discussion of how one can determine whether a passage is in formal Early Modern English or whether it is closer to spontaneous speech, see Wright (1995, 2000). Also note that all italics in the quotations indicate letters supplied for abbreviation and suspension marks in the manuscript.
3. I have been unable to trace *yerke* in any botanical literature. *Yark-rod* is recorded in Lincolnshire dialect as the ragwort *Senecio jacobea*; but *yerke* could also be a spelling for *oak*.
4. *And* in Early Modern English could introduce conditional clauses (Rissanen 1999: 281). This early modern use of *and* equates to *even if*, that is, "I will never confess it, even if I were to be stretched on the rack."
5. St Dunstons in the east. See also (59) the use, the Abbey, (72) the Guild Hall.
6. *OED* arse n.2., 3. arse-board (still *dial.*) "the tail board of a cart." *Charity Commissioners' Report* (1557 [1837]: 394, modernized spelling): "If any such shall return again to the city in roguish manner he shall openly be whipped at a cart's tail."
7. For a discussion of Early Modern English *-s* and *-th*, see Schneider (1983b), Stein (1985, 1987), Percy (1991), Kytö (1993), Ogura and Wang (1996), Nevalainen and Raumolin-Brunberg (1996).
8. For a discussion of the third-person-singular *-s* and zero in AAVE and SWVE, see Fasold (1981), Sommer (1986), Poplack and Tagliamonte (1989, 1991, 1994), Montgomery, Fuller, and DeMarse (1993), Montgomery and Fuller (1996), Winford (1998: 106), Montgomery (1999), Schneider (1983b, 1995, 1997); Viereck (1995, 1998).
9. *OED* piccadill 1. b. "an expansive collar with a broad laced or perforated border"; 2. "A stiff band or collar of linen-covered paste-board or wire, worn in the 17th c. to support the wide collar or ruff."
10. *OED* bush n.[1] 5. "A branch or bunch of ivy (perhaps as the plant sacred to Bacchus) hung up as a vintner's sign; hence, the sign-board of a tavern."
11. Fischer (1992: 350) notes "It is not quite clear what the basis was for subjunctive assignment in Middle English; different manuscripts often show different moods in

the same text and sometimes indicative and subjunctive are found side by side within the same sentence."

12. The term *blackmore* (as here written, later to become *blackamoor*) originally referred to people of sub-Saharan African origin, see *OED* blackamoor 1. "a black-skinned African."

13. *OED* pander n. 2. "a male bawd, pimp, or procurer"; see also (49).

14. *OED* frow n. 1. "a Dutchwoman."

15. *OED* house n.[1] 14.b. "a privy."

16. A *queane* was a prostitute. It is derived from the Old English weak feminine noun *cwene* "young woman" (see *OED* quean); as opposed to Old English strong feminine noun *cwēn* "wife of a nobleman" (see *OED* queen).

17. *awncyent* was a common term for describing an old person (see *OED* ancient A. adj. II. 6.).

18. *incestuous* referred to the act of having sex outside marriage (see *OED* incestuous a. I. b.).

19. Montgomery (1991: 185–7) reports that in his 1979 dissertation on Appalachian English he found nearly 300 instances of this pattern.

20. A gillyflower, wallflower.

21. Holm notes a possible overlap between West African languages and Early Modern English: "like many western Niger-Congo languages, the Atlantic creoles indicate progressive aspect with a preverbal marker which is often etymologically connected to an expression of location. This may represent a universal relationship between expressions of location and actions in progress, as in early modern English 'He is on doing it', which was reduced to 'He is a-doing it' " (Holm 1991: 236). Actually the *on-* prefix was characteristic of the Old English period, although there are still examples to be found in Middle English, see Fischer (1992: 253).

22. This is not to claim that all available variants have a sociolinguistic (or other) function at any one synchronic moment, or that all speech communities share the same distribution of variants or functions. On the contrary, any early modern London speaker at the point of departure would have had a selection of the variants described in table 3.1, which is an overview, rather than a description of an idiolect.

23. This difficult undertaking is being addressed by, for example, Bailey on the effect of the role of the cotton gin in settlement position and size, Mufwene on the arrangement of slaves' living accommodation on southern plantations, and Montgomery on the dispersal and settlement of the Scots-Irish migrants, amongst others.

Manuscript sources

London, Guildhall Library, MS Minutes of the Court of Governors of Bridewell and Bethlem: Microfilm Reels MS33011/1–2, 22 April 1559–6 May 1576; MS33011/3, 7 May 1576–19 November 1579; MS33011/4, 1 February 1597/8–7 November 1604; MS33011/5, 10 November 1604–28 July 1610; MS33011/6, 26 July 1617–3 March 1626; MS33011/7, 1 March 1626–7 May 1634; MS33011/8, 21 May 1634–7 October 1642; MS33011/9, 14 October 1642–7 July 1658.

The shared ancestry of African-American and American White Southern Englishes: some speculations dictated by history

SALIKOKO S. MUFWENE

1   Introduction

Speculations, conjectures, and hypotheses on the genetic relationship between African-American Vernacular English (AAVE) and American White Southern English (AWSE) date from the colonial period. Travelers to the American colonies often observed that blacks and whites spoke alike. Some of them even conjectured that the then emergent AWSE was influenced by its AAVE counterpart. As late as the 1990s, this view was still reflected by linguists such as Feagin (1997), who attributes to AAVE influence the southern drawl, non-rhoticity (or r-lessness), and falsetto pitch (apparent musicality).

The similarities between AAVE and AWSE are real. Non-Southerners have even often remarked that they were unable to determine whether a speaker was black or white unless they saw them. There is as yet no consensus on whether these ethnic varieties are so similar because the (descendants of) Africans influenced the speech of the (descendants of) Europeans up to the late nineteenth century or because of other reasons. I argue below, on sociohistorical grounds, that while AWSE and AAVE have undoubtedly influenced each other, their commonalities can be explained primarily by their common, coextensive histories of over 200 years during which their speakers interacted regularly with one another. Many of today's differences between the two vernaculars can be attributed to the divergence that resulted from the widespread institutionalization of segregation in the late nineteenth century.

It has also often been observed that an English koiné developed in the American colonies, which is the ancestor of at least today's American English vernaculars. Montgomery (1995, 1996b) contends that no uniform colonial koiné could have developed by the late eighteenth century. I argue below that he is certainly justified in rejecting such a uniform cross-colony koiné. However, several local or regional koinés must have developed quite early in the colonial period, due to the fact that the evolution of English in every colonial community was contact-induced. These koinés varied from, and yet resembled, each other on the family-resemblance model, because their metropolitan inputs were largely dialects of the same language with variable degrees of similarities and differences. The colonial mixes of these dialects varied from one setting to another, and this regional variation of the mixes accounts for the dialectal diversity that is typical of the construct "American English" today.

2   The shared ancestry of AAVE and AWSE

The position that AAVE represents class for class the colonial English spoken by poor whites in the South (Krapp 1924; Kurath 1928; Johnson 1930) has not been entirely abandoned. With some contextualization, this position can still be recognized in the version of the "divergence hypothesis" advocated by Bailey (1997b), Bailey and Maynor (1987, 1989), and Bailey and Thomas (1998). It presupposes a long period – from the early colonial, through the plantation, and to the post-Emancipation phases – during which (descendants of) Africans and most Europeans in the South spoke more or less the same English vernacular.[1] Different social dynamics since the passage of the Jim Crow laws (Schneider 1995), especially the adoption of residential segregation as a way of life, brought about divergent, ethnic-based evolutions of English among southern whites and African Americans (Mufwene 2000b). The introduction of the mill industry in some parts of the American South to replace the collapsing cotton plantation economy led to another regional reshuffling of the white populations (McNair 2002), hence to new dialect and language contacts, which were enhanced by new immigrations from continental Europe. These factors brought about new, twentieth-century evolutions in AWSE in which African Americans have not participated.

Compared to white vernaculars – which vary from one region to another and between the urban and rural environments – the relative homogeneity of AAVE across the United States (Labov 1972b) reflects the massive northward and westward exodus of African Americans from the South since the "Black Exodus" of the late nineteenth century and the "Great Migration" of the early twentieth century.[2] Otherwise, AAVE's birth place lies in the tobacco and cotton plantations of the American Southeast (Rickford 1998; Bailey and Thomas 1998; Rickford and Rickford 2000). Basic AAVE and Gullah seem to have changed little since the early twentieth century (Mille 1990; Mufwene 1991, 1994), and AAVE in general may largely reflect what, with the exception of varieties spoken on the rice and sugar cane plantations, American Southern English must have been like in the late nineteenth and early twentieth centuries (Bailey and Thomas 1998). One is certainly led to a similar conclusion by Poplack and Tagliamonte (2001), which summarizes their research since the late 1980s, whose consistent conclusion has in part been that earlier, nineteenth-century AAVE shares many features with white nonstandard vernaculars and could not have developed from an erstwhile creole.

To support the above version of the Divergence Hypothesis, I capitalize here on the evidence provided by the socioeconomic history of the United States. Linguistic evidence is rather indirect, lying in the ways African-American English

(AAE, including Gullah) has been represented in the media in the eighteenth century (Brasch 1981). Sources such as Wood (1974), Steeg (1975), and Coleman (1978) show clearly that the coastal South Carolina and Georgia regions, which absorbed most of these states' slave populations, developed on a different pattern from the hinterland regions, where the European populations, most of whom were yeomen, remained the overwhelming majorities until the abolition of slavery. Other sources such as Kulikoff (1986) and Perkins (1988) also indicate that in the Chesapeake colonies the African populations were higher in the coastal, swampy areas than in the hinterlands, where the European populations – most of whom where indentured servants – were the majority. The overall American history also shows that in the mid nineteenth century, the overwhelming majority of the African-American population resided in the American Southeast. In most of the northern states, the average ratio was 2 percent of the overall state populations (McPherson 1991).

Although residential segregation was widespread then, it did not really become institutionalized and strictly enforced until after the passage of the Jim Crow laws in the hinterland of the Southeast in the late nineteenth century. History suggests that, although discrimination was in place since the first English–African encounters in Virginia, segregation which bore on language evolution was a late, post-colonial state of affairs, except of course in the swampy areas of South Carolina (and later in coastal Georgia), where blacks became the majority since early in the eighteenth century on the rice fields. Gullah developed precisely in these areas, for reasons having to do less with their numerical majority than with race segregation and the rapid turnover rate in the ever-increasing slave population (Mufwene 1996b, 2001b).[3] Elsewhere, where AAVE developed as a tobacco and cotton plantation phenomenon, blacks and poor whites interacted regularly. As a matter of fact, the mulatto phenomenon was probably more common in early stages of colonization, when there were very few European females, than in the later stages. The spread of light complexion among African Americans is thus largely due to the founder principle, notwithstanding the literature on rapes of African-American women by their plantation masters and overseers.[4] The mulattoes (one of the most conspicuous manifestations of the non-linguistic creole phenomenon) must have played a greater role in the maintenance and transmission of colonial English to the Africans than has been acknowledged.[5]

The socioeconomic history thus suggests an early, eighteenth-century split between coastal and hinterland speech, with the conditions on the coast being more favorable to the development of a separate African-American ethnolect, especially Gullah, than in the hinterland. Here, most blacks and most whites still lived on small farms and regular interactions in such settings led them to develop similar colonial speech patterns, which even the greater segregation institutionalized by the Jim Crow laws managed to differentiate only minimally.[6]

History also reports that in the early stages of colonization the slave population grew more by birth than by importation (Steeg 1975; H. Thomas 1998). Growth by importation was more typical of the eighteenth century. As far as the contribution of Africans to colonial American English is concerned, this suggests that American-born blacks in especially the seventeenth century, who interacted regularly with American-born whites, spoke the same colonial vernaculars as the whites of their colonies. By the founder principle, they would become the models targeted by Africans and Europeans who joined them in the eighteenth century (even in segregated communities) and they determined most of the structural patterns that would be selected and restructured into later varieties of American English.

Although populations of African origin/descent have always been discriminated against since the colonial beginnings of North America, history also informs us that it is only toward the late seventeenth century that their status as indentured servants was changed to that of slave for life (Tate 1965). The earliest ones worked as house servants and fit in the category of those who have always been recognized in the literature to have approximated the speech characteristics of their masters. Although the proprietors of the Chesapeake colonies purchased more African laborers during the last third of the seventeenth century and used them on tobacco plantations, the Africans remained a minority, not exceeding 15 percent of the total population by the early eighteenth century. The highest proportion of population of African descent did not exceed 40 percent by the late eighteenth century (Perkins 1988). This situation on the tobacco plantations was unlike that in the rice fields of coastal South Carolina, where the African-to-European population ratio often reached 9 to 1 (Turner 1949; Joyner 1984), where social turmoil since before the Stono Rebellion (1739) and similar (threats of) slave uprisings led to early institutionalized segregation in the eighteenth century – soon after South Carolina became a Crown colony in 1720 (Wood 1974). This unique setting and its peculiar social structure produced Gullah, which is so similar to Bahamian and Caribbean plantation English vernaculars that it has been identified by analogy as a creole.

Although segregation may have existed *de facto* on the tobacco and later on the cotton plantations to which the Chesapeake colonies provided the founder slave labor, race relations did not become as rigidly constrained until the passage of the Jim Crow laws in the late nineteenth century (1877), a way of discriminating strongly against the emancipated slaves whose status relative to former indentured white servants was not (clearly) distinguished by the Constitution (Corcoran and Mufwene 1998). Perhaps the higher proportion of mulattoes from the tobacco and cotton plantations, in contrast with the rice fields, is in itself a reflection of differences in the patterns of race relations between the two kinds of colonies. Similarities between AWSE and AAVE, the vernacular which developed precisely where tobacco and cotton agriculture was the main industry, are thus due to over two centuries of close interactions between (descendants of) Africans and proletarian (descendants of) Europeans (the majority, based on Kulikoff's 1991 estimates). The similarities do not necessarily reflect influence of African-American speech on European Americans, the vast majority of whom could not afford slaves. Rather, they reflect common heritage that has been preserved among African-American and European-American Southerners since the institutionalization of segregation in the late nineteenth century as a way of life. That the similarities have been preserved for over a century is probably an indication of how deeply entrenched that common heritage is in both AWSE and AAVE.

On the other hand, the coastal rice settlements of South Carolina and Georgia developed on the Caribbean colonial model and with large and heavily populated plantations on which the Africans were the overwhelming majority. As noted above, these socioeconomic peculiarities of theirs produced a distinct colonial English ethnolect, Gullah, which has been related structurally (not necessarily genetically) to West Indian creoles.[7] Note that the term *creole* has primarily contributed to showing that there is influence external to the lexifier on the development of such colonial vernaculars. The naming practice does not *ipso facto* prove that the colonial dialects from which they have been distinguished lack such external influence on their development or that the creoles evolved from their lexifiers by any restructuring processes that did not play a role in other cases of language speciation. Thus the term *creole*, also used to argue that such offspring of the lexifier are separate languages, has played more an ideological, disfranchising role than it has served to help us understand much about language evolution in general. A closer examination of the socioeconomic historical settings of the development of these colonial vernaculars shows that differences between the structures of the "dialectal" and "creole" offspring of the lexifier are consequences of how the relevant colonial societies developed, including what models of the lexifier were accessible to non-native speakers, what patterns of social interaction existed between fluent speakers of the lexifier and those who were acquiring it, and especially whether the proportions of fluent speakers of the local vernaculars were being offset by the rapidly increasing volumes of newcomers (Mufwene 2001b).

The history of European settlements in the colonies suggests that contact was as much a factor in the development of white varieties of English as in that of African Americans (Mufwene 1996a, 2001b). If contact with other languages had not been a factor, then White American English would be like British English – though we must keep in mind that both constructed national varieties reflect evolutions since the seventeenth century. Things are actually more complex. Sociohistorical evidence also shows that the evolution of British English itself since the seventeenth century was likewise contact-induced, being a consequence of economy-instigated population movements and dialect contacts in the British Isles. Moreover, the demographic significance of dialectal inputs to all these metropolitan and colonial evolutions varied from one setting or region to another. Thus, as in all prior evolutions of the English language since the inception of Old English in the fifth or sixth century, the specifics of the contacts varied from one setting to another. If such regional variation were not a factor, then there would be no regional dialects in either the United Kingdom or North America.

In the colonial context, we must remember that migrations to the New World were basically an extension of population movements that were taking place in the metropole. What makes contacts with non-anglophone Europeans significant is the fact that places such as New England with a predominantly East Anglian founder population (Fischer 1989) still have an English variety that is more American than British, despite claims that it is the closest thing to British English. Layers of later immigrations from the United Kingdom and continental Europe appear to have affected the evolution of English in the region (see below).

We can thus come back to AWSE and its kinship to AAVE. Both varieties can be traced back to the tobacco and cotton plantations, the most important industry before the mines of the Appalachian and Piedmont mountains were exploited industrially and produced their own particular varieties. An important proportion of the indentured laborers, who worked side by side with the African slaves and interacted regularly with them, were non-native speakers of English, from Ireland and places in continental Europe, especially Germany. The same kinds of European and African influences impacted the evolution of English among both African and European Americans, although the significance of influences from the different backgrounds were probably not identical from one ethnic community to another.

One of the reasons most commonly advanced to perpetuate the myth that African Americans must have developed their own divergent variety from the early colonial days is that segregation made it difficult for African slaves to have access to the same English models as the European immigrants. However, as noted above, segregation was institutionalized later, after the Revolution (late eighteenth century) and, based on reports of visitors to the colonies (see below), apparently after distinct American English varieties had already formed.

In any case, assuming that segregation was practiced much earlier, recall that in the early stages of almost all colonies populations grew more by birth than by immigrations or importation. In the small homestead communities that the colonies started with, children of both Europeans and Africans are likely to have acquired the same colonial varieties (Chaudenson 1992; Berlin 1998). Thus, what matters in the transmission of English to newcomers in the colonies is not so much the proportion of Europeans to Africans but rather that of native to non-native speakers, regardless of race (Mufwene 2000a,b, 2001b). I maintain that while slavery denigrated people of African descent, it did not reduce their aptitude to acquire the target language any more than indentured servitude did to many European immigrants. Therefore, children of Europeans and Africans acquiring English under similar naturalistic conditions developed similar colonial varieties, though their parents had different accents (as is true of European and African immigrants today who live in the same neighborhoods). We may assume that in the tobacco and cotton plantation communities American-born descendants of Europeans and Africans spoke the same kinds of English, until the institutionalization of segregation made such similarities in their evolutionary trajectories difficult to maintain.

I also surmise that AAVE and AWSE are so similar structurally because the time of the institutionalization of segregation and its subsequent maintenance *de facto* was, in evolutionary terms, too late to make them more significantly divergent.[8] By then, it was no longer necessary for blacks to interact regularly with whites in order for features that had originated in one group to be transmitted within the other, though other social factors may have led members of different ethnic groups to identify some variants as either xenolectal or more properly theirs.

During the time when segregation was institutionalized there were no additional migrations from Africa (Bodnar 1991), which makes it implausible to invoke late African substrate influence to justify the divergence of white and black vernaculars in North America. One would have to show first that the "new" phenomenon was not attested during the pre-segregation period and/or could not be due to the internal ecology of AAVE itself. All such linguistic-ecology considerations suggest that the reason why AAVE and AWSE share so many of their structures is not only because the inputs to restructuring into colonial English varieties were so similar, but because African slaves and European indentured servants participated in the restructuring processes together – at least during the protracted seventeenth-century founder period in Virginia, during which most colonists and their indentured/slave laborers lived in small farm holdings. Both Europeans and Africans living so closely and/or intimately influenced each other's speech patterns. Moreover, they continued to interact regularly with each other until the late nineteenth century, despite increased discriminatory measures against the African Americans.

Those who cherish relating AAVE to Gullah and creoles of the Caribbean should note the following: (1) cotton plantation colonies such as Alabama, Tennessee, Mississippi, and even the hinterlands of South Carolina and Georgia imported their initial black slave labor from the Chesapeake tobacco colonies, which had been developed earlier and had slave populations (though they were the minority), but not from coastal South Carolina and Georgia;[9] (2) under the social interaction conditions described above – which involved no *de jure* segregation – the population movement history suggests a continuity with less extensive restructuring of the colonial English that was targeted by newcomers; (3) it is also noteworthy that overall African Americans sound more like other Americans of their corresponding socioeconomic class and level of education than like Caribbeans of the corresponding socioeconomic class and level of education. White Caribbeans too sound more like black and brown Caribbeans, the majority counterparts of white Americans, than like white Americans.[10] It would be very informative to compare educated American English as spoken by the average European and African Americans from non-integrated neighborhoods. Are there (not) minor differences that under stronger segregated conditions could lead to somewhat distinct English varieties? Or is there more foundation to Spears' (1988, 1998) position that there is a "standard AAVE" that is distinct from "standard White American English?"[11]

I have referred several times to a colonial vernacular spoken alike by the early Europeans and Africans – although it should perhaps be identified as a plurality of varieties. I am avoiding being more specific here, because a large proportion of European immigrants during the seventeenth century were small farmers and indentured servants – 50–75 percent of the European population in the seventeenth-century Chesapeake colonies (Kulikoff 1991). The Africans came initially as indentured servants and lost this status in the Chesapeake colonies only toward the last third of the seventeenth century (Tate 1965). This information also highlights both the significantly proletarian ancestry of many European Americans and the non-standard origins of European-American vernaculars. It should also make obvious why AAE is so different from standard/educated English, as it inherited its features from non-standard vernaculars.

We should never forget that several indentured servants did not speak English natively, as they came from Germany, Ireland, France, and some other places in continental Europe. Ireland was then just shifting from an exploitation colony (on the model of India and African British colonies in the nineteenth and twentieth centuries) to a settlement colony (on the North American model), as explained in Mufwene (2001b).[12] The appropriation of English as a vernacular (rather than as a lingua franca) among the Irish was just beginning then and a significant proportion of them did not speak it fluently (if at all), including some of those who wound up in the New World colonies. All this information highlights the fact that, contrary to a well-established myth among both linguists and lay people, European-American vernaculars have not been inherited wholesale from the British Isles but are colonial contact-based phenomena, like AAE (Mufwene 1999).

I am assuming that external influence on a language need not consist of elements imported from another language but may involve only the role played by that language in determining what features from varieties of the target language will be selected into the emergent vernacular (Mufwene 1993). Accordingly, European-American English vernaculars must bear influence from the contact of British English vernaculars with continental European languages and, in some places, with African languages, depending especially on the composition of each colony's founder population and the kinds of demographic stochastic events that marked each population's growth over the following centuries. Constructions such as *go to the store* vs. *go to school* and *watch (the) TV* (with reference to the activity that the referent is associated with rather than to the referent itself) may very well reflect differences between the native English system and continental European ones, in which the article is usually used in their translations. (In British English, such constructions tend all to be used in the *non-individuated* delimitation, without an article.)[13]

Where the presence of African populations was significant especially during the late seventeenth and the eighteenth centuries, such as in the southeastern parts of the United States, African substrate influence cannot be ruled out by fiat, at least in the sense of speakers having favored options in English that were more consistent with (some) African languages, such as the monophthongization of some vowels (e.g. /ay/ and /aw/) and the absence of rhoticism (which blurs the distinction between *farther* and *father*).[14] This is independent of the fact that similar features have sometimes been selected in settings where contact with Africans during the initial formative period was minimal, such as non-rhoticity in New England.

During the founder period, there were no large plantations. Africans worked as domestics in places such as Williamsburg or on farms, where they interacted regularly with members of the families that employed them. During the same period, the black population grew more by birth than by importation (Wood 1974; Thomas 1998). Both African and European children were looked after together, while their parents worked in the field. Thus all of them acquired the same colonial vernaculars. It is these creole slaves that Berlin (1998) identifies as important power brokers: they knew how to negotiate some status and privileges thanks to their command of the master's language. By the early eighteenth century, large plantations increased in number, and the African slave population increased dramatically by importation of new slaves. Segregation was either institutionalized (as in coastal South Carolina) or loosely adopted as a way of life (presumably in places such as east-central Virginia). However, there was already a substantial number of creole slaves to function as models to African newcomers. The creole slaves transmitted the colonial vernaculars in the same way as American-born Europeans did or would have, since one's command of a language is not conditioned by race as a biological notion. Where segregation was more rigid and the African slaves were the overwhelming majority since the early eighteenth century, divergence of African- and European-American vernaculars must have started as early as the first half of the eighteenth century.[15] The evidence lies in Gullah. However, the reason for the divergence misidentified as "creolization" is not the absence of white speakers of the local koiné.[16] It had to do with the reduction of the proportion of fluent speakers of the koiné (consisting of both creole and seasoned slaves). As the plantations grew bigger and work became more intense, harsher living conditions increased infant mortality and reduced both the birth rate and the average life expectancy. A consequence of these factors was a rapid turnover in the ever-increasing population. Thus, newcomers increasingly learned the local vernacular from less fluent speakers, a condition that fostered more and more restructuring away from the original lexifier. As the (descendants of) Africans got to communicate more among themselves than with non-Africans, there was more room for influence from African languages to find its way into the evolving vernaculars (Mufwene 1996b, 2001b).

Although similar demographic factors affected the development of tobacco and cotton plantations, they were statistically less dramatic. The numerical disproportions between European indentured servants and African slaves were smaller. Regular interactions continued between them and countered the significance of the divergence that influence from African languages could have inflicted on the then emergent AAVE. Recall that it was only in the late nineteenth century that segregation was institutionalized, after the passage of the Jim Crow laws. It is also important to note that rice fields generally required a larger labor force than tobacco and cotton plantations. Rice fields had 200 or more slaves, whereas the largest tobacco plantations had about eighty laborers, and the cotton plantations often had no more than twenty laborers. Aside from the fact that on average the disproportions of African slaves to European indentured laborers were much lower on the tobacco and cotton plantations (where the Africans were typically the minority) than in the rice fields, the smaller sizes of the tobacco and cotton plantation communities themselves and the looser dynamics of *de facto* segregation on them could hardly be as effective in the hinterland communities as in the coastal communities in fostering divergent linguistic patterns between African Americans and European Americans. Besides, descendants of coastal plantation whites sound more like descendants of coastal black slaves and like Bahamians than like hinterland white Southerners, just as white and black Caribbeans sound alike, class for class, and as white and black Southerners also sound similar, class for class.[17]

These similarities suggest regionalized shared inheritances and evolutions rather than the much more commonly held myth that the speech of white Southerners has been influenced by that of their black nannies. What comes close to the truth about it is that coexistence with African indentured servants and slaves must have influenced the selection of features that Europeans made into colonial English from the larger pool of native and xenolectal features that they were exposed to. Such an interpretation is consistent with the fact that most, if not all, the features associated with AAE can be identified in some white English vernacular that may not have a connection with African slaves, for instance, the fact that Gullah's aspectual *duh* [də] is also used as a progressive marker in nonstandard Southwestern British English.

3   The nature of (early) colonial American English

Although features of American-English vernaculars have been traced to different regional dialects of British English, no American dialect has been identified that is systemically coextensive with a particular British dialect.[18] Therefore, the following important question can be asked: what was the nature of (early) colonial American English? Was it one or were there many? Historical dialectology research since Kurath (1928) suggests that there were several early colonial varieties. This conclusion is backed by economic historical studies such as those by Bailyn (1986a) and Fischer (1989), which show that the initial colonies or clusters thereof tended to start with settlers and indentured servants from particular parts of the British Isles. For instance, the founder population of New England consisted primarily of East Anglians, whereas that of the Chesapeake colonies combined mostly Southern and Southwestern English with the Irish, aside from the other continental Europeans who joined them. Until the stochastic migration events that affected their evolutions, the initial colonial varieties were largely influenced by the metropolitan origins of these founder populations. Moreover, many later immigrants went to places where there were earlier immigrants from their own places of origin (Bailyn 1986a; Montgomery 1996b).

Those varieties have also been identified as koinés, for instance by Dillard (1975, 1992). However, as noted in section 1, Montgomery (1995, 1996b) has expressed reservations about the existence of such a koiné, at least as a uniform one spoken across all colonies, by the eighteenth century. He advances very plausible arguments in support of his position, as summarized below.

Bailyn (1986a: 4) observes that the colonization of North America consisted of a "centrifugal Volkerwanderung that involved an untraceable multitude of local small-scale exoduses and colonization." Montgomery adds that up to the late eighteenth century the American population was not only heterogeneous but quite mobile. These factors made difficult the development of a large-scale, stable, and uniform colonial English variety that would have been spoken by all colonists (1996b: 214). This state of affairs was fostered in part by the fact that many European immigrants preferred to go where there were already colonists of their own backgrounds, although they would later mix with other colonists of different backgrounds (1996b: 232). Still, they moved about frequently in search of "better land and better situations for themselves," thus keeping their metropolitan dialects continuously in contact with other dialects and languages, therefore subjecting their own varieties to continuous restructuring. These kinds of contacts would, accordingly, not have produced the kind of "leveling" and "simplification" traditionally associated with koinéization. He observes that "the 'uniformity' of language across a territory as extensive as the colonies is logically impossible" (1996b: 218).

According to Montgomery, travelers' comments about a uniform North American colonial English may have had to do with "the more monotonic quality of American speech when compared to that of Britain" (1996b: 219) and they "undoubtedly tell us more about variation in Britain than in North America" (1996b: 218). I may also conjecture that such observations are probably more a testimony to the fact that, like today, the continuum of varieties that formed American English sounded different from metropolitan English varieties. They could not really inform us about the uniformity of the emergent American varieties. In the first place, as in the metropole, communicative conditions probably made difficult the emergence of such a uniform koiné (see below). Montgomery concludes: "Koinéization undoubtedly occurred in American English, but that the language of Colonial North America, especially through the whole of the colonies, was a koiné is extremely doubtful" (1996b: 230). Then he also remarks that the Subject–Verb Concord system of Appalachian English is different from the Irish English system in which both the Subject-Type constraint and the Proximity-of-Subject-to-Verb constraint apply. In the Appalachian English system, only the Subject-Type constraint applies. He argues that the change seems more like a "'shift' from one type of concord system to another" than like a simplification associated with koinéization (Montgomery 1996b: 230). In the next to last paragraph of his essay, Montgomery states that "Colonial American English was probably not a koiné in many places; rather dialect diversity, especially reflected in style shifting, was the rule" (1996b: 233). This position is also consistent with the following observation of his:

> Americans were multi-style speakers from the beginning, and dialect rivalry/contact may well have made them more so. We must assume the existence of dialect continua for individual speakers both before and particularly after dialect contact. Koinéization proceeded much more quickly for writing than for speech ... In published documents from the [eighteenth] century it is indeed difficult to detect many regionalisms, but this points to the regularization of written English throughout the colonies and early nation. (1996b: 231)

We must also recall that Montgomery's arguments against positing a single uniform colonial koiné from which today's American English varieties started are directed primarily against the conception of a koiné as a variety that has developed from the leveling out of differences among dialects of the same language. This explains his account of the development of the Appalachian English Subject–Verb Concord system in terms of shift rather then leveling (the usual explanation for koinéization). However, it also finds support from Mufwene's (1996b, 2001b) characterization of "koiné" as a variety that has evolved from the competition and selection that took place in a setting involving contact of dialects of the same language. Hence, we can say Appalachian English selected only one of the constraints that applied. It should be informative to find out whether Gaelic, which was still the mother tongue of several (Scots-)Irish immigrants, had any influence on this particular selection and others.

My interpretation is in fact consistent with the following other observations of Montgomery's:

> Following the colonial era, the verb concord rule observed [in] Irish emigrant letters may have been maintained most strongly in Appalachian varieties of American English, but this cannot be attributed to relative geographical isolation alone. In fact, there is considerable evidence that both the Subject-Type and Proximity constraints on verbal concord operated in letters throughout the nineteenth century, not only in Appalachia or the Upper South region of the United States, but also throughout the American South, in the speech of both whites and blacks. (1996b: 229)

In the spirit of the competition-and-selection model proposed in Mufwene (1996b, 2001b), speakers typically selected into the emergent variety variants that were available to them in the feature pool provided by the different varieties in contact (see below). The challenge is to figure out what ecological features (linguistic or ethnographic) influenced these selections.

Montgomery is right in arguing that there could not have emerged a uniform koiné spoken in all the eighteenth-century colonies. The socioeconomic conditions of colonization described above by Bailyn (1986a) and also by Fischer

(1989) were not conducive to the development of such a widespread koiné or any contact variety used everywhere by colonists.

I will attempt to reinterpret Montgomery's arguments regarding what he identifies as language shift. Contact situations in the colonies brought together dialects that had not necessarily been in regular contact with each other in the metropole (see also Algeo 1991). The new colonial contacts produced larger feature pools and ecologies in which conditions for selecting one particular option or another available for particular variables were also novel. The choices made were not necessarily consistent with each other, so that feature F_1 in a particular colonial vernacular may have its origin in a different metropolitan variety than feature F_2, etc. In the same vein, vernacular V_1 need not have made selections that were coextensive with those of vernacular V_2. Of course the variants were not necessarily selected in absolute exclusion of other alternatives and the different vernaculars may have diverged primarily in the statistical significance of some of the variants or in the strengths of constraints regulating their distribution, as Montgomery's account of the Subject–Verb Concord system in Appalachian English shows, consistent with research in quantitative analysis over the last few decades.

What is especially critical here is that koinés developed apparently by the same competition-and-selection processes that produced varieties such as Gullah and AAVE, although in these cases the speakers who produced them had to deal with the additional contribution of African languages to the new feature pool mentioned above (Mufwene 2001b). Colonial contact ecologies were not identical from one colony to another or even from one part of a colony to another, because the ethnolinguistic groups involved were not identical in terms of language varieties represented or in the demographic strengths of their speakers. Therefore the selections made were not identical. In this sense, Montgomery's position against positing an across-the-board eighteenth-century American koiné is quite well justified.

On the other hand, note that Bailyn speaks of several local colonies, so to speak. The colonists constituted what in macroecology is known as a metapopulation, an ensemble of smaller populations connected by dispersing individuals. It is plausible to assume that each local colony developed its own local/regional vernacular, which was structurally related to other emergent English vernaculars mostly by the fact that the inputs to these outcomes of restructuring were both similar and different on the family resemblance model. A local or regional vernacular may have differed from another as much by the particular combination of structural features it selected into its system as by the probability of usage of features that were attested in another vernacular. One finds evidence of this by observing some of the probability maps developed by Kretzschmar (1996) which make him "hesit[ate] to assume the existence of dialect areas" (36). The reason is that the features do not spread continuously over geographical areas and tend to hop from one subarea to another. Where there seems to be geographical continuity, the probabilities of usage vary from one location or subarea to another, suggesting also coexistence with other alternates. This is as true of the regional distribution of *pail* versus *bucket* as of *way* versus *ways* in *a little way(s)*, and postvocalic /r/-constriction in *fourteen*. Moreover the geographical distributions of different features are not coextensive. One can thus expect places where postvocalic /r/ is almost always constricted, locations where it is seldom constricted, and areas where there is a lot of alternation or variation in the presence or absence of constriction but in different ways from one location to another. The geographical area of alternation need not coincide with a traditional dialect boundary area. All this supports Montgomery's position against the development of a uniform colonial American English koiné in the eighteenth century.

However, one cannot disregard the effect of the founder principle, according to which features of the variety developed by the founder population tend to become deeply entrenched in the speech of a community, subject to stochastic events that have affected the community's evolution (Mufwene 1996b, 2001b). The reason for this is what Wimsatt (2000) has named "generative entrenchment," according to which what came earlier has a better chance of establishing deeper roots in a system than what was adopted later. In the case of language, speakers are very accommodating. Dispersing individuals in a metapopulation find it easier to accommodate the locals in adopting their speech habits than to maintain their own traits, unless they are numerous enough to overwhelm the current local population or are not (sufficiently) integrated in it.[19] An overwhelming influx of colonists from backgrounds that are different from those of the founder population may account for the development of New England's English as different from the largely homogeneous East Anglian background of its founder population. In the vast majority of cases, however, colonial populations grew by moderate increments, so that immigrants' children born in a colony became native speakers of the local (emergent) vernacular and increased the number of its transmitters to later learners. As their parents died, while the population increased both by birth and immigration (and there were children among immigrants) the founder population's features became more and more deeply entrenched, even if overall the original system was gradually being restructured under the influence of newcomers. This scenario lends plausibility to Kurath's (1928) observation that the boundaries of American regional dialects, i.e. their regional distributions (consistent with Kretzschmar's 1996 observation that dialect areas lack clear boundaries), reflect the settlement patterns of the earliest successful colonists, although the dialects were no longer the same.

As a matter of fact, Montgomery is correct in suggesting that American English was still in development by the end of the eighteenth century. We may in fact observe, perhaps not trivially, that the development of American English is still in process, because every living language is in constant evolution. The ongoing

,ci shifts in American northern cities and in the South, on which Labov (1994) and others have commented, are just evidence of this ongoing evolution. Stronger evidence for Montgomery's position lies, however, in the emergence of new regional dialects since the nineteenth century, corresponding to the westward expansion of the United States. This produced, for instance, Mid-Western English.

Still, Montgomery's denial of a uniform colonial American koiné by the end of the eighteenth century does not entail that no koinés had developed at all by then. He clearly admits that "koinéization undoubtedly occurred" (1996b: 230). In agreement with this concession, my conception of the American colonial population as a metapopulation consisting of smaller populations marked by local and regional boundaries makes allowance for the development of local and/or regional koinés. With the exception of early New England, the British populations of the early American colonies were heterogeneous and brought with them different regional dialects. At the local and/or regional levels in the colonies, what developed from the contacts of these various metropolitan regional dialects are what the literature has identified as koinés. They developed from the competition of variant features (forms and rules) from dialects of the same language. By the founder principle (or generative entrenchment), vernaculars spoken by earlier colonists would have contributed a large share of features to the American dialects that developed later.

4   Conclusions

More empirical research may substantiate these plausible conjectures on the evolution of English in North America, as has been shown on a smaller scale in, e.g, Newfoundland vernacular English (Clarke 1997a, b) and Appalachian English (Montgomery 1989b). However, such an undertaking generally entails adopting a research program that is not too different from the sociohistorical approach that has been adopted in research on the development of creoles. This approach makes the colonization of the world outside Europe and the concurrent development of new language varieties a consequence of population movements triggered by specific economic conditions, which dictated specific modes of social interaction. Out of each ecological setting evolved a particular language variety, including AAVE, Gullah, and AWSE. Making contact a central factor in language evolution and speciation, each new variety developed gradually by the same contact-based language restructuring equation, with cross-variety differences attributable to differences in the values assigned to the variables of the algebraic equation (Mufwene 1996a, 2001b). The specific form of the equation remains to be articulated, if it ever will be. In any case, American southern whites shared much of the colonial and antebellum ecology that produced AWSE with African Americans. It is thus not surprising that AAVE and AWSE have similar structures even a little over a century after segregation was institutionalized and permitted divergence between them. The founder principle still prevails.

Notes

1. Some scholars have identified this as a koiné – which I discuss in section 3.
2. The putative homogeneity may be considered contrary to feelings among African Americans that AAVE varies regionally from the North to the South and from the east to west coasts. However, compared to varieties spoken among white Americans and excluding Gullah, AAE can justifiably be claimed to vary less from one region to another. This fact undoubtedly justifies identifying it as an ethnic variety.
3. Another exception is coastal, east-central Virginia, where the proportion of Africans often reached 60 percent (AuCoin 2002). However, as explained below, the estates here were much smaller than in coastal South Carolina and Georgia, and segregation was perhaps not as rigidly enforced either. The proportion of mulattoes or light-skinned blacks is generally a reflection of the kinds of race relations during the (early) colonial days, if not all the way to the late nineteenth century.
4. According to the founder principle, adapted here from population genetics, the people who successfully settle earlier in a colony and form a critical mass have a greater chance of widely spreading their features in their new community than those who arrive later, assuming the community is integrated. From a biological perspective, some of the newcomers, who come by installments, interbreed with the locals. Their offspring, who inherit the founder traits, increase the number of their transmitters to offspring of some of those who arrive later. From a linguistic perspective, it is easier for the newcomers to target the local vernacular and be integrated in the local community than to make a new one, barring cases of hostility. Children born to the new community acquire it natively and increase the number of those who transmit it with minimal modifications to those who immigrate later. As adult newcomers die with their xenolectal features, and more and more children are born to the community, the original features continue to be transmitted, being modified only minimally, as the community undergoes some influence from adult immigrants. As long as native speakers remain the ideal models for newcomers, the founder population features have a greater chance of prevailing.
5. Berlin's (1998) discussion of the role of creole populations as sometimes power brokers in the development of the colonies is very informative on this question. I return to this reference below.
6. Segregation is viable in highly populated settings, such as cities and large plantation communities, but not on homesteads and farms. Unfortunately the literature has not made this distinction and has focused on the overall numerical differences between ethnic groups. Such undifferentiated discussions of population growth in the colonies and their linguistic consequences have presented inaccurate one-for-all explanations for situations that varied one from the other. An important function of the ecological approach presented in Mufwene (2001b) is to highlight such internal variation even within the same colony.
7. This is not to say that Gullah was brought over from Barbados (Cassidy 1980, 1986) or anywhere else in the West Indies, nor that its development was significantly influenced by West Indian creoles (Rickford 1997; Rickford and Rickford 2000). The similarities are attributable to similar inputs and to evolutions under similar ecological conditions (Mufwene 1999b).
8. Aside from the fact that segregation in American southern states had to be decreed by law, there is other indirect evidence for the argument that Europeans and Africans

interacted regularly and closely, if not always intimately, with each other. From the late seventeenth century to the mid eighteenth century, several laws were passed that prohibited whites from marrying black women or having children with them, in response to the fear that the colonies were "blackening." Laws were also passed that not only declared blacks slaves for life but also established more dehumanizing forms of punishments for them. It would not have been necessary to pass such laws if the living conditions of the whites and blacks had been different in the beginning. For colonies such as those of the Chesapeake, such measures were enacted up to about 100 years after the first Africans were brought in, several decades after the African population had increased largely by birth and a critical mass of native speakers of colonial English had established roots in the relevant communities.

9. An important reason for this disparity is the fact that the tobacco industry required a smaller labor force than the rice fields, which were booming when the cotton industry started. The rice industry depended almost exclusively on slave labor, whereas, like the emergent cotton industry, the tobacco industry depended on both indentured and slave labor, due in part to the fear of having colonies or states with black majority populations.

10. Socially, Emancipation seems to have worked in opposite directions in the United States, with its white majority, and in the Caribbean, with its non-white, black and brown majority. In the latter, it led to more racial integration within the relevant economic classes, whereas in the United States, the Jim Crow laws actually institutionalized segregation, which can be noticed even in northern cities, more obviously in the residential distribution of the population. Such segregation accounts for the maintenance of speech differences between African and European Americans in the North and/or for the divergence of their vernaculars, especially in the South. In the Caribbean, speech varies more according to one's socioeconomic class and level of education than according to race.

11. The quotation marks simply reflect my uneasiness in conflating the notions of "standard" and "educated" speech as one and the same. I think that "educated" speech is more real than the construct that "standard" stands for.

12. Exploitation colonies are those where European colonists worked on fixed-year terms and exploited the colony to enrich the metropole, which remained their home. In settlement colonies, the colonists established new roots and homes. If the colonists imposed their language in exploitation colonies, it was only on a small elite that interfaced between them and the Native majority and it was transmitted as a lingua franca through the school system. In settlement colonies, the whole economic system was set up to function in the colonists' language and this was appropriated as a vernacular naturalistically in any of its nonstandard varieties. The linguistic consequences of these different modes of language transmission and appropriation are thus different, with indigenized Englishes being more typical of exploitation colonies and creoles and other new native Englishes more typical of settlement colonies. Pidgins, often mistakenly identified as ancestors of creoles, developed in trade colonies, associated with sporadic contacts between the trading parties.

13. The French translations of these examples require a definite article: *aller au magasin*, *aller à l'école*, and *regarder la télévision*. (*Au* is coalesced from *à le*.) German translations involve a camouflaged definite article when the preposition is *zu*, as in *zur Schule gehen* and *zum Markt gehen*, in which *zur* comes from *zu der* and *zum* from *zu dem*. German offers options with an article, as in *auf den Markt gehen*, which is in contrast with

zu der Schule gehen (with reference to a specific school). Watching TV has a specific verb *fernsehen*, though there are also alternatives without an article such as *Fernsehen gucken/schauen/sehen*.

14. According to Bailey and Thomas (1998), differences between African- and European-American vernaculars in respect to such features reflect later developments among European Americans, which have contributed to the divergence of AAVE from AWSE.

15. This is precisely as early as Brasch (1981) could identify evidence of a divergent black form of speech, based on literary representations. As the Africans had been discriminated against since the early seventeenth century, there would be seventeenth-century representations of their peculiarities if their colonial English had diverged in any significant way that made it a distinct ethnolect. There were, indeed, several second-language approximations of English, spoken by both Europeans and Africans, which were contributing to the emergent American colonial koinés (see section 3).

16. I argue in Mufwene (2000) that "creolization" is a social, not a structural, process. There is no particular restructuring process that can be singled out as such. The processes that have produced creoles are the same that have been identified in other cases of language evolution resulting in speciation into new varieties (Mufwene 2001b).

17. AuCoin (2002) reports that in the east-central counties of Virginia, the African slaves were sometimes the majority in the eighteenth century. However, such a majority, which is limited to the coastal area, was reached only after a protracted homestead period during the seventeenth century. Since the coastal plantations were also generally smaller than the hinterland plantations, nothing close to Gullah developed along the Virginia tidewater, although that regional AAVE variety apparently contains some of the features attested in Gullah (Sutcliffe 1998).

18. Even Appalachian English does not match Irish English, although its peculiarities have largely been associated with predominantly (Scots-)Irish settlements during the colonial period. For instance, it does not have a consuetudinal or invariant *be* (as in *he be hollerin' at somebody every time I come to visit*), which is attested in AAVE's and Gullah's time-reference systems (Montgomery 1989).

19. Incidentally, these principles account for the development of AAVE and Gullah (a combination of both in the latter case), and they may account for the development of other American vernaculars.

5 The complex grammatical history of African-American and white vernaculars in the South

PATRICIA CUKOR–AVILA

1 Introduction

In October 1981 Michael Montgomery and Guy Bailey organized the first conference on Language Variety in the South (LAVIS I) at the University of South Carolina, Columbia, where for the first time scholars discussed research and exchanged ideas about the history of and relationship between Southern American English (SAE) and African-American Vernacular English (AAVE).[1] The general consensus from the research presented at the conference, and later chronicled in a volume of essays (Montgomery and Bailey 1986), was that SAE is a far more complex variety than had previously been noted, specifically in regard to the shared social and linguistic histories of African Americans and whites and their resulting vernaculars. Establishing the relationship between AAVE and the vernacular English of southern whites, referred to here and elsewhere as Southern White Vernacular English (SWVE), has proven to be a difficult task, and as a result there are still many unresolved issues surrounding the origins of AAVE – specifically its phonological and grammatical history – and how that history relates to the history of SWVE. Not surprisingly, the debates that have emerged over the past half century can oftentimes be attributed to methodological practices (and sometimes malpractices) in the research that have led to varying hypotheses concerning the relationship of these two varieties.

2 Dialect geography

The first concentrated effort to investigate linguistic variation in the South was by dialect geographers who analyzed spoken data from African Americans and whites in an effort to counter the racist views, popularized in the late nineteenth and early twentieth centuries, that genetic inferiority and cultural deprivation of African Americans were the principal causes for differences between black and white speech.[2] Data from interviews with older rural African Americans and whites (i.e. folk speakers) included in the fieldwork from the Linguistic Atlas of the Middle and South Atlantic States (LAMSAS) led these researchers to conclude that there were minimal differences between black and white folk speech and that these differences were more quantitative than qualitative; thus they suggested that southern African Americans and whites spoke essentially the same variety of English (cf. Kurath 1949; Atwood 1953). These data were somewhat problematic, however, since they came from only one generation of speakers and furthermore underrepresented the speech of African Americans, even in areas where they made up a significant percentage of the population. For example, of the 1,162 informants interviewed for LAMSAS, only 41 African Americans from five states – Maryland, Virginia, North Carolina, South Carolina, and Georgia – were included in the survey (Kretzschmar et al. 1994). Despite these methodological shortcomings, however, the contribution that the dialect geography research made to offer scholarly opposition to claims of African-American linguistic inferiority cannot be overlooked. Furthermore, the data from atlas surveys comprised the key evidence to a new hypothesis that variation in black and white speech could be traced to British dialects, the so-called "Anglicist" position (McDavid and McDavid 1951).

2.1   Creole studies

During the early 1960s the Anglicist position was challenged by a new strand of research on pidgin and creole languages, specifically those found in West Africa and the Caribbean. This "creole hypothesis" stated that contemporary AAVE derived from a plantation creole and not from earlier dialects of British speech (cf. Bailey 1965; Stewart 1967). Further attestation of the creole origins of AAVE was elaborated by Dillard (1972) whose conclusions about the historical and social origins of this variety were drawn from anecdotal evidence and the written records of eighteenth- and nineteenth-century travelers who were "observers of Southern culture" (Montgomery and Bailey 1986: 11). The early creolists tended to focus on sociohistorical factors as the most likely explanation for black/white speech differences, providing an "external" rather than an "internal" description of AAVE (Wolfram 1973). However, follow-up studies (cf. Rickford 1974, 1975, 1977; Baugh 1980; Holm 1984) and more recent work (Rickford 1997, 1998) have concentrated more on linguistic similarities and differences between AAVE and creole languages in order to study linguistic change. One of the linguistic features that perhaps has received the most scholarly attention by these researchers in this regard is copula absence.[3] Thus for creolists, AAVE and white vernaculars differ because they have different histories, and the many similarities that do exist between the two are primarily a consequence of the "decreolization" of AAVE, that is the movement of AAVE towards "standard English" over time (Bailey 2001).

2.2   Sociolinguistic studies

The innovative methodology designed to study the quantitative nature of linguistic variation and change (Labov 1963, 1966) became the benchmark for sociolinguistic research and analysis, much of which influenced the study of AAVE, particularly in northern urban centers (cf. Loman 1967; Wolfram 1969; Fasold 1972, 1981). The study of AAVE spoken by preadolescent and adolescent peer groups in Harlem (Labov et al. 1968) challenged the creolist position that differences between black and white speech were manifested at the level of deep structure. Instead, they argued that these differences resulted from "low-level rules which have marked effects on surface structure" (Labov et al. 1968: v), suggesting that AAVE "is best seen as a distinct subsystem within the larger grammar of English" (Labov 1972a: 63–4). The application of quantitative analysis and innovative field methods to the study of AAVE led to a plethora of linguistic information about this variety of English (Labov et al. 1968; Wolfram 1969; Fasold 1972; Wolfram and Fasold 1974; Baugh 1983), much of which was also used by educators to gain an understanding of the complexities of the dialect (Burling 1973). However, much of the early sociolinguistic research on AAVE focused on urban northern African Americans, leaving still unanswered the questions about the relationship between generations of African-American and white vernacular speakers in the South.[4]

Despite the substantial methodological contributions of the sociolinguists, whose research focused on resolving the issue of the relationship between AAVE and SWVE, they too, like the creolists, were making comparisons of AAVE to an undefined "standard English" usually spoken by northern whites often from middle-class socioeconomic backgrounds (Wolfram 1971, 1974 is an exception). This was coupled with the fact that these early sociolinguistic studies ignored possible generational differences and focused almost exclusively on the speech of children, based on the assumption that these speech varieties have always had fairly stable relationships and have responded to linguistic changes in the same way (Montgomery and Bailey 1986: 21).

2.3   Innovative approaches to variation

The beginning of the 1980s marked a new era in the research which combined the methods of dialect geography, creole studies, and sociolinguistics, and which focused on resolving both diachronic and synchronic issues in the relationship between southern African-American and white speech. As the number of in-depth, ethnographic community studies increased (cf. O'Cain 1972; Miller 1978; Feagin 1979; and Nix 1980), the old notion that race alone could account for linguistic differences was seriously called into question, as data from these and other studies suggested that factors such as education, age, and social class were also significant in determining linguistic choices. There was also more specific linguistic research on creole languages spoken in the South, such as Gullah on the Sea Islands and Afro-Seminole Creole in southwest Texas, in order to determine the history of these languages and their possible relationship to southern AAVE (cf. Jones-Jackson 1983, 1986; Nichols 1983, 1986; Mufwene 1991; Rickford 1986b; Hancock 1986), as well as more thorough investigations on the processes of creolization and decreolization (Hancock 1986; Rickford 1986b). Additionally,

a number of written sources of early southern speech, such as collections of letters, diaries, and other records of nineteenth-century white overseers (Hawkins
1982), including the transcribed narratives of ex-slaves (Rawick 1972, 1977,
1979), provided researchers with diachronic evidence of a period in southern
speech crucial to the understanding of black/white speech relationships in the
South.[5]

In fact, as the 1980s unfolded there was a growing consensus among linguists
about the relationship between African-American and white vernaculars based
on the following generalizations (Bailey 2001):

i.   AAVE is a subsystem of English with a distinct set of phonological and
     syntactic rules that are now aligned in many ways with the rules of other
     dialects.
ii. AAVE incorporates many features of southern [white] phonology, mor-
     phology, and syntax; blacks in turn have exerted influence on the dialects of
     southern whites where they lived.
iii. AAVE shows evidence of derivation from an earlier creole that was closer
     to the present-day creoles of the Caribbean.
iv. AAVE has a highly developed aspect system, quite different from other
     dialects of English, which shows a continuing development of its semantic
     structure (Labov 1982: 192).

The consensus quickly dissolved by the mid 1980s when independent research
by both Labov and his associates in Philadelphia (Labov 1987) and Bailey and
Maynor in Texas and Mississippi (Bailey 1987) suggested that, contrary to popular belief, AAVE appeared to be diverging from rather than converging with
white vernaculars. This became known as the "divergence hypothesis" and set
off a new round of bitter polemics in the field.

2.4   The divergence controversy

The evidence for divergence came from both phonological and syntactic sources.
Phonological evidence cited by Labov was based on the fact that sound changes in
white vernaculars in Philadelphia are not affecting the African-American speech
community there (Labov, Yeager, and Steiner 1972).[6] Bailey and Maynor (1987)
suggested a similar pattern in the use of postvocalic /r/ in the South: whereas
postvocalic /r/ is being restored in white southern speech,[7] this process is not
occurring for southern AAVE speakers. Grammatical evidence cited by both research teams centered on the syntactic reanalysis of two existing present-tense
features in vernacular English, third-singular verbal -s and invariant be. The
data from Philadelphia suggested that AAVE speakers there had reanalyzed the
function of the verbal -s inflection from that of marking person/number agreement in the present tense to functioning as a marker of narrative structure for
third person, similar to the historical present described in Wolfson (1979) and
Schiffrin (1981) (cf. Myhill and Harris 1986; Labov and Harris 1986; Labov
1987).[8] Bailey and Maynor's data suggested that a reanalysis of the present-tense

aspectual system of AAVE was occurring, so that *be₂* (all instances of invariant *be* that cannot be accounted for by *will/would* deletion, e.g. *He('d) be coming around every day*), was being reanalyzed by young urban speakers as a marker of habitual action when used before V+*ing* constructions. Their data showed that while *be₂* was present in all age groups, including the white folk speakers, the syntactic constraints for its use were significantly different between the oldest generations and the urban children. For the oldest AAVE speakers, *be₂* was used for actions and states occurring at a single point in time as well as for habitual, durative, and permanent states and actions (Bailey 1993: 306), but for the urban children, *be₂* was primarily used before V+*ing* to indicate habitual actions (Bailey and Maynor 1987, 1989; Bailey 1987, 1993).

However, not all linguists who were doing research on AAVE at the time initially supported the divergence hypothesis (Vaughn-Cooke 1986, 1987; Rickford 1987a; Wolfram 1987; Butters 1989). Arguments came from both sides of this issue, which became known as the "divergence controversy".[9] The divergence controversy fueled a new era in the study of both African and white vernaculars, one in which a great deal of historical evidence on early African-American and white speech has been uncovered and analyzed (cf. Poplack and Sankoff 1987; Poplack and Tagliamonte 1989, 1991, 1994, 2001; Poplack 2000; Tagliamonte and Poplack 1988; Schneider 1989; Schneider and Montgomery 2001; Abney 1989; Bailey and Ross 1988; Bailey and Smith 1992; Bailey, Maynor, and Cukor-Avila 1989, 1991; Paparone and Fuller 1993; Montgomery 1993c; Montgomery, Fuller, and DeMarse 1993; Tagliamonte and Smith 1998; Bailey and Cukor-Avila forthcoming; Wolfram and Thomas 2002), in which new approaches to fieldwork have been developed (Cukor-Avila 1995, 1997a; Cukor-Avila and Bailey 1995a), and new social parameters have been explored (Mufwene 1996b and this volume).

3   Current polemics

Despite the vast amount of research on both AAVE and SWVE linguists are still far from agreement about the relationship between these two varieties of English. The creole origins issue is still under debate as evidence from diaspora varieties and early British dialects sheds new light on the linguistic history of AAVE (Poplack 2000; Poplack and Tagliamonte 2001). In addition, recent research on AAVE grammar has revealed structures not present in white vernaculars or in earlier varieties of AAVE (Cukor-Avila 1999; Cukor-Avila and Bailey 1995b; Rickford and Rafal 1996; Labov 1998) serving to keep the divergence hypothesis alive (although the term *divergence* has been replaced in the literature by *linguistic innovations*). Bailey (2001) suggests four reasons for the continued absence of a consensus in the research:

i.   the larger political contexts in which views about these relationships have been expressed;

ii.   the early tendency to compare AAVE to northern white vernaculars or a hypothetical standard English, an approach that conflated regional and ethnic differences and failed to account for the sociohistorical context in which AAVE emerged;

iii. the lack of data from comparable groups of African Americans and whites;
iv. the failure to recognize that black/white speech relationships are evolving rather than static.

This last factor, which stresses the importance of time depth in sociolinguistic studies, will be the focus of the remainder of this chapter through a qualitative overview of the relationship over time between AAVE and SWVE grammars in a rural Texas community, followed by a quantitative analysis of the evolution of a grammatical feature in AAVE that at one time had similar constraints in both vernaculars.

4   The relationship between AAVE and SWVE grammar in Springville

4.1   The research site

The east-central Texas community of Springville has been the focus of an ongoing longitudinal ethnolinguistic study, now in its thirteenth year, designed to document linguistic variation and change in rural southern speech over time (Cukor-Avila 1995; Cukor-Avila and Bailey 1995a). Springville is an insular, rural community organized around a general store. It is a contemporary relic of the plantation agriculture that developed during tenancy and was typical of the post-Civil War South; in fact, many of the community's approximately 150 residents either worked as tenant farmers or are their descendents. During its prime in the first four decades of the 1900s, Springville typified the classic southern plantation culture where the population consisted of whites and African Americans: white landowners and African-American field hands, with a small segment of the population made up of white tenant farmers. It was a thriving community with a large population, three cotton gins, three stores, a café, two schools, and two churches (one for the whites and one for the African Americans), and was a scheduled stop on the passenger train that connected Springville to larger towns in the county.

The post-World War II era brought demographic changes to Springville that were similar to what was happening in many other communities throughout the rural South during this period. Urban areas began offering increased economic opportunities and freedom from the tenant farming system; however, these opportunities were mainly reserved for whites only. Thus, Springville whites began their exodus in the late 1940s, and by the time farming had become completely mechanized in the early 1960s, the community's white population had diminished drastically, and the African-American population had begun to decline too. It was during this period of population shift that Mexican immigrants, mainly undocumented workers, began to settle in and around the Springville area, offering the local farmers a cheaper alternative for manual labor. They slowly replaced the

African Americans who had previously worked in the fields, who now were either too old to do manual labor or who had found employment in service jobs in the surrounding communities.

Today, about 10 percent of the population of Springville is white with the remainder almost evenly divided between African Americans and Hispanics. Although the tenant farming system is no longer operative, the organization of the community still bears its imprint: most of the land and many of the former tenant houses are owned by a woman who is a descendent of one of Springville's original white residents. She also owns the only store in town and, up until her retirement in 2000, had been the postmaster for some forty years. She maintains financial control over much of the community – many residents still pay their utility bills directly to her, borrow money, and purchase items from the store on "credit," reconciling their tabs on the first of the month after she cashes their government checks.[10]

Thirteen years of fieldwork in Springville have provided opportunities to record conversations with African-American, Hispanic, and white residents born between 1894 and 1996, thus enabling the documentation of 100 years of Springville speech in apparent time collected over more than a decade of real time. The Springville recordings represent a variety of interview contexts: individual, peer group, site studies, community fieldworker, and diary studies (Cukor-Avila 1995, 2002; Cukor-Avila and Bailey 1995a). Many of the community's residents have been recorded numerous times over the course of the project; moreover, most have been recorded in more than one context and several have been recorded in the first four contexts listed above.

4.2   A qualitative analysis of Springville AAVE and SWVE

Table 5.1 is a list of thirty-two grammatical features included in a qualitative analysis of the relationship between AAVE and SWVE grammars in Springville (Cukor-Avila 2001) that illustrate changing relationships over time in these two vernacular varieties of English. The real- and apparent-time data shown in table 5.2 suggest that the grammars of AAVE and SWVE speakers in Springville were much more similar (at least for the thirty-two features analyzed) in the first half of the 1900s than they are today. In order to illustrate the changing relationship of these vernaculars as they have evolved over time, table 5.2 is divided into five sections, each one representing a different component of the relationship between AAVE and SWVE in Springville: (1) features that are shared in older varieties of AAVE and SWVE but that are not shared in younger varieties; (2) features that are stable over time in AAVE and shared in older varieties of SWVE; (3) features that are stable over time in AAVE and SWVE; (4) features found only in AAVE; and (5) innovative features of AAVE that evolved since World War II. The first section of table 5.2 illustrates seven features shared in the speech of older African Americans and whites which have disappeared in the speech of younger whites born after World War II and have disappeared or

Table 5.1 *Selected grammatical features of AAVE and SWVE (adapted from Cukor-Avila 2001)*

Feature	Example
1st/2nd-person -*s*	I *likes* livin' out in the country.
plural verbal -*s*	Those boys *works* for me.
is for *are*	So many people *is* movin' in.
non-habitual invariant *be*	You don't *be* a Lewis until you get married.
for to	Somethin' *for to* snack on down the road.
a+verb+*ing*	They'd be happy an' *a-singin'*.
would deletion	They 0 make cheese when I was a boy.
zero-subject relative pronoun	I got some friends 0 do that.
singular copula absence	Bobby 0 not workin' this summer.
zero 3rd-singular -*s*	She *live* right down the road.
non-recent perfective *been*	I *been knowin'* her all my life.
be done	I come home an' he *be done* clean up an' cooked.
yall	*Yall* don't make any sense.
fixin' to/*fitna*	We're *fixin' to* go to the store.
multiple modals	I *might could* help you later today.
zero pl/2nd-singular copula absence	You 0 taller than Sheila. They 0 gonna leave today.
was for *were*	We *was* at the house all day.
have/*had* deletion	That school 0 been there a long time.
irregular preterits	I *knowed* her when she was a baby.
unmarked preterits	They *come* in here last night.
inceptive *get*/*got to*	I *got to* thinkin' about that.
multiple negation	She *don't never* buy *nothin'*.
ain't	I *ain't* seen him since yesterday.
existential *it*	*It's* one lady that lives in town.
perfective *done*	I *done drank* all my coffee now.
demonstrative *them*	*Them* peaches are ripe.
ain't for *didn't*	I *ain'* even had a price on it.
habitual invariant *be*	He *be* in the house all summer.
zero possessive -*s*	She think she *everybody* mama.
zero plural -*s*	You want some *pea*?
be+verb+*ing*	Those boys *be messin'* with me all the time.
innovative *had*+past	Today I *had went* to work.

are disappearing in the speech of young African Americans, however, somewhat later than in the speech of Springville whites. For example, auxiliary deletion (in this case deleted past habitual *would*), is a recessive feature in the speech of the post-World War II generations of AAVE and SWVE speakers; in fact, *would* as a past habitual rarely occurs in the speech of the youngest speakers since, for them, *would* in this context has been replaced by the grammaticalized

Table 5.2 *The relationship between AAVE and SWVE grammar in Springville (adapted from Cukor–Avila 2001)*

Gram. feature	AAVE speakers							SWVE speakers				
	Mary (1913)	Wallace (1913)	Lois (1941)	Bobby (1949)	Vanessa (1961)	Sheila (1979)	Brandy (1982)	Mabel (1907)	Ester (1917)	Ron (1941)	Pam (1949)	April (1982)
(1) 1st/2nd-person -s	−	+	+	+	+	−	−	−	−	+	−	−
non-hab. *be*	+	+	+	+	+	−	−	−	−	−	−	−
for to	−	+	+	+	+	−	−	−	−	−	−	−
a+verb+*ing*	+	+	+	+	+	−	−	+	+	−	−	−
would del.	+	+	+	+	+/−	+/−	+/−	−	+	−	−	−
pl. verbal -s	+	+	+	+	+	(+)	(+)	+	+	+	−	−
is for *are*	+	+	+	+	+	[+]	[+]	+	+	−	−	−
(2) sing. cop. abs.	+	+	+	+	+	+	+	+	−	−	−	−
zero 3rd-sing. -s	+	+	+	+	+	+	+	+	+	+	−	−
zero subj. rel.	+	+	+	+	+	(+)	(+)	+	−	−	−	−
perf. *been*	+	+	+	+	+	+	+	+	−	−	−	−
be done	−	−	−	+	+	+	+	−	−	−	−	−
(3) *yall*	+	+	+	+	+	+	+	+	+	+	+	+
fixin to/*fitna*	+	+	+	+	+	+	+	+	+	+	+	+
mult. modals	+	−	+	+	+	+	−	+	−	?	?	?
zero pl/2nd cop.	+	+	+	+	+	+	+	+	+	+	−	{+}
was for *were*	+	+	+	+	+	+	+	+	+	+	+	−
have/*had* del.	+	+	+	+	+	+	+	+	+	+	−	+

irreg. pret.	+	+	+	+	+	+	+	+	+	+	+
unmarked pret.	+	+	+	+	+	+	+	+	+	+	+
get to/got to	+	+	–	+	–	+	+	+	–	–	–
mult. negation	+	+	+	+	+	+	+	+	+	+	+
ain't	+	+	+	+	+	+	+	+	+	+	+
existential it	+	+	+	+	+	+	+	–	+	+	–
perf. done	+	+	+	+	+	+	+	+	+	+	+
dem. them	+	+	+	+	+	+	+	+	+	–	+
(4) ain't for didn't	+	+	–	+	–	+	+	–	–	–	–
hab. invar. be	+	+	+	+	+	+	+	–	–	–	–
zero poss. –s	–	+	+	+	+	+	+	–	–	–	–
zero pl. –s	–	+	+	+	+	+	+	–	–	–	–
(5) be+verb+ing	–	–/+	+	+	+	+	+	–	–	–	–
had+past	–	–/+	+	+	+	+	+	–	–	–	–

( ) used rarely; [ ] used mostly after existentials and compound NPs; { } used mostly before *gonna* and *v+ing*; +/– recessive; –/+ innovative form *useta* which is undeletable. Similarly, plural verbal -*s* and *is* for *are* occur only sporadically in the speech of the youngest AAVE speakers and in more restricted environments than for older generations. For example, *is* for *are* is found primarily after existentials as in, *There's two or three new kids in the eighth grade* and compound NPs as in, *Barbara Bush an' bein' a president is the firs' thing he thought of.* This usage is common in other vernacular varieties of English as well. Finally, although there are no recorded instances of first/second-person -*s*, non-habitual *be*, and *for to* in the speech of the two oldest SWVE speakers, previous research on southern white vernaculars has documented their existence in comparable informants (cf. McDavid and McDavid 1951; Feagin 1979; Bailey and Maynor 1985); therefore these features are included in this section.

The second section includes four features, singular copula absence, zero third-person-singular -*s*, zero-subject relative pronouns, and non-recent perfective *been*, which are stable across generations of AAVE speakers, but which are shared, at a much lower rate of frequency, only by older SWVE speakers. In SWVE these are features which are typically associated with older, rural, working-class speakers (Feagin 1979). The fifth feature listed, *be done*, is not found in the speech of older AAVE and SWVE speakers in Springville;[11] similarly, Myhill (1995), finds no occurrences of this feature in the recordings of the former slaves. However, *be done* has been attested in the speech of older Liberian settlers (Singler 1998), and it also occurs in the speech of elderly LAGS informants.[12] *Be done* does occur in the speech of younger Springville residents[13] and is consistent with the innovative use of this feature outlined by Dayton (1996) and Labov (1998: 132).

The first two sections of table 5.2 also illustrate variability within the grammars of the two oldest SWVE speakers, Mabel and Ester. Even though they have similar social histories – they both are Type I speakers,[14] they have always lived in rural areas, and both of their husbands worked as tenant farmers – Mabel's speech is much more similar to the speech of older AAVE speakers than is Ester's. Their vernaculars share many features associated with SWVE, such as *is* for *are*, *was* for *were*, demonstrative *them*, and irregular and unmarked preterits (listed in the third section of table 5.2), yet only Mable has a fair amount of the features typical of AAVE such as third-singular copula absence and non-recent perfective *been*. She also consistently lacks tense marking on third-singular present tense verbs with rates of -*s* absence equal to that of the older AAVE speakers in Springville (see section 5). These data demonstrate the importance of looking at individual speakers even within the same generation and from the same community, since individual differences, which may reveal important facts about language, are often masked by the effects of group analysis. Therefore, the data suggest coexisting grammars within generations of SWVE, a situation that must be accounted for in comparisons of African-American and white vernacular speech. This same situation is relevant for AAVE speakers as well, as will be shown in section 5.2.

The third section of table 5.2 includes fourteen features which occur across all generations of Springville AAVE and SWVE speakers. These are stable features of southern vernacular speech which exhibit some individual variation within the SWVE speakers born after 1941. For example, two established features of SWVE, multiple modals and *ain't*, are not accounted for in the speech of three of the SWVE speakers. This could either result from the topics of conversation, more than likely the cause for the lack of multiple modals which have a low frequency rate, or could possibly be caused by style shifting, as in the case of *ain't*. Despite these inconsistencies, the overall occurrence of these fourteen features by both AAVE and SWVE speakers has remained steady over time.

The fourth section of table 5.2 includes four grammatical features unattested in the speech of Springville SWVE speakers. Except for habitual invariant *be*, which previous research by Bailey and Maynor (1985) and Bailey and Bassett (1986) shows to occur in older Type I SWVE speakers, these features have historically been associated only with AAVE (cf. Fasold 1981 and Myhill 1995).

The final section of table 5.2 lists two features which occur only in AAVE yet not in the speech of the older generations studied, *be*+V+*ing* and *had*+past.[15] In fact, these innovative features only begin to emerge in Springville AAVE around the time of World War II or sometime thereafter.

Of the thirty-two grammatical features listed in table 5.2, twenty-six, or 81 percent, are features that have been shared, at one time or another, by both AAVE and SWVE speakers in Springville. Moreover, nearly half of the features (those listed in the third section of table 5.2) are still characteristic of both vernaculars. Only six of the features studied are unique to AAVE, at least two of which have emerged within the past sixty years. This suggests that in the recent past (mid nineteenth to early twentieth century) the grammars of Springville AAVE and SWVE speakers were much more similar than they were different, and it is only over the last few decades that change has caused an independent development in the grammar of AAVE.[16] Thus, while contemporary AAVE shares many features with earlier AAVE, it seems apparent that it is being transformed by new developments within the AAVE grammatical system itself. This point is illustrated more clearly by the following quantitative overview, based on longitudinal data from Springville, of the loss of tense marking on present-tense verbs.

5   Verbal -*s*

The origin, distribution, and function of verbal -*s* in AAVE have been the focus of numerous studies and a source of controversy among linguists over the past four decades (cf. Labov et al. 1968; Wolfram 1969; Fasold 1972; Pitts 1981; Brewer 1986; Myhill and Harris 1986; Bailey, Maynor, and Cukor-Avila 1989; Poplack and Tagliamonte 1989, 1991, 1994, 2001; Rickford 1992; Montgomery, Fuller and DeMarse 1993; Montgomery and Fuller 1996; Poplack 1999; Singler 1999). Explanations offered for its occurrence (and non-occurrence), as in examples (1) and (2), have been varied and often contradictory:

Table 5.3 *Five generations of Springville residents*

1900–20	1920–40	1940–60	1960–75	1975–90
Audrey b. 1907	Slim b. 1932	Lois b. 1941	Vanessa b. 1961	Sheila b. 1979
Mary b. 1913	Pinkie b. 1936	Bobby b. 1949	Travis b. 1965	Brandy b. 1982
Wallace b. 1913	Elsie b. 1939		Lonnie b. 1965	

(1)   His sister *go* where she *need* to go.
(2)   They *tells* me that it's too hard on 'em an' that they get tired of gettin' up
        every mornin'.

Most of the discussion of verbal -*s* has centered on the question of whether this feature is present in the underlying grammar of AAVE speakers. While early studies (Labov et al. 1968) suggested that verbal -*s* was not an underlying part of the AAVE grammatical system and was subject to an -*s* insertion rule (Fasold 1972), more recent research (Poplack and Tagliamonte 1989, 1991, 2001) shows that -*s* was much more robust in earlier varieties of AAVE than linguists originally thought. If this is the case, then -*s* has not been inserted over the years but rather lost, since contemporary urban vernacular speakers show high rates of -*s* absence (Labov et al. 1968; Myhill and Harris 1986; Rickford 1992). The following analysis explores this issue by examining the factors concerning the loss of verbal -*s* in AAVE by documenting its gradual disappearance over time, and by outlining the social and linguistic contexts that have fostered its loss.

The data for this analysis present a total of 8,516 occurrences of present-tense -*s* and zero in the speech of a representative sample of AAVE speakers from five generations of Springville residents listed in table 5.3.

All present-tense verbs in concord and non-concord contexts were included, as in examples (3) through (6):

(3)   She *spends* money like, like it goin' outta style.
(4)   I *cooks* for him sometime when I *stay* all night with him.
(5)   Well I got some friends, yeah they *fools* with 'em.
(6)   It *take* courage don' it.

Present-tense marking for *do* and *have* show considerable variation, as in examples (7) and (8); however, because these verbs involve phonological changes when inflecting for third-person singular, and in the interest of comparability with previous studies of verbal -*s*, the results presented below do not include data from these irregular verbs. In addition, the analysis does not include present-tense marking for *say* as a dialogue introducer, as in example (9), since it usually refers to past tense and is used almost categorically in the uninflected form. Examples of *say* as a main verb, however, as in example (10) are included. Other instances not counted include *know* and *think* when used as discourse markers as in examples (11) and (12).

(7)   We *does* all that stuff.

(8)   She *have* nightmares about, you know, scary things.

(9)   I *say*, "I wasn't married to him."

(10) Yeah he's still . . . no she *say* she don' want him never no more.

(11) She thought, *you know*, they tell you uh, the firs' call is free.

(12) Angie in the car, I *think*.

Table 5.4 outlines the apparent-time distribution of present-tense marking for the five generations studied. These data show a wide range of variation in verbal -*s* usage from the oldest to the youngest speakers: -*s* occurs in all persons yet the frequency of its occurrence changes over time. There is a significant increase in the use of -*s* in first- and third-singular and third-plural contexts between the first two generations which then gradually decreases over time, so that for the youngest speakers -*s* is found mainly in the third singular, but at a relatively low rate of occurrence. However, the presentation of the data in table 5.4 gives little insight on two important processes that have affected Springville speech: the weakening and subsequent loss of the NP/PRO constraint and the increasing loss of -*s* for speakers with strong urban connections.

5.1   *The loss of the NP/PRO constraint*

In earlier varieties of English the NP/PRO constraint, also referred to as the "Northern subject rule" (Montgomery, Fuller and DeMarse 1993; Montgomery and Fuller 1996; Filppula 1999; Tagliamonte 1999) was a determining factor in present-tense marking, such that a preceding noun phrase (NP) subject favored the presence of an -*s* ending in third-person plural, whereas a preceding personal pronoun (PRO) favored zero. Bailey, Maynor, and Cukor-Avila (1989) show that this constraint was also a factor for marking third-person-singular verbs, and in addition, was also operative for present-tense copula marking. Recorded evidence from the former slaves (Bailey, Maynor, and Cukor-Avila 1991) and written evidence from overseers' letters (Schneider and Montgomery 2001) suggest that the NP/PRO constraint was a significant factor in mid to late nineteenth-century AAVE and SWVE. Residual effects of this constraint are also found in the speech of rural African Americans who were born a generation before the oldest speakers in the Springville corpus (Bailey, Maynor, and Cukor-Avila 1989). However, by the beginning of the twentieth century, the strength of the NP/PRO constraint appears to have weakened substantially as data from speakers born in the 1900–20 generation in Springville suggest (table 5.5). Although the percentages of -*s* after NP for these speakers are higher in both singular and plural contexts neither of these differences is significant. In fact, a comparison of the strength of person/number (the operative constraint in "standard" English varieties) and NP/PRO for these data shows an almost equal effect for these constraints, as is illustrated in table 5.6. Table 5.7 shows the subsequent loss of the NP/PRO constraint in the next generation of Springville speakers.

Table 5.4 *Person/number distribution of present-tense verbal -s over time for Springville AAVE*

		1900–20			1920–40			1940–60			1960–75			1975–90		
		N	% 0	% -s	N	% 0	% -s	N	% 0	% -s	N	% 0	% -s	N	% 0	% -s
sing.	1st	743	97.2	2.8	252	92.1	7.9	319	95.0	5.0	574	97.7	2.1	888	99.8	.2[a]
	2nd	271	98.9	1.1	132	99.2	.8	173	99.4	.6	221	98.6	1.4	355	99.7	.3
	3rd	360	82.2	17.8	207	71.5	28.5	357	75.4	24.6	644	81.8	18.2	1217	82.4	17.6
pl.	1st	22	95.5	4.5	7	85.7	14.3	35	100		60	98.3	1.7	227	99.6	.4
	2nd	[4	75.0	25.0]	2	100		2	100		9	100		34	100	
	3rd	261	96.6	3.4	107	91.6	8.4	204	94.6	5.4	327	97.6	2.1	503	99.2	.8
Total		1,660			707			1,090			1,835			3,224		

All tokens of second-person plural are instances of *yall*.

[a] Both of these tokens are emphatic

Table 5.5 *Percentage of third-singular and third-plural verbal -s following NP and PRO for speakers in the 1900–20 generation*

		NP ____	PRO ____
singular	-s	(21) 20.2%	(43) 16.8%
	0	(83) 79.8%	(213) 83.2%
	N=	104	256
plural	-s	(6) 11.5%	(3) 1.4%
	0	(46) 88.5%	(206) 98.6%
	N=	52	209

Table 5.6 *Effect of person/number and NP/PRO on third-singular and third-plural verbal -s for speakers in the 1900–20 generation*

Person/Number	NP/PRO
sing. -s 64/360 = 17.8%	NP + -s = 26/156 = 16.7%
plural -s 9/261 = 3.4%	PRO + -s = 47/465 = 10.1%

Table 5.7 *Percentage of third-singular and third-plural verbal -s following NP and PRO for speakers in the 1920–40 generation*

		NP ____	PRO ____
singular	-s	(7) 12.3%	(52) 34.7%
	0	(50) 87.7%	(98) 65.3%
	N=	57	150
plural	-s	(3) 9.7%	(6) 7.9%
	0	(30) 90.3%	(70) 92.1%
	N=	31	76

As the strength of the NP/PRO constraint diminishes for speakers in the oldest generation, -s also begins to lose its association with person/number agreement, which historically competed with the NP/PRO constraint in black and white folk speech and eventually became established as the sole constraint on -s usage in white speech (Bailey, Maynor, and Cukor-Avila 1989). Table 5.4 shows an increased use of -s by speakers in the 1920–40 generation; in fact, the overall use of -s (i.e. with all person/number subjects) more than doubles from 6 percent in the 1900–20 generation to 12.7 percent in the 1920–40 generation. However, the expanded use of this form is not a systematic increase in the use of -s for subject/verb agreement; rather it is a proportional increase of -s in all environments where it occurs for speakers in the previous generation. The expansion of -*s* for these speakers, then, results in a more unsystematic distribution of verbal -*s* than for previous generations of AAVE speakers (Myhill 1995 reports only 1 percent -*s* in the first singular and 5 percent -*s* in the third plural in the speech of the former slaves). Even though speakers in the 1920–40 generation use significantly more -*s* than speakers in the previous generation in concord environments to mark third-singular verbs, they use more -*s* in non-concord environments as well. The increased use of -*s* in all environments suggests that for these speakers the function of verbal -*s* agreement has become less clear, and as a consequence, the status of -*s* as a present-tense marker is confused. This fact is best exemplified by example (13), which is an excerpt from a conversation about tamales with Slim (born 1932):

(13)   S: See it's a lady, it's a girl, it's a girl that'll bring some by. An' this morning I was in Johnson up there an' she brought a whole plate of 'em in there.

    FW: Really?

    S: She got 'em up there hot an' mil' you know. An' she [L. overlaps]

    L: A dollar seventy-five.

    S: What's her, what's her name that *cooks* 'em? She a real young girl. She *bring* 'em in every mornin'. An' they, an' they *sells* 'em, an' they *sells* 'em for that girl there in that store.

    FW: Really?

    S: Uh huh. They be hot when she firs' *bring* 'em in.

    FW: What store?

    S: In Johnson. The onlies' store they got in Johnson an' she *comes* in every mornin' with 'em. Real good.

    FW: Are they flour or corn?

    S: What is it? They could be flour [unintelligible]. Yeah, yeah. An' I guess, I think she *makes* those, them things she got from up here. An' she *makes* them herself.

5.2   Urban influences on rural speech

The unsystematic use of verbal -*s* shown in example (13), which is typical of speakers in the 1920–40 generation, starts to shift in the 1940–60 generation and is all but gone in the speech of Springville residents born after 1960. As speakers in the 1960–75 generation begin to resolve the confusion surrounding the use of -*s*, it begins to disappear everywhere as the constraints on its use as a tense marker are lost. There is a significant decrease in the overall occurrence of -*s* (in all person/number environments) from 12.7 percent in the 1920–40 generation to 7.6 percent in the 1960–75 generation. Table 5.4 shows that there is also much less variation in the use of -*s* for these speakers as the occurrence of -*s* in non-concord environments decreases along with a 10.3 percent decrease in the use of third-singular -*s*.

The overall percentages for the use of verbal -*s* actually mask a significant amount of intragroup variation. The use of -*s* in the 1960–75 generation is influenced by competing urban/rural norms similar to the use of other innovative AAVE features (Cukor-Avila 1995; Cukor-Avila and Bailey 1995b, 1996). The data from Travis (born 1965), who has both rural and urban ties, clearly illustrate this competition. Travis was no longer living in Springville all year round at the time he was recorded but he still maintained fairly strong ties to the community and its rural values. He had also spent time in the city, and, as a result, he had acquired one of the most salient features of urban AAVE, the use of *be*+V+*ing*. However, the variable use of verbal -*s* in his speech is very different from that of Vanessa (born 1961), who also has ties to the city; in fact, Travis' use of -*s* is more similar to the frequency and distribution reported for speakers born in the two previous generations. This is illustrated in examples (14a) and (14b):

(14) a.   FW: Do a lot of people you know fool with drugs?
       T: Well I got some friends, yeah they *fool* with 'em. They drink an' they be smokin', you know, the pots an' stuff. You know I got some friends do that.
      FW: Are there a lot in Springville that take drugs you think?
       M: Yeah, mos' of the older ones *does* it.
   b.   I mean it, you know, it's jus' like I don', like me, say I don' pick on nobody I don' bother anybody, I *tends* to my own business, you know I, I, I, like I said, I got a lot of frien', I can get along with a lot of people, I *gets* along with a lot of them. But when you, when you be aroun' a lot of bullies you know, you can', you can' control yourself.

Intragroup variation in the use of third-singular -*s* also characterizes the youngest generation of Springville speakers, the 1975–90 generation. There is less variation in -*s* marking than in the previous generation as the use of this feature continues to decline. The apparent stability for third-singular -*s* between the two generations born after 1960, however, is an artifact of the manner in which the data from the youngest speakers are presented. Previous analyses of real-time data from Sheila and Brandy (Cukor-Avila 1995b, 1999; Cukor-Avila and Bailey 1995b, 1996) show that as their social networks expand out of rural Springville into neighboring urban areas they quickly adopt urban speech patterns and acquire the use of innovative AAVE features such as *had*+past and *be*+V+*ing*. An analysis of the loss of third-singular verbal -*s* data over time reveals the same pattern for this feature.

In 1988/89, before Sheila develops extensive urban ties, she has verbal -*s* on 27.4 percent of her singular tokens – a figure comparable to that of rural adults. However, as she develops urban ties and an urban identity, she adopts the urban linguistic pattern as well. In 1991/92 she begins to spend a considerable amount of time with other teenagers from Attmore and Wilson, two neighboring urban

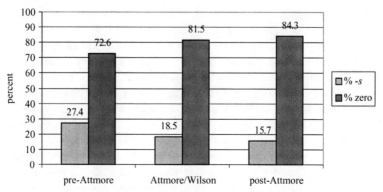

Figure 5.1 Percentage of third-singular -s over time for Sheila (born 1979)

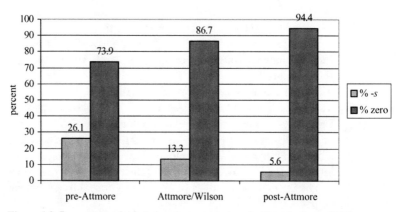

Figure 5.2 Percentage of third-singular -s over time for Brandy (born 1982)

areas. During this period her use of verbal -s decreases almost 9 percent to 18.5 percent. As Sheila's urban connections become stronger her ties to Springville and rural life grow significantly weaker as she identifies more and more with her urban friends and their urban lifestyle.[17] The data from the post–Attmore period, 1996–2000, show that her verbal -s usage remains low, decreasing slightly from earlier years to 15.7 percent. The changes in Sheila's use of verbal -s are shown in figure 5.1.

The changes in Brandy's social network orientation, which ultimately lead to the gradual loss of third-singular verbal -s in her speech, are parallel to those seen in Sheila. This is illustrated in figure 5.2. In the pre–Attmore period, 1988 to mid 1996, her use of verbal -s, 26.1 percent, is only slightly less than other Springville adolescents, including her sister Sheila, whose ties to rural networks remain strong. At the age of twelve in 1994, Brandy is just beginning to spend extended time away from Springville visiting friends and relatives in neighboring Wilson and hanging out with them at the Boy's and Girl's Club there. However, her urban ties strengthen when she goes to high school in Attmore, and she

Table 5.8 *Stages in the loss of verbal -s for Springville speakers (adapted from Cukor-Avila 1997b)*

Stage 1	Stage II	Stage III
1900–20 generation	1920–40 generation	Post-1940 generations
*subject/verb and NP/PRO constraints weaken *variable -s usage	*loss of NP/PRO constraint *-s begins to lose its function *frequency of -s increases *use of -s is unsystematic	*frequency of -s decreases *-s loses its meaning *loss of -s relates to the strength of urban ties

begins to change her attitude about life in Springville. This is reflected in her use of verbal -s which decreases by almost half to 13.3 percent during the period from mid 1996 to 1998. By the time she graduates from high school Brandy has solidified her urban identity and disassociated herself from her rural roots; in fact, during the last half of her senior year she moved from her house in Springville to live with friends in an apartment in Wilson. Again, her speech reflects these lifestyle changes – during the period from 1988–2000 her verbal -s usage declines significantly, occurring only 5.6 percent of the time.

5.3   An overview of the loss of -s over time in Springville

The gradual loss of verbal -s over time for speakers in Springville is best described as a three-stage process, illustrated in table 5.8. In the first stage there is a weakening of the subject/verb and NP/PRO constraints that formerly affected verbal -s. This leads to the type of variation exhibited in the speech of the 1900–20 generation. In stage II, in response to the weakening of these constraints, the overall frequency of -s increases and its use becomes unsystematic as speakers try to sort out its function (1920–40 generation). In stage III, the frequency of -s declines and -s loses its meaning as a present-tense marker (post-1940 generations). The extent to which -s is lost for speakers born after 1960 depends on the development and strength of their urban network ties.

The data from Springville further suggest that as verbal -s is lost it initially disappears in the first singular, next in the third plural, and lastly in the third singular. The ordering for the loss of -s (see figures 5.3 and 5.4) roughly corresponds to the frequency of -s in the speech of the oldest generation. In other words, -s disappears first where it's least common (e.g. in the first singular and third plural) and it disappears last where it's most common (e.g. in the third singular). However, as is shown by the longitudinal data from Sheila and Brandy, the degree to which third-singular -s is lost for young Springville speakers directly correlates with their association in the vernacular speech community in the two neighboring urban areas of Attmore and Wilson. Interestingly, the most striking aspect of the changes in Sheila's and Brandy's vernacular is that those changes

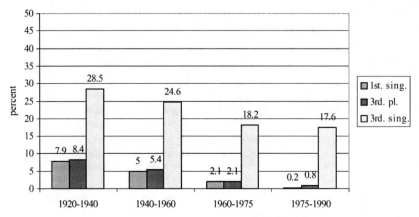

Figure 5.3 Use of -*s* by grammatical person in four generations of Springville speakers

FIRST-SINGULAR > THIRD-PLURAL > THIRD-SINGULAR

Figure 5.4 Implicational scale for the loss of verbal -*s* in Springville

recapitulate ongoing real-time change in Springville speech. In fact, when the data from Sheila and Brandy are considered in the light of the data from the community as a whole, they suggest that the vernacular in Springville is undergoing a general restructuring.

In addition, the analysis of verbal -*s* over time also reveals important methodological implications for data analysis in general. As the data from the 1960–75 and 1975–90 generations show, analysis of grouped data can often mask conflicting grammatical processes, as individuals often have different social orientations and different linguistic norms.

6   Conclusion

The qualitative data over time from Springville (section 4.2) suggest that different sociohistorical contexts correlate closely with linguistic differences in both AAVE and SWVE. Table 5.9 outlines some of those correlates. In the pre-World War II period there was significant contact between southern African Americans and whites, and as a result there were many shared linguistic features. The post-war era saw a significant reduction in the contact and consequently a reduction in the linguistic similarities. It should be clear that because both vernaculars are changing over time as reflexes of their sociohistorical context, making generalizations about the relationship between AAVE and SWVE grammars is difficult at best. Moreover, as the evidence on the reanalysis of verbal -*s* in Springville (section 5) and the evidence on the reanalysis of other vernacular features in both African-American and white grammars

Table 5.9 *Social situations and linguistic correlates over time in AAVE and SWVE (adapted from Cukor-Avila 2001)*

Pre-World War II	*Linguistic correlates*
A lot of contact between African Americans and southern whites because of working conditions (i.e. through tenancy and share cropping)	1. AAVE and SWVE shared many grammatical features: plural verbal *-s*, zero 2nd sing./pl. copula, *is* for *are*, *ain't*, *was* for *were*, negative concord, irregular and unmarked preterits, perfective *done*, zero 3rd singular *-s* 2. AAVE has some grammatical features which are infrequent or not shared in SWVE: zero 3rd sing. copula, habitual *be*, remote time *been*
Post-World War II	*Linguistic correlates*
Reduced contact between African Americans and southern whites because of the development of mechanized farming, the influx of Mexican labor, and the subsequent development of inner cities.	1. Many shared older grammatical features are still shared: *was* for *were*, *ain't*, demonstrative *them*, perfective *done*, multiple negation, irregular and unmarked preterits 2. Some shared older grammatical features have all but disappeared in both AAVE and SWVE: plural verbal *-s*, *is* for *are* 3. Some shared older grammatical features are primarily found in AAVE: zero 2nd sing./pl. copula, zero 3rd sing. *-s* *4. Some shared older features are primarily found in SWVE: no existent data 5. Some older grammatical features of AAVE that weren't shared in SWVE are still present in AAVE: zero 3rd sing. copula, remote time *been*, *ain't* for *didn't* 6. Grammatical features have evolved in AAVE that are not present in SWVE: *be+V+ing*, *had+*past

show (cf. Bailey 1993, 1997b, 2001; Bailey, Wikle, Tillery, and Sand 1996; Cukor-Avila 1995, 1997b, 1999; Cukor-Avila and Bailey 1995b), AAVE and SWVE continue to develop; thus any comparison must take into account the evolving linguistic relationship between these two varieties of vernacular English.

Notes

The research for this chapter and for the Springville Project has been generously supported by the National Science Foundation (BNS-8812552, BNS-90099232, and BNS-9109695), the University of Michigan, Texas A&M University, the University of North Texas, the National Endowment for the Humanities (FA-35429-99), and the American Council of Learned Societies (A06 01-02 7301).

1. Twelve years later in April 1993, Auburn University hosted the second Language Variety in the South conference (LAVIS II) organized by Cynthia Bernstein, Thomas Nunnally, and Robin Sabino. (See also Bernstein, Nunnally, and Sabino 1997).

2. This viewpoint was later formalized and known as the "deficit hypothesis" (cf. Bereiter and Englemann 1966; Deutsch, Katz, and Jensen 1968; Jensen 1969). Evidence for this hypothesis came mainly from non-linguistic observations by educators and psychologists and the results from standardized tests that were often racially biased (Labov 1969). Although the deficit hypothesis has been successfully refuted by linguistic research over the past fifty years, there are still people who argue for its validity (cf. Orr 1987; Rickford and Rickford 2000 for their discussion of newspaper articles and editorials that appeared during the Ebonics controversy in Oakland, CA).

3. See Bailey and Thomas (1998) and Thomas and Bailey (1998) for a discussion of phonological similarities between early varieties of AAVE and creole languages.

4. The gap in the research on Southern AAVE was partially filled by several studies in the late 1960s and early 1970s (cf. Anshen 1969 (Hillsborough, North Carolina); Houston 1969, 1970, 1972 (north Florida); Summerlin 1972 (northern Florida and southern Georgia); Fetscher 1971 (Atlanta, Georgia); Dunlap 1974 (Atlanta, Georgia); Graves 1967 (east-central Alabama), and Wolfram 1971, 1974 (Mississippi)).

5. The validity of the Rawick data has been called into question, specifically by Maynor (1988) and Montgomery (1991).

6. Subsequent research by Labov (1991) suggests that AAVE speakers are also not participating in sound changes that are evolving in white speech.

7. The absence of postvocalic /r/ in white southern speech here refers to speakers from the lower South and not to those persons residing in the Piney Woods and the Appalachian regions, who are, for the most part, r-ful.

8. While loss of the verbal -s inflection has been documented for both rural and urban speakers in Bailey and Maynor's corpus, the reanalysis of this feature proposed by Myhill and Harris (1986) has not. A possible explanation could be that, similar to the reanalysis of he, the reanalysis of -s as a marker of historic present is an urban feature, perhaps originating in northern cities. An analysis of verbal -s by Cukor-Avila (1990) in Southern AAVE suggests that for both old and young rural speakers, third-singular -s is present approximately 33 percent of the time and -s does not occur in narrative constructions, while for urban speakers third-singular -s occurs less than 10 percent of the time; however, none of these occurrences are in narrative constructions.

9. For a more in-depth discussion of the divergence controversy see the special issue of American Speech volume 62 and Bailey and Maynor (1989).

10. The country store in the post-Civil War South played a major part in shaping the lives of rural people and served as the foundation for the economy of the New South (Clark 1944). As the role of the country store became increasingly more important in the lives of southern planters, so did the role of storekeepers who were no longer just the purveyors of merchandise, but were also the agents of credit and the collectors of debts. Naturally, with this new role came a type of power over the members of communities never before held by country merchants (cf. Ayers 1992; Atherton 1949). This type of power brokering is still very much a part of the relationship between the owner of the Springville Store and the community's residents, a situation that has remained

virtually unchanged since the time of tenancy when her father was the owner and postmaster.

11. The Springville data include two examples of *be done* in the speech of an African American male born in 1932, but his data are not included in the analysis for the present study.

12. There are several examples of *be done* in the speech of older African-American and white LAGS informants. For example, *Nex' morning that cotton be done popped outta there* (85-year-old white male from Arkansas) and *All those houses here got people that supposed to be done come torn 'em down* (72-year-old African-American male from Florida).

13. An example from Vanessa illustrates this usage: *He might be done stop gardenin' now that he got his woman.*

14. The categorization of informants by types originates with the *Linguistic Atlas of New England* (Kurath 1949) where the distinction was made between Type I, II, and III speakers. Type I informants live primarily in insular, rural communities. They typically have few, if any, social contacts outside of their communities, mainly because of limited travel/work experiences. Type I speakers also have limited educational experiences, the majority of whom only attend school up to the middle-school grades.

15. The use of *had*+past as a past-tense marker has been a relatively understudied feature of AAVE until recently (Cukor-Avila 1995; Cukor-Avila and Bailey 1995b; Rickford and Rafal 1996). Data from Springville speakers suggest that, similar to *be*+V+*ing*, *had*+past began to grammaticalize around the time of World War II. Cukor-Avila and Bailey (1995b) suggest that the use of *had*+past as a simple past-tense form emerges first in narrative discourse, primarily in orientation and evaluation clauses and that, over time, its discourse function shifts from expressing traditional backgrounded events to expressing narrative backgrounded and foregrounded events. *Had*+past further grammaticalizes when its use expands out of narrative discourse and into non-narrative contexts; this use is primarily associated with Springville speakers born after 1970.

16. Recent research by Cukor-Avila (2001) suggests that the relationship over time between the grammars of Springville African Americans and whites can be generalized to a large extent for AAVE and SWVE speakers outside of this community.

17. In fact, Sheila drops out of school in 1994, less than half-way through the tenth grade.

6　Grammatical features of southern speech: *yall*, *might could*, and *fixin to*

CYNTHIA BERNSTEIN

1　Introduction

Michael Montgomery has pointed out that Southerners "maintain grammatical categories and structures having no exact equivalent or paraphrase elsewhere in American English" (Montgomery 1996a: 1–2). There are gaps in Standard English, and Southern English has creative ways of filling them. This chapter explores three uniquely southern structures and the special meanings associated with them. Singled out by Reed and Reed (1996) in *1001 Things Everyone Should Know About the South*, *yall*, *might could*, and *fixin to* represent three grammatical features particularly associated with southern speech. They appear in popular dictionaries of southern speech (Mitchell 1976, 1980), in literary works representing Southern dialect (Burkett 1978), and in films including southern characters (Herman 1947).

Of course, not every Southerner speaks the same variety of Southern English. Regional and social factors contribute to dialect variation. Some varieties are associated with mountainous areas, others with coastal communities; some with the city, others with the country; some with African Americans, others with European Americans; some with men, others with women; some with upper socioeconomic classes, others with middle and working classes. Even the same individual varies his or her speech according to the formality of the occasion, the listeners who are present, the subject being discussed, and so on (cf. Labov 1972b; Wolfram and Fasold 1974). Consequently, the syntactic features explored here will not characterize all southern speakers.

Yall, *might could*, and *fixin to* are what Wolfram and Fasold (1974) refer to as "socially diagnostic" features, in that their use identifies social characteristics of the speaker. The terms are often avoided by well-educated Southerners conscious of speaking "standard" English in formal contexts. Otherwise, their use is spread widely among regional and social dialects within the South. They are not associated with one particular variety of Southern English, the way, for example, habitual *be* characterizes African-American Vernacular English (cf. Fasold 1981). At the same time, they are more characteristic of southern speech than

106

are other socially diagnostic forms, such as *ain't* and double negatives, which are shared by those outside the South (cf. Wolfram and Schilling-Estes 1998). Although Southern English remains stigmatized as the one variety of English that is definitely *not* standard (Preston 1997), some non-Southerners have seen value in adopting characteristically southern expressions.

2   Yall

No feature has been more closely identified with southern speech than the use of *yall*. What I will refer to generally as *yall* in this discussion actually includes several variants in structure, spelling, and punctuation – *you-all* (with the accent on the first syllable), *y'all, ya'll, yawl* – and there has been a good deal of research interest in what those variants are, where they might have come from, and how they might be changing. The problem stems from a gap in the pronoun reference system of Modern English. Some languages have different pronouns for the singular and plural forms of the second person. Spanish, for example, has *tu* (singular, familiar), *usted* (singular, polite), *vosotros* (used in Spain, plural, familiar), and *ustedes* (plural). In English, *thou* used to function the way *tu* does in Spanish, but its use has dropped out of Modern English. So, how can one distinguish between singular and plural second-person pronoun reference? Today *yall* competes not only with *you* but also with *you'uns*, heard in Pittsburgh and in the Smoky Mountains, and with *youse* and *you guys*, heard primarily in the northeastern United States (cf. Wolfram and Schilling-Estes 1998).

Some researchers have found regional distinctions in pronoun choice to be blurring. The use of *you guys*, for example, may be spreading to the South. I became aware of this one evening in an Atlanta restaurant in November, 1993, where I was having dinner with a group of linguists – five women and one man. I was surprised to hear the waiter ask, "Can I get you guys something to drink?" Toward the end of the meal, I had a chance to speak to him of my interest in his use of *you guys*. He explained that he used it instead of *yall* because he thought it was more polite, and, besides, although he was originally from a town in rural Georgia, he did not want to sound southern. The spread of *you guys* is confirmed by a survey conducted by Natalie Maynor in 1999 of university students in Mississippi, Alabama, North Carolina, and South Carolina. She found "a surprisingly large number of respondents who said they might use *you-guys*" (Maynor 2000).

Likewise, *yall* seems to be gaining popularity among non-Southerners. A recent article in *Southern Living* expresses one Bostonian's discovery of the usefulness of the southern pronoun (Patton 1999). Linguists have shown that its popularity is shared by others outside the South. Tillery, Wikle, and Bailey (2000) report that an increasing number of non-Southerners participating in Southern Focus Poll surveys acknowledge using *yall* or *you all*: 44 percent in 1994, and 49 percent in 1996. Interestingly, this study also shows increasing usage among Southerners: 79 percent in 1994, and 84 percent in 1996. Although these figures may not be strictly comparable, there is no doubt that the form is widespread.

Table 6.1 *Usage of* yall *in* LAGS *by age*

Age	Percent	using *yall*
13–45	57%	(112/196)
46–65	40%	(85/210)
66–76	36%	(96 /266)
77–99	34%	(83/242)

Table 6.2 *Use of* yall *in 1996 Southern Focus Poll by age*

Age	Percent using *yall*	
	Outside the South	Inside the South
18–24	43%	68%
25–44	24%	62%
45–64	18%	54%
65+	7%	35%

Time seems to be favoring *yall* over *you all*. Maynor (1996) summarizes data from the *Linguistic Atlas of the Gulf States* (Pederson et al. 1991): of 196 informants aged 13–45, only 33 percent used *you-all*, compared to 57 percent who used *yall*. For every age group, older informants were less likely to use *yall* than were younger informants. Table 6.1 shows how the figures broke down.

This pattern is repeated in results reported by Tillery, Wikle, and Bailey (2000) for the Southern Focus Poll of 1996. For both Southerners and non-Southerners, *yall* is an option chosen more often by younger respondents than by older ones. Summarizing their data and rounding the percentages yields the results shown in table 6.2 for respondents who acknowledge using *yall*.

Tillery and her co-authors speculate that the reason for the increasing popularity of *yall* among young people, both in the South and elsewhere, is the usefulness of the feature. Unlike *you-all* (and, similarly, *you-uns* and *you guys*), all of which require more than one morpheme, *yall* may be construed as a single element. The authors regard *yall* as the result of *fusion*, or *grammaticalization*, referring to a word resulting from the merger of words or of grammatical elements that attach to words (cf. Hopper and Traugott 1993). The fused variant can then be used for emphasis in such phrases as *both yall* or *all yall*.

The structural origin of *yall* is a subject of considerable scholarly interest. Some people regard *yall* as a contraction of *you+all* and typically put an apostrophe after the *y*. Others put the apostrophe after the *a* and think of it either as a contraction of *ya+all* (with *ya* being *you* in fast or informal speech) or as a grammaticalized form not involving the contraction of *you* (Montgomery 1989c, 1996a). Montgomery (1992) suggests the possibility that *y'all* derives from the Scots-Irish *ye aw*. He points out that the stress pattern does not favor the contraction of *you+all*; since *you* has the primary stress and *all* the secondary stress, contraction would tend to produce *you'll*, not *y'all*. Also, even though *all* is a productive morpheme in southern speech (we have *what-all*, *who-all*, *we-all*, and so on), no other combination with *all* has led to a contracted or fused variant. Lipski (1993) traces the grammaticalization of *yall*, through literary dialect and other early sources, to the influence of African slaves. Literary dialect also gives us *yawl*, which similarly conceals any association with *all* and suggests a grammaticalized form.

There is general agreement about most of the potential uses for *yall* (cf. Montgomery 1996a). Besides referring to more than one addressee, it can function as an "associative plural" (cf. Richardson 1984), meaning something like "you and the rest of your family or friends"; as an "institutional" pronoun, as in "Do y'all have any french fries?"; as a kind of indefinite *yall*, which refers to one of several people, but the speaker doesn't know which one; as a sign of friendliness in greetings, partings, invitations, or attention-getters; and, in contrast to *you-all*, as a mark of intimacy or informality.

There is disagreement, though, among southern non-linguists as well as among linguists, as to whether *yall* can have primarily singular reference. The issue has been resurfacing for more than one hundred years. It was raised in 1899 in *The Nation* (Garner 1899, cited in Montgomery 1992). It came up as notes in *American Speech* in the 1920s, 30s, and 40s (Axley 1927, 1929; Morrison 1928; Perkins 1931; Vowles 1944). It appeared several more times since in the 1970s, 80s, and 90s (Spencer 1975; Richardson 1984; Butters and Aycock 1987; Maynor 1996). Much of the commentary has focused on how non-Southerners misrepresent Southerners as using *yall* consistently to refer to a singular addressee. Although recent studies have shown that such usage may be acceptable to some Southerners (Tillery, Wikle, and Bailey 2000), its occurrence is relatively rare.

In the last few years, evidence of interest in the southern second-person pronoun has appeared on the internet. There was a flurry of mail on the American Dialect Society mailing list in 1995 and again in 1999–2000. There were attestations on both sides of the singular–plural debate. In addition, contributors identified various forms of the possessive that they have heard: *yall's*, *yalls's*, *you all's*, *your all's*, *all of yall's*, and so on. This ongoing discussion was on my mind, when in April 2000 at a barbecue restaurant in Gatlinburg, Tennessee, our group of two men and two women was asked by the waitress, "Are you ready for your all's check?" It is unlikely that we have heard the last of this multi-faceted topic.

3   Might could

The expression *might could* (cf. Schneider in this volume) – as in "I might could do it", meaning something like "Maybe I could do it" – is used by Southerners to express a degree of uncertainty and politeness. The structure falls into the more general category of *double modals* or *multiple modals*, that is, the use of two or more modal auxiliaries within the same verb phrase. Modal auxiliaries include present- and past-tense pairs *may/might*, *shall/should*, *will/would*, and *can/could*, although most present-day speakers use these terms without regard to tense (and some linguists do not treat them as tensed pairs). Some modals, such as *must*, have no past-tense equivalent. Modals are generally not followed by an infinitive marker, but *ought* may be (compare "They ought to go"/"They ought not go"). All of these differ from other auxiliaries in that they are not marked for third-person singular; that is, we say "He might go," not *"He mights go." Modals differ from other verbs also in that they do not form gerunds (*her mighting) or participles (*he is mighting, *he has mighted); they do not combine with the infinitive marker *to* (*to might); and they do not combine with periphrastic *do* (*they do not might). (For further discussion of the difference between modals and other verbs, see Nagle 1993.)

Standard English is said to have a limit of one modal auxiliary per verb phrase. Southern English, however, permits not only *might could* but other combinations involving two or three modal auxiliaries. The most common combinations involve a choice of either *may* or *might* for the first modal and a choice of *can, could, should, will*, or *would* for the second. The occasional triple modal usually involves *ought to* (or *oughta*), as in *might should oughta*. (For lists of multiple modals used in Southern American English, see Montgomery and Nagle 1993; Mishoe and Montgomery 1994; Di Paolo 1989; Boertien 1986; Fennell and Butters 1996.) With so many possible modal combinations, Southerners have a tool for expression not available to speakers of Standard English.

Double modals are not limited to present-day speakers in the American South. Researchers have found examples in Middle English, in several varieties of Scottish and British English, and in Caribbean creoles. Although Nagle (1993) sees double modals as a development of Modern English, Feagin (1979), citing Visser (1969) and Traugott (1972), traces their origins to Middle English. Feagin notes that numerous examples from Scotland and England may be found in Wright (1898–1905). Fennell and Butters (1996) also see the likelihood of the form having been brought to the New World from Great Britain, whereas Montgomery and Nagle (1993) speculate that multiple modals may have been brought to the southern United States by Scots-Irish settlers. The language variety spoken in Ulster, in the north of Ireland, by Scottish settlers was not used very often in written communication, so it is difficult to find direct evidence of its characteristics. One interesting written source noted by Montgomery and Nagle is a guide published by a schoolteacher which describes the Ulster Scots dialect as incorrectly combining *will* and *can* in negative sentences. Although this was probably the predominant double modal in Ulster Scots, other combinations are in the inventory, including *might could* (Montgomery and Nagle 1993: 102). Fennell and Butters (1996) show that double modals may be found not only in English but also in German and Swedish. They note double modals in Jamaican Creole (Cassidy 1961; Bailey 1966; Christie 1991), in Bahamian Creole (Holm and Shilling 1982), and in Gullah (Wentworth 1944; Cunningham 1970). Feagin (1979) likewise cites Bailey (1966) for Jamaican Creole but adds that double modals are not present in Guyanese Creole (Rickford 1986a).

Within the United States, evidence suggests that use of *might could* extends to states outside the South. Citing a variety of sources (Atwood 1953; Wolfram and Christian 1976; Randolph and Wilson 1953) as well as anecdotal accounts, Feagin (1979) reports occasional usage of *might could* in New Jersey, Pennsylvania, West Virginia, Arkansas, Missouri, Iowa, North Dakota, and Nebraska. Di Paolo (1989) adds examples from Utah. Using data from the *Linguistic Atlas of the Middle and South Atlantic States* (*LAMSAS*), Montgomery (1998) points out that double modals are associated with twenty-one (of 158) speakers from Pennsylvania; thirty-one (of fifty-nine) from Maryland; nine (of seventeen) from Kentucky; and from one to four in New Jersey, West Virginia, Ohio, and Delaware. Although percentages are higher for speakers in Virginia, North Carolina, South Carolina, Georgia, and Florida, *LAMSAS* evidence does show that usage occurs outside the South. Among speakers of African-American Vernacular English (AAVE), usage of double modals is common both within and outside the South (Labov et al. 1968; Labov 1972b; Feagin 1979; Fennell and Butters 1996).

One must be cautious in drawing conclusions about frequency in use of double modals. Measuring their frequency is not an easy task, since not very many examples occur naturally in the limited context of a linguistic interview (cf. Fennell and Butters 1996). Just because no double modals arise during any given conversation, one cannot be certain that the interviewee does not use them. To avoid this problem, some researchers have interviewees judge the acceptability of sentences containing double modals. However, in order to study pragmatic context and linguistic structure of double modals, other researchers compile naturally occurring double modals heard or overheard in conversations (Feagin 1979; Mishoe and Montgomery 1994). In linguistic atlas surveys, the methods used are not always consistent. For this reason, Montgomery (1998) cautions against making inferential statistical judgments based on atlas data. Still, atlas data can be used to determine that a given person or group does use a given form. (See Bailey and Tillery 1999 for a discussion of methodology in eliciting *might could*.)

Within the South, double modals are used by all segments of the population. Analysis of data from the *Linguistic Atlas of the Gulf States* (*LAGS*) in Montgomery (1998) shows that multiple modals are used within each regional sector: Upper East Texas, Lower East Texas, Arkansas, West Louisiana, East Louisiana/Gulf Mississippi, Upper Mississippi, Lower Mississippi, West Tennessee, Middle Tennessee, East Tennessee, Upper Alabama, Lower Alabama, Gulf Alabama/West Florida, East Florida, Upper Georgia, and Lower Georgia. They are used almost equally by men and women, blacks and whites. Montgomery does find some difference in usage according to social class: although double modals are used by upper-, middle-, and lower-class speakers, the percentage of usage in *LAGS* increases as class decreases. Again, though, one must be tentative in drawing conclusions based on percentage comparisons from atlas data.

Whether or not any stigma is attached to double modals is the subject of some debate. Atwood (1953, 1962) suggests that more educated or cultured speakers avoid *might could*, preferring *might be able*, but other studies find that *might could* "is heard from the mouths of illiterates and graduate students in college" (Kroll 1925, quoted in Montgomery 1998). Feagin (1979) does find statistically significant differences in the frequency of double modals between upper- and working-class whites in Alabama; still, she concludes that no stigma is attached to their use. Interestingly, Montgomery (1998) finds that usage of double modals is actually greater for linguistic atlas subjects who are characterized as being particularly conscious of correct speech than for those who are not. Generally speaking, then, Southerners of all social classes use *might could* without attaching stigma to its use.

The form seems also to be distributed widely among different age groups. In *LAGS* interviews, which were conducted between 1968 and 1983, *might could* was used by speakers born in every decade represented, from the 1870s through the 1960s (Montgomery 1998: 118). Usage of multiple modals in general increases dramatically for speakers born after the 1910s, dropping off for speakers born after 1940, but, again, Montgomery cautions against relying only on *LAGS* data to determine whether or not usage is increasing over time.

Differences represented by age of informant can reflect change in progress. The theory underlying this assumption, known as "apparent time," is that "unless there is evidence to the contrary, differences among generations of adults mirror actual diachronic developments... The speech of each generation is assumed to reflect the language as it existed at the time when that generation learned the language" (Bailey et al. 1991: 242). Applying this principle to data from the Grammatical Investigation of Texas Speech (GRITS), Bailey et al. attempt to judge whether or not usage of certain southern features is expanding. GRITS is a 1989 telephone survey of approximately 1,000 randomly selected residents of Texas. Since all respondents had the opportunity to judge the extent to which they would use *might could*, it is a more suitable vehicle than *LAGS* for making judgments regarding increase in usage. Bailey et al. find that *might could* is used more often by respondents in the 18–29 age range than by those in the 62–95 group, a difference that increases dramatically when only native Texans are considered. It is their conclusion that *might could* is an expanding feature.

The extent to which non-native Southerners acquire *might could* is a matter of some dispute. On the one hand, Di Paolo asserts, "some Northerners who migrate to Texas begin to use DM's within a year of their arrival, thus indicating that Northern English can easily accommodate DM's" (Di Paolo 1989: 196-7). On the other hand, Montgomery claims,

> Some Northerners (i.e. non-native speakers) may adopt *might could* as a fixed phrase or idiom, but this acquisition is far from the same as being a user of multiple modals. Thus, while some Northerners may adopt one or two multiple modals, these are likely to be quite few. That Northerners (as well as Southerners without a native command of them) do not learn the combinability of multiple modals can be supported by their nonuse of these patterns, their nonacquisition of them after moving to the South, and their difficulty in paraphrasing them. (Montgomery 1996a: 16)

Data from GRITS show that approximately 18 percent of non-native Texans acknowledge using *might could*, compared to about 37 percent for lifelong residents. Of course, not everyone who uses the form will acknowledge doing so. Di Paolo believes that all Southerners have used a double modal at least once; Montgomery claims that there are some whose dialect does not include double modals.

Both Southerners and non-Southerners recognize *might could* as a salient feature of southern dialect. One source of evidence of this is its appearance in literary dialogue. Mishoe and Montgomery (1994) cite seven examples extracted from the files of the *Dictionary of American Regional English*; they add six additional examples from the fiction of Eudora Welty and Flannery O'Connor. Montgomery (1998) notes eighteen examples from a novel by Californian novelist Harry Turtledove. Bernstein (2000) shows that the feature is sometimes used in literary dialogue in ways that run counter to the native southern speaker's intuitions. In *The Outside Man*, Richard North Patterson identifies the feature as an indication of southern "lapses" in speech. One character, speculating on the motive for a murder, says, "It might could be rape." Such usage lacks the intentionality of the speaker, which native Southerners associate with the phrase.

The use, or misuse, of *might could* might be described by answering three questions. The first is a question of semantics: does the phrase mean something that a native speaker would mean when using it? The second is a question of pragmatics: is the phrase used in a context in which a native speaker would use it? The third is a question of syntax: is the phrase structured within the sentence in a way that the native speaker would structure it?

The question of semantics may be addressed by considering the range of meanings that have been attributed to modals in general. There are three such *modalities* (cf. Palmer 1990; Smith 1999). *Deontic* modality expresses a range of permissibility from obligated to forbidden. A teacher telling a student, "You **must** turn in the assignment by Tuesday" is employing deontic modality. *Epistemic* modality expresses a range of probability from certain to impossible. A friend sympathizing with another's sad story by saying, "That **must** have been difficult for you" is employing epistemic modality. *Dynamic* modality expresses ability or volition. A researcher telling a colleague, "I **can** get that information at the library" is employing dynamic modality. Judgment surveys reported by Di Paolo (1989) show that the most accepted function of *might could* is to indicate ability (dynamic); the possibility (epistemic) sense is ranked low; and the permission sense (deontic) is ranked in-between. It makes sense to see *I might could do it* as combining a degree of willingness and ability (dynamic modality) with a degree of uncertainty (epistemic modality); that is, "I'm willing to do it, but I'm not sure I have the ability." A sentence such as "It might could be rape" sounds wrong to native Southerners because it has only epistemic value; it lacks the dynamic function associated with *might could*.

The second question in judging usage is that of pragmatics. This question is explored by Mishoe and Montgomery (1994). This study isolates two pragmatic functions of the double modal. One is in one-on-one conversations, particularly those that take the form of negotiation. The second is during a conversation in which there is a threat to "face" (following Goffman 1967) of one or more speakers. Di Paolo (1989) affirms especially the first of these conditions. She observes that sales clerks would use *might could* especially when they wanted to offer a suggestion that might run counter to her own wishes as a customer, in other words, in the one-to-one context of negotiation. The general point is that *might could* is a mark of politeness in conversation. It is used so that the listener will not feel threatened by possible lack of agreement on the part of the speaker.

The third question is the matter of structure. The question has both theoretical and practical interest. Double modals are of theoretical syntactic interest because they appear to violate the phrase structure rule that allows only one modal in the verb phrase. One approach has been to consider them not as combinations of modals but as combinations of a modal and an adverb. Di Paolo (1989) suggests treating them as idioms or compounds. In practice, researchers' findings agree as to the formation of questions and negatives. Questions are formed by moving the second modal *could* in front of the subject of the sentence, as in "Heather, could you might find you a seat somewhere?" (Di Paolo 1989: 216), or "Could you might possibly use a teller machine?" (Mishoe and Montgomery 1994: 11). Negatives are formed, in general, by inserting *not* after *might*: "I might not could understand you." If the negative is contracted, however, it attaches to could: "I was afraid you might couldn't find it" (Di Paolo 1989: 216). Interestingly, native Southerners in Memphis claim that they would be less likely to use double modal questions and negatives than they would affirmative declarative statements (Chtareva 1999).

4   *Fixin to*

In a sentence such as, "I was just fixin to leave," *fixin to* means something like "about to." It expresses the intention to do something within a relatively short period of time. Just where the expression came from and why its use is chiefly southern is hard to say. Dialect dictionaries regularly include the term, defining it most often with the synonyms *preparing to* or *intending to* and specifying that it is associated with southern speech (cf. Cassidy and Hall 1991; Hendrickson 1986, 1993; Garber 1976; Wentworth 1944). *Fixin to* in *The Dictionary of American Regional English* (*DARE*) is not limited to the South; outlying examples are cited from Michigan, California, Pennsylvania, and New Jersey. *DARE* includes several variants, which confirm a link between *fixin to* and the verb *fix*:

to fix to go to Boston
to fix for the trip
busy fixing for company tomorrow
fix up for the drought
fixed to stay a week
fix for going to the school house
fixing up for a storm
all these people I've got to fix for

Table 6.3 *Use of* fixin *to in* LAGS *by sector*

LAGS sector	Sector total	Number using *fixin to*	Percent using *fixin to*
Upper Texas	54	31	57%
Lower Texas	40	17	43%
Arkansas	82	20	24%
West Louisiana	62	37	60%
Western Gulf (MS and LA)	61	25	41%
Upper Miss.	49	10	20%
Lower Miss.	47	22	47%
West Tenn.	34	6	18%
Mid Tenn.	47	14	30%
East Tenn.	60	6	10%
Upper Alabama	53	13	25%
Lower Alabama	62	15	24%
Eastern Gulf (FL and AL)	34	7	21%
Upper Georgia	87	24	28%
Lower Georgia	78	22	28%
East Florida	64	16	25%

Data compiled from *LAGS* (Pederson et al. 1986–92), vol. 1, p. 22 and vol. 4, pp. xvi and 240.

These examples suggest that *fixin to* may have been grammaticalized, starting from a productive set of tensed verbs and prepositions and blending, like *yall*, into a fused form (cf. Zeigler 1997, 1998). Rather than considering *fixin to* as a verb+infinitive, then, some linguists analyze the structure as *quasimodal* (Ching 1987: 343).

Data available in *LAGS* suggest that its use is widespread among all regional sectors and social groups. As with *might could*, one must exercise caution in drawing statistical conclusions from atlas data. The form is similarly difficult to elicit, and methods of elicitation may have varied from one atlas interview to another. Nevertheless, evidence is sufficient to suggest that *fixin to* was common throughout the South during the period of the atlas interviews. Table 6.3 shows its frequency among the *LAGS* sectors. The social distribution of *fixin to*, as shown in table 6.4, is also broad.

Overall, the form is acknowledged by about 31 percent of the respondents in *LAGS*. Usage is divided almost equally between men and women, blacks and whites. Two general trends are suggested by the remaining social figures. First, the form may be used slightly more often by younger people than by older people; second, it may be used more often by those with less education and social status than those with higher levels.

Table 6.4 *Use of* fixin to *in* LAGS *by social factors*

	Number	Number using *fixin to*	% Using *fixin to*
Gender			
female	422	125	30%
male	492	160	33%
ethnicity			
black	197	61	31%
white	717	224	31%
Age			
13–45	196	68	35%
46–65	210	68	32%
66–76	266	78	29%
77–99	242	71	29%
Education			
0–7 years	234	77	33%
8–10 years	216	78	36%
11–12 years	224	57	25%
13+ years	240	73	30%
Social status			
lower	194	70	36%
lower middle	369	119	32%
upper middle	279	78	28%
upper	72	18	25%

Data from *LAGS* (Pederson et al. 1986–92) vol. 4, pp. xvi, 240.

A trend of increasing usage of *fixin to* is suggested by more recent survey research conducted in Oklahoma. Bailey et al. (1993) find that young people use the form significantly more than their older counterparts. Young people have carried this usage from rural areas, where the form is prevalent, to urban ones. The authors find, too, that usage of the form is a marker of southern identity. Those who have resided in the state less than ten years were much less likely to adopt the expression.

Those less familiar with *fixin to* may not capture its nuances of meaning. Ching (1987) details some of the more subtle distinctions in the semantics of the expression. The majority of his Tennessee respondents favor usage in sentences such as *I'm fixin' to wash the dishes* or *I'm fixin' to do it now* and disfavor usage in *I'm fixin' to leave in the next five years* or *I'm fixin' to get married some day*. In other words, the phrase is appropriate when the action is imminent, not when it is indefinite or in the distant future. In some ways, *fixin to* resembles other southern expressions that refer to initiation of an action, as in, *He'd* go to (*or* get to) *talking and we'd never hear the end of it* (cf. Montgomery 1980, 2000a; Bean 1991). Such verbs are said to be *inchoative* in aspect, in that they refer to action that is just beginning. *Fixin to* differs slightly, in referring to activity prior to an action's beginning.

In some ways, then, the expressions discussed here convey meaning that cannot satisfactorily be communicated by standard words or phrases. The same may be said for the many other grammatical features that are associated with southern speech. *Ain't* enjoys such popularity in part because Standard English has no satisfactory contraction for *am not*. Unconjugated *be*, associated with African-American Vernacular English, can distinguish between a habitual action as in *She be home by six* (usually or every night) and a one-time occurrence. If some of these forms seem to be spreading among younger generations and to populations outside the South, it may be that their usefulness has come to outweigh any negative prestige that has traditionally accompanied them.

5   Other prominent grammatical features

The three grammatical features discussed here are among the most likely to be associated with Southern American English and least likely to be identified with a particular regional, ethnic, or social group within the South. Even though they are among the most salient features of southern grammar, however, they are not the only features. Ideally, we would list all the relevant features associated with any given dialect; in practice, it does not work out that way. Any list of features such as the one compiled according to atlas data by McDavid (1958) is likely to become outdated or applied too rigidly. A good place to start, though, for a broad listing of morphological and syntactic features associated with Southern English is *American English: Dialects and Variation*, especially the grammatical section of the "Appendix: Inventory of Socially Diagnostic Structures" (Wolfram and Schilling-Estes 1998: 331–43). Here, the reader can find grammatical features, in addition to the ones already mentioned, that figure prominently in at least some varieties of southern speech:

- irregular verb patterns in the rural South (*Something just* **riz** *up right in front of me*);
- completive *done* in AAVE and in Anglo American vernaculars (*I* **done** *forgot what you wanted*);
- *be+s* in some parts of the South influenced by Highland Scots and Scots-Irish (*Sometimes it* **bes** *like that*);
- remote time *béen* (stressed) in AAVE to denote distant past (*I* béen *known her*);
- indignant *come* in AAVE (*He* **come** *telling me I didn't know what I was talking about*);
- *a*-prefixing in Appalachian English and other rural varieties (*Kim was* a-*drinkin'*);
- *are* absence in Southern Anglo and AAVE (*You ugly*);
- singular *s* on plural verbs in rural Upper and Lower South (*Me and my brother get*s *in fights*);
- *-s* absence on third-person-singular forms in AAVE (*The dog stay outside in the afternoon*);
- *-ly* absence in Appalachian and Ozark English (*I come from Virginia* **original**);

- intensifying adverbs in Southern English (*She is* **right** *nice*);
- *steady* in AAVE (*They be* **steady** *messing with you*);
- plural -*s* absence with measurement nouns, especially in isolated southern areas (*The station is four mile↲down the road*);
- possessive -*s* absence in AAVE (*The man↲hat is on the chair*);
- *mines* as possessive pronoun in AAVE (*It's* **mines**);
- possessive forms ending in -*n* in phrase-final position in Appalachian English (*Is it* yourn?);
- relative pronoun absence in subject position in southern-based varieties (*That's the dog ↲bit me*);
- existential *they* in southern-based vernaculars (**They**'*s a good show on TV*).

Of course, *yall*, *might could*, and *fixin to* are included in the appendix, as are habitual *be*, *ain't*, and multiple negation, which have already been mentioned. The point must be reiterated, though, that not all members of a group will use all of these grammatical features to the same degree.

6   Conclusion

The reader who wants to find more detailed discussion of particular features or more elaboration of features confined to a limited regional, ethnic, or social group should turn to James McMillan and Michael Montgomery's *Annotated Bibliography of Southern American English* (1989). Chapter 5 of this important resource is devoted entirely to references concerning morphology and syntax. Entries cover 100 years of research, from 1888 through 1987. There are collections of articles on varieties of Southern English that contain important work on syntax: Montgomery and Bailey (1986); Bernstein, Nunnally, and Sabino (1997); Montgomery and Nunnally (1998). Several volumes of Publications of the American Dialect Society (PADS) are devoted to syntax or include grammatical structures within a particular region of the South: Christian, Wolfram, and Dube (1988); Cunningham (1992); Little and Montgomery (1994); Wolfram, Hazen, and Schilling-Estes (1999); Hazen (2000). The internet, too, has become an important medium for the exchange of ideas. Discussions on the American Dialect Society List can be helpful in compiling data on regional English and in suggesting new avenues of research. (See www.americandialect.org for information on joining the list or on searching through past discussions.) In the end, the researchers themselves are the best source of information, that is, next to the people of the South whose language varieties we take such pleasure in discovering.

7 Sounding southern: a look at the phonology of English in the South

GEORGE DORRILL

I know noble accents
And lucid, inescapable rhythms;
But I know, too,
That the blackbird is involved
In what I know.
    (Wallace Stevens, "Thirteen Ways of Looking at a Blackbird")

1 Sounding southern

There is doubtless no limit to the number of ways that a blackbird may be looked at, but Wallace Stevens in his poem "Thirteen Ways of Looking at a Blackbird" demonstrates that there are at least thirteen. The same is true of Southern American English (SAE) phonology. There is really no limit to the ways of sounding southern and to the ways of describing those "noble accents," but there are surely at least eight to explore in this look at the phonology of English in the southern United States.

Michael Montgomery's revision of James B. McMillan's *Annotated Bibliography of Southern American English* (McMillan and Montgomery 1989) lists over 600 items concerned in whole or in part with the phonetics or phonology of English in the South. Two inferences can be drawn from this fact. First, it is difficult to provide both a comprehensive and a detailed picture of SAE phonetics and phonology in a brief overview. However, it is possible to draw a broad picture of SAE phonology that is both understandable to the general reader and accurate in its depiction of the scene. Michael Montgomery has done just that in his articles "English language" in the *Encyclopedia of Southern Culture* (Montgomery 1989a) and "Language variety in the South: a retrospective and assessment" in *Language Variety in the South Revisited* (Montgomery 1997a). This chapter draws substantially from these two sources.

The second inference that can be drawn from the large number of items on phonetics and phonology in the McMillan and Montgomery bibliography is that there is no lack of interest in SAE phonetics and phonology. Montgomery

(1989a: 761) notes, "[T]he South is the most distinctive speech region in the United States," and "When Lyndon Johnson and Jimmy Carter ran for president, the country and the media gave extraordinary attention to their accents." The fact that the country focused on the two presidents' accents points to the salience of phonology as the most distinctive feature of the speech of the "most distinctive speech region in the United States," as does the widespread use of the term "southern drawl." However, despite the folk use of such terms as "southern accent" or "southern drawl," it is not easy to assign a particular set of phonological features indicative of southern speech; rather, it should not be surprising to find that there is as much variation in southern speech as there is in other varieties of American English. Again, as Montgomery (1989a: 761) points out, "Linguistic research cannot . . . identify any common denominator that can safely be termed a 'southern accent' or a 'southern dialect.'"

While no single explanation can be given for what it means to sound southern, there are a number of studies that have examined various aspects of SAE phonology. In what follows, a brief history of the systematic study of the phonetics and phonology of Southern English is given, along with the major findings, first of regional patterns, and then social and ethnic patterns. A more detailed look at certain phonetic and phonological features follows, along with a brief description of the historical dimension.[1]

2   The systematic study of the phonetics and phonology of Southern English

2.1   The Linguistic Atlas of the South Atlantic States

Although there has been a long history of studies of Southern English phonology (see, for example, Read 1909, 1911), the first large-scale, systematic investigation of the speech of the South came with the Linguistic Atlas of the South Atlantic States. This project, proposed by Hans Kurath in 1929 as part of an investigation of the area of American colonial settlement, was later combined with the Linguistic Atlas of the Middle Atlantic States to form the Linguistic Atlas of the Middle and South Atlantic States (LAMSAS).[2] Fieldwork for the Linguistic Atlas of New England (LANE) was carried out from 1931 to 1933, and a preliminary survey of the South Atlantic states was conducted by the principal LANE fieldworker, Guy Lowman, during 1933 and 1934. Lowman completed sixty-eight interviews, primarily in the states of Maryland, Virginia, North Carolina, South Carolina, and Georgia, using a modified version of the LANE questionnaire with about 700 items designed to elicit variations in pronunciation, usage, and vocabulary.

In 1935, Lowman began a systematic survey of the South Atlantic states. He had completed the fieldwork in Maryland, Virginia, and North Carolina by the time of his death in 1941. Kurath hired Raven I. McDavid, Jr., to complete the fieldwork, but McDavid was able to complete only a few field records in

South Carolina before World War II interrupted the survey. After the war, McDavid resumed fieldwork, completing the survey of South Carolina, eastern Georgia, and northeastern Florida by 1949. In 1949, Kurath published the first major analysis of the survey data, *A Word Geography of the Eastern United States*. In this work, he divided the Atlantic coast into three large regions on the basis of differing word usage: Northern, Midland, and Southern. He further subdivided the Midland area into two large regions, North Midland and South Midland. He noted that his identification was to a certain extent tentative: "It may well be that the South Midland, which has very few distinctive terms of its own but shares some of them with the South, may have to be regarded in the end as a sub-area of the South rather than the Midland" (Kurath 1949: 37).

In 1961 Kurath and McDavid published the follow-up to Kurath 1949, *The Pronunciation of English in the Atlantic States* (*PEAS*). This is the most accessible source for the phonetic data found in LANE and LAMSAS. In chapter 2, "Regional dialects of cultivated speech," Kurath and McDavid devote three sections to SAE pronunciation: 2.7, the South Midland (the Appalachians and the Blue Ridge from the Pennsylvania line to northern Georgia); 2.8, the Upper South (with the Virginia Piedmont the center); and 2.9, the Lower South (chiefly South Carolina and Georgia). Kurath and McDavid also note, "Within the Lower South the Low Country [coastal plain] of South Carolina and the adjoining coast of Georgia and Florida form a rather distinctive sub-area" (1961: 21). A summary of their chief findings follows. They focus mainly on the pronunciation of vowels and postvocalic /r/. In the South Midland, postvocalic /r/ is kept, and /r/ frequently intrudes in *wash* and *Washington* among folk and common speakers; these features are also present in North Midland speech. Postvocalic /r/ is lost in both the Upper and Lower South. Their treatment of vowel variation is discussed in section 3 of this chapter, "A synopsis of the regional varieties of SAE phonology."

2.2   The Linguistic Atlas of the Gulf States

The Linguistic Atlas of the Gulf States (LAGS) is "the largest and most inclusive research project on southern speech" (Bailey 1989: 788). Directed by Lee Pederson and begun in 1968, the interpretive results were published in seven volumes between 1986 and 1992, the 1,118 protocols (transcribed field records) having been published on microfiche in 1981, based on 5,300 hours of recorded speech stored at Emory University in Georgia. Michael Montgomery (1997a: 10) makes the strong claim that "LAGS is undoubtedly one of the half-dozen most important scholarly achievements in American English in the twentieth century." LAGS was a follow-up to and an extension of the methodology developed in Kurath's Atlantic coast surveys. More attention was paid both to urban speech and to African-American speech (22 percent of the sample) than had been the case in the earlier surveys. Younger informants were interviewed as well.

Pederson et al. (1986) provides some major findings. In the eight-state area surveyed (Tennessee, Georgia, Florida, Alabama, Mississippi, Louisiana, Arkansas, and eastern Texas), at least eleven major subregional dialects and as many as fourteen urban dialects were identified, including the Piney Woods of the Lower South and the Mississippi Delta.[3]

2.3   The Dictionary of American Regional English

Although primarily intended as a lexicographical resource, the *Dictionary of American Regional English* (*DARE*) contains much of phonetic and phonological interest, particularly in the pronunciation of individual words. *DARE*, though conceived as early as 1889, really came into being in 1962 under the leadership of Frederic Cassidy. A questionnaire was developed, and workers were sent into the field between 1965 and 1970 to collect data from across the United States. In addition to the questionnaire, 1,843 audiotapes were collected, each of approximately thirty minutes, of the chief informants of each community speaking freely on familiar topics and also reading a passage called "Arthur the Rat," designed to elicit known variations in pronunciation. In the Introduction to volume 1 of *DARE* (Cassidy 1985), there is a summary of the major pronunciation findings, including four maps: absence or weakening of postvocalic /r/, weakening and flattening of the diphthong /ai/, diphthongization of /ɔ/ before voiceless consonants, and the merger of /ɔ/ and /a/. The southern region is strongly involved in the first three of the maps.

2.4   Other surveys and studies

The major survey that is ongoing at present is the Atlas of North American English, under the tutelage of William Labov at the University of Pennsylvania (cf. Feagin in this volume). Another survey, just of a single state, but a large state, is the Phonological Survey of Texas, reported on in Bailey and Bernstein (1989) and Bernstein (1993). An innovation of this project is "piggybacking" on another telephone survey. This methodology was also used in the Survey of Oklahoma Dialects, also under the leadership of Guy Bailey (Bailey 1997a).

There are also a number of studies dealing with smaller regions and individual communities. Earlier studies tended to focus on isolated or relic areas, such as the Smoky Mountains of North Carolina/Tennessee, the Outer Banks of North Carolina, the Chesapeake Bay islands, etc.[4]

3   A synopsis of the regional varieties of SAE phonology

From a perusal of the results of these surveys and studies, a general picture of the phonology of SAE emerges. As was pointed out earlier, there is no single set of features that distinguishes SAE phonology from the rest of the United States. There is, however, a perception that such a thing exists. This perception probably relies on a combination of elements. Bailey (1996) provides a useful list of possible phonological factors. Probably the closest thing to a generally identifying feature would be the "flattening" or monophthongization of the /ai/ diphthong, but that turns out to be a quite complicated phenomenon, with much variation depending on environment (word end, following voiceless consonants, following voiced consonants, etc.). If a fundamental division is made between South Midland (or Inland Southern) and Southern (or Coastal Southern), then postvocalic /r/ becomes very salient: it is present in the former, absent in the latter. (However, its absence is shared with New England speech, and its presence is shared with most other varieties of North American English.)

Other features of southern phonology noted by Bailey (1996) include the following: upgliding /ɔ/, fronted back vowels, certain vowel mergers including front vowels before nasals (*pen* and *pin*), the "southern drawl" (lengthening of certain vowels and intrusion of /ə/ between the vowels and following consonant) and the "breaking" of some vowels, so that *steel* is pronounced like *stale* and *stale* like *style* (discussed more thoroughly in Feagin's chapter in this volume). Bailey focuses on vowels, but there are also some consonant variations characteristic of SAE, such as the simplification of final consonant clusters (including [st], [sk], [sp], [nd], etc.).

4   Socioeconomic varieties

Obviously social and economic factors play a large factor in language variation, but syntax and morphology often seem to be more socially diagnostic than phonology. However, an early study (McDavid 1948) focused on the social dimension of a phonological variable. McDavid's study revealed a complicated pattern of the presence or absence of postvocalic /r/ in South Carolina correlating with social mobility and prestige dialects. He predicted a change in the pattern resulting from changed social conditions. A student of McDavid's, Raymond O'Cain, found this change occurring in his dissertation research, which was a social dialect study of Charleston, South Carolina (O'Cain 1972).

5   Ethnic varieties

The most notable ethnic variety of SAE is African-American Vernacular English (AAVE), and much has been written about it and its relation to white varieties of English (including several discussions in this volume). By 1974, enough had been written for a book-length bibliography to be compiled (Brasch and Brasch 1974), and the flow continues unabated. A good source for a balanced picture of the subject is Montgomery and Bailey (1986). Two articles dealing with the phonology of AAVE and its relationship to other varieties of SAE in the volume are Dorrill (1986) and Miller (1986). Dorrill looked at the stressed vowels of paired African-American and white speakers interviewed for LAMSAS. He found a greater tendency for monophthongized vowels and a greater regional uniformity among the African-American speakers. Miller looked at the pronunciation of the plurals of words ending in the consonant clusters [sp], [st], and [sk] in Augusta, Georgia. He found disyllabic plurals in both black and white speech of older generations and found that unmarked plurals are the norms for both blacks and whites.

6   The pronunciations of individual words

Probably the most salient variation in the pronunciation of a single word is the /s/-/z/ alternation in *greasy*, commented upon as early as 1896 by George Hempl. Kurath and McDavid (1961) includes a map showing the basic north/south disjunction between the two variants (/s/ – north; /z/ – south), the line separating them roughly moving northwestward from middle Delaware to northwest Pennsylvania. There are of course numerous other words exhibiting similar variation, such as *git-get* and *Miz-Misiz* (Mrs.); Kurath and McDavid (1961) contains a number of maps focusing on individual word pronunciations.

7   The "southern drawl"

There are two distinct interpretations of the term "southern drawl": the common or folk notion and the linguistic definition (Montgomery 1989a: 761). In common parlance, the southern drawl is a synonym for southern accent or southern speech and refers to the putative slowness of southern speech, often attributed to the heat or to the laziness of its speakers. It is thus often used derogatively, as is the term "brogue" or even the term "dialect" itself. In contrast, linguists use the term to refer to "the lengthening and raising of accented vowels, normally accompanied by a change in voice pitch. It involves the addition of a second or even a third vowel but does not necessarily entail a slower overall speech tempo" (Montgomery 1989a: 761). The classic treatment of the southern drawl is Sledd (1966).

8   The historical dimension

The historical dimension of SAE phonology obviously cannot be ignored. It is hard to describe a moving target, and SAE phonology is a moving target. Like everything else in language, it is undergoing change. Some of the features we take as very characteristic of SAE turn out to be quite recent, such as the merger of /ɪ/ and /ɛ/ before nasals. Bailey (1996) is a good discussion of earlier SAE, and Feagin in this volume describes the ongoing southern vowel shift.

9   Conclusion

The South is the home of "noble accents / And lucid inescapable rhythms" and the study of these accents and rhythms is a noble task. There is still much to know about the phonology of English in the southern United States and many ways of looking at the many ways of sounding southern.

Notes

1. For a more detailed examination of southern phonological features, please see the chapter by Crawford Feagin in this volume.
2. For a brief description of LAMSAS, see Dorrill 1989; for a more detailed look, see Kretzschmar et al. 1994.
3. A useful summary of the accomplishments of LAGS can be found in the volume edited by Michael Montgomery and Thomas Nunnally (1998).
4. For a comprehensive listing of these studies, refer to McMillan and Montgomery (1989a).

8   Vowel shifting in the southern states

CRAWFORD FEAGIN

1   Introduction

In 1972 it was first realized that there was a general shift in the vowels of not only the southern states, but all the southern varieties of English around the world – southern England, the southern states of the United States, New Zealand, Australia, and South Africa. What was especially remarkable about this shift in the United States was that the direction of the rotation of the vowels was completely opposite to the direction of a vowel shift going on simultaneously in the northern cities, producing yet more differences between northern and southern varieties in the United States over time.

This very interesting research was done by William Labov, Malcah Yaeger, and Richard Steiner and presented in a National Science Foundation report (1972) as well as in other publications and presentations. The southern states data on which it was based came from seventeen conversational interviews carried out by Labov in central and west Texas, Georgia (Atlanta), and eastern North Carolina (including the Outer Banks) in 1969. In more recent work, Labov has revised and expanded his earlier research, and has attempted to place it in a larger context (Labov 1991, 1994). Data collected by Ash in 1988 and 1990 from twenty lower-middle-class and working-class young adults and teenagers in Birmingham, Alabama, has also played a part in the work on this topic (Labov and Ash 1997).

Figure 8.1 shows the Southern Shift schematically, in Labov's 1994 version. Here, the front vowels are exchanging positions between the traditional diphthongs of /iy/ and /ey/ and their traditionally short counterparts, /i/ and /e/. The movement of the back vowels to the front is not interpreted as a chain shift, but rather as parallel movements toward the front of the high back vowel /uw/ and the mid back vowel /ow/.

Since Labov's pioneering work on vowel shifting in the South, a growing number of researchers have examined this phenomenon in different parts of the South – my own work in Alabama (1987), Fridland's in Memphis (1998, 1999, 2001, in progress), and Baranowski (2000) in Charleston, South Carolina.

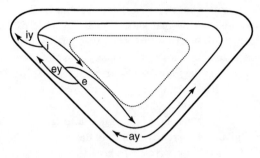

Figure 8.1 Southern Vowel Shift (Labov 1994: 209)

Moreover, Labov and his team have conducted a telephone survey of the entire South as part of their larger Telsur project, a massive telephone survey of the United States and English-speaking Canada, resulting in the *Atlas of North American English* (Labov, Ash, and Boberg, forthcoming).

Other work in which vowel shifting is only a part of wider-ranging investigations include a number of studies based on data from Texas (Thomas and Bailey 1998; Bailey and Thomas 1998), North Carolina (Wolfram and Schilling-Estes 1996; Schilling-Estes 1997), and Maryland (Schilling-Estes 1997), and of African Americans (Bailey 1997b; Thomas 1997). Since the focus of these studies is more on the shifting of particular vowels (generally /ay/ or /aw/) or on the direction (or existence) of their glides, these studies will enter the discussion only marginally.

Separate mention must be made of Thomas (2001) which presents vowel charts for 116 speakers across the South, plus thirty-three African Americans.[1] Extensive references to work connected with all these varieties accompany the vowel charts, as well as some remarks concerning vowel shifting. Thomas' inventory of vowels across the South undoubtedly will provide data for many more general analyses in the future, but is not intended to address the specific topic of vowel shifts. For that reason it will not be mentioned further with the exception of its material on African-American vowels – the most extensive study of African-American vowels to date.

First, I will discuss the place of African-American vowels in these studies. Then I will present the overview of the South provided by Labov et al. (forthcoming). Next I will discuss Baranowski's and Fridland's work in Charleston and Memphis, and then my own work in Alabama. Lastly, I will discuss the interrelations of these various projects, especially their differing methodologies, including selection of speakers.

2   African-American vowel shifting

African Americans across the South, like their counterparts in the rest of the US (Labov 1991, 2001: 506–8), show a limited influence from whites of the same community (see Bailey and Thomas (1998), and Thomas and Bailey (1998)). Thomas' (2001) thirty-three vowel charts from African Americans come mainly from Texas (fourteen) and North Carolina (thirteen). In general, African Americans avoid the sound changes observed in the white community, so it should not be surprising that the Southern Shift is not taking place in the black community. On the other hand, the shifting of back vowels to the front can be observed both in Thomas' North Carolina and Texas speakers.

Because of this distinction, none of the following studies have included African Americans, though Fridland is currently exploring the vowels of the black community in Memphis (Fridland in progress). In her early analyses, she has found some fronting of back vowels among her speakers (personal communication, July, 2001).

3   The Atlas of North American English: the South

In presenting an overview of vowels in the southern states, Labov, Ash and Boberg define the South linguistically as that area which monophthongizes /ay/ before voiced segments and in final position – the vowel of *sigh*, *sign*, *side*. This encompasses geographically most of the South, excluding, however, (east to west) most of Florida except Jacksonville; Charleston, SC; most of the eastern coastal areas; the area north of Richmond, Virginia; the area north of Charleston, West Virginia; the area north of Lexington and Louisville, Kentucky (i.e. north of the Ohio River); and the area north of Springfield, Missouri. Moving west, the line excludes Tulsa and Oklahoma City, Oklahoma. It includes Amarillo, Lubbock, and Odessa, Texas, but excludes El Paso.

Within this area, Labov et al. describe the defining features of southern speech as found in the "active rotation of vowels termed the Southern Shift." The original view of the Southern Shift (Labov, Yaeger, and Steiner 1972; Labov 1991) presented a combination of three common vowel shift patterns: the chain shift of back vowels upwards before /r/; the fronting of back upgliding vowels; and the chain shift of front vowels in which the long or peripheral vowels centralize and fall, while the short vowels move toward the front and rise.[2] This last shift alone is what is now called the Southern Shift by Labov (Labov 1994; Labov et al. 2001).

Within the South, as defined by the monophthongization of /ay/, are two core areas, the Inland South and Inland Texas. The Inland South – defined by the reversal of /e/[2], /ey/, and /i/, /iy/; back gliding /oh/, in addition to the monophthongization of /ay/ – focuses on three cities: Knoxville and Chattanooga, Tennessee; and Birmingham, Alabama. This area extends from east Tennessee to western North Carolina and northern Alabama. To a lesser extent it includes Charlotte, NC, and Greenville, SC, and extends north to northwest West Virginia and Kentucky, and south to Linden and Montgomery, Alabama. For Inland Texas these features are most characteristic of Dallas, Lubbock, and Odessa. However, it appears that large-scale immigration of Northerners to Atlanta and Dallas may be influencing the speech there, so they may no longer share the features of their nearby core areas. (On Dallas as well as other metropolitan areas in Texas, see Thomas 1997.)

The data of the Atlas come exclusively from a telephone survey (Telsur) carried out between 1992 and 2000. The complete sample consists of almost 800 speakers, selected to represent the urbanized areas of English-speaking North America, particularly those speakers who are the most advanced in regard to phonological change. This has resulted in interviews with speakers from 161 urbanized areas, most with a population of over 200,000, with a few smaller cities selected in areas of sparse population (see Ash 2001). In the South, the speakers number over 100, from forty-one cities. The speakers were chosen to represent the dominant national ancestry groups of each area, with names selected from telephone books or their website equivalent after research on national ancestry figures from the 1990 census.

The telephone interview itself (recorded with permission) was carefully scripted to elicit phonological contrasts or vowel shifts of interest, resulting in up to an hour of recorded speech. Interviewers included Southerners, non-Southerners; men and women. A letter followed with a word list; the speaker was contacted soon after and asked to read the word list over the telephone. All interviews were impressionistically coded for all variables elicited on mergers and near mergers, as well as syntactic and lexical variables. The resulting phonological data were then submitted to vowel analysis (using the Kay Elemetrics' Computerized Speech Laboratory), with normalization, and added to the pool of speakers to be charted via PLOTNIK, a vowel-plotting program.[3] This study is likely to become highly influential, the benchmark of all subsequent work on southern speech.

In contrast, those other studies which concentrate on single cities provide more detail than would be possible – or desirable – in the massive Atlas. These three quite different cities – Charleston, SC; Memphis, Tennessee; and Anniston, Alabama, contrast sharply in history, economics, demography, and size. To begin with, neither Charleston nor Memphis is located in core areas, linguistically. Vowel shifting in these two places has been examined in detail by Baranowski (2000) and Fridland (1998, 1999, 2001, in progress). A third, smaller city, Anniston, Alabama, is located in what the Atlas calls the Inland South; this has been the locale of my own research on vowel shifting (Feagin 1986, forthcoming.).

4   Charleston

In his study of change over time in Charleston, SC, Baranowski (2000) bases his work on four speakers: the older speaker is a sheriff from Beaufort, SC, not far from Charleston, interviewed by William Labov in 1965 (no age indicated, but the man was probably born around 1905). This was a conversational sociolinguistic interview of the sort pioneered by Labov. The younger speakers are three women, ages twelve, thirty-four, and forty, all interviewed in 1996 by Christine Moisett as part of the Telsur (telephone survey) project at the University of

Pennsylvania. These younger speakers, selected randomly from the urbanized Charleston area, were interviewed by telephone in accord with the Telsur (now Atlas of North American English) project format – continuous speech, elicited items, and minimal-pair tests. All four recordings were analyzed using the Kay Elemetrics' LPC routine of the Computerized Speech Laboratory as well as being examined by ear.

While all three women were born and raised in Charleston, the twelve-year-old girl is a Native American, her father from Charleston, her mother from Canada. The forty-year-old woman moved to Columbia, SC, after high school where she was living at the time of the interview. Her mother was from Charleston, her father from New York. The thirty-four-year-old was born and raised in Mount Pleasant, a suburb of Charleston, with both parents from Charleston.

Regardless of age, none of these speakers have /ay/ monophthongization, which has never been part of Charleston speech, setting it apart from the rest of the South. Furthermore, the older male speaker has monophthongal or possibly ingliding /ey/ with only a few upglides out of twenty-seven tokens; monophthongal /iy/, back monophthongal /ow/, and fronted, but monophthongal /uw/ – all characteristic of traditional Charleston speech as reported by Primer (1888), McDavid (1955), and Kurath and McDavid (1961). In the younger female speakers, the /ey/ and /ow/ are no longer monophthongs. Moreover, /ow/ and /uw/ have fronted considerably, /ow/ more so than any other variety in America today (Baranowski 2000: 29). However, in regard to the front vowels, Charleston still does not appear to be engaged in the Southern Shift. Furthermore, there is no laxing or monophthongization of /ay/.

Consequently, it can be said, based on these data, that Charleston has lost its distinctiveness so far as the vowel system is concerned, but still does not share most of the features characteristic of the South, making it a marginal southern city, like Savannah and New Orleans, so far as its speech is concerned.

5   Memphis

Using data from twenty-five speakers from Memphis, Tennessee, Fridland (1998, 1999, 2001), has found that vowel shifting in Memphis does not follow the typical pattern described by Labov (Labov et al. 1972; Labov 1994) for southern vowel shifting. This should not be surprising, since, in the Atlas data, Memphis, while southern, does not lie in the Inland South core linguistic area, and so cannot be expected to participate in every shift found in the core area. Since Fridland did not find certain vowel shifts, she has questioned particular aspects of vowel shifting in the South, both the ordering of the changes and whether chain shifting is the mechanism taking place at all here.

What she found was that while the back movements were in place, the front shift was much less in evidence than she had expected. In fact, the only shifting she found in the front had to do with the interchange of /e/ and /ey/, with no evidence of change in /i/ and /iy/.

Looking at the social dimension of vowel shifting in Memphis, Fridland (2001) found that for the Southern Shift (i.e. the front vowels) mid-middle-class males had the shift in the mid-front vowel classes /ey/ and /e/, while the mid-middle-class women strongly disfavor it. On the other hand, lower-middle-class and upper-working-class women tend to shift /ey/ and /e/ more than either their male counterparts or mid-middle-class women. The only Memphis speakers who shift /iy/ and /i/ – even slightly – are lower-middle-class and upper-working-class males. Fridland attributes this pattern of social distribution in regard to the front vowels to the conflict between southern rural speech norms which represent local identity and non-local, non-southern prestige forms. Local identity norms prove to be more attractive to the men while mid-middle-class women tend to follow the prestige forms which are non-local. This fits in with previous studies showing that men tend to favor less polished forms as being more masculine, while middle-class women prefer the more elegant prestige forms (Trudgill 1972). Fridland suggests that the lack of /iy/ or /i/ shifting comes from an attempt to separate the Memphis region from the neighboring southern areas where that shift occurs.

In regard to the back vowels, Fridland found that males fronted the /uw/ class much more than females, regardless of age group, suggesting that men initiate and disseminate this shift in Memphis. It begins in the lower middle class then spreads to the rest of the male community. Unlike the /uw/ shift, which is led by the lower middle class, the fronting of /u/ and /ow/ is a mid-middle-class phenomenon. While this, too, is more of a male shift, there is a greater participation of women in the forward movement of /u/, and even more so with /ow/.

What is interesting about Fridland's findings is her suggestion that the front shifts (the Southern Vowel Shift) are motivated by local identity connected with the rural South, while the fronting of the back vowels has a different social motivation, perhaps related to national norms.

6 Alabama vowels

In contrast to the studies of Charleston and Memphis, my own work on change in progress among whites in Anniston, a small city in Alabama, not only confirms Labov's earlier hypotheses, but adds time depth to detailed attention to sex and social class differences in regard to the rate and direction of those changes. It is interesting to note that Anniston lies in what Labov has termed the Inland South, the core area of southern speech.

My work is based on data from twenty individuals, two per category of age, sex, and social class. For each of those twenty people, between 100 and 150 vowels per person were extracted from tape-recorded interviews, analyzed, and plotted, for a total of between 2,000 and 3,000 vowels. Speakers range from the generation born in the 1880s to the generation born in the 1950s; social backgrounds vary from urban lawyers and bankers and their children, to rural sharecroppers and urban millworkers and their children. Distribution by gender was equal for both age and social class; all speakers were European Americans native to the area.

The results are astounding, in that they conform in detail to Labov's original description of vowel change in the South. While this appeared to be the case when I presented early results some years ago (Feagin 1985), adding a second speaker per category as well as the local upper class confirms my own earlier work, giving more solidity to my conclusions.

We will first devote our attention to the back vowels moving to the front, then to the chain shift in the front vowels.

7   Back vowels to the front

For all working-class speakers,[4] (iw) as in *dew* or *tune* is the highest, most fronted vowel, across the generations. The movement of the back vowels to the front refers to the vowels of (uw) as in *boot* or *school* and (ow) as in *coat* or *sew*. Looking at the earlier movement of the back vowels to the front, the most conservative system for the working class is found in a rural man born in 1881 (see figure 8.2). Although his system is the "earliest," his (uw) is located in the high central area, in front of the other back vowels – (ow) and (oy) (as in *boy*) – so it has already begun to move. Meanwhile (ow) is still a back vowel, but forward of (oy). In a rural woman, born 1887, (uw) is slightly forward of the 1881 rural man's; (ow) is

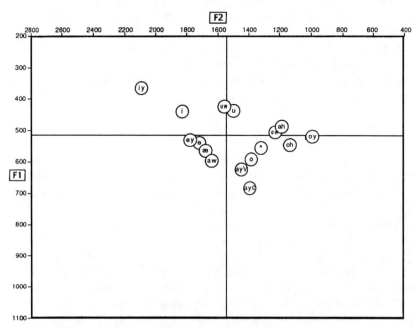

Figure 8.2 Anniston working-class rural man, age ninety-two (born 1881)

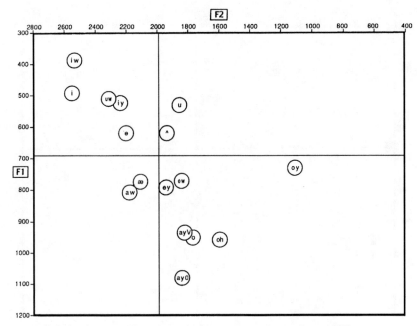

Figure 8.3 Anniston working-class urban woman, age sixteen (born 1957)

still a back vowel. While the rural speakers show that (uw) fronting has definitely begun in the country for speakers born after 1881, the urban working-class older speakers have yet more fronting of (uw). Here (uw) is coming up behind (iw) and (iy). For the urban man, born 1892, (ow) has moved forward, while for the urban woman (born 1899) (ow) is still in the back.

Skipping forward more than fifty years, the back vowels of the working-class urban young man (born 1955) show (uw) as in about the same location as for the older generation, while (ow) is back, but moving toward the front. In contrast, the most advanced speakers in regard to the movement of back vowels to the front are two urban young women born in 1953 and 1957, roughly the same age as the young man (see figure 8.3 for one). In both speakers, (uw) is now a high front vowel. Similarly, both women (teenagers at the time of their interviews) have fronted (ow) just behind (ey) for the one born in 1957. So here, the two young women are leading the two young men, especially in regard to the fronting of (ow).

What about the local upper class? Do they share in these vowel changes? After all, their ages are similar to the working-class speakers. As in the working class, there is a difference of more than fifty years in the ages of the generations. In the speakers discussed here[5], there are two cross-generational comparisons: one grandfather/granddaughter (figures 8.4 and 8.5), one grandmother/grandson.

Even for the upper-class man born in 1882, the movement of (uw) toward the front can be observed (see figure 8.4). The other back vowels, however, are still

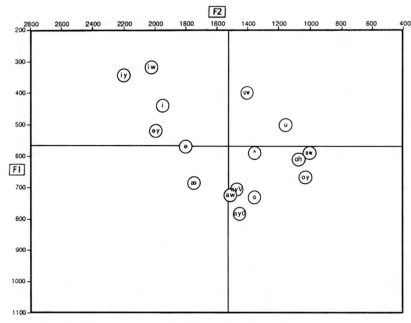

Figure 8.4 Anniston upper-class urban man, age eighty-six (born 1882)

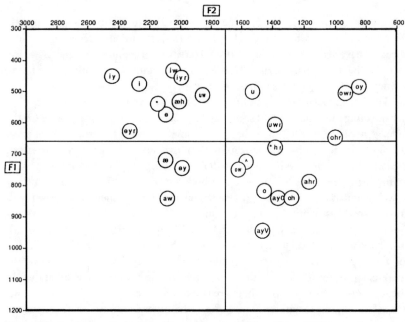

Figure 8.5 Anniston upper-class urban woman, age fifteen (born 1953)

in the "normal" places. The woman born in 1890 shows (uw) as a high central vowel, but (ow) is in a solid back position. The grandchildren's generation has definitely progressed in the shift. The young man (born 1956) has fronted (uw), not far behind (iy); (ow) has moved forward, nearly to central postion. The young woman displays yet more progression of the back shift, with (uw) just behind the front vowels, while (ow) is behind the front vowels almost overlapping central (ʌ) (see figure 8.5). In general, it seems that this old shift is not moving so rapidly in the upper class as in the working class.

8   Front shift

Beginning with the older rural working-class man (born 1881), only the earliest stages of the front shift can be observed, with the (ey) located just forward of (e) (see figure 8.2). Otherwise, the front vowels are in their expected places. It is now clear that at that time, women led change in the front vowels of the working class. The older rural woman (born 1887) not only has completed the exchange of (e) and (ey), but (i) has already moved behind (iy), in almost as high a position. Meanwhile, the urban men (born 1892, 1899) are behind the urban women (both born 1899) in this shift, with (ey) in its "normal" location. The two urban women show interesting individual differences, though they are both "ahead" of the men in regard to the front shift. For one, the flip flop is just beginning: (e) is forward of, but below (ey). In contrast, the other woman has (i) below, but almost equally fronted in regard to (iy), while (ey) is below and behind (e).

What is most remarkable here is the tremendous change over the following fifty years. For each of the four urban working-class speakers born in the 1950s, the front shift has gone to completion, though the resulting configuration of vowels is more extreme for the two boys (born 1955) than for the two girls (born 1953, 1957). That is, for all four, short (i) is definitely a high front vowel; (e) is a mid-front vowel; while (iy) and (ey) are central vowels (see figure 8.3). So, for the boys (iy) is now behind (e), while (ey) is behind (ae). Meanwhile, for the girls (iy) is below and behind (i), while (ey) is behind (ae).

In regard to the front shift in the upper class, no change from the "normal" positions of (iy), (i), (ey), (e) can be observed in the older upper-class man (born 1882) (see figure 8.4). As in the working class, women are leading this change at the early stages. One woman (born 1890) shows the movement of (ey) to the non-peripheral track, to a slightly more central position, while (e) is in the peripheral track, more fronted. This is only just beginning, since the (ey) and (e) almost overlap. (i) has moved to a higher position just barely below and behind (iy). The other woman (born 1897) shows a similar pattern.

In the grandchildren's generation, the grandson (born 1956) of the older woman (born 1890) shows a clear progression in the lowering and centralization of (ey). (i) is raised to the level of (iy), but is definitely behind it. The granddaughter (born 1953) of the older man (born 1882) and another young woman (born 1954) are the most advanced of their social class in the front shift (see figure 8.5). For both, the (e) and (ey) have exchanged places, while the (i) is now behind (iy). In this respect, their front vowels resemble those of working-class women born in the 1880s and 1890s, whether urban or rural.

As one might expect, the working class is leading the upper class in regard to vowel shifting. What is interesting, however, is that the upper class does indeed share the shifts, though they are not as advanced as – and therefore less colorful than – those of the working class.

9   Ordering

The ordering among the Anniston speakers appears to be the following:
    For the back shift:

1.   Back (uw) moves forward, followed by short (u) and (ʌ).
2.   Later, (ow) moves forward, becoming a central vowel, nearly overlapping shifted (ey).

For the front shift:

1.   Short (e) moves forward and up.
2.   Long (ey) drops down and back to a central position.
3.   Short (i) rises to a position behind (iy).
4.   Long (iy) backs and falls, leaving (i) in high front position.

The vowel charts of the men born in 1881 (figure 8.2) and 1882 (figure 8.4) and the women born in the 1950s (figures 8.3 and 8.5) show the earliest and latest stages of those changes by social class among the speakers I analyzed.

What is intriguing to me is that, contrary to Labov's suggestion, there does not appear to be any connection between the position of the vowels in (ay) and (ae) and the front shift, nor between the parallel fronting of the back vowels and the front shift. The peaks of (ay) and (ae) stay in approximately the same location, regardless of the other changes going on.

The only relationship that I can determine is a possible association between vowel breaking or gliding (as in *man* ['mæ'yən]) and the front shift. That is a very interesting topic which warrants a separate study in its own right.

10   Comparison to Labov, Fridland, and Baranowski

Now that I have reported on my own results, where does that leave us in comparison to the work of Labov and his team, Fridland, and Baranowski? One advantage I have over their work is time depth and social range in a single community.

Since the patterning of my data matches what Labov and his team have found, both in the 1972 study and for the Atlas's Inland South, though some of my tentative conclusions do not, I will not discuss their work further. Instead, the question I will address here is this: why is the vowel shifting data from Memphis,

Charleston, and the Telsur project outside the Inland South so different from my work and that of Labov, Yaeger and Steiner (1972)?

Several explanations can be offered for the differences in the various results. First is dialect geography; a second explanation concerns methodology which encompasses the comparability of speaking style (conversation vs. reading passages and word lists), speaker selection, and interviewer effect. A last explanation involves the size of cities and the directionality of such changes between smaller and larger places.

First and foremost, is dialect geography. Charleston, SC, has always prided itself on being different from the rest of the South. The speech of the white community has always shared Caribbean features (influenced by Gullah) which included lack of gliding for (iy), (ey), (uw), (ow), and a glided (ay). Change over time appears to be eliminating some of the distinctiveness; nevertheless, the newer phonology is not aligning itself with the rest of the South. Similarly, Memphis differs from many places in the South because of its position on the Mississippi River, opening it to influences both from the north and from the south. (New Orleans is also an anomaly in its speech, so far as the South is concerned.) In fact, neither Carver in his mapping of vocabulary nor the Labov team in their mapping of phonology place Memphis and Birmingham (or Anniston, which is not far from Birmingham) in the same dialect area (cf. Carver 1987; Labov et al. 1999). So it should not be surprising that vowel shifting would pattern differently in Memphis from what was found in Alabama and other points in the South examined by Labov and his team.

Secondly, the material used for both the Memphis study and the Telsur work (which formed the data base for Baranowski as well as for the Atlas) consisted of reading passages (for Memphis) and word lists (for both), though the earlier Charleston speaker data are conversational, as are some of the data from the younger speakers. Such attention to language is well known to have an effect on speech, moving the whole situation to a more formal status, and perhaps producing less advanced vowel variants (cf. Yaeger 1975; Labov 1986; Ash 1999). My own data were entirely from conversational interviews, often two speakers and myself, a native speaker from the town. The Labov, Yaeger and Steiner work (1972) was also based on conversational interviews.

Another methodological point to address concerns the question of interviewer effect. A similar discrepancy has appeared in the work of Nancy Niedzielski (1997) in regard to (ae) raising in the northern cities. She has found that many people have almost no (aeh) raising, in contrast to the results first discussed by Labov, Yaeger and Steiner in 1972, and found in recent years by Ash to be expanding. Malcah Yaeger-Dror (personal communication) reports that this (ae)-raising exists in most middle-class, middle-age speakers from, say, Buffalo. Yaeger-Dror attributes the difference between the Niedzielski results and that of others to interviewer styles and consequently to the extent of accommodation to the interviewer. That may also be the case in regard to Fridland's, Baranowski's, and the Telsur results.[6]

In yet another aspect of differing methodologies, the speakers in the various studies are not altogether comparable: two of Baranowski's three 1990s speakers have one parent who is not from the South. Payne (1980) has shown that the effect of a non-native parent can reduce the ability of children to learn the local dialect in all its complexity. In addition, one of Baranowski's female speakers is a Native American. In North Carolina a number of studies have shown that Native Americans pattern differently from the rest of the community, whether white or black (e.g. Wolfram and Dannenberg 1999; Schilling-Estes 2000b). The background of the many Phonological Atlas speakers is mainly middle class and middle aged in the 1990s, therefore comparable to the Anniston speakers born in the 1950s. While Fridland gives ranges of ages and general labeling of social class, without more detail it leaves us unable to say whether what she calls "upper working class" is comparable to the Anniston working class, and what she calls "lower middle class" is comparable to the Birmingham lower middle class. Since she carried out the interviews in 1996, her "middle-aged people" – those aged thirty-two to forty-eight – are about the same age as my "teenage" speakers who were born in the 1950s. Understandably, she does not have any people as old as my oldest generation. And until I analyze the data I have gathered from Anniston speakers born in the 1970s, there is no way to compare her results from the younger group (those under twenty-five) to mine. So in the end, two of her speakers are roughly comparable in age to eight of mine, the working- and upper-class younger speakers who were born in the 1950s. The rest simply don't match up. Actually, the vowel charts of those two Memphis speakers look very much like those of my two younger upper-class speakers, whose vowels resemble those of the Anniston working class born in the 1890s!

Aside from questions of dialect geography and methodology, perhaps this is a question of the directionality of change. We can guess that the Memphis speakers are simply behind the Alabama speakers in these changes, so that the shifting of the position of vowels in vowel space is going from smaller places to larger places. Charleston is certainly larger than Anniston, while Memphis is a much larger city than Anniston or even Birmingham. (It is about one and a half times the size of Birmingham, in fact.) I would therefore speculate that these vowel shifts, as well as vowel breaking, are changes from below – certainly below the level of consciousness and to some extent from below in the social hierarchy. Such a change from below might include the size of cities – with smaller cities and rural areas ranking below larger cities – as well as social class within those cities. This certainly appears to be the case in Texas, according to Thomas (1997).

On the other hand, it is also possible that the diphthongization and vowel shifts are perceived negatively as "country" or small town – or maybe just old fashioned – so perhaps big cities such as Memphis and Atlanta, and smaller cities such as Charleston, will continue to reject them, maintaining both lesser breaking (diphthongization) and very moderate vowel shifts. This in fact was suggested to me by James Sledd (personal communication 1988) in his comment that breaking (diphthongization) was more a characteristic of speakers from small towns rather than an urban phenomenon. Informal comments of upper-class Atlanta teenage girls concerning the speech of relatives in smaller cities in Alabama reinforce this (Ruth and Margaret Baldwin 1985, personal communication). More recently, Fridland (2001) suggests that the front shift might be associated with the rural South, an evaluation which plays a part in its place in Memphis speech. Along the same lines, Thomas (1997) shows that a contrast between metropolitan areas in Texas (such as Dallas–Fort Worth) and smaller towns and rural areas has developed, displayed in the contrasting distribution of gliding in (ay) and in lowering of (ey). It is, of course, a matter of speculation as to whether the greater urban areas will dominate the development of phonology in the South, or whether the more rural and small towns will influence the metropolitan areas. If the South resembles other areas, it is likely that the metropolitan variety will become dominant. However, it is not clear how much that dynamic will play out in the South, which has managed to keep its culture separate from the rest of the nation up to this point.

11   Conclusion

While attention to location of vowel peaks in phonological space and the movement in regard to those locations across time and space is essential, the results of such studies present only half the story. The other equally important part is the breaking and gliding (or diphthongization) of the vowels or their monophthongization. The patterns of diphthongization in the American South are in many ways quite distinct from such patterns in many or perhaps most other varieties of English. (See Feagin 1996 for distinctive (ae) gliding; Thomas 2001 provides many examples of glides across the South.) Consequently, the combination of vowel shifting and diphthongization results in an extremely complex phonology, marking off the region from the rest of the United States.

On the other hand, over time, the rise of cities in the South – with the crosscurrents of southern speech from various locales mixed with non-southern varieties and with the social mobility which cities promote – suggests a coming homogenization and consolidation within the South: not an assimilation to northern patterns but the development of a modified southern speech, a koiné of sorts, with some of the distinctiveness filtered out. This is clearly what has happened in Charleston and Memphis from the reports of Baranowski and Fridland, as well as the more general findings of Labov et al. This, too, is what C.-J. Bailey has predicted (1996: 259) – that a mixture of several varieties of a language will generally produce leveling, an outcome confirmed in work of Kerswill (Kerswill 1994; Kerswill and Williams 2000) in both Norway and England, and in the research of Trudgill (Trudgill et al. 1998) in New Zealand. This indeed seems to be the direction in which Southern States English is headed, with its growing metropolitan centers. Such a development, however, has yet to be fully realized, but should provide plentiful material for future research.

Notes

1. The 116 Southerners are distributed as follows: 36 from the Southeast (Maryland 1, Virginia 4, South Carolina 1, Georgia 1, Alabama 4, Tennessee 1, North Carolina 24), 47 from the south central states (New Orleans 1, Arkansas 1, Oklahoma 4, Texas 41). The thirty-three African Americans are from Texas (14), North Carolina (13), Tennessee (2), Ohio (1), Alabama (1), Virginia (1), and Georgia (1).
2. The selection of slants (for phonemes) versus parentheses (for variables) is a theoretically loaded statement concerning the nature of the item under consideration (see Feagin 1998). The vowels in my own data are treated as variables, not phonemes.
3. PLOTNIK, developed by William Labov in 1992, and continuously updated since then, can be obtained through the United States Regional Survey, Linguistics Laboratory, University of Pennsylvania, 3550 Market Street Suite 201, Philadelphia, PA 19104.
4. Total working-class sample: twelve speakers: six men, six women. Rural speakers born in 1881 (m), 1887 (f); 1906 (m), 1911 (f). Urban speakers born in 1892, 1899 (m); 1899, 1899 (f); 1955, 1955 (m); 1953, 1957 (f). Ages mentioned refer to age at the time of the interview.
5. Total upper-class sample: eight speakers born in 1882 (m), 1894 (m); 1890 (f), 1897 (f); 1955 (m), 1956 (m); 1953 (f), 1954 (f).
6. See also the discussion in Weldon (1998: 267) concerning the different outcomes of her interviews in the black community of rural Kershaw County, SC, as an insider and those of the North Carolina State University team in rural North Carolina, all outsiders and/or white.

9 Enclave dialect communities in the South

WALT WOLFRAM

1 Introduction

Contrary to the popular stereotype, there is great dialect diversity within the speech folkways of the regional South. No situation is more reflective of this diversity than the so-called *dialect enclave*, in which a speech community has been historically disconnected from the wider sociospatial, dominant population groups in the region. There are a number of these situations in the Mid-Atlantic and South, located in areas that range from the islands off of the Atlantic coast to the inland highland regions of Appalachia. Although such dialect situations have always been of interest to dialectologists, their significance seems to have heightened over the past couple of decades.

Dialect enclaves have now been considered as a primary database for the reconstruction of prominent vernacular varieties in the United States, based on the assumption that linguistic change will be conservative and that these dialects will remain relatively immune to changes diffusing throughout the wider population. Enclave varieties of English might thus provide a window into the earlier structure of evolving vernacular varieties such as Appalachian Vernacular English (Montgomery 1989b; Montgomery and Hall forthcoming) and African-American Vernacular English (AAVE) (Poplack 1999; Poplack and Sankoff 1987; Poplack and Tagliamonte 1989, 1991, 2000). In fact, transplant enclave communities of African Americans have provided essential spoken-language evidence for revising the historical reconstruction of AAVE over the past couple of decades.

Another reason for the recent interest in dialect enclaves is related to the moribund status of some of these varieties. In some cases, historically isolated communities have been undergoing rapid economic and social transformation due to the changing demographics of American society and the increased accessibility of these communities to outsiders. As historical sociocultural and linguistic traditions have been subjected to increasing external influence, the dynamics of dialect change and maintenance in so-called *endangered dialect communities* (Wolfram and Schilling-Estes 1995; Schilling-Estes and Wolfram 1999) has come under greater scrutiny. Accordingly, there has been increasing concern for documenting the traditional form of these dialects before they are lost, or at least restructured to accommodate more recent language influences.

In the following sections, I describe some of the dialect traits of enclave dialect communities by surveying some representative situations in the eastern region of the Mid-Atlantic and southeastern United States in order to examine the historical dialect base, or *founder effect* (Mufwene 1996b) that provided input into the early establishment of these dialect communities, the historical language-contact situations that helped define them, and the independent language development that has taken place within these communities over time. Before doing so, however, it is necessary to examine the notion *enclave dialect* as a sociolinguistic construct, since it has sometimes been used in imprecise and inconsistent ways in the sociolinguistic literature (Montgomery 2000b).

2   The sociolinguistic construction of dialect enclaves

Although practically all studies of enclave dialect situations provide the specific details of historical settlement, migration, and development that have led to the disconnection of particular communities from more widespread, dominant populations, few have attempted to propose a general set of physical, demographic, historical, sociocultural, and sociolinguistic conditions associated with such communities. On the one hand, it might be assumed that the circumstances defining these situations are self-evident and that there is no need to describe the general attributes of a dialect enclave. On the other hand, it might be assumed that each situation is so particularized that, in fact, there are no common conditions that unite different situations. Both of these assumptions seem unjustified. Montgomery (2000b: 45–6) points out the inconsistencies and imprecision in the current application of the term "historical isolation" and the corresponding delimitation of the dialect enclave community.

> While often invoking the concept of isolation, linguists have yet to define it in a way that is sociologically respectable (based on valid, measurable criteria), or anthropologically sensitive (involving analysis of the community on its own terms and based on community perceptions and behavior – what is remoteness for the investigator may not be perceived as such by residents) . . . In sum, we can see that American linguists have recognized several types of isolation, but have done little to examine it critically or explore its many dimensions.

In Wolfram (forthcoming) and Wolfram and Schilling-Estes (forthcoming), we have attempted to set forth some of the physical, sociocultural, and sociopsychological attributes that are implicated in the definition of the notion of historical isolation and dialect enclave. These may be summarized as follows:

Geographic: Geographical remoteness often plays a significant role in cases of historical isolation and enclave dialect communities because bodies of water, mountains, and other features of the topography may serve to foster separation and hence create communication discontinuities.

Economic: Economic self-sufficiency is necessary for a community to maintain insular status over an extended period of time; in fact, one of the reasons that fishing communities are implicated so often in historically isolated situations is because of the combination of geographic location and their potential for economic self-sufficiency.

Historical continuity: There must be sufficient time depth and historical continuity for the establishment of linguistic divergence from wider sociospatial population groups; in many cases, residents can trace their genealogies back to the earliest inhabitants of the area.

Migration: Although some communities may undergo considerable out-migration at various periods in their histories, there is limited in-migration. Some periods of in-migration may be tolerated, but sustained periods of in-migration would typically end the insular status of the community.

Interactional: High-density, multiplex social networks (Milroy 1987) are more likely to be found in enclave dialect communities than in larger, more densely populated areas. However, there are a number of social network constellations that may be found in such communities, from concentrations of entire communities within a small geographic locale to the dispersion of subcommunities or families living in locales quite remote from other units within the community.

Status: Enclave dialect communities are usually socially subordinate to "mainstream" regional and national groups. Even when such groups have control of local governing institutions and enjoy some measure of economic prosperity, they remain vulnerable to more powerful regional, state, and national institutions that have ascribed them "non-mainstream" status.

Identity: Social distinctions between "insiders" and "outsiders" are endemic to enclave communities. The local construction of "us" versus "them" often results in indexical labeling that embodies important distinctions extending beyond physical, social, and historical conditions *per se.*

Norms: Focus on community-internal social and linguistic norms often competes with external norms, thus setting up sociopsychological (and often linguistic) barriers against the encroachment of the outside world.

While it may be possible to set up an inventory of characteristic traits such as those identified here, there are many qualifications that need to be made about these attributes. It thus seems theoretically and methodologically questionable to establish an invariant set of physical, social, and psychological attributes characterizing an enclave community. As observed in Wolfram and Schilling-Estes (forthcoming), particular situations represent different configurations of these traits. Perhaps the most constant attributes are those related to identity and norming, but they, in turn, are connected to various historical circumstances and physical conditions. It might be possible to objectify these traits and arrive at a quantitative "index of insularity" but subjective evaluations by community members and investigators would ultimately serve as the basis for such a quantitative index. At its base, *historical isolation* and *enclave speech community* are socially constructed notions, negotiated by those within and outside the community. This constructed identity appears to play an important role in the development and maintenance of the community's language, as witnessed by the fact these communities may reshape and perpetuate dialect distinctiveness during less insular periods, just as they maintain dialect distinctiveness during periods of greater isolation. As a part of this construction, enclave communities often develop a strong, positive sense of group identity related to the phenomenological notion of "place." Johnstone (forthcoming) notes, "Identification with a region is identification with one kind of 'imaged community.'" If nothing else, all of the communities that we include here have a strong sense of localized place that has at various points in their history been symbolically manifested in dialect traits.

It is also essential to recognize that insularity is a relative notion and that, accordingly, the conception of an enclave community is "more of a popular – and social science – fiction than a historical fact" (Schilling-Estes 2000b: 144). Contact and connections pervade society, and cultures do not come in neatly packaged, independent entities. Similarly, so-called enclave dialect communities have linkages and interrelationships with other communities, and their interrelatedness is reflected in their dialect configurations. As we shall see, it is not unique dialect structures *per se* that typically define enclave dialect communities, but a constellation of structures. Very few of the dialect structures found in a given enclave community are unique to that variety; the vast majority of structures are found in other dialects as well, so that it is the combination of structures rather than individual structures that sets enclave communities apart.

3   Structural traits of enclave dialects

There is a range of enclave dialect situations that might be catalogued for the Mid-Atlantic and the southern United States, highlighting various physical and social attributes delineated in the previous discussion. Our current studies have investigated representative island communities on the Outer Banks of North Carolina (Wolfram and Schilling-Estes 1995, 1997; Wolfram, Hazen, and Schilling-Estes 1999, 2000a) and the Chesapeake Bay area of Maryland and Virginia (Schilling-Estes 1997; Schilling-Estes and Wolfram 1999), mainland mono-ethnic communities (Gantt 2000), bi-ethnic enclaves (Wolfram forthcoming; Wolfram, Thomas, and Green 2000; Wolfram and Thomas 2002), and one tri-ethnic situation involving Lumbee Native American Indians (Wolfram 1996; Wolfram and Dannenberg 1999; Dannenberg 1999). Earlier investigations included highland regions of Appalachia (Wolfram and Christian 1976) and some of its dialect extensions (Christian, Wolfram, and Dube 1989). More current descriptions of southern Appalachia, the Smoky Mountain region in particular,

Figure 9.1 Map of representative enclave dialect communities

are found in Montgomery (1989b; Montgomery and Hall forthcoming). The location of these communities is given in the map in figure 9.1.

These representative situations serve as the empirical basis for the comparative overview and observations about the patterning of dialect maintenance and change. Notably absent in this presentation are creole situations, such as that of Gullah, spoken along the coastal islands of South Carolina and Georgia. These situations involve a quite different dimension in terms of dialect comparison and are deserving of descriptive attention in their own right.

In the following sections, we consider the sample of enclave dialect varieties in terms of grammatical, phonological, and lexical items. Our focus is on the ways in which these varieties compare with each other rather than on providing a comprehensive description of particular enclave communities as such. The goal is to illustrate their unity and diversity and to understand the kinds of general sociolinguistic principles that might account for their dialect maintenance and development.

3.1 Grammatical structures

A comparison of representative enclave dialect communities indicates several distinct types of grammatical patterning. First, there is a set of structures that unite these dialect communities not only with each other but also with a relatively wide range of vernacular dialects. For example, most of the enclave dialect communities examined here share a generalized core of structures with vernacular dialects of English throughout the United States (Wolfram and Schilling-Estes 1998) and elsewhere (Cheshire 1991). For example, traits such as negative concord or multiple negation (e.g. *They didn't do nothing about nobody*), past-tense *be* regularization (e.g. *We was there yesterday*), regularized plurals (e.g. *sheeps, oxes*), and irregular-verb restructuring (e.g. past for perfect as in *They had went there*, participle for past as in *They seen it*, or regularized past as in *They knowed it*), objective demonstrative forms (e.g. *them shoes*), and so forth occur in socially subordinate varieties of English wherever they are found throughout the world. A combination of linguistic and sociolinguistic principles may be invoked to account for such cross-dialectal uniformity. Given the disfavored social status of such communities, there will be reduced social pressure to preserve socially marked, linguistic irregularities within English, thus opening the pathway for the application of natural principles of language change such as analogical leveling, regularization, and rule generalization. The end result of this language change leads to parallel dialect configurations in quite disparate vernacular dialect communities, including historically unrelated enclave dialects and vernacular dialects in general. Two principles seem to be operative here, the PRINCIPLE OF VERNACULAR DIALECT CONGRUITY and the PRINCIPLE OF SOCIAL MARGINALIZATION (Wolfram forthcoming). The former principle relates to the system-internal pressure that preordains certain natural linguistic changes because they involve structural exceptions or patterns susceptible to structural generalization. The latter principle relates to the social status of most enclave dialect communities, relegating them to non-mainstream, marginalized subordinate sociolinguistic status. In this asymmetrical social relationship, natural language changes taking place within these varieties will therefore be socially disfavored and resisted by speakers of socially favored, mainstream varieties.

A second set of grammatical structures shared by many enclave dialect communities involves structural traits that were once fairly widespread in colonial America but have since receded among broader sociospatial populations. One might assume that communities manifesting these structural traits have simply resisted the changes that they have undergone in other populations, reflecting conservative language change. Such forms have often been labeled RELIC FORMS in dialectology. For example, the use of *a*-prefixing in structures such as *She was a-huntin'* or *They make money a-fishin'* has been documented not only in the enclave communities of the Mid-Atlantic and South considered in this description but also in outlying rural contexts in New England (Kurath 1939–43) and the midwestern United States as well (Allen 1973–6). Further, it was widely distributed in the earlier English of the British Isles (Trudgill 1990: 80), including Irish English. Complements such as *for to* as in *He's looking for to stop now* or *I want for him to quit* and perfective *be* structures such as *I'm been there* "I've been there" or *You're lost some weight* "You've lost some weight" also would seem to fit into this category.

While we recognize that such forms reflect the persistence of structures once widespread throughout colonial America, thus indicating a kind of linguistic conservatism, it is important to understand that these structures have not simply been retained in an unmodified, static state. Enclave dialect communities may, in fact, selectively retain and develop putative dialect structures in ways that result in structural divergence even when the varieties are the product of a common founder effect (Mufwene 1996b). Although such dialects may, in fact, show conservatism in change for some dialect structures, they may simultaneously reveal progressive change for others, in accordance with the PRINCIPLE OF SELECTIVE LANGUAGE CHANGE (Wolfram forthcoming). For example, many enclave dialects in English have perfective *be* alternating with the auxiliary *have*, reflecting the fact that there was widespread fluctuation with perfective *be* and *have* well into the seventeenth century (Rydén and Brorström 1987). However, while perfective *be* is now relatively infrequent in most enclave dialects in the United States, the use of perfective *be* remains a robust, productive form in one of the varieties examined, Lumbee Vernacular English – even among younger Lumbee speakers. Furthermore, its development in this variety distinguishes it from other varieties (Sabban 1984; Kallen 1989; Tagliamonte 1997). Perfective *be* is structurally restricted to contracted finite forms (e.g. *I know I'm been here* but not*? *I know I am been here*), and it has expanded semantically to apply to some simple past constructions (e.g. *I'm forgot the food yesterday*). Though enclave dialects may retain structures found in earlier stages of English, the trajectory of change and structural composition for such items may be markedly different for particular enclave communities.

Finally, there are regionalisms reflected in enclave dialect communities, that is, forms that have come to typify enclave communities in a particular region or even a single enclave community. These structures may reflect distinctive dialect traits in the putative founder dialects for the development of English in the United States or they may reflect the independent development of forms in particular communities. For example, the attachment of *-s* to verbs co-occurring with third-person-plural subjects, particularly if the subject is a noun (e.g. *The dogs barks*) as opposed to a pronoun (e.g. *They barks*), can be traced to regional patterns of distribution in the dialects of England. In colonial American English, these patterns might have shown regional distribution as well, as groups from particular regions of the British Isles tended to settle in particular locales within America. For example, the concord pattern attaching *-s* to verbs occurring with plural noun-phrase subjects has been attributed to varieties in northern England, including the dialects of the Ulster Scots-Irish immigrants who were a dominant population in the highland areas of Appalachia (Fischer 1989; Montgomery 1989b). The assumed regional origin of such features in the British Isles does, however, raise important questions about the occurrence of these features in the enclave dialects of southern and mid-Atlantic coastal dialects in the United States, where Ulster Scots immigrants and speakers from northern England, though certainly part of the overall mix, were not nearly as concentrated in the historical population as they were in other areas such as the highland South. One possibility is that some of the earlier varieties of English in colonial America diffused well beyond the areas of their original concentration. It is also possible that some of these regional features of the British Isles may have become part of an early American English koiné that subsequently retracted into regional varieties within North America. If this was the case, then the dialect features would be expected to persist in varieties that have had no significant contact with each other for a couple of centuries, such as the highland South and the southeastern coastal islands. The question of donorship with respect to the traits of enclave dialect communities involves not only the identification of dialect traits brought originally from particular regions of the British Isles, but also the subsequent development of general American English and its formative regional varieties. The dialect traits of various settlement groups from the British Isles, the development of an earlier general American English variety, and the subsequent regional developments within American English must all be kept in mind in sorting out questions of donorship in enclave dialect communities in North America.

Issues of migration and the formation of earlier regional varieties become more apparent with respect to features showing a common regional distribution among enclave dialects. The most prominent example of this type of regionalism in our survey is the case of the regularization of past *be* to *weren't* (e.g. *It weren't me*; *she weren't there*) as discussed in Schilling-Estes and Wolfram (1994), Wolfram and Sellers (1999), and Wolfram and Thomas (2002). In most vernacular varieties in the United States, past *be* is regularized to *was*, as in *We was home* or *You wasn't there* (Wolfram and Schilling-Estes 1998). However, in a subset of the dialect communities considered here, we find an alternate pattern in which past *be* is leveled to *was* in positive contexts (e.g. *We was there*) but to *weren't* in negative sentences (e.g. *I weren't home*). This pattern represents a restructuring of the two past *be* stems, such that *was* is now used as a marker of affirmative rather than singular meaning, and the *were*-stem is now used as a marker of negativity rather than plurality. Within our sample, the *was/weren't* pattern is robust among groups as geographically and culturally disparate as the European Americans of Smith Island in the Chesapeake Bay (Schilling-Estes 1997, 2000a) and the Lumbee Indians of the Coastal Plain of North Carolina (Wolfram and Sellers 1999). At the same time, there is little indication that the polarity-based pattern is found to any extent among current cohort rural communities in the neighboring Coastal Plain region or enclave dialect communities in the highland South. Perhaps even more striking is the fact that it is not generally found elsewhere in transported dialects of English around the world (Cheshire 1991), although leveling to *were(n't)* has been amply documented in current and past vernacular varieties of English spoken in the British Isles (Cheshire 1982; Trudgill 1990; Britain 2002).

Where might this form have come from, and why is it so robust in the particular enclave communities considered here? Although one can only speculate, it does not seem likely that regularization to *weren't* is due to a simple, direct effect from a founder dialect in the British Isles. The feature was present in some of the varieties brought to regions of the eastern seaboard of America, including those varieties that originally came from southwest England (Orton, Sanderson, and Widdowson 1978). From that point, it probably developed into a regional feature of the coastal Delmarva dialect region (Shores 2000). As people from the Delmarva region moved to various coastal sites, including islands in the Chesapeake and Outer Banks, the *was/weren't* pattern was perhaps diffused along the mid-Atlantic and southern coasts. Thus, an important aspect of regularization to *weren't* is its apparent development in an earlier regional variety of American English and its subsequent diffusion to other areas through migration by speakers who subsequently became disconnected from more broadly based populations.

A similar type of regionalism has developed with respect to the use of personal pronouns in non-attributive position, such as *That's how he made hisn* and *It's yourn*. Along with this is the use of second-person-plural *youns*, which distinguishes the Smoky Mountain and some other southern Appalachian dialect communities from those that have adopted the general southern *y'all* form for second plural. A more specific type of grammatical regionalism is the use of finite *be* (e.g. *That's how it bes, They be taken them away*). This form is found only among groups in the southeastern Coastal Plain of North and South Carolina (Dannenberg and Wolfram 1998; Montgomery and Mishoe 1999). The region saw a concentrated influx of Scots-English during its formative European settlement period in the mid 1700s, as well as some Scots-Irish, and it may well be that a founder effect from this input dialect heritage is responsible for this distinctive dialect structure. Whereas one cannot be certain of its origin, there is evidence that it is quite regionally restricted among some enclave dialect communities.

Different configurations of grammatical structures for the enclave dialect communities considered here are summarized in table 9.1. The list is selective and somewhat oversimplified, and does not take into account some of the quantitative differences among varieties, but it does reflect the different kinds of affinities among the representative communities. Included in the list are island communities such as those on the Outer Banks and Chesapeake Bay, highland communities of southern Appalachia, and mainland ethnic enclave varieties that coexist with their cohort European-American varieties, in particular, mainland coastal Hyde County African-American speech and Lumbee Vernacular English of Robeson County, NC. A check ✓ indicates the presence of the structural feature and (✓) indicates infrequent or "vestigial" usage. Table 9.1 demonstrates that enclave dialects, like other dialects of American English, are typified for the most part by the constellation of dialect structures rather than distinctive dialect forms. Many of the structures are shared by vernacular dialects in general, others are shared by other enclave dialect communities; and still others are regionally restricted to a subset of enclave dialect communities. While there are occasional distinctive structures for particular enclave communities, it is the differential selection processes and varying rates of change and development that account for the major grammatical differences observed among the representative dialects.

Table 9.1 *Comparative dialect profile of selective grammatical variables*

Grammatical structure	Outer Banks	Chesapeake Bay	Mainland coastal Euro. Am.	Mainland coastal African Am.	Lumbee English	Southern Appalachia
negative concord e.g. *We didn't like nothing*	✓	✓	✓	✓	✓	✓
irregular verb						
(1) generalized past/part. e.g. *She had came here*	✓	✓	✓	✓	✓	✓
(2) generalized part./past e.g. *She done it*	✓	✓	✓	✓	✓	✓
(3) bare root as past e.g. *She give him a dog*	✓	✓	✓	✓	✓	✓
(4) regularization e.g. *She knowed him*	✓	✓	✓	✓	✓	✓
(5) different irregular e.g. *He retch up the roof*	(✓)	(✓)				✓
double modals e.g. *He might could come*	✓	✓	✓	✓	✓	✓
for to complement e.g. *I want for to get it*	(✓)	(✓)	✓	✓	✓	✓
was/regularization e.g. *We was there*	✓	✓	✓	✓	✓	✓
weren't regularization e.g. *It weren't me*	✓	✓	(✓)	✓	✓	
regularized plural e.g. *sheeps, oxes*	✓	✓	✓	✓	✓	✓
a-prefixing e.g. *He was a-fishin'*	(✓)	✓	(✓)	(✓)	✓	✓
3rd plural -s marking e.g. *The dogs barks*	✓	✓	✓	✓	✓	✓
perfective *be* e.g. *I'm been there* *I might be done it*	(✓)	(✓)	(✓)	(✓)	✓	(✓)
measurement noun -s abs. e.g. *twenty mile_*	✓	✓	✓	✓	✓	✓
3rd plural -s agreement e.g. *The dogs gets upset*	✓	✓	✓	✓	✓	(✓)
General plural absence e.g. *Lots of bird*				✓		
Possessive -s absence e.g. *Walt hat*				✓		
Copula absence e.g. *They nice, She nice*				✓	(✓)	
finite *bes* e.g. *She bes there*				✓		
3rd singular absence e.g. *She like_ cats*				✓		
2nd plural *youns* e.g. *How youns doing?*						✓
Non-attributive -n e.g. *It's hisn*						✓

3.2   Phonological structures

The phonological structures of enclave dialect communities show the same distribution patterns as those found for grammatical structures. As with the grammatical features, there is a set of structures that unites these varieties with a wide array of vernacular varieties in the United States and elsewhere because of the operation of parallel, independent processes. Thus, the phonetic weakening of interdental fricatives such as [ð] and [θ] to their corresponding stops in syllable-onset position (e.g. [dɪs] "this" [tɪn] "thin") is a general trait of vernacular English dialects around the world. Interdental fricatives are also quite vulnerable to variant phonetic productions in other syllable positions as well, but there is more variation in terms of their phonetic form and their social distribution. For example, in syllable-final position and in intervocalic position within a word, a labiodental fricative [f] or [v] may be used for the standard English interdentals, as in *toof* for *tooth*, *aufor* for *author*, *smoov* for *smooth*, and *brover* for *brother*. At the same time, a corresponding stop may also be used in some varieties, as in *oder* for *other* or *broder* for *brother*. Similarly, the fronting of [ŋ] to [n] in unstressed syllables such as *swimmin'* for *swimming* or *comin'* for *coming* is quite widespread in virtually all enclave dialect communities, as it is in other vernacular dialect communities around the world. The levels of usage may be higher than those found in other vernacular dialect settings, however, reflecting the fact that final [n] seems to represent the retention of an earlier variant in English rather than a contemporary process in which [ŋ] becomes [n] in unstressed syllables.

Conservative language change in enclave dialects is reflected in the fact that there are a number of phonological patterns found in these dialects that have receded in the varieties spoken by wider population groups. Thus, the retention of the initial *h* in *(h)it* and *(h)ain't* appears in most of the enclave communities surveyed here, as does the lowered production of the vowel of *there* or *bear* (closer to that of *thar* and *bar*). The rate of change in different dialect enclaves, however, may be quite varied. For example, some communities surveyed retain an older backed and raised vowel nucleus in the /aɪ/ of *tide* [tɑɪd] and *time* [tɑɪm], whereas other varieties have moved away from this pronunciation. For some areas of the Outer Banks of North Carolina, this retention has assumed iconic status, so that speakers are referred to as *hoi toiders*, an approximate (but not phonetically accurate) mimicry of their pronunciation of *high tiders*. In other enclave varieties, this older pronunciation has receded completely, often being replaced by the newer, unglided production (e.g. [a] as in [tad] for *tide* and [tam] for *time*) now found throughout a large area of the South, or the [ai] production of *tide* found in other areas of the South. Similarly, the retention of the *t* with final *s* or *f* in items such as *oncet*, *twicet*, and *clifft* in a number of enclave communities is obviously related to the retention of a dialect trait transplanted from the British Isles that has now disappeared from other varieties.

At the same time, we must recognize that enclave varieties may engage in localized changes that intensify the use of certain traits. For example, among older speakers in the Chesapeake Bay region and the Outer Banks, the /au/ diphthong may be produced with a distinctive front-gliding vowel, so that words like *brown* and *pound* approximate *brain* and *pained* respectively in their pronunciation. In the Chesapeake Bay area, this change has been fortified in recent generations while it has receded among the dialects of the Outer Banks of North Carolina. This pattern of selective language change is one of the characteristics that distinguishes enclave communities from one another over time. Theoretically, it is important to understand the potential for ongoing, phonetic change in different enclave communities that leads to distinctiveness, even when they may have been more similar at an earlier stage in their development.

Some of the phonological similarities and differences in representative enclave communities are summarized in table 9.2, where the check ✓ again indicates the presence of a particular dialect trait and the (✓) indicates the limited occurrence of the structure.

As with the grammatical profile, we see a large number of shared features among different enclave dialect communities as well as subsets of varieties that share features. We also notice a few distinctive traits that are manifested in only one or a couple of the representative communities.

One of the noteworthy observations is the fact that most of the enclave communities we have surveyed are rhotic in postvocalic position (e.g. *car*, *beard*), in opposition to the surrounding *r*-less dialect regions of the South in the nineteenth and first half of the twentieth centuries. Of the representative varieties examined closely in this survey, only the enclave African-American community indicated postvocalic *r*-lessness to any degree, and even then it was reduced by comparison with African-American varieties spoken elsewhere (Rickford 1999). In part, this may be due to the founder dialects implicated in the development of these varieties, such as the rhotic dialects of Irish English or the southwest region of England. But the rhotic status of these dialect enclaves may also be due to the fact that their early insularity inoculated them against the diffusion of postvocalic *r*-lessness that spread throughout large regions of the South in the nineteenth century (Bailey 2001).

Some of the distinctive traits in selective enclave dialects also may be attributable to substratal effects from language-contact situations. For example, there are a number of phonotactic differences that distinguish the African-American enclave community on the coast of North Carolina from other communities: the reduction of consonant clusters such as *st*, *sk*, *ld*, and *nd* before vowels (e.g. *wes' en'* for *west end*, *fin' it* for *find it*), the use of initial *skr* for *str* clusters (e.g. *skraight* for *straight*), and *ks* for *sk* in *aks* for *ask*. Wolfram and Thomas (2002) argue that these distinctive traits of the African-American enclave community in this region may be due to the vestigial effects of the original contact situation between Africans and English speakers a few centuries ago. Similarly, Torbert (2001) has hypothesized that the increased levels of prevocalic consonant cluster reduction for Lumbee English speakers might have derived from

Table 9.2 *Comparative profile of selective phonological variables*

Phonological Structure	Outer Banks	Chesapeake Bay	Mainland coastal Euro Am.	Mainland coastal African Am.	Lumbee English	Southern Appalachia
dental fricative stopping e.g. [dɪs] "this"	✓	✓	✓	✓	✓	✓
[h] retention in "it," "ain't" e.g. [hɪt] "it"	✓	✓	✓	✓	✓	✓
[æ] lowering e.g. [bar] "bear"	✓	✓			(✓)	✓
final [θ] labialization [bof] "both"	✓		✓	✓	✓	✓
[ɪz] following s+stop [postɪz] "posts"	✓	(✓)	✓		✓	✓
[aɪ] backing/raising e.g. [tʌɪd] "tide"	✓	✓	✓	✓	(✓)	
[ayr]/[awr] reduction e.g. [tar] "tire"	✓	✓	✓		✓	
intrusive r, unstr. final [o] e.g. [fɛlɚ] "feller"	✓	✓	✓		✓	✓
postvocalic r loss [ka] "car"					(✓)	
Final unstressed [ə] raising e.g. [sodi] "soda"	✓	✓			(✓)	✓
unstressed initial [w] del. [yʌŋ#ənz] "young uns"	✓	✓	✓		✓	✓
Front-glided /aw/ e.g. [dæɪn] "down"	(✓)	✓	(✓)			
ks metathesis e.g. [æks] "ask"				✓		(✓)
prevocalic cluster red. [wɛs##ɛn] "west end"				✓	(✓)	
Initial skr for str clusters [skrit] "skreet"				✓		
w/v merger [ʋɪ] "we"			(✓)	(✓)		

the ancestral Native American language(s) once used by the Lumbee. Thus, we see that historical language-contact situations might also be one of the reasons for the distinctions in phonologies revealed in different communities.

Our comparison of phonological features shows that enclave dialect communities may share a variety of features because of conservative language change while simultaneously distinguishing themselves because of differential rates of change and independent language change. Furthermore, different historical contact situations may add to the distinctive mix that sets various enclave communities apart from one another.

3.3   Vocabulary

It is difficult to do justice to the lexicon of enclave dialect communities given the enormity of lexical differences in the dialects of American English. For example, Montgomery and Hall's (forthcoming) dialect dictionary of Smoky Mountain speech features well over 1,000 items for this region, and the *Dictionary of Regional American English* (Cassidy et al. 1986, 1991, 1996) will include six huge volumes when it is finally completed in the next decade. At best, we can only hope to illustrate selectively some of the trends found in the respective lexicons of enclave dialect communities.

To begin with, we observe that there are relatively few lexical items restricted to a single dialect community. In studies of historic enclave situations such as Ocracoke (Wolfram and Schilling-Estes 1997), Tangier Island (Shores 2000), the Smoky Mountains (Montgomery and Hall forthcoming), and Lumbee English (Locklear, Wolfram, Schilling-Estes, and Dannenberg 1999), there is a relatively short list of items that are exclusively used in these respective communities. Local geography and labels for "insiders" and "outsiders" are, however, among those usually on the list of unique items, along with some terms for local activities. Thus, only on the Outer Banks, particularly in Ocracoke, is the term *dingbatter* used for an outsider. The term *dingbatter* was adopted from the TV sitcom *All in the Family* to refer to anyone who cannot trace their genealogy to several generations of island residency, whereas *O'cocker* is reserved for ancestral islanders. In some small rural communities of Appalachia and the Southeast, the term *foreigner* as "someone from another country" is metaphorically extended to include any person who is not from the community, regardless of their place of origin. Local geography and social relations are often implicated in labels so that *on the swamp* is used for "neighborhood" among the Lumbee Indians in Robeson County, and the local terms *brickhouse Indian* "high-status community member" and *swamp Indian* "common community member" refer to relative social position within the community. Similarly, *Creekers* and *Pointers* refers to local neighborhoods on the island of Ocracoke, with an implied historical difference in status, and the term *yarney* is used by both Tangier Islanders and Smith Islanders in the Chesapeake Bay to refer to residents of the other island.

Local activities and objects may also have community-specific labels. For example, we have not found terms like *meehonkey*, the traditional Ocracoke version of "hide and seek" and *Russian rat*, the local label for the marshland rodent "nutria" outside of this community. Similarly, we have not found the Lumbee term *ellick* "coffee with sugar" to be used anywhere outside of this community. At the same time, we have to be cautious in our conclusions. On a number of occasions, we have concluded that a term was community-specific only to find out later that its use was somewhat more widespread than we assumed originally. We found, for example, that the term *juvember* "slingshot" is used not only by the Lumbees of Robeson County but also by other social and ethnic groups in southeastern North Carolina; similarly, we found the term *call over the mail* for "delivering the mail" used not only by Ocracokers (Wolfram and Schilling-Estes 1999) but by residents in other island communities where the mail was announced at the dock when the mailboat arrived. The list of unique terms in the enclave communities we have studied firsthand turns out to be in the dozens rather than the hundreds or thousands.

Enclave dialect communities also tend to participate in broader-based regional dialect vocabulary. All of the enclave communities we have investigated share in a more general southern lexicon that extends from the use of *carry* for "accompany" or "escort" (e.g. *She carried him to the store*), *cut on/off* for "turn on/off" (e.g. *Cut off the light now*) and *mash* for "push" (e.g. *Just mash the button*) to the use of *kin(folk)* for relatives and *young 'uns* for "children." Of course, there are also dialect vocabulary items that may be shared among enclave communities because of occupational or ecological affinity, as in marine-based economies that share fishing terminology (e.g. *peeler, jimmy*, etc. for types of crabs) or terms for coal mining in some areas of Appalachia (e.g. *sprag* "block of wood for stopping mine cars," *laggin'* "lumber for support," *strippin' hole* "hole from strip mining,"etc.).

Though enclave communities may share regional lexical forms and create new lexical items as the need arises, they again also exhibit a tendency to retain some older forms that have been lost in other varieties of English. For example, lexical items such as *mommuck, quamish, token, vittles*, and so forth have been retained in some of the enclave communities we examined long after they disappeared from the speech of other English dialects. However, this does not necessarily mean that their meanings have remained fixed in relation to their earlier uses. For example, in seventeenth-century English, the term *mommuck* meant "to tear or shred" in a literal sense, but on the Outer Banks its meaning has been extended metaphorically to refer to "physical or mental tormenting," as in *The parents were mommucking their children*. Meanwhile, on the island communities of the Chesapeake and in southern Appalachia it refers to "making a mess," as in *He was mommucking the house*. Over time, enclave communities may broaden or narrow the semantic meaning of so-called relic words, or metaphorically extend their reference.

Table 9.3 offers a selective list of some of the lexical items representing different enclave communities and the different alignment patterns among representative communities. For this comparison, the dialect category "general Southern" has been added to the representative list of language varieties in order to give an idea of the presence of more broadly based regional dialects in the lexicon of enclave dialect communities.

Some of the alignment patterns show natural affinities, such as the alliance of some lexical items in island communities in the Chesapeake Bay and Outer Banks, but others show more disconnected affinities, such as those between southern Appalachia and coastal islands. And all of the communities show an overarching affinity with lexical items characterizing the broad-based South.

Although we have focused on individual lexical items in our survey, we cannot ignore the fact that that it is also possible for enclave communities to distinguish

Table 9.3 *Comparative dialect profile of selective lexical items*

Lexical item	Outer Banks	Chesapeake Bay	Coastal African Am.	Lumbee English	Southern Appalachia	General South
meehonky "hide and seek"	✓					
call the mail over "deliver the mail"	✓					
buck "(male) friend"	✓					
buckram "semi-stiff shelled crab"		✓				
fuzz cod "gale"		✓				
progin' "looking for arrowheads"		✓				
pone bread "corn bread with molasses"			✓			
juniper "Atlantic white cedar"			✓			
ellick "coffee with sugar"				✓		
juvember "slingshot"				✓		
on the swamp "neighborhood"				✓		
boomer "red squirrel"					✓	
bald "natural meadow"					✓	
hollow "small valley"					✓	
slick cam "smooth water"	✓	✓				
fatback "menhaden"	✓	✓	✓			
jimmy "mature male crab"	✓	✓	✓			
token/toten "omen, ghost"	✓			✓		
gaum "mess"				✓	✓	
kernal "bump"				✓	✓	
mommuck "mess up"		✓		✓	✓	
mommuck "harass"	✓		✓			
fixin' to "intend, plan"	✓	✓	✓	✓	✓	✓
y'all "you pl."	✓	✓	✓	✓	✓	✓
carry "accompany"	✓	✓	✓	✓	✓	✓
cut on/off "switch on/off"	✓	✓	✓	✓	✓	✓
tote "carry"	✓	✓	✓	✓	✓	✓
young 'uns "children"	✓	✓	✓	✓	✓	✓
mash "push"	✓	✓	✓	✓	✓	✓

themselves through language-use routines. Thus, in a couple of enclave communities, the designation *talking backwards* or *over the left* refers to a fairly developed verbal ritual involving semantic inversion, for example, saying, "It sure is a nice day" or "It ain't raining none" on a very rainy day. The use of the phrase *over the left* on Tangier Island (Shores 2000) to describe this activity derives from an older reference related to "over the left shoulder," or "contrariwise." Although a type of semantic inversion has been noted for other varieties of English (Holt 1972), such as the use of some descriptive adjectives in African-American English (e.g. *bad* for "good"; *uptight* for "nice"), island communities such as Tangier Island, neighboring Smith Island (Schilling-Estes, personal communication), and Harkers Island (Prioli 1998) on the Outer Banks of North Carolina have a more developed, recognized verbal ritual that sets these communities apart from the traditional use of irony or semantic inversion in other speech communities. The routine apparently involves flouting conversational maxims of quality and/or relevance in evaluative speech acts related to complimenting and criticizing and is reinforced through a set of prosodic features as well as paralinguistic cues. Certainly, descriptions of different levels of dialect in enclave dialect communities should include language-use routines as well as traditional levels of language organization such as phonology, grammar, and lexicon.

4   Conclusion

Our survey of selective enclave dialects reveals a number of differences and similarities in the configuration of these varieties. As we noted repeatedly, differential combinations of dialect structures define these varieties more than the existence of unique structures. It is also important to observe that these communities are often characterized by a set of sociolinguistic conditions that affect their development and maintenance of language. Some of these are captured in the kinds of principles set forth in Wolfram (forthcoming), selectively summarized briefly as follows:

Principle of dialect exclusion. Discontinuities in regular communication networks with outside groups impede enclave dialect communities from participating fully in ongoing dialect diffusion that is taking place in more widely dispersed and socially dominant population groups.

Principle of selective change. Enclave dialects may selectively retain and develop putative dialect structures in ways that result in divergence from other varieties, even when a common founder variety is implicated; selective conservatism with respect to some structures, however, may be combined with accelerated change for others.

Principle of regionalization. Founder effects and selective independent language change may lead to divergence among enclave dialects as well as from more broadly based regional dialect communities, thus resulting in a type of regionalization for particular enclave communities.

Principle of social marginalization. The relegation of enclave dialect communities to subordinate, "non-mainstream" social status leads to a marginalized sociolinguistic status for the speakers of such varieties; accordingly, the linguistic forms found in these varieties will be socially disfavored.

The principle of vernacular congruity. Natural linguistic processes that involve analogical leveling, regularization, and generalization may lead to parallel dialect configurations in quite disparate enclave dialect communities.

Principle of localized identity. Community members in small, historically isolated communities may embrace language distinctiveness as an emblematic token of local identity even in a post-insular state; this manifestation may range from selective dialect focusing to overall dialect intensification.

As noted at the outset of this discussion, insularity is a relative notion and the dialects of enclave communities are dynamic rather than static in their composition.

In fact, some of the situations we have surveyed are undergoing rapid change due to the transformation of economic and social conditions affecting these communities. This dynamic is not captured by the focus on traditional dialect features most often found among older, vernacular dialect speakers. The reality of the change trajectory we have observed is actually much different from this unidimensional model. For example, on the Outer Banks of North Carolina, the traditional Outer Banks dialect is clearly dissipating, found mostly now only among the elderly and some middle-aged speakers but rarely among younger speakers (Wolfram and Schilling-Estes 1995). By the same token, in the Chesapeake Bay, the dialect seems to be intensifying among younger speakers, even as the population of the islands decline and the communities become more open (Schilling-Estes 1997, 2000a; Schilling-Estes and Wolfram 1999; Shores 2000). The reasons for such dramatic differences in the trajectories of change are often multi-dimensional, involving demographic, economic, social, and linguistic conditions. In an important sense, the language dynamic of each community has to be described in its own right as communities react to changing circumstances in different ways. Although we have focused on some of the unifying sociolinguistic conditions of these situations and highlighted the similarities and differences in dialect traits found in such situations, it is necessary to recognize the unique social and linguistic circumstances that characterize each speech community and their effect on language change and maintenance within that community.

10 Urbanization and the evolution of Southern American English

JAN TILLERY AND GUY BAILEY

1 Introduction

Southern American English (SAE) has long been regarded as a conservative variety preserved in large part by the rural, insular character of the region. As a result, until recently most researchers have attempted to explain the distinctive character of SAE by focusing on its settlement history and its roots in the various regional dialects of Great Britain.[1] At its worst, the view of SAE as a conservative variety and the focus on British roots has led to the assertion that SAE is pure Elizabethan or pure Shakespearean English. At its best, it has led to the kind of careful research exemplified by Michael Montgomery's (1989b) exploration of the connections between the patterns for the use of verbal -s in southern Appalachia and those in northern Britain. While the work of scholars like Montgomery has helped clarify the origins of some SAE features, a growing body of research over the last ten years has shown that many other characteristics of SAE cannot be traced to British roots or correlated with settlement history.[2] In fact, this research suggests that many of the prototypical features of SAE either emerged or became widespread during the last quarter of the nineteenth century or later and that many older SAE features have been disappearing rapidly. The ultimate consequence of such research is that innovation and change, rather than preservation and stability, may well be the most important factors in the development of SAE. Innovation and change are so widespread that Schneider (forthcoming) has suggested a distinction be made between "traditional" and "new" SAE. An examination of the work that documents rapid and widespread change in SAE more than justifies such a distinction and suggests a history of SAE that shows a dialect characterized by its dynamism, adaptability, and responsiveness to demographic and cultural change rather than a variety mired in its past.

2 Some studies that document change in SAE

The studies that document widespread change in SAE examine a broad range of both phonological and grammatical features. Figures 10.1–10.11 summarize the

159

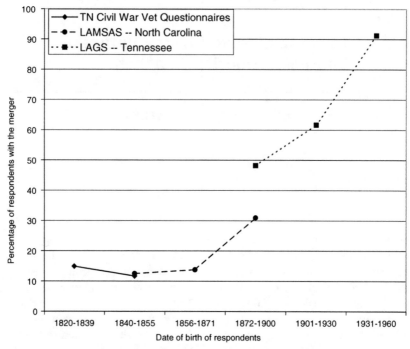

Figure 10.1 The evolution of the *pin/pen* merger in Tennessee (Brown 1991)

results from eight of these studies as well as additional data on change in SAE from the *Linguistic Atlas of the Gulf States* (*LAGS*). The work of Brown (1991), figure 10.1, on the merger of /ɛ/ and /ɪ/ before nasals (so that *pen* becomes homophonous with *pin*) provides a clear demonstration of a stereotypical feature of SAE that only became widespread after 1875. To explore the merger, Brown used three primary sources of evidence: (1) the Tennessee Civil War Veterans' Questionnaires, (2) the *Linguistic Atlas of the Middle and South Atlantic States* (*LAMSAS*), and (3) *LAGS*. The data from these three sources show that before 1875 the *pen/pin* merger was relatively infrequent in the South. After 1875 the merger began to expand rapidly until by World War II more than 90 percent of the informants Brown examined had the merger. The convergence of evidence from these three different sources and from supplementary tape recordings of informants whose dates of birth span the period from 1844 to 1974 lends credence to Brown's (1991) conclusions.

The merger of /ɛ/ and /ɪ/ before nasals, however, is not the only linguistic change in SAE to have begun in the last quarter of the nineteenth century. While Brown's study shows the rapid expansion of a phonological stereotype of SAE after 1875, the work of Krueger (2001), figure 10.2, shows the rapid decline in the use of a grammatical stereotype, perfective *done* (as in *we've done fixed it*), during the same time period. Using evidence from *LAGS*, Krueger's study shows that

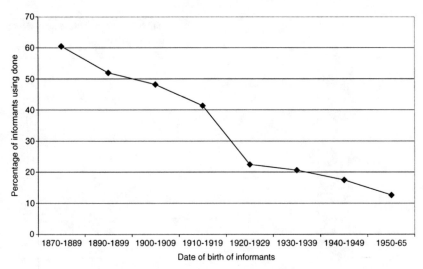

Figure 10.2 Apparent-time distribution of perfective *done* in LAGS (Krueger 2001)

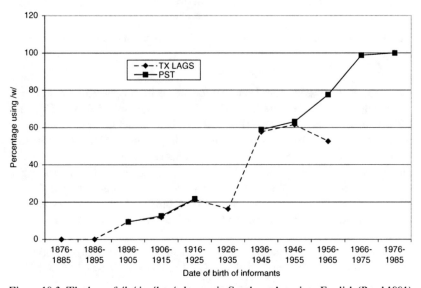

Figure 10.3 The loss of /h/ in /hw/ clusters in Southern American English (Reed 1991)

more than 60 percent of the informants born before 1890 use perfective *done*, but less than 15 percent born after 1950 use the feature.

The work of Reed (1991), figure 10.3, on the loss of /h/ in initial /hw/ clusters (which makes *which* homophonous with *witch*) shows the decline of another well-known feature of SAE phonology; however, the time frame for the

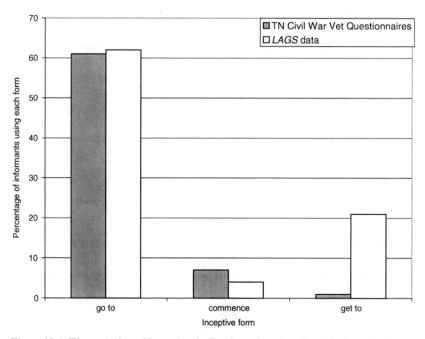

Figure 10.4 The evolution of inceptives in Southern American English (Bean 1991)

loss of this feature is different from that for the decline of perfective *done*. Based on evidence from the Tennessee Civil War Veterans' Questionnaires, *LAGS*, and a Phonological Survey of Texas (PST), Reed (1991) concludes that before 1890 the preservation of /h/ was almost universal in the South. After 1890 the loss of /h/ began to spread gradually, but Reed's data suggest that the expansion of this feature was primarily a post-1935 development. As figure 10.3 shows, in the cohort born between 1926 and 1935, slightly less than 20 percent have the loss of /h/. Among the cohort born between 1936 and 1945, almost 60 percent lost /h/ in /hw/ clusters. The loss of /h/ among Reed's informants born after 1966 was nearly universal.[3]

Two other studies parallel Reed's in demonstrating rapid change in SAE beginning around the time of World War II. Bean (1991), figures 10.4 and 10.5, examines the development of SAE inceptives such as *go to* as in *I went to laughing and couldn't stop* and *get to* as in *we got to talking and missed the bus*. Using evidence from the Tennessee Civil War Veterans' Questionnaires and *LAGS*, Bean shows that *go to* was by far the dominant form in earlier SAE. After 1900, and especially after 1940, *get to* began to expand rapidly at the expense of *go to*. Our data from a Survey of Oklahoma Dialects (SOD) suggest that *get to* is now the inceptive of choice in SAE. In the SOD telephone survey, 79.3 percent of the respondents prefer *get to* to *go to*; in the field survey, 88.9 percent do.[4]

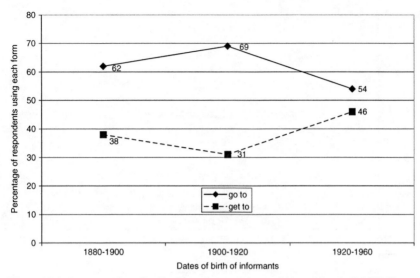

Figure 10.5 Apparent-time distributions of *go to* and *get to* in inceptives in LAGS (Bean 1991)

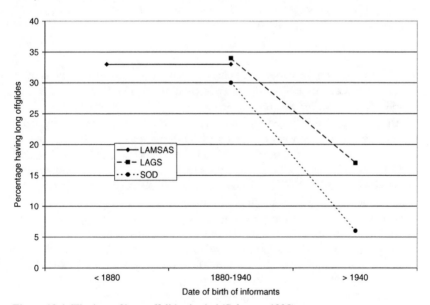

Figure 10.6 The loss of long offglides in /æ/ (Schremp 1995)

The work of Schremp (1995), figure 10.6, on the occurrence of long offglides in /æ/ (so that /bæg/ is pronounced [bæɪg]) again shows rapid change in progress after World War II. Before World War II, pronunciations such as [bæɪg] were relatively common in the South, occurring among roughly a third of the *LAMSAS*,

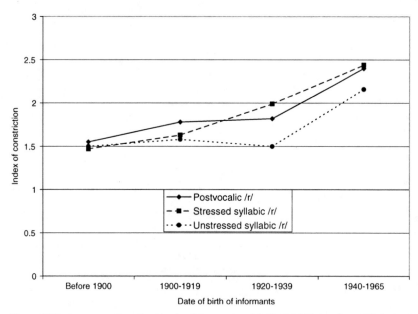

Figure 10.7 Apparent-time distribution of constricted /r/ in LAGS data from Mississippi and east Louisiana (Lambert 1995)

LAGS, and SOD informants that Schremp examined. Less than 20 percent of the LAGS informants and less than 10 percent of the SOD informants born after World War II, however, had pronunciations of /æ/ with long offglides.

Rapid change has affected regionally restricted as well as more generalized southern features. The work of Lambert (1995), figure 10.7, on the pronunciation of postvocalic /r/ (e.g. in *four* and *ford*) and syllabic /r/ (e.g. in *fur, first*, and *father*) in Mississippi and Louisiana shows the expansion of *r*-ful or constricted /r/ in these traditionally *r*-less areas. Lambert analyzes tokens of postvocalic and syllabic /r/ using a constriction or *r*-fullness scale, with zero indicating tokens with no constriction and four indicating those with full constriction. As figure 10.7 illustrates, *r*-ful pronunciations have expanded rapidly in all environments in this traditionally *r*-less area since World War II.

Taken as a whole, then, the work of Brown (1991), Krueger (2001), Reed (1991), Bean (1991), Schremp (1995), and Lambert (1995) suggests widespread and rapid change in SAE, with changes gathering momentum during two time periods: the last quarter of the nineteenth century and the time around World War II. An examination of evidence from LAGS on eight more features of SAE provides additional confirmation of the results of these studies.

Figures 10.8 and 10.9 provide apparent-time data from LAGS on five recessive and three innovative features of SAE. The data for both figures are taken directly from LAGS, volume 6: *The Social Matrix* (Pederson et al. 1991). The five

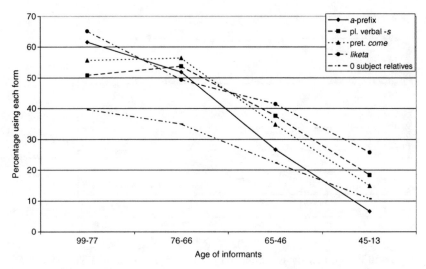

Figure 10.8 Apparent-time distribution of five grammatical features of Southern American English (*LAGS*, vol. 6)

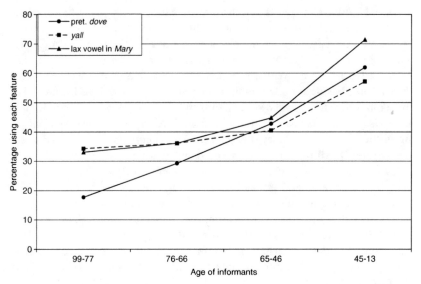

Figure 10.9 Apparent-time distribution of three Southern American English features (*LAGS*, vol. 6)

recessive features include (1) *a*-prefixing as in *They were a-laughing and a-singing*; (2) plural verbal *-s* as in *The children knows they have to do their chores*; (3) preterit *come* as in *He come down here last week*; (4) preverbal *liketa* as in *I liketa fell out of my chair*; and (5) zero-subject relatives as in *The people live next door are real*

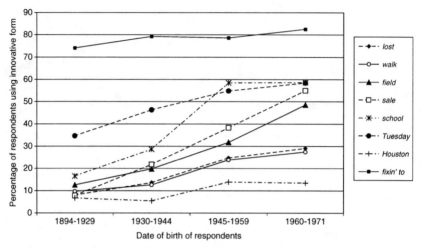

Figure 10.10 Apparent-time distribution of innovative features in PST and GRITS (Bailey et al. 1991)

friendly. Figure 10.8 suggests that three of these five features, *a*-prefixing, *liketa*, and zero-subject relatives, have been steadily declining since the last quarter of the nineteenth century, when the oldest cohort of *LAGS* informants was born. The use of preterit *come* and plural verbal -*s* seems to have begun to decline in the early part of the twentieth century, but the *LAGS* evidence suggests that their decline has been no less rapid than that of the other three features. The three innovative features shown on figure 10.9 include (1) *yall*, (2) preterit *dove* as in *He dove into the pool*, and (3) the use of lax vowels before heterosyllabic /r/ in the proper name Mary (i.e. the pronunciation [mɛɚi] as opposed to the earlier [meɹi]). All three features have expanded rapidly since 1930, when the oldest members of the youngest *LAGS* cohort were born. Their initial expansion may have begun even earlier than figure 10.9 suggests, but the lack of pre-1870s evidence makes it difficult to determine an exact point in time.

Finally, data from PST and a Grammatical Investigation of Texas Speech (GRITS) provide an even clearer picture of the importance of World War II as an impetus for linguistic change in the American South. Figure 10.10 illustrates the apparent-time distributions of eight innovative features in Texas; figure 10.11 shows apparent-time distributions for three recessive ones. Table 10.1 provides a key to the features in figures 10.10 and 10.11. As figures 10.10 and 10.11 show, the most dramatic expansion of almost all of the innovative features and the most dramatic decline of the recessive ones began around World War II. As we have shown in detail elsewhere (cf. Bailey, Wikle, Tillery, and Sand 1996), World War II has reshaped SAE more than any other event in its 400-year history.

In light of the extensive lexical and grammatical changes that took place between 1875 and 1945, by the middle of the twentieth century perhaps the most

Table 10.1 *PST and GRITS features*

Target item	Process	Innovative form	Conservative form
lost	merger of /ɑ/ and /ɔ/	[lɑst]	[lɔst]
walk	merger of /ɑ/ and /ɔ/	[wɑk]	[wɔk]
field	merger of /i/ and /ɪ/ before /l/	[fiɫd]	[fɪld]
sale	merger of /e/ and /ɛ/ before /l/	[sɛɫ]	[sel]
school	merger of /u/ and /ʊ/ before /l/	[skʊɫ]	[skul]
Tuesday	loss of /j/ after alveolars	[tuzdi]	[tjuzdi]
Houston	loss of /h/ before /j/	[justn]	[hjustn]
fixin to	use of quasimodal	*fixin to*	_____
Washington	intrusive /r/	[waʃɪŋtən]	[waɚʃɪŋtən]
forty-a	variation between /ɑ/ and /ɔ/ before /r/	[fɔɚri]	[fɑɚri]
forty-b	unconstricted postvocalic /r/	[fɔɚri]	[fɔɚi]

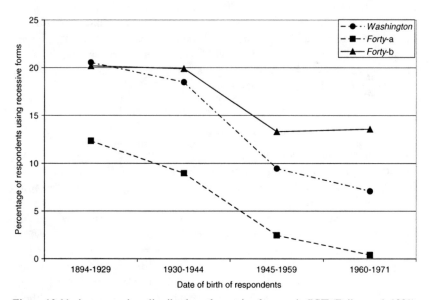

Figure 10.11 Apparent-time distribution of recessive features in PST (Bailey et al. 1991)

distinctive and widespread characteristics of SAE were the cluster of phonological features known as the Southern Shift.[5] Although there is some dispute as to exactly what features comprise the shift, the following six features have, at one time or another, been associated with it:

- Glide-shortened or monophthongal /ai/
- Fronted onsets of /au/
- Fronted /u/
- Fronted /ʊ/
- Lowered and retracted /e/
- Fronted and sometimes lowered /o/

The work of Bailey and Thomas (1998) and Thomas (2001) shows clearly that these Southern Shift features developed primarily after 1875. (See Feagin in this volume for an overview.) Thomas (2001) provides analyses of the vowel systems of three Southerners, one from eastern Virginia, one from White County, Arkansas/Dallas, Texas, and another from Gatlinburg, Tennessee, all born in the middle of the nineteenth century. Except for some fronting of /u/ in the vowel system of the Virginian, none of these systems show evidence of the Southern Shift. In all three vowel systems, /e/ remains to the front of /ɛ/, both /o/ and /u/ remain back vowels, onsets of /au/ remain central, and /ai/ is diphthongal, although the offglides are weaker before voiced obstruents than before voiceless ones. Southern Shift features begin to appear only during the last quarter of the nineteenth century, but they expand rapidly thereafter until by World War II they are general features of SAE (see Thomas 2001 for extensive documentation). Like other features of SAE, their history suggests a dialect characterized by innovation and adaptation rather than preservation.

3   The social motivation for change in SAE

In light of the widespread belief that SAE and southern culture in general are essentially conservative and the long-standing focus on settlement history and British roots, the extensive data showing that many stereotypes of SAE are recent developments and that most inherited features have been disappearing for quite some time are surprising. The results are remarkably consistent, however, and they occur in data sources such as linguistic atlases that oversample the most insular areas and the most conservative speakers of the region as well as in random sample surveys that are designed to reflect the current demographic make-up and residential patterns of the region. Moreover, Schneider's (forthcoming) test of some of the results against a body of overseers' letters essentially confirms those results. Table 10.2 provides a summary of the results of Schneider's test, along with our notes on evidence from the *Dictionary of American Regional English* (*DARE*) when it clarifies the results of the test. As table 10.2 indicates, the data from overseers' letters are generally consistent with the results outlined above,

Table 10.2 *Diachronic distribution of ten grammatical features in earlier SAE*

feature	illustration	period distribution (Bailey 1997)			overseers' letters (sample)
		before 1875	1875–1945	1945–1980	
a+verb+*ing*	*he left a-running*	+	+/−	−	+
pl. verbal -*s*	*folks sits here*	+	+/−	−	+
liketa	*I liketa died*	+	+/−	+/−	−[a]
perf. *done*	*she's done left*	+	+	+/−	+ (?}[b]
you-all/yall	*we saw yall*	−/+	+	+	−[c]
fixin to	*I'm fixin to eat*	−/+	+	+	−
multiple modals	*I might could do it*	?	−/+	+	−[d]
inceptive *get to*	*I got to talking*	−	−/+	+	−/+ (?)
dove "dived"	*they dove in*	−	−/+	+	−
drug "dragged"	*he drug it*	−	−/+	+	−

[a]note that the *Dictionary of American Regional English* (*DARE*) documents *liketa* as early as 1808 in Virginia, 1845 in Georgia, and 1886 in the southern Appalachians. The *DARE* evidence suggests that at one time *liketa* occurred in non-southern as well as southern varieties of English. See Bailey and Ross (1988) for evidence of *liketa* in earlier Ship English.
[b]*DARE* includes citations of perfective *done* from 1827 on in the South.
[c]*DARE* files include evidence of *you-all*, but not *yall*, from the first half of the nineteenth century.
[d]*DARE* includes one ambiguous citation of *might could* before 1900: "I know I might could & should enjoy myself" (an 1859 citation taken from Eliason 1957). *DARE* editors suggest that this may actually be "I might, could, and should ... "
Source: Schneider, forthcoming, with notes added by Tillery and Bailey

and when those data are ambiguous or unenlightening, the *DARE* evidence usually provides clarifications which confirm the position elaborated in this chapter. The question that remains, then, is why the linguistic history of SAE has evolved as it has.

The two periods during which the linguistic changes described above have gathered the most momentum provide a clue as to the social motivation for change in SAE – they were major periods of urbanization in the South. Figure 10.12 summarizes the growth of the urban population in the South and includes data from the United States as a whole for comparison. It is important to remember here that the US Census Bureau's definition of urban place included all locales with populations of 2,500 or more. As figure 10.12 shows, throughout the nineteenth century the urban population in the South grew steadily but quite slowly so that in 1880 about 12 percent of Southerners lived in urban areas. Most of the urban growth, however, was in a few relatively large cities such as New Orleans, Charleston, and Richmond. Beginning about 1880, urbanization accelerated rapidly as (1) industry, including cotton mills, lumber production

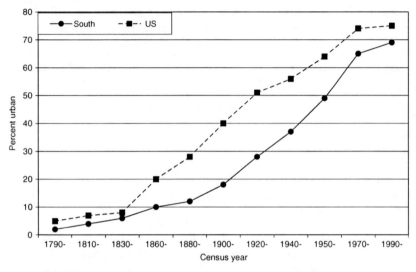

Figure 10.12 Growth of the urban population in the American South

facilities, and mining and steel factories began to move south to take advantage of low wages and (2) the rail system began to expand until by early in the twentieth century it covered much of the South.[6] Most of the urbanizing population during this period came from the rural South, and prominent among the urbanizing places were the small cities and towns where the cotton and lumber mills were built. Further fueling the expansion of small towns and cities in the period after 1880 was the widespread emergence of country stores, and subsequently the villages around them, which sometimes in turn developed into towns with the advent of the railroads. Concurrent with the development of villages and towns was the emergence of farm tenancy after 1880, which not only preserved the plantation system of agriculture, but also brought about much more extensive contact among whites and African Americans than in earlier periods as small white farmers increasingly descended into farm tenancy. All of these developments created contexts in which dialect contact became the major sociolinguistic fact of life in the American South after 1880. Dialect contact, in turn, may have been a major impetus for innovation and change in SAE. The coming of World War II saw a second major period of urbanization (and hence dialect contact) in the South, but in this case urban growth came primarily in large cities, especially those near military installations or with defense-related industries.[7] This population growth in both larger and smaller metropolitan areas included not only Southerners from the surrounding countryside, but also significant numbers of non-Southerners brought to the South by the consequences of the war. Moreover, whereas the urbanization that took place during the last part of the nineteenth century did not lead to a decline in real numbers in the rural population, after World War II the rural population began to decline numerically as well as proportionately.[8]

Metropolitanization and the decline of the rural population continue to be major demographic trends in the South today, but over the last two decades much of the metropolitan growth has been concentrated in the largest cities in the region, and the new industries and businesses moving to the South are as likely to be corporate headquarters of concerns like JC Penny and Southwestern Bell as they are to be Nissan and Mercedes Benz factories.

4 Conclusion

Recent research on the evolution of SAE, then, suggests not a conservative dialect bound to its past, but rather a dynamic, innovative variety that has experienced rapid, fundamental change over the last century and a quarter. Much of that change coincides with two major periods of urbanization in the South and with the dialect contact that resulted from urbanization. In many respects, the development of SAE over the last 125 years provides a striking parallel to the development of southern music during that time. The following passage from historian James Cobb (1999) could as easily have been written about Southern English as about southern music:

> Noting the "tangled genealogy" of southern musical styles, Edward L. Ayers [1992] insisted that southern music became *more* rather than *less* southern in the late nineteenth and early twentieth century as "older styles and newer fashions mixed and cohered, as musicians of both races learned from one another." Ayers clearly had both early country music and the blues in mind when he observed that "what the twentieth century would see as some of the most distinctly southern facets of southern culture developed in a process of constant appropriation and negotiation. Much of southern culture was invented, not inherited." (1999: 198)

The inventiveness of southern music and language are signs not of cultural decline, but of cultural resiliency. The following passage, again from James Cobb, best sums up SAE as well as southern culture in general. Quoting Levine (1978), he notes that:

> Culture is not a fixed condition but a process: the product of interaction between past and present. Its toughness and resiliency are determined not by a culture's ability to withstand change, which may indeed be a sign of stagnation not life, but by its ability to react creatively and responsively to the realities of a new situation. Where cultural identity is concerned, Levine pointed out, "The question . . . is not one of survivals but of transformations." (1999: 193)

The history of SAE is largely one not of survivals, but of transformations, of creative and responsive adaptation to new situations. That is why it is still around.

Notes

1. McMillan and Montgomery (1989b) provide extensive documentation of the view of SAE as a conservative variety and also the focus on the British roots of the variety.
2. Bailey and Ross (1992) term the assumption that differences among contemporary dialects must reflect differences in the source dialects from which they derive the "roots fallacy" and suggest that this assumption has misguided much of the research on SAE and the related African American Vernacular English.
3. Figure 10.3 omits the data from the Tennessee Civil War Veterans' Questionnaires since Reed (1991) finds no evidence of the loss of /h/ in that source.
4. As Bailey, Wikle, Tillery, and Sand (1996, 1993) point out, the effects of World War II in Oklahoma are almost identical to those in Texas. See those sources for additional data.
5. Compare Johnson (1996) for a discussion of lexical change in SAE.
6. See Bailey (1997b) for a more extended discussion of the historical context and the linguistic developments in the South after 1880. See Ayers (1992) for an excellent discussion of the historical developments.
7. See Bailey, Wikle, Tillery, and Sand (1996) for a more extensive discussion of the linguistic consequences of World War II.
8. The migration of rural Southerners to southern cities was, of course, accompanied by the migration of both black and white Southerners to the urban North beginning about the time of World War I and accelerating during World War II. The historical migration from South to North was reversed after 1970 with the advent of the Sunbelt phenomenon – the movement of business and industry from the high-wage North to the low-wage South.

11   The Englishes of southern Louisiana

CONNIE C. EBLE

1   Introduction

Sometime in the mid 1980s at a meeting of the Southeastern Conference on Linguistics, a presentation by Michael Montgomery led me to think about how the perceptions, feelings, and opinions of users contribute to the workings of language. Montgomery on that occasion analyzed a number of popular works on southern speech, mostly humorous illustrated booklets of the sort available at convenience stores and restaurant chains along the nation's highways. His point was not to list the errors and scholarly shortcomings of these works but to demonstrate that such linguistic descriptions by amateurs constitute important ancillary evidence to the understanding of regional variation by professionals.

Since that time, and largely because of the research of Dennis Preston (e.g. 1989, 1993, 1999), sociolinguists have come to understand better the importance of the shared beliefs of members to the language life of communities. According to Preston (1997: 312), "What linguists believe about standards matters very little; what nonlinguists believe constitutes precisely that cognitive reality which needs to be described – one which takes speech community attitudes and perception (as well as performance) into account." In her contribution to the seventy-fifth anniversary issue of *American Speech*, Barbara Johnstone uses a popular booklet on Pittsburghese to develop the thesis that popular representations of local dialects will become even more significant in the expanding global economy and culture:

> To a certain extent, the leveling forces of increased dialect contact, which encourage people to sound more like people elsewhere, may be counteracted by attempts to cling to local identity by preserving at least one or two features that sound local. Representations of local speech are a key part of this process, because parodies, performances, and other representations are the mechanisms by which people tell each other what sounds local. (2000: 392)

Any characterization of contemporary varieties of the English of southern Louisiana based on secondary sources rather than on original fieldwork must rely heavily on popular representations. Aside from *LAGS* and *DARE*, accessible descriptions by linguists and other kinds of scholarly observers are almost non-existent. James B. McMillan and Michael Montgomery's monumental *Annotated Bibliography of Southern American English* (1989) contains over 3,600 entries. Of these, 181 (fewer than 5 percent) pertain specifically to Louisiana. And a third of these concern personal and place names. Of the thirty-eight Master's and doctoral theses on Louisiana language topics reported in McMillan and Montgomery, none has been published and only a handful have resulted in any type of scholarly publication. Published works listed in McMillan and Montgomery are mostly brief commentaries on particular vocabulary items, like *lagniappe* and *pecan*, or on history, folklore, or cultural practices.

Despite the lack of attention from academics, the language practices of southern Louisiana have not gone without notice or commentary. The people of southern Louisiana consciously perform language and hold strong beliefs about language as a part of their identity. They consider their culture unique, inherently interesting, and more fun than that of fellow Southerners who live in the Bible Belt north of Alexandria, Louisiana, and across northern Mississippi and Alabama. Their cultural and linguistic affinities run east and west along the Gulf of Mexico, and northern Louisiana might as well be a separate state. This divide shows up in the pronunciation of the state name, with northern Louisiana favoring four syllables beginning [luz-] and southern Louisiana favoring five syllables beginning [luiz-]. The people of southern Louisiana revel in the stereotypes of a mixed non-Anglo-Saxon heritage of passion and pageantry that brought great saints and sinners together in a swampy paradise. They love to maintain, revive, and invent occasions for eating, drinking, story telling, gaming, and public festivity. All southern Louisianans, Cajun or not, espouse the Cajun motto, *Laissez les bons temps rouler!* "Let the good times roll!" Language is an important element of the communal self-image of southern Louisiana.

Today the vast majority of southern Louisianans are monolingual speakers of English. A hundred years ago the dominant public language was likewise English, though then a large percentage of the people of southern Louisiana were likely to have known some form of French, Spanish, German, Italian, or Native American tongue instead of or in addition to English. Two hundred years ago, just before the Louisiana Purchase, the dominant language was French, though the colony had been administered by Spain for almost forty years and groups of Spanish speakers from the Canary Islands (now known as the Isleños and Brulés) had established settlements in Louisiana with the encouragement of the Spanish authorities (Lipski 1990; Holloway 1997). Slaves in the colony at that time appear to have spoken an approximate variety of French, Louisiana Creole, an African language, or some combination of these (Klinger 1997).

All varieties of English in southern Louisiana developed against the backdrop of French. When Louisiana was purchased by the United States in 1803, the colonial population descended from Europeans and Africans was clustered in the southern portion of the vast Louisiana territory near the Gulf of Mexico and the mouth of the Mississippi River. Their language was French. In less than a decade, in 1812, Louisiana became the eighteenth state of the United States of America. Three years later the final victorious battle of the war of 1812 against the British took place just downstream from the city of New Orleans. Americanization and the English language came quickly to New Orleans. In the course of the nineteenth century, the port city absorbed the same immigrant groups that helped to build the urban centers of the north – the Germans, Irish, and Italians. Many of the new Americans adopted customs and cultural perspectives that had been established when the city was French without adopting the French language. The prairies and swamplands south and west of the Mississippi had been settled beginning in 1765 by French-speaking Acadians displaced from Nova Scotia. Acadian Louisiana remained largely inaccessible by road until the middle of the twentieth century, and French remained the language of everyday life there much longer than in New Orleans. Now, however, all varieties of Louisiana French are endangered, though the traces of French language and heritage are evident in all the Englishes of southern Louisiana.

Despite the rapid decline in the number of speakers in the second half of the twentieth century, Louisiana French has been more thoroughly studied than has Louisiana English. The Center for Louisiana Studies at the University of Louisiana at Lafayette (formerly University of Southwestern Louisiana), with the leadership of folklorist Barry Ancelet and historian Carl Brasseaux, has led in the study of all facets of Louisiana francophone culture. The 1990s saw great progress in the study of language too. Sylvie Dubois and her students at Louisiana State University undertook original fieldwork among speakers of Cajun French (also called Acadian French), funded in large part by the National Science Foundation. An excellent brief overview of the status of Cajun French was written by Michael Picone in response to an email query to the American Dialect Society from a student in the Netherlands and was published in the society's newsletter (Picone 1994). French in Louisiana today includes not only Cajun French but creole, a term that now, when applied to language in Louisiana, refers to varieties developed by descendants of Africans. The complexities of distinguishing creole from other kinds of French or English in Louisiana are explored in Megan Melançon's doctoral dissertation (2000) and in Dubois and Melançon (2000). In 1997, with support from the Lurcie Charitable Trust and the National Endowment for the Humanities, Albert Valdman of Indiana University published *French and Creole in Louisiana*. This essential reference tool collects original essays that not only describe varieties of French in Louisiana historically and socially but also set forth new methods and directions for recording and studying them. An interdisciplinary team, mostly of younger scholars, is currently working under Valdman's direction on an NEH-funded project to create a database of lexical and lexicological research for Louisiana French (Picone 2001). The study of Louisiana French by trained scholars has never been more intense, organized, or directed towards publication.

The Englishes that developed in the formerly French-speaking regions of Louisiana offer patterns of dialect variation almost as difficult to distinguish as do French varieties. Many monolingual English speakers in the areas that maintained French as the principal community language until World War II speak a recognizable variety called Cajun English. Yet other lifelong residents of towns like Abbeville, Ville Platte, or Thibodeaux show no trace of Cajun affinity in their speech, though their brothers or sisters might. Distinct from Cajun English also are the varieties of English spoken in New Orleans, Baton Rouge, and on the northern shore of Lake Pontchartrain. Within greater New Orleans, dialects can vary by race, neighborhood, schooling, or socioeconomic factors. Although the Englishes of southern Louisiana provide a living laboratory of the consequences of language contact, racial and ethnic diversity, and severe social and economic stratification, they are almost unstudied. Following popular characterizations, this chapter considers two varieties, Cajun English and New Orleans English.

2   Cajun English

In 1933 in *American Speech*, Claude Merton Wise of Louisiana State University published a broad phonetic transcription of the story of Grip the Rat as pronounced in "French-English," or "Cajan" (Wise 1933). The following summer Wise was one of four scholars from southern universities chosen to receive intensive training in phonetics and fieldwork practices at Brown University from Hans Kurath, Bernard Bloch, and Miles Hanley. On his return to Baton Rouge, Wise began at least fifteen years of work on the "Dialect Atlas of Louisiana" (Wise 1945), eventually amassing at least eighty-six dialect interviews from almost fifty communities in thirty-three parishes (George 1952: 86). At least a dozen Master's theses and five doctoral dissertations on Louisiana speech resulted. Yet only a few brief articles on this extensive work made it to print (for example, Perritt 1943; Abel 1951; George 1952). Years later workers on the *Linguistic Atlas of the Gulf States* consulted seventy-four of the field records made in Louisiana under Wise's supervision (Leas 1981). Wise's plan for a dialect atlas of Louisiana ultimately came to nought. For about forty years, with the exception of Mima Babington's unfinished study (Babington and Atwood 1961), research projects specifically on the Englishes of Louisiana never reached an audience beyond a seminar class or a thesis or dissertation committee.

The Cajun English area, however, is included in two of the most careful and rigorous American dialect projects of the twentieth century, *DARE*, the *Dictionary of American Regional English* (1985–), and *LAGS*, the *Linguistic Atlas of the Gulf States* (1986–92). The *DARE* fieldworker for Louisiana in the mid 1960s was August Rubrecht, who used the results of his interviews in eighteen communities as the basis of his dissertation on phonology (Rubrecht 1971). He also published his observation that linguistic isoglosses and the boundaries of cultural features – like drinking dripped, dark-roasted coffee in demitasse cups – are roughly congruent in southern Louisiana (Rubrecht 1977), confirming the triangle-shaped provenance that most Louisianans assign to Cajun English. *LAGS* includes transcriptions of interviews with thirty-five informants from the twenty-two Acadian parishes plus five others who are described with some notation of French influence on their English (Eble 1993a). Data in the *DARE* archives and in the Basic Materials of *LAGS* provide a unique resource for the study of Cajun English waiting to be tapped.

The 1990s saw the beginning of the professional study of Cajun English under that rubric. The first published work of any scope was a collection of eight essays by students and faculty at the University of Louisiana at Lafayette (formerly University of Southwestern Louisiana), edited by the late Ann Martin Scott (Scott 1992). The essays are directed at educators in order to increase their understanding of the linguistic situation in southern Louisiana and to describe the main characteristics of Cajun English (Eble 1993b). With a view to addressing educational issues in the region, a doctoral dissertation by Deany-Marie Cheramie (1998) documented the presence of Cajun English features in student writing. Whereas the first conference on Language Variety in the South in 1981 included no discussion of the linguistic situation in Louisiana, the second LAVIS conference in 1993 included presentations on Cajun French, Louisiana Creole, the speech of New Orleans, and Cajun Vernacular English.

The most promising advance in the recording and analysis of the English varieties spoken in French Louisiana is the project currently being carried out by Sylvie Dubois and her students at Louisiana State University, with the aid of Barbara Horvath of Sydney University. The Cajun English project builds on fieldwork undertaken as part of Dubois' NSF-funded Cajun French project, expanded to include the English of African-American creole speakers and the English of monolingual Cajuns. Although some attention is given to regional variation, the project is essentially an ethnographic and sociolinguistic one. It investigates the development of Cajun English as an ethnolect springing from a situation of language contact and correlates features of pronunciation and grammar with such external variables as age, gender, and race. Already Dubois and Horvath have shown that phonological features that arose from interference from French among the oldest generation were stigmatized and suppressed for the middle generation and are now markers of Cajun identity among the youngest adult generation. They also find gender to be an important but not easily interpretable factor because it is conditioned by age and by changing sociohistorical contexts (Dubois and Horvath 1998a; 1998b; 2000).

The Cajun Renaissance that began in the 1970s and the growth of tourism as one of the most important components of the regional economy have bolstered Cajun identity. Cajuns are proud of things Cajun, including their distinctive kind of English. A folk linguistics industry has placed Cajun joke books, tall tales, ghost stories, and dictionaries next to the cash register in almost every gift shop and restaurant in Cajun country.

The two most readily available popular treatments of Cajun speech are *Cajun Dictionary* (Sothern 1977) and *Speaking Louisiana* (Martin and Martin 1993).

The 1977 glossary contains only 177 entries. With few exceptions (*may* < *mais;* *pooldoo* < *poule d'eau; Fee Folay* < *feu folie; Roogaroo* < *loup garou*), French phrases, etymons, and spellings are lacking. Even terms widely known in their French spelling in southern Louisiana are anglicized, for example, *booray* for the card game *bourré* and *gree gree* for the curse *gris gris.* By 1993 the Cajun Renaissance was in full swing. The glossary authored by the Martins, a transplant from South Carolina and her Cajun husband, contains over 1,100 entries. About 500 are standard French words and expressions, for example, *yeux* "eyes," *tout de suite* "quickly," *soulier* "shoe," *matin* "morning," *lit* "bed," *hier soir* "last night," and *allons* "let's go." More than 300 are place names or surnames from the region, for example *Tchefuncta River, Calcasieu Parish*, and *Bonnet Carré Spillway*, and family names like *Arceneaux, Gauthier*, and *Ledet*. Of the remaining entries, fully a third are word-for-word duplicates of entries in Sothern (1977). Generally, entries in the 1993 booklet are fuller and often contain cultural information, as with the entry for *grillades*, "beef or veal steak, browned and simmered until tender in brownish tomato gravy. Grillades and grits is a common Louisiana brunch."

The pronunciations of Cajun English suggested by the entries in these two popular glossaries show foremost that the dialect is transmitted and preserved orally. As a result, many of the so-called peculiarities of pronunciation are simply widespread colloquial practices, particularly in the South. For example, Cajun English *cause* "cost," *tole* "told," *stan* "stand," and *swif* "swift" show loss of a final consonant from a cluster. *Cam* "calm," *guff* "gulf," and *vote* "volt" show loss of [l] from a cluster. *Ion* "iron," *jaw* "jar," *junya* "junior," *tied* "tired," and *tunda* "thunder" represent *r*-less variants common in the South. Several malapropisms and folk etymologies also show that Cajun English is rooted in oral communication, not writing: *gang warden* is the "game warden" (Sothern 1977: 14); the *loopey long* (Sothern 1977: 18) is the Huey P. Long bridge across the Mississippi River; *palometta* (Sothern 1977: 22) is "palomino," probably inspired by the plant *palmetto*; and *Emmet N. Domangue* (Sothern 1977: 12) personifies "eminent domain."

Because Cajun English is oral, attempts at writing it often result in inconsistent spelling: *cooyon* "stupid, dumb, educated but foolish" in Sothern (1977: 11) but *couillon* in Martin; *chew* "rear end" in Sothern (1977: 9) but *cu* in Martin; and *pooldoo* "swamp hen" in Sothern (1977: 14) but *poule deau* in Martin.

For the most part, unconventional spellings point to consistent patterns of variation between the consonants and vowels of Cajun English and other English dialects of southern Louisiana. The voiceless interdental fricative [θ], as in *think, throw, teeth, north*, shows up in Cajun English as a voiceless dental stop [t], spelled *tink, trow, teet, nort*. The voiced interdental fricative [ð], as in *that, this, other* corresponds in Cajun English to the voiced dental stop [d], spelled *dat, dis, udder*. In the two glossaries, the pronoun *I* is spelled *ah*, *my* is spelled *ma*, and *like* is spelled *lak* – suggesting the monophthongization of the diphthong [ai]. The replacement of interdental fricatives by dental stops was shown in Wise's

1933 phonetic transcription of "Cajan." This feature and [ai] > [a] are two of six typical features of current Cajun English identified by Dubois and Horvath (1998b: 163).

The spellings *ball* for *boil* and *all* for *oil* suggest the monophthongization of [ɔɪ], but the spellings *coil* for *call* and *oil* for *all* suggest the reverse. The spelling of *plane, plate, same,* and *pave* as *pleen, pleet, seem,* and *peeve* indicate raising of [e] to [i]; and the spelling of *in* and *itch* as *een* and *each* show tensing of [ɪ] to [i]. Conventional *lunch* and *punch* are spelled *launch* and *paunch,* [ə] to [ɔ].

By far the most frequent and consistent vowel correspondence is the occurrence of [æ] in Cajun English where other dialects have [ɛ], as in *ag* for *egg, vary* for *very, harry* for *hairy, tan* for *ten, ranch* for *wrench, shad* for *shed, pansil* for *pencil,* and many others. Although this is not one of the six typical features identified by linguists, it is certainly a caricatured feature used when imitating Cajun English speakers.

How do the words and phrases presented as localisms in *Cajun Dictionary* and *Speaking Louisiana* compare with the findings of *DARE* and *LAGS*? The three published volumes of *DARE* (A-O) mark 165 entries with the provenance Louisiana or New Orleans (*An Index by Region* 1993; Von Schneidemesser 1999). From the A-O entries in the General Index to *LAGS,* two more can be added. Of these 167 entries, thirty-seven are recorded in one or both of the popular dictionaries (see Appendix 1). The largest segment of the terms from the popular dictionaries comprises food terms familiar throughout southern Louisiana and now spreading nationally with Cajun cuisine: *andouille, beignet, boudin, crawfish bisque, crawfish boil, dirty rice, filé, gumbo, jambalaya, king cake,* and so forth. (As pointed out in *Speaking Cajun,* every fan of the Louisiana State University Tigers knows the word *cush cush* "fried cornmeal mush eaten as a cereal," even if they have never tasted the food, from the cheer "Hot boudin, cold cush cush, Come on, Tigers, PUSH, PUSH, PUSH!" The cheer also verifies the pronunciation, which is often obscured by the variant spellings *cous cous, cousch cousch,* and others.) Many terms from *DARE* and *LAGS* not listed in the popular works refer to topographical features and wildlife, for example, *coupé* "channel," *flottant* "floating island," *caouane* "alligator turtle," *goujon* "type of fish," and *latanier* "palm tree." Specific outdoor vocabulary of this sort, which was once central to Cajun life, is undoubtedly on the decline in southern Louisiana, for most contemporary Cajuns no longer make their livelihood on the bayous or in the fields. Their salable identity to outsiders depends mainly on their food and their music, both of which can be exported beyond Acadiana.

3   New Orleans English

Although the underworld may have christened New Orleans *The Big Easy,* natives prefer *The Crescent City* because of its niche in a bend of the Mississippi River or *The City That Care Forgot* because of its fun-loving outlook on life. A strip of alluvial land five feet below sea level, between a mighty river and a shallow lake,

New Orleans has always considered itself *sui generis*. New Orleans native Ronnie Virgets expresses the sentiment (1997: 31).

> No other American subgroup thinks they are more original than New Orleanians. More singular too. More discerning, savvy. Our rivers and roller coasters are better than yours. Our ice is probably colder than yours, and if it isn't, we make better use of it – Sazeracs and snowballs, for instance. We are like Texans and New Yorkers about all this, except our bragging is softer and usually reserved for ourselves alone . . .

To be sure, New Orleans shares many linguistic features with its neighbors in other parts of southern Louisiana. Most New Orleanians would recognize, if not use, at least three-quarters of the words listed as Cajun English in Appendix 1. Others like *armoire, mosquito bar, china ball tree, creole cream cheese, lost bread,* and *mirliton* are used throughout southern Louisiana, both in Cajun country and in New Orleans and environs. But New Orleans and Cajun dialects of English sound quite different.

The best record of the dialects of New Orleans is the 29-minute documentary film *Yeah you rite* produced for the Center for New America Media by Louis Alvarez and Andrew Kolker (1984) and funded in part by the Louisiana Committee for the Humanities. Consultants for the film were Mackie Blanton, Viola King, George Reinecke, Martha Ward, and Walt Wolfram. The voices of the film ring true to natives of the city, who often complain that the movies never get the New Orleans accent right. Chuck Taggert (2000), who maintains the most complete website devoted to New Orleans speech, calls *Yeah you rite* "a perfect example and portrayal of a unique regional dialect." In the film, anthropologist Martha Ward calls New Orleans "a very self-conscious city," and the natives interviewed confirm that characterization. They are quick to give their opinions about linguistic distinctions based on class, color, and neighborhood, assenting to the popular perception that New Orleans has three dialects: uptown white, downtown white (also known as *Yat*), and black. The late George Reinecke wrote a Master's thesis on New Orleans pronunciation in 1951 and remained the expert on the dialect for the next half century. In *Yeah you rite* Reinecke observes that at the time of filming the self-conscious use of New Orleans dialects was on the increase. That was just about the time that New Orleanians were reinforcing their linguistic awareness through the comic strips of Bunny Matthews (1978), whose characters sounded just like the waitress at the neighborhood restaurant who asks, "Ya want dat po-boy dressed, dawlin?" The current proliferation of websites extolling the unique culture and vocabulary of New Orleans appears to support Barbara Johnstone's hypothesis that in a global economy popular representations of speech serve to let people know what sounds local.

Local identity is a performance art in New Orleans, and people work at it. An email circulating among displaced New Orleanians lists hundreds of ways that "You know you're from New Orleans." Many are linguistic. You cringe every time you hear an actor with a southern or Cajun accent in a New Orleans based movie or TV show. You know it's *ask*, but you purposely say *ax*. You call tomato sauce *red gravy*. You *wrench* your hands in the *zinc* with an onion to get the crawfish smell off. You write *eaux* for the sound *o*, as in *Geaux Zephyrs* or *Alfredeaux sauce*. You know how to mispronounce street names like *Chartres*, *Melpomene*, and *Terpsichore*. You can pronounce *Tchoupitoulas* but can't spell it.

Despite the apparent social importance of the local varieties, New Orleans English has been the topic of few studies. Two brief encyclopedia entries by Mackie Blanton (1989) and by Richard W. Bailey (1992) summarize the well-known characteristics of New Orleans speech and the complex cultural heritage that still influences it. Students of Blanton and Reinecke at the University of New Orleans have written Master's theses on the English of New Orleans and its environs (Douglas 1969; Malin 1972; Wilson 1973; Auber-Gex 1983). The thesis by Malin is particularly useful, as it establishes a questionnaire of lexical items used in New Orleans. Malin's New Orleans questionnaire serves as the starting point of Wilson's study of St. Tammany Parish and Auber-Gex's study of the English of Creoles.

Two more recent studies consider the ways that the language is used rather than its features. An article in *Language in Society* (Wolf et al. 1996) examines the pronunciation of French surnames and the bearers' feelings about the ways their names are pronounced. Felice Coles (1997) shows how callers to a radio talk show identify themselves as local by using language in locally identifiable ways.

Aside from *Yeah you rite*, perhaps the best source for the flavor of the language of New Orleans is John Kennedy Toole's Pulitzer Prize winning novel *Confederacy of Dunces* (1980), the story of the lunatic adventures of Ignatius J. Reilly, gargantuan failed theologian and hotdog vendor. Almost every review of the book comments on the dialog: "The real sounds and smells and flavors of the streets of New Orleans are in this book, along with its many dialects" (Larson 1999: 104). Local journalist Ronnie Virgets also writes perceptive vignettes of life in New Orleans, sometimes slipping into comfortable vernacular vocabulary from childhood, like *razoo!* "everything in sight is up for grabs" or *pe-lay* "knock an adversary out" (1997: 162–3).

Over the past twenty years, a name has taken hold for the distinctive lower- and middle-class vernacular of whites in New Orleans. It is called *Yat*, and for the first time merits an entry in the *American Heritage Dictionary* (2000). Popular lore has it that *Yat* is a shortening of the familiar New Orleans greeting "Where you at?." *Yat* applies to the speakers as well as the speech, as in the title of the novel *Yats in Movieland* (Russo 1997). It has the derived adjective *yatty*, as in, "You surely sound *yatty* on your answer machine."

Many websites are dedicated to the cultivation of a New Orleans identity. Most are allied to tourism and seek to present New Orleans as unique, carnal, and exotic – a place in the United States that even has a high-caloric way of talking the English language. Such websites customarily include lists of New Orleans words, expressions, and pronunciations – mostly terms for food, drink, and local color gift items that tourists might encounter. However, one site, maintained by Chuck Taggert, is an earnest but light-hearted effort to document the language, *Yat-Speak: A Lexicon of New Orleans Terminology and Speech*. From its entries can be extracted much about New Orleans vocabulary and pronunciation.

DARE (A-O) lists seven terms with the designation *New Orleans*: *cala* "fried rice cake," *camelback* "house with one story in the front and two stories in the back," *islet* "city block," *king cake* "wreath-shaped coffee cake eaten during the Mardi Gras season," *krewe* "members of a carnival organization," *Mardi Gras* "Tuesday before Ash Wednesday, season from Twelfth Night through Fat Tuesday," and *oven* "cemetery vault that stacks vertically." Of these, *islet* and *oven* seem to have fallen into disuse, as they show up neither in Malin (1972) nor in any of the popular recent glossaries that I have turned up. I have found *cala* only on one website (http://www.neworleansrestaurants.com). The other four terms show up regularly in current sources. A website devoted to Mardi Gras has a section explaining *king cake, krewe, Mardi Gras*, and many other words pertaining to the season (http://www.mardigrasunmasked.com/mardigras/mardispeak.htm). Appendix 2 lists a selection of words and expressions used in New Orleans, drawn from Malin (1972) and websites available in 2000.

Most of the popular glossaries of New Orleans English try to provide some guidance in pronunciation, usually by suggestive respellings: *andouille* is *an-doo-E; do-do* is *dough-dough; etoufée* is *A-two-fay; grilliades* is *gree-yods; John* is *Jawn*; and so forth. Taggert's *Yatspeak* webpage is the most thorough and consistent, and uses @ for schwa [ə]. It includes words whose local pronunciations are not obvious to outsiders from the spelling, for example, *mayonnaise* as MY-nez, *mirliton* as MEL-lee-tawn, *pecan* as p@-KAWN, and *praline* as PRAH-leen, and the infamous *ask* as AX. Five "major standard local pronunciations" of *New Orleans* are given: new OR-l@ns, new AW-l@ns, new OR-lee-'@ns, new AH-lee-@ns, and nyoo AH-lee-'@ns. Taggert adds, "The fabled 'N'Awlins,' pronounced <NAW-l@ns >, is used by some natives for amusement, and by some non-natives who think they're being hip, but actually I've come across very few locals who actually pronounce the name of the City in this way." *Yatspeak* also includes a guide to the pronunciation of place names, like *Burgundy Street*, pronounced *bur-GUN-dee*, and *Milan Street*, pronounced MY-lan. The phonetic approximations in *Yatspeak* suggest the lack of [r] after vowels, for example, CHAW-muh for *charmer*. Thus, for many New Orleanians, *water, quarter, and oughtta* rime, and *autistic* and *artistic* are homophones. The suggested rhyming of *John* and *lawn* shows [ɑ] > [ɔ], and the voiced interdental fricative [ð] > [d], is shown by *da QUAW-tah* for *the Quarter*. The most parodied and stigmatized pronunciation is [ɔɪ] as [ər], shown by the spellings *berl, earl, ersters*, and *turlet* for *boil, oil, oysters*, and *toilet*. This is also a stigmatized feature of New York speech, further evidence for Dorrill's claim (in this volume) that all "southern" features are found elsewhere as well. Another feature of New Orleans speech is the placement of word stress on the first syllable in *adult, cement, insurance*, and *umbrella*.

4   Conclusion

Language variety is alive and well and perhaps even profitable in southern Louisiana. This sketch of two types of English used there today exemplifies what linguists have been saying all along: the regional dialects of the United States are not in imminent danger of becoming one homogenous variety. At the same time that unprecedented kinds and amounts of contact between speakers of different varieties of English appear to favor leveling, speakers of regional varieties of English are preserving, and perhaps even exaggerating, at least some local features of their dialect – allowing them to retain identity with a community smaller than the global family and to derive some sort of value from that more local identity.

Appendix 1 A glossary of Cajun English, A–O

These terms appear in one or both of the popular glossaries of Cajun English (Sothern 1977; Martin and Martin 1993) and in either *DARE* (A–O) or *LAGS* (General Index, vol. 2) or both.

andouille   sausage made with pork and garlic
beignet   square, deep-fried doughnut, usually sprinkled with powdered sugar
boucherie   communal gathering to slaughter hogs
boudin   sausage of pork, rice, and seasoning
bourré   Cajun card game
Cajun   person of Acadian French origin
Catahoula [hog/hound] dog   hound dog native to Louisiana
chalon   floating boat store
choupique   mudfish
coonass   Cajun. Sometimes considered derogatory.
couillon   foolish or inept person
crawfish bisque   soup that contains crawfish heads stuffed with meat and seasoning
crawfish boil   social gathering at which crawfish are boiled and eaten
creole   native to Louisiana, e.g. *creole tomatoes*
cuite   thick syrup at the bottom of the pot
cush-cush   browned cornmeal eaten as a cereal
dirty rice   rice cooked with liver and gizzards, onions, and parsley
do-do   sleep. *make do-do* go to sleep
étouffée   method of cooking shrimp or crawfish in a rich sauce
fais-dodo   party featuring Cajun music, dancing, and food
filé   powder made from dried sassafras leaves, often sprinkled on gumbo
grillade   beef or veal steak in browned tomato gravy
gris gris   magic formula to bring bad luck, e.g. *put the gris gris on something*
gui-gui   country bumpkin

gumbo   thick stew of seafood or meat and vegetables
jambalaya   mixture of meat or shrimp, vegetables, and rice cooked in a single pot
king cake   wreath-shaped coffee cake served during the Mardi Gras season
Lafitte skiff   shrimp boat with decks specifically designed for attaching trawling
      nets
lagniappe   something extra
loup-garou   werewolf
mais   but
make groceries   shop for food
maque-chou   dish made from corn cut from the cob and fried
Mardi Gras   Tuesday before Lent begins; season from Twelfth Night to Ash
      Wednesday
maringouin   mosquito
nenaine   godmother
neutral ground   grassy or paved strip in the middle of a street

Appendix 2   A New Orleans glossary

These terms are drawn from Malin (1972) and websites available in 2000, and
verified by a native speaker.

across the lake   the Mississippi Gulf Coast
alligator pear   avocado
andouille   sausage made with pork and garlic
armoire   large upright wardrobe for clothing
bad mouth   speak unfavorably of someone
ball   annual formal private social event of a carnival organization
banquette   sidewalk
batture   land between the levee and river
beads   inexpensive plastic or glass necklaces thrown to the crowds from Mardi
      Gras floats
beignet   square, deep-fried doughnut, usually sprinkled with powdered sugar
beauty seat   front seat in a bus or streetcar parallel to the aisle
big communion   solemn communion ceremony at the time of reception of the
      sacrament of Confirmation
bobo   minor sore, cut, or lump on the skin
boeuf gras   papier-maché fatted bull that appears annually as a float in the Rex
      parade
boogalee   a Cajun. Sometimes considered derogatory.
bourré   Cajun card game
by   at, as in *I'm by Jane's house*
café au lait   coffee with hot milk
call out   an invitation from a krewe member to the first round of dances at a
      Mardi Gras ball

camel back   house with one story in the front and two in the back

cap   noun of address for an unknown male. Used among men: *Say, cap, can you tell me where to park?*

captain   leader of a carnival organization

carnival   Mardi Gras

cayoodle   a dog of low pedigree

cedar robe   a chifforobe made of cedar

cher   dear, a noun of address

chickory   root that is ground and roasted and added to coffee

chifforobe   piece of furniture with drawers and a place for hanging clothes

chinaball tree   common tree in Louisiana

chunk   throw

cook down the seasoning   slowly sauté small pieces of onions, celery, and bell peppers together as a step in the preparation of many dishes

couche-couche, cush-cush   dish of browned cornmeal eaten as a cereal

couillon   foolish or inept person

court   king, queen, maids, and dukes at a carnival ball

courtbouillon   spicy fish soup

crab boil   social gathering, usually out of doors, at which crabs are boiled and eaten; the spices used to flavor the boiling crabs

crazy bone   elbow

creole   native to Louisiana, e.g. *creole tomatoes*

creole cream cheese   traditional breakfast food of milk curd and whey, sprinkled either with sugar or with salt and pepper, now available at only one grocery store in New Orleans

Crescent City Connection   the two bridges across the Mississippi River connecting downtown New Orleans with the West Bank. Also called *the GNO*

daube   pot roast of braised veal or beef

deadmen's fingers   inedible lungs of crabs

den   warehouse where Mardi Gras floats are decorated and stored

devil beating his wife   raining while the sun is shining

dirty rice   rice cooked with bits of liver and gizzards, onions, and parsley

do-do   sleep; *make do-do* go to sleep

doodlebug   little bug with lots of legs that rolls into a ball

dressed   served with lettuce, tomatoes, and mayonnaise

dubloon   round, metallic, coin-like throw usually embossed with the parade name, date, and theme

etouffé   method of cooking crawfish or shrimp in a rich sauce

faisondé   spoiled, said of fish or meat

favor   souvenir of a Mardi Gras ball given by a krewe member to a friend

flambeau   lit torch carried in night parades

flying horses   carousel, merry-go-round

fugaboo   lie, deceive, fool

funny bone   elbow

gallery   balcony, porch, stoop

GNO   greater New Orleans; the bridge connecting downtown New Orleans to the West Bank of the Mississippi River

go-cup   paper or plastic cup for drinking alcoholic beverages on the street

goose bumps   bristling of the hairs of the skin because of cold or fear

grand march   procession of the entire court at a carnival ball

grillades   beef or veal steak in browned tomato gravy

grip   suitcase

grippe   cold and fever, flu

gris gris   magic formula to bring bad luck, e.g. *put the gris gris on someone*

gumbo   thick stew of seafood or meat and vegetables

gumbo ya-ya   everyone talking at the same time

hickey   knot or bump on the head or forehead

hi-rise   elevated portion of I-10 at the Industrial Canal in New Orleans East

homestead   financial institutional that deals in home mortgages

hurricane   large alcoholic drink served in distinctive glasses at Pat O'Brien's in the French Quarter

indian fire   impetigo

jambalaya   mixture of meat or shrimp, vegetables, and rice cooked in a single pot

king cake   wreath-shaped coffee cake containing a bean or plastic baby eaten between King's Day (January 6) and Mardi Gras

lagniappe   something extra

lightning bug   firefly

little communion   reception of the sacrament of Eucharist for the first time

locker   closet

Lord of Misrule   king of the elite Twelfth Night Revelers carnival organization, whose ball on January 6 officially begins the Mardi Gras season

lost bread   French toast. Translation of *pain perdu*

make [an age]   become a specific age, e.g. *I make forty next week*

make groceries   shop for groceries

Mardi Gras Indians   groups of African Americans who dress in elaborate beaded costumes and feathers in imitation of Native Americans and participate in their own set of Mardi Gras rituals

masker   anyone in costume at Mardi Gras time

mamere   grandmother

mirliton   vegetable pear, like a squash, usually eaten stuffed with a dressing of shrimp or meat

mosquito bar   net, usually placed over a bed or child's crib, to keep mosquitoes out

mosquito hawk   dragon fly

muffaletta   large Italian sandwich of ham, Genoa salami, Provolone, and olive salad on a round, seeded bun

nanan   godmother

nectar   pink, almond-flavored syrup in a soda or on a snowball

nou-nou   pacifier

page fence   chain-link fence

pain perdu   French toast

pairoot   rummage through another's possessions

pané meat   breaded and fried veal or beef

parrain   godfather

pass by   visit briefly, e.g. *I'll pass by your house after work*

pere, pepere   grandfather

pirogue   small, lightweight boat, usually flat on the bottom with pointed ends like a canoe, developed by Native Americans and Acadians for swamps and shallow water. The pirogue "floats on the dew."

pistolet   French bread roll

plantain   banana that grows easily in many backyards in New Orleans. Usually cooked, particularly deep-fried and rolled in powdered sugar.

po-boy   sandwich of meat or fried shrimp or oysters served on crisp French bread and *dressed* with lettuce, tomatoes and mayonnaise

poule d'eau, pooldoo   marsh hen

praline   round, sugary confection made of brown sugar, heavy cream, butter, and pecans

prie-dieu   kneeling bench, usually with a shelf, generally for one person for personal or private devotion

raquecha   cockleburr

Rex   king of Mardi Gras; male chosen by the Krewe of Rex to rule over the public celebration of Mardi Gras

roux   flour and oil mixture used to start almost all Louisiana dishes

second line   mass of people who follow behind a funeral procession dancing in the streets. Now applied to a particular dance and music which has become a favorite part of wedding receptions as the bride and groom lead the assembled guests in a snake-like procession throughout the hall.

shed   small storage building

the show   movies

shoot da shoot   playground slide

shotgun   single-story house in which all rooms are on one side and are connected by a single hallway down the side

shu-shu   dead firecracker or one that failed to explode

silver dime   ten-cent piece

slaughter pole   cane pole for fishing

snowball   shaved ice in a cone drenched with syrup

stand in a wedding   serve as a bridesmaid, groomsman, or usher in a wedding

stoop   front steps, particularly of a shotgun

shoe sole   flat, glazed pastry shaped roughly like the sole of a shoe

tableau   dancing or mimed scenes following a theme and presented by the krewe for the entertainment of the court and guests at a carnival ball

throw   trinkets like beads, dubloons, and plastic cups tossed to the crowd by krewe members riding the floats in a Mardi Gras parade

tumbleset   summersault

Uptown   upriver from the intersection of Canal St. and the Mississippi River

Vieux Carre   the French Quarter; the oldest part of the city, bounded by the river, Canal St., and Esplanade

West Bank   the west side of the Mississippi River opposite the city of New Orleans

yellow mustard   milder, yellow-colored mustard as opposed to sharper brown-colored creole mustard or Zatarain's

Zatarain's   popular brand of New Orleans foods, sometimes used generically for creole mustard or the spices used to boil crabs and crawfish

Zulu   the oldest African-American carnival krewe, which for many decades paraded on Mardi Gras morning on an unplanned route mostly through African-American neighborhoods

12   Features and uses of southern style

BARBARA JOHNSTONE

1   Introduction

In a local newspaper article covering his retirement as a longstanding member of the school board of Bryan, Texas, Travis Bryan, Jr., a banker and a descendent of the European Americans who founded the city, is described as "defy[ing] stereotypes, vacillating between being a hard-nosed businessman and a God-fearing southern gentleman who is prone to tears when he talks about 'those little faces looking out of the school bus windows'" (Levey 1991: A1). To the writer of the article, a man like Bryan has to "vacillate" between acting like a businessman and being "God-fearing" and "prone to tears." Acting like a "southern gentleman" is inconsistent with being "hard-nosed," and the coexistence of the two ways of acting in one person's repertoire is evidence that he is special.

Bryan "defies stereotypes," however, only in a fairly stereotypical way. The article's characterization exemplifies an image of what it takes to be a successful Southerner that is frequently adduced in popular discourse about southernness. According to this familiar trope, a person cannot be simultaneously "hard" in the way required for practical efficacy and "soft" in the southern way, so one has to alternate between the two styles. The ideal Southerner is someone who can make effective use of both, someone who can be "hard" (like a Northerner) for strategic reasons but whose more natural style is the "soft" southern one. To give just one familiar example from popular fiction, Scarlett O'Hara, protagonist of *Gone With the Wind*, is a successful Southerner of this kind (Mitchell 1936).

The example of Travis Bryan highlights the fact that not all Southerners talk alike and that most Southerners (probably all) have more than one way of talking. Sounding like a Southerner is not, in other words, an automatic and inevitable result of being from the South. Like people everywhere, each Southerner has a repertoire of available ways of being, acting, and sounding, styles which he or she can adapt (more or less consciously and more or less freely) to the situation and the communicative purpose at hand. For some Southerners as well as for some people from elsewhere, sounding southern is a set of sociolinguistic resources (including, though by no means limited to, the kinds of phonological resources

189

outlined by George Dorrill in chapter 7 of this volume) which may be employed sometimes not at all and sometimes heavily. This chapter is about some of the linguistic aspects of styles of speaking and interacting that are alluded to in descriptions of white Southerners such as Travis Bryan, Jr., and Scarlett O'Hara. First I describe a few of the specific linguistic features which have been observed in the speech of some Southerners (and in literary and other representations of southern speech). Then I talk about some of the things people may accomplish by adopting features of southern style.

Southern white men and women have long been characterized as using language differently from others, interacting differently, and having different attitudes toward language. The characterizations have varied somewhat over time. Thomas Jefferson described Southerners (by "Southerners" he meant white southern men) as "hot-headed, indolent, unstable, and unjust" (McWhiney 1988: xiii). By the middle of the nineteenth century, however, the idea that Southerners were more polite, more easygoing, less direct in speech than Yankees, and more verbose and more eloquent seems to have become a regular feature of discourse about them, by outsiders and insiders. This idea structures much discourse about Southerners, whether the Southerners in question are from the coastal or the mountain South and whether they are men or women. Travelers from the North in the mid nineteenth century noted that Southerners had "softer" manners and that they were franker and more cheerful than Northerners, more courteous and courtly (McWhiney 1988: 109). In the early 1930s, Florida novelist Marjorie Kinnan Rawlings described the speech of "crackers" as "soft as velvet, low as the rush of running branch water" (Burkett 1978: 60). In the fictionalized voice of Bill Clinton, contemporary Arkansas novelist Bobbie Ann Mason comments on the northern tendency to "call a bull a bull." She has "Clinton" claim that "in the South, we have an expression for people who do that. We say, 'He's a person who says what he thinks.' And it's not necessarily a compliment. What you call 'waffling' is just good manners back home" (Mason 1993: 90). Southerners' love of talk, both informal small talk and formal oratory, is also often mentioned. In a letter to Malcolm Cowley, William Faulkner claimed that the "gentle folk" of the antebellum South "really did nothing: they slept or talked. They talked too much, I think. Oratory was the first art" (Ross 1989: 188). Reminiscing about her southern childhood, Shirley Abbott (Abbott 1983: 164–5) remembers "the goodbye ritual" which could take up to three hours.

Linguistic research about regional variation in discourse structure and style is still fairly sparse. By "discourse structure" I mean the grammar of units larger than sentences and the closely related issue of cohesion (Halliday and Hasan 1976), as well as discourse-marking strategies (Schiffrin 1987) by which speakers show, as they produce talk or writing, how it is to be interpreted. "Discourse style" consists of typical choices for expressing linguistic politeness (Brown and Levinson 1987) in general and for performing specific speech acts: requesting, persuading, narrating, and so on. Tannen (1981, 1984) shows how the interactional style of New York Jews is characterized by such features as the tendency to tolerate only very brief pauses in conversation and to ask rapid-fire personal questions to demonstrate friendly solidarity. Reissman (1988) talks about Puerto Rican women's narratives, and Johnstone (1990a,b) describes how white mid-westerners construct and use stories, contrasting this population with the urban northeasterners studied by Polanyi (1985) and others.

More directly relevant to the topic of southern style is the fairly extensive body of scholarship about the discourse style of African Americans, beginning with work by Abrahams (1962, 1976), Kochman (1972), and Mitchell-Kernan (1972) on such speech events as signifying, hoorawing, and styling out. Kochman (1981) describes African Americans' speech styles in aggressive talk, boasting, flirting, and handling accusations and personal information, Labov (1972a) compares lower- and middle-class African Americans' expository style and discusses teenage boys' personal narratives. Etter-Lewis (1993) discusses life stories of professional women. Erikson (1984) describes the structure of boys' conversations, and Gumperz (1982: 187–203) analyzes African-American political oratory. Heath (1983) contrasts language socialization practices in a working-class African-American neighborhood with those in a similar white neighborhood, describing differences in such things as how caregivers use questions and how children are encouraged to construct and perform narratives. It should be noted that all these studies except those of Abrahams and Heath are about northern, urban African Americans.

Whatever the particulars of the history of African-American varieties of American English and the details of the interactions between African Americans and European Americans in the South, it is clear that there has always been mutual influence. Certain aspects of southern whites' styles are similar to aspects of African-American styles. For example, Feagin (1997) suggests that the use of certain intonation patterns and of the falsetto register by southern whites can be traced to African-American influence. In this chapter, however, I focus on white Southerners, primarily because relatively little has been written about discourse-level features of southern white Americans' speech despite decades of descriptions of southern phonology, vocabulary, and grammar (cf. McMillan and Montgomery 1989). In what follows, I sketch the work that has been done on discourse styles and strategies of European-American Southerners and suggest some of the many directions in which future research could go. First I describe studies of particular features of southern discourse. These include features that can be associated with what may be characteristically southern interactional requirements, such as forms of address, greetings, indirectness, and other politeness phenomena; features associated with the southern folk poetic tradition such as oratorical style and parable-like narrative; and patterns of language socialization that may be connected to characteristically southern beliefs about how language works. Then I turn to a discussion of some of the uses to which southern style can be put, summarizing some recent work on how Texas women make strategic use of ways of sounding and interacting associated with southernness.

2   Interactional style: deferential politeness

2.1   Greetings and forms of address

Many of the features of southern style which have been remarked on have to do with how interpersonal relations are indexed and negotiated in conversation. Southerners' elaborate civility has been noted over and over, in popular and scholarly representations. Among the earliest studies of southern style is that of Spears (1974) on southern folk greetings and responses, which, as other observers have also more informally noted, are more elaborate and more obligatory than greetings elsewhere. In a study of expressions of local solidarity in New Orleans, Coles (1997) found that the use of local-sounding greetings was the strategy adopted most often by telephone callers who wanted to display their identification with radio talk-show hosts and a veterinary-clinic receptionist.

Coles also describes the use of particularly New Orleans-sounding forms of address as a solidarity-building move: *darling, doll,* and *babe* are examples. While these particular items are characteristic of New Orleans rather than the South as a whole, forms of address in general are described over and over as being different and more significant in the South than elsewhere. *Sir* and *ma'am* are among the most frequently mentioned of the forms of address with particularly southern uses. The use of *sir* and *ma'am* to one's parents, for example, as a required element of the answer to a *yes/no* question, is widespread in the South and not elsewhere, as is the use of *sir* or *ma'am* to peers or younger people. On the basis of observation, interviews, and questionnaires, Ching (1988) concluded that the central function of the southern *sir* and *ma'am* was to express deference, but that there were other uses too: emphasis, and, among younger peers and when used to someone younger than the speaker, to express friendly solidarity. Simpkins (1969) notes that the same speaker may be addressed in different ways depending on which aspects of his or her social identity are relevant at the moment. In a study of the uses of *ma'am* and *sir* in the screenplay (by Horton Foote) and film (directed by Sterling Van Wagenen) *The Trip to Bountiful,* Davies (1997) combined discourse analysis and a "playback" phase in which she asked Southerners to comment on the meanings of these address terms while watching clips of the film. Like Ching, she found that the core meaning was the expression of deferential politeness, or "negative" politeness in Brown and Levinson's (1987) terms: the creation and maintenance of culturally appropriate social distance between speakers, so that potential impositions on others' autonomy are avoided. In addition, Davies shows that shifts in the intonation accompanying the use of *sir* or *ma'am* can serve to foreground other aspects of the social relationship between speaker and hearer, so that, for example, a shift to a flatter intonation contour can index a shift to a less formal relationship. *Ma'am* and *sir* can also be used for emphasis, when the answer to a question is, for example, surprising or particularly significant. The conventional deferential meaning of *sir* or *ma'am* can, in some uses, be completely overridden, as when one of these forms is used sarcastically or in the course of a conversational negotiation for power.

Sir and *ma'am* are just two of a wide variety of address forms used by Southerners to index and manipulate social relations. In his childhood autobiography (Crews 1978), Georgia novelist Harry Crews describes a powerful feeling of connection with other generations of his family when he noticed that he was saying *yes, sir* to his uncle and being addressed by his uncle as *son*, just as his uncle addressed his own mother as *ma'am* and was addressed as *son* (1978: 164–5). Here is part of the conversation Crews re-creates, as the narrator, his grandmother, and his Uncle Alton operate on a rooster's craw:

> "Cut a little deeper in there, son," said grandma.
> "Yes, ma'am," said Uncle Alton. "Son, git that turpentine swab right here."
> "Yes, sir."
> "Clean it down in the corner, Alton."
> "Yes, ma'am," said Uncle Alton. "Son, I got the needle started, but I cain't git the end of it. See if you can."
> "Yes, sir," I said. (Crews 1978: 165)

In Crews' novel *Body* (1990), characters use a wide variety of address forms (Johnstone 1992, 1994). To older people and to strangers to whom they want to display respect, Crews' characters use *ma'am* or *sir* and *Mr.*, *Mizz*, or *Miss* plus first name, as in "*Mr. Alphonse, sir*, I have come to ask for you daughter's hand in marriage" (Crews 1990: 200). As did Crews' uncle, older men use *son* to younger men or boys, as well as *old son*, *boy*, and *bud*; men address women they know as *girl* and as *child*. Women call men *honey*, *old honey*, and *old thing*. Many uses of these address forms, particularly to elders, display a sort of ritual deference, but other uses can help to defuse tension by putting the speaker's deferential attitude on display at a key moment. Among peers, terms like *old son* and *girl* can signal closeness and solidarity, but other uses, particularly of terms such as *bud* and *son*, appear in bids for dominance or threats of belligerence, as in this response to a challenge to "talk right": " 'I come from the same part of the country you do, *old son*,' said Billy Bat, shifting on his heels. 'I'll talk any damn way I please' " (Crews 1990: 209–10).

2.2 *Conditional syntax and indirectness*

Crews' characters in *Body* also express negative politeness via a range of strategies for linguistic indirectness, rarely expressing a proposition in such a way as to take full responsibility for it or impose their view of the world on others. One of the most frequent strategies for indirectness involves the use of conditional syntax. Full *if-then* constructions, as well as conditional clauses alone, can be used to hedge assertions, as in examples (1) and (2):

(1)   I ain't got a thing if I ain't got time.
(2)   Damned if yeller [yellow] weren't always my favorite thing in the world.

Conditional syntax also appears in requests, as in (3) and (4):

(3)   I guess you could step out and git some toothpicks and a carton of camel cigarettes, if you a mind to.
(4)   If you be good enough to take the newness off it, I believe I could stand me a taste.

In (5) and (6), conditional syntax mitigates a suggestion:

(5)   I wouldn't look for'm to show up if I was you.
(6)   I'd think that whiskey'd be a trifle hot.

In (7) conditional syntax is part of a more forceful suggestion, and in (8) and (9) conditional syntax appears in threats:

(7)   You gone [gonna] marry into the Turnipseed family, you gone have to learn not to be a asshole.
(8)   You do and you can make you a pallet on the floor.
(9)   There'll be trouble if you can't learn to keep a civil tongue about my family.

Conditional syntax creates distance between the hearer and the claim or action which is conventionally performed by what he or she is saying. It can thus serve to mitigate impositions, serving, like forms of address, to express negative, deferential politeness. By the same token, however, the use of conditional syntax reflects characters' heightened awareness of the social distinctions that make politeness necessary, so it often occurs at socially tense moments in the story.

2.3   Evidentiality

Crews' characters' utterances often include predicates such as *believe*, *reckon*, *think*, *guess*, *have the feeling*, and so on: superordinate "evidential" predicates which indicate how the knowledge asserted or interrogated in the embedded clause was acquired or how certain it is (Chafe and Nichols 1986). For example, in (10), the evidential clause *I believe* embeds the assertion "you already said that oncet [once]." Other examples are in (11)–(13).

(10)   You already said that oncet *I believe*.
(11)   *I wouldn't want to guess*, but *I have the feeling* we'll know soon enough.
(12)   *You reckon* we ought to get help?
(13)   *I don't believe* I've ever known one.

Reckon is the most common evidential predicate in the novel in questions, *believe* or *don't believe* in assertions.

Evidentials are required in many genres of discourse, and they are not, of course, exclusively southern (although the verb *reckon* and the expression *I don't believe* with a sentential complement may be more common in traditional southern speech than elsewhere). But their frequency and their specific function in these southern characters' speech is distinctive (Johnstone 1992; Johnstone 1994). This is in part because only two of the hundreds of evidentials in the novel express the speaker's complete security in his knowledge: "*One thing's for sure*, he cain't last much longer like he is," and "Now *I know* that is right *for a dead solid fact*." Evidentials are overwhelmingly in the negative (*I don't believe*, *I don't misdoubt, I don't guess, I can't say as, I don't know as*), and/or conditional (*I wouldn't know about, I'd say*), and when they are not, the semantics of the predicates expresses insecurity (*think, believe, have the feeling, strike someone as, expect, seem, make x to be, look to be*). In other words, the evidential predicates almost always have the effect of hedging assertions and allowing respondents to hedge theirs. Characters say what they believe to be true and describe how things seem to be rather than telling what they know and how things are. Like conditionals, evidentials can leave space between speakers and the meaning of their utterances. By hedging assertions, evidentials protect speakers from the social embarrassment that would result if the assertion turned out to be false. They are also deferential. Speakers who hedge assertions avoid imposing their version of the world on others. Hedged assertions are not, literally, claims about how the world is, but only claims about how the speaker sees it.

2.4   *Reasons for southern civility*

Other strategies for the expression of deferential politeness in Crews' *Body* include speaking at a higher level of generality than might be expected if the Gricean cooperative maxims were all that mattered, as well as the frequent use of conventional formulas such as "I don't mean to pry" before requests for information and "I wish" to introduce requests for action, and the phrasing of some requests as questions. These strategies also help to mitigate possible threats to a person's need to be treated as autonomous and not imposed on. The use of question intonation in assertions, which McLemore (1991) calls "uptalk," has also been identified as southern, and particularly characteristic of the discourse style of young women (Ching 1982; McLemore 1991), although it appears to have spread rapidly in the US since these studies in Tennessee and Texas were done. Mitigating the directness of an assertion is among the functions of this feature, too.

Deferential negative politeness (as opposed to friendly expressions of "positive" solidarity) is especially important when there are potential threats to negative face – when it is especially likely that people might offend or bother one another. This means that negative politeness can be used either to avoid offense or to display the fact that offense is likely – in other words, to threaten. This is why it is possible for "If I was you, I don't know as I'd . . . " to serve, depending on the context of its utterance, either as a deferential suggestion or as a warning of potential violence. Southern politeness has in fact often been linked, in popular accounts, with the threat of violence. In a popular-press book, for example,

McKern (1979) describes southern culture as "a tradition that routinely pairs civility and violence." A nineteenth-century English woman, writing about a trip through Texas and the Gulf States, describes the use of polite address forms in confrontational discourse (McWhiney 1988: 163):

> [E]ngaged in a dispute, however violent may be the discussion, the courtesy of the "sir" is never omitted. On the contrary it is repeated at every third word, and mixed up as it is with oaths and denunciations, with which they always interlard their discourse, the effect is curious enough.

McWhiney (1988) attributes the tendency toward violence among southern male "crackers" or "rednecks" to their Celtic heritage. People often attribute a tendency to violence to people whom they perceive as different and less "civilized," however. Thus explanations such as these cannot be taken at face value. The only thing we can be sure of is that the presence of the kinds of elaborate deferential politeness we have seen indicates the need for them. The kind of Southerner whose style is characterized in the studies summarized in this section is one for whom social boundaries are significant and personal autonomy must be maintained. Deferential negative politeness provides ways of renegotiating boundaries and reclaiming autonomy in every interaction.

3   Southern verbal artistry

Southerners have often been characterized as particularly artistic with language, skilled in speechmaking, preaching, storytelling, and writing. Many of the most canonical figures in American literature are or were from the South. It would be impossible in the space of this chapter to review all the research there is about the literary style of southern authors, and studies of southern verbal artistry in non-literary contexts are sparse and do not by any means cover the territory. I will touch in this section on just two areas: oratory and storytelling.

3.1   Oratory

Ross (1989: 185–233) talks about southern oratory in the context of an exploration of the sources of William Faulkner's style. (Another study of southern oratory is Braden 1983.) According to Ross, "oratory was deeply embedded in the South's ideology, as a 'style', yes, but also as a way of establishing and enforcing relationships among people, as a way of critiquing and commemorating assumed values, as a way of gaining and maintaining power" (1989: 188). The memorization of passages from famous classical orations and the study of elocution and declamation were key elements in the education of young white southern gentlemen. Before the Civil War, oratory was the principal vehicle of political discourse (often at large picnics and "oratorical feasts"), journalism and other printed material playing a much smaller role than they did in the northern states. After the war, when the South's political power was at an ebb, public oratory became less deliberative and more ceremonial, functioning to buttress cultural values and for entertainment, as orators were more likely than before to be speaking to people who already agreed with them. Post-Civil War southern oratory was "a ritualistic, discursive performance, a celebration not only of the participants' values, but also . . . a celebration of the *language* in which those values were couched" (Ross 1989: 192). Interestingly, Ross points to a connection between oratory and violence, pointing out that southern demagogues sometimes expressed domination not only through vocal eloquence but also through gesture and were sometimes "known to carry their messages physically into the audience" (1989: 195).

Ross contrasts the "colloquial" oratorical style of the South with classical Ciceronian speech-making, which was more pre-planned and hence structurally more balanced and rounded, both on the sentence level and on the level of the speech as a whole. Southern orators needing to hold an audience's attention, sometimes for hours, had to cultivate ways of adding and improvising as they spoke. One of these, according to Ross (1989: 198–202), was amplification, a set of techniques for adding to phrases or sentences at points where they might otherwise end. This could be done by appending appositive phrases, relative clauses, and other elements, or via anaphora, the repetition of the beginning of the previous phrase as a way of starting a new, parallel one. We see a variety of amplification techniques in use in this excerpt from a speech by a Senator Morgan (1900: 5) in support of the coinage of silver. Ross discusses this passage on page 199; I have expanded the analysis somewhat, lining up examples of anaphora and underlining successive examples of appended material.

> Another leading reason why I have so earnestly favored the full and free coinage of silver is that it is gathered by the toil of man in the deep and dangerous mines;
>> it is converted into coin by the highest art of the chemist;
>> it is the gift of God, <u>who made silver and gold alone for use as money in their functions of real value</u>, and
>> it is the reward in money, not in promises to pay, of the laborer; the reward of each day's work <u>when the night shuts in</u>.
>> It is the fruit of the pick and the shovel, and it is not the product of some artful brain in a bank parlor that is busy with contrivances <u>to deceive the world</u> <u>into the belief</u>
>> <u>that his credit is better for the people than this gift from heaven, and</u>
>> <u>that his wisdom has made a back number of the omniscience of God.</u>

Another rhetorical trope used in the service of amplification is *expeditio*, or the rejection of all but the last of a set of alternatives, as in this excerpt from a speech by Benjamin H. Hill (1909–13: 176), which I have again reformatted somewhat:

> Immediately after the close of the late war a gentleman of northern birth, raising, and education, one who had been a brave and faithful soldier with

the northern army throughout the war, came to make his home in the South.
He did not come to rob us in our helpless condition.
He did not come to boast over the humiliation of our defeat.
He did not come to breed strife between the races for the purpose of office and power.
He came as a citizen, as a gentleman, as a patriot, to identify himself with us and with ours.

Amplification can also be achieved via the use of balanced compounds, pairs of synonyms or words of closely related meaning connected with *and* such as *energy and animation, idleness and wantonness*, or *evil and remorse*. (This figure of speech is sometimes called "hendiadys.") Ross points out (1989: 202) that Faulkner sometimes made creative use of this technique, using pairs of words that contrast in a surprising way, such as "tranquil and astonished" or "wild and reposed."

The style of southern oratory was sometimes not unlike that of a family of related speech genres employed in church settings. Orator Gene Talmadge of Georgia, for example (Ross 1989: 194), was described as using the "call and response" technique of revivalist preaching to draw his audience in. In the contemporary South, highly developed interactive oratorical style is associated both with the African-American church and with some fundamentalist white denominations. Titon (1988), for example, describes how the pastor and the members of a Baptist church in the Virginia Appalachians compose prayers and sermons on the spot, using various kinds of pre-formed phrases and structures, and Clements (1974) describes the rhetoric of Pentecostal radio sermons in northeast Arkansas.

4   Narrative

One of the religious speech genres Titon describes is the offering of personal "testimony" (1988: 359–407). This occurred in the church Titon studied at a set time during worship services, when the pastor invited members of the congregation to testify or "witness" about "what the Lord's done for you" (1988: 360). Such testimonials sometimes included personal reminiscences, as congregation members recounted youthful or recent events and told how they were "saved" from error through God's intervention. In her work comparing the roles of language and literacy in two working-class communities in the Piedmont Carolinas, Heath (1983) suggests that children in the white community were trained to tell personal narratives in somewhat the same way in secular contexts, too. In "Roadville," as Heath calls the white neighborhood, narratives of personal experience were meant to be "a piece of truth" with a moral. "Stories" were not to be fanciful and were to make some point about error on the part of the teller and a lesson learned. For example, a story taken up as appropriate in a conversation among a group of women is one about how a recipe failed because the cook had interrupted herself to gossip on the telephone. Its moral, expressed as the story-ending "coda"

(Labov and Waletzky 1997), is "Guess I'll learn to keep my mind on my own business and off other folks' " (Heath 1983: 152). The story is told without exaggeration, highlights a personal weakness on the part of the narrator, and ends with an
implicit warning, in this case about gossip, an activity which in this community is
publicly disfavored (though nonetheless sometimes practiced). It is, Heath points
out, like a parable, depending on analogy for its interpretation (1983: 154–5).
Children's narratives are guided by adults into this mold; making up fictional
tales about personal experience is not accepted and is referred to as lying.

In all these respects, Roadville storytelling contrasts with narrative practices
in "Trackton," the African-American community Heath studied, where highly
fanciful, entertaining stories are explicitly encouraged. "Expressive lying" is, of
course, part of the repertoire of some white Southerners as well. Bauman (1986:
11–32), for example, describes the uses of exaggeration and untruth in stories
told by white Texas dog traders at a county fair. Bauman does not focus on what,
if anything, is particularly southern about this practice, claiming instead that this
sort of storytelling is widespread in the American folk tradition. The difference
between the moralizing storytellers of Roadville and the comic liars of Canton,
Texas, has to do, at root, with differences in language ideology (Schieffelin,
Woolard and Kroskrity 1998), or people's beliefs about what language is, what it
is for, and what its roles in their lives should be. People in Roadville, according to
Heath, are literalists, believing that there is a single correct word for each object
and a single correct way of recounting each event. For them, language is not a
resource for play or humor.

The contrast between the Southerners Heath studied and those Bauman studied underlines, once again, the fact that there is not just one southern style of
discourse, because there is not just one style of Southerner or set of southern
beliefs, attitudes, and purposes. Although the South's historical reliance on the
spoken word rather than print in political and social life may have encouraged
verbal artistry in some situations, the reliance on written text (scripture) in fundamentalist religious belief may encourage literalness in other situations. The
underlying explanations for southern style have to do not with region per se
(Southerners do not use language as they do because they are Southerners), but
with particular facts about history, belief, social structure, and communicative
purpose which may vary from group to group, person to person, and situation
to situation.

5   Uses of southern style

To illustrate the variety of things "sounding southern" can consist of and accomplish, let us now turn to a set of brief case studies that illustrate some of the
variety of ways in which women from Texas orient to and use southern-sounding
speech.[1] Historically, economically, and culturally, Texas is both a southern state
and a western one. Many Anglo-Texan settlers came from the coastal or mountain
South, bringing their plantation or small-farming economy and their southern or

south midland ways of talking with them. White Texans owned slaves and fought on the side of the pro-slavery southern confederacy in the Civil War of the 1860s, and the post-Civil War history of Texas was like that of other southern states.

Anglo-Texans tend to think of themselves primarily as Texans and Americans, and as Southerners only incidentally. Southern speech is part of white Texans' sociolinguistic world, however, whether or not they identify themselves in the first instance as Southerners. People talk, sometimes out of a vaguely nostalgic wishfulness and sometimes for very specific strategic purposes, about "Texas speech," but it is obvious to most Texans that Anglo-Texans who sound stereotypically like Texans also sound like Southerners. While there are phonological features that are notably rarer (postvocalic *r*-lessness, for example) or more common (monophthongal /ai/ before voiceless obstruents) than in southern speech elsewhere (cf. Bailey 1991), the features Texans tend to think of as particularly Texan (such as the use of *y'all*) are actually pan-southern, and people who feel that they have "an accent" are aware that it sounds southern in some ways. Anglo-Texans, particularly those from the eastern part of the state, can say they are not Southerners, but many of their forebears were from the South, and, sometimes, some of them sound like Southerners. Anglo-Texans thus have to deal with southernness in a way others do not, and, for some, southernness can function as a strategic resource.

The idealized Southerner who was the focus of traditional regional dialectology – rural, non-mobile, older, with limited contact with information or people from elsewhere – is a person for whom sounding southern could not serve any strategic function, because she would have no other way of sounding. For such speakers, sounding southern would be invariable and automatic. Because sounding and acting southern would not contrast with any other way of sounding and acting, it could not be a rhetorical (or, in Gumperz's (1982) terms "metaphorical") resource.[2] Such speakers probably do not really exist, since no one is completely monostylistic, but there are certainly Texas women for whom southern style in discourse is relatively invariable and automatic.

One such speaker is Sophie Austin. She was born in the early 1920s and was seventy when she was interviewed as part of a study of Texas women's speech (Bean 1993; Johnstone 1995, 1998, 1999; Johnstone and Bean 1997). She is a retired journalist, now active in historic preservation in the small east Texas town where she lives. Miss Sophie (as she would be addressed there) thinks of herself as combining western directness with southern indirectness: "We can be direct, but [we] know how to couch [what we say] with courtesy and consideration. We took that [southern] gentility and we blended it" with ways of acting encouraged by "the expanse of Texas," "freedom," and "the outdoors." Texans are "windchesty" (they have opinions about things and "have a way of getting to the point"), she says, but, raised as "a lady," she has always felt it important to be, or to orient to expectation that she be, "retiring." McLeod-Porter (1992) describes some of the ways Miss Sophie's interactional style illustrates this blend of regionally marked ways of talking, with particular reference to her uses of indirectness, euphemism, and literary-sounding metaphor in samples of her speech and writing.

Miss Sophie's southern-sounding speech features were acquired during a childhood in a relatively homogeneous, isolated setting. It makes sense to attribute the fact that Miss Sophie sounds southern at least in part to the fact that she is from east Texas, where most people she was exposed to as a child sounded and acted southern. This is to say that there were, in her youth, relatively few other models for how to sound and act, or at least relatively few models she would have been able to adopt.[3] Furthermore, Miss Sophie's education encouraged her to adopt a style that was both expressive of gentility in a traditionally white southern way and relatively invariant. Being "ladylike," stressed especially at home, required the former. As Miss Sophie put it, "I knew that when I was with Mother, I was to be like Mother, which was quiet and dignified." She learned in school that there was one "correct" way to be, act, and speak, and that eloquence and expressiveness required consistency, encouraged invariance. Miss Sophie's education took place well before teachers and curricula began to suggest the possible acceptability of strategic adoption of various ways of talking, and Miss Sophie is very explicit about her belief that "Standard English" is the way to talk and that "slang," which is her term for any nonstandard way of speaking, is an indication of "vulgarity."

Although Miss Sophie probably sometimes sounds southern simply because it is her default way of sounding, her professional life has included situations in which she is aware that sounding like a southern lady has been strategically useful. For example, as they discussed a recent TV interview, McLeod-Porter (1992) asked her to comment on her "very quiet, low-keyed style." Miss Sophie commented, "You choose your strategies for what's ahead of you, right?" and claimed she could "act as well as anyone." A more direct, less "retiring" and less southern-sounding way of talking would be more appropriate if she were asking for money for a project, for example: "I would be very direct. I'm here to do so and so, matter of fact, business-like, right?"

The kind of speaker who is best captured in variationist sociolinguistic research is one like Tracy Rudder, a college student who was twenty years old when she was interviewed, born in the early 1970s (about fifty years after Miss Sophie). Her use of southern-sounding speech is more variable and is related to her private, "vernacular" identity rather than her public identity. She switches toward southern-sounding forms relatively unselfconsciously when the situation is right. Accommodation theory (Giles and Powesland 1975) probably accounts for her behavior well. Here she talks about sounding southern with her friends, but less in more academic contexts:

> I probably feel most natural when I'm with my friends. I mean, the ugly truth is that I'm becoming more and more educated. How is it possible to read Hemingway and turn around and talk like an inbred backwoods redneck? My friends know I'm southern – so are they, though. That's okay. I just wouldn't want them to think I was some backwoods redneck or that I'm just some big funnel that my culture and education are running through. . . . [W]e kind of keep a check on each other.

Unlike Miss Sophie, Tracy is oriented here to what is stigmatized about southern-sounding speech as well as to what may be rhetorically effective about it. "Sounding country" is clearly desirable in some contexts, for some purposes (Johnstone 1998). Some students in Texas high schools and universities adopt southern-sounding ways of talking (together with other markers of ruralness such as stylized cowboy dress, country music and dancing, and pick-up trucks) to express their allegiance to traditional "small-town" values, whether or not they actually come from small towns. But Tracy's set of attitudes about her variety (it is not an educated way of sounding, but it is appropriate with friends, who understand its uses) is also very common, and probably more typical of people of her generation than of people of Miss Sophie's. Southern speech was less known and recognized outside the South in Miss Sophie's day than it is now, due in part to large-scale migrations of Southerners to the West during the 1930s and to the North after World War II, and to the increasing visibility of Southerners in national politics and the media. Southern-sounding speech is thus probably more stigmatized now, by outsiders and Southerners alike, than it was earlier. Migration of people from elsewhere into Texas during several oil booms has created an enhanced need for an "in-group" way of talking by which people who consider themselves "real" Texans can identify themselves to and with each other. Bailey (1991) shows, for example, that certain phonological and lexical features associated with sounding like a Texan are increasing in use with the need for Texans to distinguish themselves from northern in-migrants.

Orienting to southernness somewhat differently, Janet Wilson claims not to use southern-sounding speech ("I think I've probably tried to minimize it"), not so much because she thinks it sounds uneducated as because she thinks it sounds rural. Having spent most of her life in Houston, she thinks of herself as urban and identifies southern style with the country. ("[Y]ou have to be urban, you know, and not get the accent going"). But in the course of a summer workshop in a northern state, Wilson (a middle-aged teacher and truant officer, born in the early 1950s) realizes that her southern sound "is there, no matter what." One form she uses, *y'all*, comes to index her as a Southerner, which becomes obvious to her when the Northerners hail her as "y'all." *Y'all* is "just a very *south*ern thing," Wilson says, thinking back about the experience, "that I wasn't aware of." So while her initial answer to our question "Is there some value ... in sounding like you're from Texas?" is "No," talking through the Rhode Island experience makes her realize that she likes the "familiarity" associated with that way of being seen.

Janet Wilson:	[W]hen I was in Rhode Island I realized you c- you know, it's it's there
Delma McLeod-Porter:	Umhm
JW:	no matter what.
DP:	Is there some value (when you're somewhere else) of sounding like you're from Texas?

JW:	No, I, ah, w- except, the uses of uh y'all.
DP:	Umhm
Barbara Johnstone:	What did, what did they think of that?
JW:	They got a lot of, they they thought, they couldn't believe that people actually did say that, they thought it was a television thing
((laughter))	
Judith Mattson Bean:	Oh really?
JW:	from movies and
BJ:	Umhm
JW:	So I'd walk in the room and they'd say "Hi y'all." You know, w- we talked about y'all, as a form, and I consider it, very useful, I can't understand why people in, from the North don't use it, it's very familiar, it's, and it has its place in our language.
DP:	Uh huh. Uh huh.
BJ:	Uh huh.
??:	[( )]
BJ:	[And they] tended to think that you just used it wholesale instead of you.
JW:	Yees, they didn't understand the familiarity and you know that sort of thing and and how you use it. I I I don't know, it's just a very southern thing, that I wasn't aware of, I I guess I was aware of it but it's just it still strikes me as odd that, people everywhere don't ((laughing)) use it.

In Janet Wilson's case, a nearly invariable southern feature becomes an index in a new way, coming to identify her as a Southerner and with a relaxed, practical way of using language. Wilson's use of *y'all* before her encounter with the Northerners was fairly automatic, but afterwards she could (and may) have used *y'all* as a strategic way of displaying her southernness for rhetorical and self-expressive ends, to accomplish interactional goals that sounding southern might help with and to show who she is and how she wants to be seen.

Terri King is a telephone salesperson in her twenties whose "southern drawl makes [her] $70,000 a year," in her words. In selling mailing lists over the telephone, she finds the strategy of switching into a southern-sounding way of talking and interacting to be particularly useful with men. As she puts it, "It's hilarious how these businessmen turn to gravy when they hear it. I get some of the rudest, most callous men on the phone, and I start talkin' to them in a mellow southern drawl, I slow their heart rate down and I can sell them a list in a heart-beat" (Stevens 1996: E1). King's use of southern discourse features represents a more fully stylized (Rampton 1999) use of southern-sounding speech. She draws on one specific model for southern femininity, the model of the "southern belle." The southern belle as a literary type is of course most famously represented in Margaret Mitchell's 1936 novel – and the subsequent movie – *Gone with the Wind*; a description of this female type that gets used over and over is "an iron fist in a velvet glove." As Shirley Abbott (1983) explains it, this image of the wealthy white southern lady – the plantation mistress, physically delicate but mentally tough, tenderly concerned with the well-being of the slaves and fiercely devoted to her family – served in part to make slavery appear palatable or even desirable. It is part of what Tindall (1980: 162) refers to as "the romantic plantation myth of gentility." Abbott suggests that one reason for the image's survival after the Civil War is that it involves a set of "managerial techniques" that can be effective (1983: 106). The belle acts helpless, dependent, dumb, and passive to get a man, over whom she exerts control through his weakness, by virtue of the fact that she can forgive him. Abbott herself, who is from the South, "grew up believing... that a woman might pose as garrulous and talky and silly and dotty, but at heart she was a steely, silent creature, with secrets no man could ever know, and she was always – always – stronger than any man" (1983: 3). Texas women talk about sounding like a southern belle in similar ways, claiming that it is particularly useful as part of a sexually charged manipulative strategy.

When asked to show how southern belles talk, people often adopt higher-than-usual pitch, a wider-than-usual intonation range, and exaggerated facial and hand gestures, in addition to trying to sound polite, tentative, loquacious, and cute. Monophthongal /ai/, at least in the pronouns *I* and *my*, is almost invariably part of the performance, even for speakers who find the variant difficult to produce. King claims that her "southern drawl" can be turned on and off as needed. "Turning on the southern charm" in this way is something many southern women, not just Texans, talk about doing, claim they do, and can be heard to do. It should be noted, of course, that the same speakers can make various uses of southern-sounding speech. King may well sound southern in other contexts too, for other reasons, including ones such as those discussed above.

These examples illustrate just four points on a continuum of ways in which southern discourse style can function for women in Texas, from the relatively automatic to the quite consciously strategic. Each of these women draws on somewhat different aspects of southern style in her bid to "sound southern." The resources of southernness are available to these women because of where they are from: they have heard people sounding like Southerners all their lives and can do so themselves in native-sounding ways, and, because they are in some ways members of the core group to whom southern speech "belongs" (namely, people who were born and/or grew up in the south), they can adopt southern style without its seeming parodic or "inauthentic" for them to do so. Yet their uses of southern discourse features are in some ways performances, just as are anyone else's uses of southern discourse features. Being southern and sounding southern are, for those who have access to them, resources for the "performance of self" (cf. Goffman 1959; Johnstone 1996), sometimes in general (Miss Sophie's sense of self requires her to be "ladylike," for example) and sometimes for very specific, fleeting purposes (such as selling a business service to a man who wants you to flirt, or getting a particular loan from Daddy).

6   Needed research

As the preceding overview makes clear, there is still a great deal of room for research about southern discourse styles and strategies. And it continues to be important that this work be done, because some Southerners continue to orient to language and use language differently from people elsewhere, and some people from elsewhere continue to draw on stereotyped notions of what southern speech means as they evaluate and interact with Southerners and the South. There are many aspects of discourse which have been studied in other contexts but never explicitly in connection with southern speech. For example, there are features connected with how sentences combine into paragraphs and paragraph-like spoken units, such as patterns of cohesion (Halliday and Hasan 1976). There are features connected with how people coordinate the activity of talk, such as topic introduction and topic shift (Sacks, Schegloff and Jefferson 1974), conversational repair (Jefferson 1974), or discourse marking (Schiffrin 1987). There are features connected with verbal artistry, such as the use of the formulaic comparisons that are so often caricatured in popular representations of southern speech ("lower than a snake's belly"; "slower than a crippled turtle"; "rich as cream gravy on Sunday"), as well as other kinds of figurative language. There are features connected with interactional style: when and how, for example, is the dominant mode of interaction solidarity-building "positive" politeness rather than the deferential negative politeness described above? What are southern greetings like, and how do they differ from greetings elsewhere? There are other speech events as well which may be characteristically southern and would repay study in the framework of the ethnography of communication.

Most of the studies I have drawn on in this chapter have been based on literary texts, and although these have all been chosen, in part, because they were thought to represent southern discourse well and interestingly, the sample of discourse with which discourse analysts have worked is not representative of the range of ways in which Southerners use language. It would be interesting to focus, in future research, on other sorts of examples: transcripts of conversation, for example, or non-literary prose. Doing this would be likely to draw out the range of variation in talk and writing in the South, both within and among speakers, and to highlight the contexts in which sounding southern is neutral or detrimental to the task at hand and those in which sounding southern is a useful resource. In the latter kind of situation, it would be interesting to see how people stylize southern speech: which features get highlighted as indices that a person means to sound southern, and what sounding southern can conventionally mean. I have explored some of the things it can mean to women to sound southern; what, for example, can it mean for men? When Southerners "cross" (Rampton 1995) into other ways of sounding, what can be thereby accomplished? What can it accomplish for non-Southerners to sound southern? Choices about sounding and acting southern have, for example, played a key strategic role in several recent US presidential campaigns, and country/western music relies heavily on southern imagery and on representations of southern ways of talking.

As the South becomes less and less isolated from other parts of the US and more and more similar in economy and mass culture, the topic of language change becomes interesting in new ways. Just as one can ask what happens to regional phonology in the face of dialect contact, one can wonder what happens to regional styles of interacting and speech events thought of as regional. Leveling of differences and the eventual obsolescence of non-dominant varieties is of course one possibility. But social theory suggests that one reaction to globalization may be to attempt to reorient to local identity. Cultural geographers recognize the continued persistence and importance of traditional sources of meaning such as localness (Entrikin 1991: 41). Evidence of the continued value of localism can be seen in activities that are aimed at perpetuating it, or even creating it. Localness can, for one thing, become a commodity, which gives rise to competitions over the control of what localness means or over its uses. What it means to be "here" or "from here" can, for example, be the site of arguments about how local economic development should proceed (e.g. Cox and Mair 1988), and we are all familiar with advertising that makes strategic use of nostalgia for neighborhood, local community, or region (cf. Sack 1988). Local contexts of life may still be tied to human identity in more immediate ways, too. As Stuart Hall points out (1991: 33–6), globalization is not, after all, a new phenomenon, and "the return to the local is often a response to globalization . . . It is a respect for local roots which is brought to bear against the anonymous, impersonal world of the globalized forces which we do not understand." In the South, renewed orientation to regional identity in the face of homogenizing pressures may play out linguistically in various ways. Guy Bailey (1991), in Texas and Oklahoma, and Michael Montgomery (1993b) in the Southeast, have shown, for example, that certain features can become symbols of local identity and then be preserved and even spread in the face of in-migration from elsewhere. It will be interesting to see whether, and if so how, the more global features of southern discourse which have been considered in this chapter are preserved in the face of pressures on Southerners to act more like people from elsewhere.

Notes

1. This section is adapted from Johnstone (1999), which examines strategic uses of southern discourse style in the context of theories of "language crossing" (Rampton 1995) and "styling" (Rampton 1999; Hill 1999).
2. Even a (hypothetical) monostylistic speaker of a southern-sounding variety could be taken by others to be using it strategically – to be *acting* southern rather than just *being* southern. Someone who unintentionally puts on a show simply by acting the only way

they know how to act is a potential source of humor, and southern characters often have this role in fiction and film and on television. (Forrest Gump, in the film of the same name, is one example.)

3. Miss Sophie would certainly have interacted throughout her life with many African Americans as well as with Anglo-Americans like herself. As far as pronunciation goes, southern blacks and whites of Miss Sophie's generation are difficult to distinguish (Haley 1990). But there are differences in interactional style. Due to the racism and social hierarchy of the day (and to a considerable extent of this day, too), Miss Sophie would, however, have found it inconceivable to adopt features of African-American interactional style in public contexts. Thus, while African-American speech ways were arguably more available to Miss Sophie than they are to contemporary Anglo-American teenagers like the ones studied by Cutler (1996, 1999) and Bucholtz (1997), they were less likely to become useful expressive resources for her, thus less likely to be adopted. "Contact" in the sense of mere contiguity does not necessarily imply influence, unless people have a use for the other variety they are exposed to.

References

Abbott, Shirley 1983. *Womenfolks: Growing Up Down South*, New York: Ticknor and Fields.

Abel, James W. 1951. "About the pronunciation of six freshmen from Southern University," *Southern Speech Journal* 16: 259–67.

Abercrombie, David et al. (eds.) 1964. *In Honour of Daniel Jones. Papers Contributed on the Occasion of His Eightieth Birthday 12 September 1961*, London: Longman.

Abney, Lisa 1989. "Preterites in early Southern White English," *SECOL Review* 13: 180–93.

Abrahams, Roger D. 1962. "Playing the dozens," *Journal of American Folklore* 75: 209–18. 1976. *Talking Black*. Rowley, MA: Newbury.

Aertsen, Henk and Robert J. Jeffers (eds.) 1993. *Historical Linguistics 1989: Papers from the Proceedings of the 9th International Conference on Historical Linguistics*, Amsterdam: Benjamins.

Ahlers, Jocelyn, Leela Bilmes, Joshua S. Guenter, Barbara A. Kaiser, and Ju Namkung (eds.) 1995. *Proceedings of the Twenty-first Annual Meeting of the Berkeley Linguistics Society*, Berkeley: University of California, Department of Linguistics.

Alatis, James E. (ed.) 1969. *Georgetown Monograph Series on Languages and Linguistics*, Washington, DC: Georgetown University Press.

Algeo, John 1991. "Language," in Foner and Garraty (eds.), 637–40.
  (ed.) 2001 *The Cambridge History of the English Language*, vol. 6: *English in North America*, Cambridge University Press.

Allen, Harold B. 1973–6. *The Linguistic Atlas of the Upper Midwest*, 3 vols. Minneapolis: University of Minnesota Press.

Alvarez, Louis, and Andrew Kolker 1984. *Yeah you rite!* Narrated by Billy Dell, New York: Center for New American Media, film.

The American Heritage Dictionary of the English Language, 4th. edn. 2000. Ed. Joseph P. Pickett. Boston: Houghton Mifflin.

Anshen, Frank 1969. "Speech variation among negroes in a small Southern community," New York University dissertation.

Arends, Jacques (ed.) 1995. *The Early Stages of Creolization*, Amsterdam: Benjamins.

Arnold, Jennifer, Renée Blake, Brad Davidson, Scott Schwenter, and Julie Soloman (eds.) 1996. *Sociolinguistic Variation: Data, Theory, and Analysis*, Stanford: Center for the Study of Language and Information (CSLI) Publications.

Ash, Sharon 1999. "Word list data and the measurement of sound change," paper presented at the New Ways of Analyzing Variation in Language (NWAV) Conference, Toronto.
　　2001. "The Atlas of North American English: methods and findings," in Mesthrie (ed.), 412–18.
Atherton, Lewis 1949. *The Southern Country Store 1800–1860*, Baton Rouge: Louisiana State University Press.
Atwood, E. Bagby 1953. *A Survey of Verb Forms in the Eastern United States*, Ann Arbor: University of Michigan Press.
　　1962. *The Regional Vocabulary of Texas*, Austin: University of Texas Press.
Auber-Gex, Madeline 1983. "A lexical study of the English of New Orleans Creoles based on the Malin questionnaire," University of New Orleans master's thesis.
AuCoin, Michelle 2002. "Colonial and antebellum slave settlement patterns: a demographic and linguistic study of early African American English," University of Chicago dissertation.
Axley, Lowry 1927. "'You all' and 'we all' again," *American Speech* 2: 343–5.
　　1929. "One word more on 'you all,'" *American Speech* 4: 347–51.
Ayers, Edward L. 1992. *The Promise of the New South: Life After Reconstruction*, Oxford University Press.
Babington, Mima, and E. Bagby Atwood 1961. "Lexical usage in Southern Louisiana," *Publications of the American Dialect Society* 36: 1–25.
Bailey, Beryl Loftman 1965. "Toward a new perspective in Negro American dialectology," *American Speech* 40: 171–7.
　　1966. *Jamaican Creole Syntax: A Transformational Approach*, Cambridge University Press.
Bailey, Charles-James N. 1996. *Essays on Time Based Linguistic Analyses*, Oxford: Clarendon.
Bailey, Guy 1987. "Are Black and White vernaculars diverging?," papers from the NWAV–XIV panel discussion, *American Speech* 62: 32–40.
　　1989. "Linguistic Atlas of the Gulf States project," in Wilson and Ferris (eds.), 788.
　　1991. "Directions of change in Texas English," *Journal of American Culture* 14: 125–34.
　　1993. "A perspective on African-American English," in Preston (ed.), 287–318.
　　1997a. "Southern American English: a prospective," in Bernstein, Nunnally, and Sabino (eds.), 21–31.
　　1997b. "When did Southern American English begin?," in Schneider (ed.), 255–75.
　　2001. "The relationship between AAVE and White vernaculars in the American South: a sociocultural history and some phonological evidence," in Lanehart (ed.), 53–92.
Bailey, Guy and Marvin Bassett 1986. "Invariant *be* in the Lower South," in Montgomery and Bailey (eds.), 158–79.
Bailey, Guy, and Cynthia Bernstein 1989. "Methodology for a phonological survey of Texas," *Journal of English Linguistics* 22: 6–16.
Bailey, Guy and Patricia Cukor-Avila forthcoming. *The Development of African American Vernacular English: The Evolution of a Grammar*, Cambridge University Press.
Bailey, Guy and Natalie Maynor 1985. "The present tense of *be* in white folk speech of the Southern United States," *English World-Wide* 6.2: 199–216.
　　1987. "Decreolization?," *Language in Society* 16: 449–73.

1989. "The divergence controversy," *American Speech* 64: 12–39.

Bailey, Guy, Natalie Maynor, and Patricia Cukor-Avila 1989. "Variation in subject–verb concord in Early Modern English," *Language Variation and Change* 1: 285–301.

Bailey, Guy, Natalie Maynor and Patricia Cukor-Avila (eds.), 1991. *The Emergence of Black English: Text and Commentary*, Amsterdam: Benjamins.

Bailey, Guy and Garry Ross 1988. "The shape of the superstrate: morphosyntactic features of ship English," *English World-Wide* 9.2: 193–212.

Bailey, Guy and Clyde Smith 1992. "Southern English in Brazil, no?," *SECOL Review* 16: 71–89.

Bailey, Guy and Erik R. Thomas 1998. "Some aspects of African-American vernacular English phonology," in Mufwene, Rickford, Bailey, and Baugh (eds.), 85–109.

Bailey, Guy, and Jan Tillery 1999. "The Rutledge effect: the impact of interviewers on survey results in linguistics," *American Speech* 74: 389–402.

Bailey, Guy, Tom Wikle, Jan Tillery and Lori Sand 1991. "The apparent time construct," *Language Variation and Change* 3: 241–64.

1993. "Some Patterns of Linguistic Diffusion," *Language Variation and Change* 5: 359–90.

1996. "The linguistic consequences of catastrophic events: an example from the American Southwest," in Arnold, Blake, Davidson, Schwenter, and Soloman (eds.), 435–51.

Bailey, Richard W. 1992. "New Orleans," in McArthur (ed.), 690.

Bailyn, Bernard 1986a. *The Peopling of British North America: An Introduction*, New York: Random House.

1986b. *Voyagers to the West: A Passage in the Peopling of America on the Eve of the Revolution*, New York: Knopf.

Baker, Philip and Adrienne Bruyn (eds.) 1998. *St. Kitts and the Atlantic Creoles: The Texts of Samuel Augustus Matthews in Perspective*, London: University of Westminster Press.

Baranowski, Maciej 2000. "Changes in the vowel system of Charleston, S.C.," University of Pennsylvania master's thesis.

Barber, Charles 1976. *Early Modern English*, London: André Deutsch.

Baugh, John 1980. "A re-examination of the black English copula," in Labov (ed.), 83–106.

1983. *Black Street Speech*, Austin: University of Texas Press.

Bauman, Richard 1986. *Story, Performance, and Event: Contextual Studies of Oral Narrative*, Cambridge University Press.

Bean, Judith Mattson 1991. "The evolution of inchoatives: *go to* and *get to*," *SECOL Review* 15: 69–86.

1993. "True grit and all the rest: expression of regional and individual identities in Molly Ivins' discourse," *Journal of Southwestern American Literature* 19: 35–46.

Bereiter, Carl and Siegfried Engelmann 1966. *Teaching Disadvantaged Children in the Pre-School*, New Jersey: Prentice Hall.

Berlin, Ira 1998. *Many Thousands Gone: The First Two Centuries of Slavery in North America*, Cambridge, MA: Harvard University Press.

Bernstein, Cynthia 1993. "Measuring social causes of phonological variation in Texas," *American Speech* 68: 227–40.

2000. "Misrepresenting the American South," *American Speech* 75: 339–44.

(ed.) 1994. *The Text and Beyond: Essays in Literary Linguistics*, Tuscaloosa: University of Alabama Press.

Bernstein, Cynthia, Thomas Nunnally, and Robin Sabino (eds.) 1997. *Language Variety in the South Revisited*, Tuscaloosa: University of Alabama Press.

Blake, Norman (ed.) 1992. *The Cambridge History of the English Language*, vol. 2: *1066–1476*, Cambridge University Press.

Blanton, Mackie 1989. " New Orleans English," in Wilson and Ferris (eds.), 780–1.

Bodnar, John 1991. "Immigration," in Foner and Garraty (eds.), 533–8.

Boertien, Harmon S. 1986. "Constituent structure of double modals," in Montgomery and Bailey (eds.), 294–318.

Boorstin, Daniel J. 1958. *The Americans: The Colonial Experience*, New York: Random House.

Braden, Waldo W. 1983. *The Oral Tradition in the South*, Baton Rouge: Louisiana State University Press.

Brasch, Ila Wales and Walter Milton Brasch 1974. *A Comprehensive Annotated Bibliography of American Black English*, Baton Rouge: Louisiana State University Press.

Brasch, Walter Milton 1981. *Black English and the Mass Media*, New York: University Press of America.

Brewer, Jeutonne P. 1986. "Durative marker or hypercorrection? The case of -*s* in the WPA ex-slave narratives," in Montgomery and Bailey (eds.), 131–48.

Britain, David 2002. "Diffusion, leveling, simplification, and reallocation in past tense BE in the English Fens," *Journal of Sociolinguistics* 6: 16–43.

Britton, Derek (ed.) 1996. *English Historical Linguistics 1994: Papers from the 8th International Conference on English Historical Linguistics*, Amsterdam: Benjamins.

Brooks, Cleanth 1985. *The Language of the American South*, Athens: University of Georgia Press.

Bronstein, Arthur (ed.) 1998. *Conference Papers on American English and the International Phonetic Alphabet*, Publication of the American Dialect Society 80, Tuscaloosa: University of Alabama Press.

Brown, Penelope and Stephen C. Levinson 1987. *Politeness: Some Universals in Language Usage*, Cambridge University Press.

Brown, Vivian 1991. "Evolution of the merger of /ɛ/ and /ɪ/ before nasals in Tennessee," *American Speech* 66: 303–15.

Bucholtz, Mary 1997. "Borrowed blackness: African American Vernacular English and European American youth identities," University of California at Berkeley dissertation.

Burkett, Eva M. 1978. *American English Dialects in Literature*, Metuchen, NJ: Scarecrow.

Burling, Robbins 1973. *English in Black and White*, New York: Holt, Rinehart, and Winston.

Butters, Ronald R. 1989. *The Death of Black English: Divergence and Convergence in Black and White Vernaculars*, Frankfurt: Lang.

2001. "Grammatical structure," in Algeo (ed.), 325–39.

Butters, Ronald R., and S. Campbell Aycock 1987. "More on singular *y'all*," *American Speech* 62: 191–2.

Carver, Craig M. 1987. *American Regional Dialects: A Word Geography*, Ann Arbor: University of Michigan Press.

Cassidy, Frederic G. 1961. *Jamaica Talk*, London: Macmillan.

1980. "The place of Gullah," *American Speech* 55: 3–16.

1986. "Barbadian creole: possibility and probability," *American Speech* 61: 195–205.

(ed.) 1985. *Dictionary of American Regional English*, vol. 1, Cambridge, MA: Belknap Press of Harvard University Press.

Cassidy, Frederic G. and Joan Houston Hall 2001. "Americanisms," in Algeo (ed.), 184–218.

(eds.) 1991, 1996. *Dictionary of American Regional English*, vols. 2 and 3, Cambridge, MA: Belknap Press of Harvard University Press.

Chafe, Wallace, and Johanna Nichols 1986. *Evidentiality: The Linguistic Coding of Epistemology*, Norwood, NJ: Ablex.

Chambers, J. K., Peter Trudgill and Natalie Schilling-Estes (eds.) 2001. *Handbook of Variation and Change*, Malden, MA, and Oxford: Blackwell.

Charity Commissioners' Report. 1837. London. (no author listed)

Chaudenson, Robert 1992. *Des Îles, des Hommes, des Langues: Essais sur la Créolisation Linguistique et Culturelle*, Paris: L'Harmattan.

Cheramie, Deany-Marie 1998. "Cajun vernacular English and the influence of vernacular in student writing in south Louisiana," University of Southwestern Louisiana dissertation.

Cheshire, Jenny 1982. *Variation in an English Dialect*, Cambridge University Press.

(ed.) 1991. *English around the World: Sociolinguistic Perspectives*, Cambridge University Press.

Ching, Marvin K. L. 1982. "The question intonation in assertions," *American Speech* 57: 95–107.

1987. "How fixed is *fixin' to?*," *American Speech* 62: 332–45.

1988. "*Ma'am* and *sir:* modes of mitigation and politeness in the Southern U.S.," in Thomas (ed.), 20–45.

Christian, Donna, Walt Wolfram, and Nanjo Dube 1989. *Variation and Change in Geographically Isolated Communities: Appalachian English and Ozark English*, Publication of the American Dialect Society 74, Tuscaloosa: University of Alabama Press.

Christie, Pauline 1991. "Modality in Jamaican Creole," in Edwards and Winford (eds.), 223–39.

Chtareva, Anguelina 1999. "The use of double modals in Memphis, TN," unpublished manuscript.

Clark, Thomas D. 1944. *Pills, Petticoats, and Plows: The Southern Country Store*, New York: Bobbs-Merril.

Clarke, Sandra 1997a. "English verbal -*s* revisited: the evidence from Newfoundland," *American Speech* 72: 227–59.

1997b. "On establishing historical relationships between New and Old World varieties: habitual aspect and Newfoundland vernacular English," in Schneider (ed.), 277–93.

Clements, W. M. 1974. "The rhetoric of the radio ministry," *Journal of American Folklore* 87: 318–27.

Cobb, James C. 1999. *Redefining Southern Culture: Mind and Identity in the Modern South*, Athens: University of Georgia Press.

Cole, Johnetta B. (ed.) 1988. *Anthropology for the Nineties: Introductory Readings*, London: Collier Macmillan.

Coleman, Kenneth 1978. *Georgia History in Outline*, revised edn., Athens: University of Georgia Press.

Coles, Felice A. 1997. "Solidarity cues in New Orleans English," in Bernstein, Nunnally, and Sabino (eds.), 219–24.

Corcoran, Chris and Salikoko S. Mufwene 1998. "Sam Matthews' Kittitian: what is it evidence of?," in Baker and Bruyn (eds.), 75–102.

Cox, Kevin R. and Andrew Mair 1988. "Locality and community in the politics of local economic development," *Annals of the Association of American Geographers* 78: 307–25.

Crews, Harry 1978. *A Childhood: The Biography of a Place*, New York: Harper and Row.
    1990. *Body*, New York: Poseidon.

Cukor-Avila, Patricia 1990. "Narrative -s in rural BEV," paper presented at the New Ways of Analyzing Variation (NWAV) Conference, Philadelphia, PA.
    1995. "The evolution of AAVE in a rural Texas community: an ethnolinguistic study," University of Michigan dissertation.
    1997a. "An ethnolinguistic approach to the study of rural Southern AAVE," in Bernstein, Nunnally, and Sabino (eds.) 447–62.
    1997b. "Change and stability in the use of verbal -s over time in AAVE," in Schneider (ed.), 295–306.
    1999. "Stativity and copula absence in AAVE: grammatical constraints at the sub-categorical level," *Journal of English Linguistics* 27: 341–55.
    2001. "Co-existing grammars: the relationship between the evolution of African American vernacular English and White vernacular English in the South," in Lanehart (ed.), 93–127.
    2002. "'She *say*', 'she *go*', 'she *be like*': verbs of quotation over time in African American Vernacular English," *American Speech* 77: 3–31.

Cukor-Avila, Patricia and Guy Bailey 1995a. "An approach to sociolinguistic fieldwork: a site study of rural AAVE in a Texas community," *English World-Wide* 16: 159–93.
    1995b. "Grammaticalization in AAVE," in Ahlers, Bilmes, Guenter, Kaiser, and Namkung (eds.), 401–13.
    1996. "The spread of urban AAVE: a case study," in Arnold, Blake, Davidson, Schwenter, and Solomon (eds.), 469–85.

Cunningham, Irma Aloyce Ewing 1970. "A syntactic analysis of Sea Island Creole ('Gullah')," University of Michigan dissertation.
    1992. *A Syntactic Analysis of Sea Island Creole*, Publication of the American Dialect Society 75, Tuscaloosa: University of Alabama Press.

Cutler, Cecelia A. 1996. "Yorktown crossing: a case study of the influence of hip hop culture on the speech of a white middle class teenager in New York City," New York University master's thesis.
    1999. "Yorkville crossing: white teens, hip hop, and African American English," *Journal of Sociolinguistics* 3: 428–42.

Dalton-Puffer, Christiane and Nikolaus Ritt (eds.) 2000. *Words: Structure, Meaning, Function: A Festschrift for Dieter Kastovsky*, Berlin: Mouton de Gruyter.

Dannenberg, Clare 1999. "Sociolinguistic constructs of identity: the syntactic delineation of Lumbee English," University of North Carolina at Chapel Hill dissertation.

DARE. Dictionary of American Regional English. 1985–. Vol. 1 (A–C), ed. Frederic G. Cassidy. Vols. 2 (D–H) and 3 (I–O), ed. Frederic G. Cassidy and Joan Houston Hall. 3 vols. to date, Cambridge, MA: Belknap Press of Harvard University Press.

Davies, Catherine 1997. "Social meaning in southern speech from an interactional sociolinguistic perspective: an integrative discourse analysis of terms of address," in Bernstein, Nunnally, and Sabino (eds.), 225–41.

Davis, Lawrence M. 1983. *English Dialectology: An Introduction*, Tuscaloosa: University of Alabama Press.
  (ed.) 1972. *Studies in Linguistics in Honor of Raven I. McDavid, Jr.*, Tuscaloosa: University of Alabama Press.
Dayton, Elizabeth 1996. "Grammatical categories of the verb in African-American Vernacular English," University of Pennsylvania dissertation.
D'Costa, Jean and Barbara Lalla (eds.) 1989.*Voices in Exile. Jamaican Texts of the 18th and 19th Centuries*, Tuscaloosa: University of Alabama Press.
DeCamp, David and Ian F. Hancock (eds.) 1974. *Pidgin and Creole Linguistics: Current Trends and Prospects*, Washington, DC: Georgetown University Press.
Deutsch, Martin, Irwin Katz, and Arthur Jensen (eds.) 1968. *Social Class, Race, and Psychological Development*, New York: Holt, Rinehart and Winston.
A Dictionary of the Queen's English. n.d. Raleigh, NC: Travel and Tourism Division, Department of Commerce.
Dillard, J. L. 1972. *Black English: Its History and Usage in the United States*, New York: Random House.
  1975. *All-American English: A History of the English Language in America*, New York: Random House.
  1992. *A History of American English*, London: Longman.
Di Martino, Gabriella and Maria Lima (eds.) 2000. *English Diachronic Pragmatics*, Naples: Cuen, 79–102.
Di Paolo, Marianna 1989. "Double modals as single lexical items," *American Speech* 64: 195–224.
Dorrill, George T. 1986. "A comparison of stressed vowels of black and white speakers in the South," in Montgomery and Bailey (eds.), 149–57.
  1989. "Linguistic Atlas of the Middle and South Atlantic States," in Wilson and Ferris (eds.), 788–9.
Douglas, Connie Woodruff 1969. "A linguistic study of the English used by New Orleans speakers of Creole," University of New Orleans master's thesis.
Dubois, Sylvie and Barbara Horvath 1998a. "Let's tink about dat: interdental fricatives in Cajun English," *Language Variation and Change* 10: 245–61.
  1998b. "From accent to marker in Cajun English: a study of dialect formation in progress," *English World-Wide* 19: 161–88.
  2000. "When the music changes, you change too: gender and language change in Cajun English," *Language Variation and Change* 11: 287–313.
Dubois, Sylvie and Megan Melançon 1997. "Cajun is dead – long live Cajun: shifting from a linguistic to a cultural community," *Journal of Sociolinguistics* 1: 63–93.
  2000. "Creole is, creole ain't: diachronic and synchronic attitudes toward creole identity in southern Louisiana," *Language in Society* 29: 237–58.
Dunlap, Howard G. 1974. *Social Aspects of a Verb Form: Native Atlanta Fifth-Grade Speech – The Present Tense of Be*, Publication of the American Dialect Society 61, 62. Tuscaloosa: University of Alabama Press.
Eaton, Roger, Olga Fischer, Willem Koopman, and Frederike van der Leek (eds.) 1985. *Papers from the 4th International Conference on English Historical Linguistics*, Current Issues in Linguistic Theory 41, Amsterdam: Benjamins.
Eble, Connie 1993a. "Prolegomenon to the study of Cajun English," *SECOL Review* 17: 165–77.

1993b. "Review of *Cajun Vernacular English: Informal English in French Louisiana*, Ann Martin Scott, ed. *Louisiana English Journal*, special issue 1992," *SECOL Review* 17: 180–2.

Eckert, Penelope (ed.) 1991. *New Ways of Analyzing Sound Change*, New York: Academic.

Edwards, Walter F. and Donald Winford (eds.) 1991. *Verb Phrase Patterns in Black English and Creole*, Detroit: Wayne State University Press.

Eliason, Norman E. 1956. *Tarheel Talk: An Historical Study of the English Language in North Carolina to 1860*, Chapel Hill: University of North Carolina Press.

Elliott, Colleen Morse and Louise Armstrong Moxley 1985. *The Tennessee Civil War Veterans Questionnaires*, Easley, SC: Southern Historical Press.

Ellis, Michael 1994. "Literary dialect as linguistic evidence: subject–verb concord in nineteenth-century southern literature," *American Speech* 69: 128–44.

Ellis, Stanley (ed.) 1968. *Studies in Honour of Harold Orton on the Occasion of his Seventieth Birthday*, University of Leeds, School of English.

Entrikin, J. Nicholas 1991. *The Betweenness of Place: Towards a Geography of Modernity*, Baltimore: Johns Hopkins University Press.

Erikson, Frederick 1984. "Rhetoric, anecdote, and rhapsody: coherence strategies in a conversation among Black American adolescents," in Tannen (ed.), 81–154.

Etter-Lewis, Gwendolyn 1993. *My Soul Is My Own: Oral Narratives of African American Women in the Professions*, London: Routledge.

Fasold, Ralph W. 1972. *Tense Marking in Black English: A Linguistic and Social Analysis*, Washington, DC: Center for Applied Linguistics.

1981. "The relationship between black and white speech in the South," *American Speech* 56: 163–89; reprinted in Michael D. Linn (ed) 1998. *Handbook of Dialects and Language Variation*, San Diego: Academic, 475–500.

Fasold, Ralph W. and Roger W. Shuy (eds.) 1975. *Analyzing Variation in Language*, Washington, DC: Georgetown University Press.

Feagin, Crawford 1979. *Variation and Change in Alabama English: A Sociolinguistic Study of the White Community*, Washington, DC: Georgetown University Press.

1986. "More evidence for major vowel change in the South," in Sankoff (ed.), 83–95.

1996. "Peaks and glides in Southern States short-a: towards a social science of language," in Guy, Feagin, Schiffrin, and Baugh (eds.), 135–60.

1997. "The African contribution to southern states English," in Bernstein, Nunnally, and Sabino (eds.), 123–39.

1998. "Representing Southern States English: pitfalls and solutions," in Bronstein (ed.), 78–95.

Fennell, Barbara A. and Ronald R. Butters 1996. "Historical and contemporary distribution of double modals in English," in Schneider (ed.), 265–88.

Fetscher, Margaret Elisabeth 1971. "The speech of Atlanta school children: a phonological study," University of Georgia dissertation.

Filppula, Markku 1999. "Plural verbal -s in Southern Hiberno-English," paper presented at the Tenth International Conference on Methods in Dialectology, St. Johns, Newfoundland.

Fischer, David Hackett 1989. *Albion's Seed: Four British Folkways in America*, Oxford University Press.

Fischer, Olga 1992. "Syntax," in Blake (ed.), 207–408.

Fisiak, Jacek (ed.) 1995. *Linguistic Change Under Contact Conditions*, Berlin: Mouton de Gruyter.

Foner, Eric and John A. Garraty (eds.) 1991. *The Reader's Companion to American History*, Boston: Houghton Mifflin.

Fought, Carmen (ed.) forthcoming. *Identities and Place: Sociolinguistic Approaches*, Oxford University Press.

Fridland, Valerie 1998. "The Southern vowel shift: linguistic and social factors," Michigan State University dissertation.

1999. "The Southern shift in Memphis, Tennessee," *Language Variation and Change* 11: 267–85.

2001. "The social dimension of the Southern vowel shift: gender, age and class," *Journal of Sociolinguistics* 5: 233–53.

in progress. "Social and perceptual dimensions of the Southern vowel shift," National Science Foundation grant # BCS 0001725.

Gantt, Amy 2000. "The sociolinguistic significance of peripheral island communities: the case of Crusoe Island, North Carolina," North Carolina State University master's thesis.

Garber, Aubrey 1976. *Mountain-ese: Basic Grammar for Appalachia*, Radford, VA: Commonwealth.

George, Donald 1952. "Graduate study and research in linguistic geography: some Louisiana isoglosses," *The Southern Speech Journal* 18: 87–95.

Gerritsen, Marinel and Dieter Stein (eds.) 1992. *Internal and External Factors in Syntactic Change*, Berlin: Mouton de Gruyter.

Giles, Howard, and Peter F. Powesland 1975. *Speech Style and Social Evaluation*, London: Academic.

Goffman, Erving 1959. *The Presentation of Self in Everyday Life*, Garden City, NY: Doubleday Anchor Books.

1967. *Interaction Ritual: Essays in Face-to-Face Behavior*, Chicago: Aldine.

Gordon, Elizabeth 1998. "The origins of New Zealand speech: the limits of recovering historical information from written records," *English World-Wide* 19: 61–85.

Gordon, Elizabeth and Peter Trudgill 1999. "Shades of things to come: embryonic variants in New Zealand English sound changes," *English World-Wide* 20: 111–24.

Graves, Richard Layton 1967. "Language differences among upper- and lower-class Negro and white eighth graders in East Central Alabama," Florida State University dissertation.

Gumperz, John J. 1982. *Discourse Strategies*, Cambridge University Press.

Gumperz, John J. and Dell Hymes (eds.) 1972. *Directions in Sociolinguistics: The Ethnography of Communication*, New York: Holt, Rinehart and Winston.

Guy, Gregory, Crawford Feagin, Deborah Schiffrin, and John Baugh (eds.) 1996. *Variation and Change in Language and Society*, Amsterdam: Benjamins.

Haley, Kenneth 1990. "Some complexities in speech identification," *SECOL Review* 14: 101–13.

Hall, Joan H., Nick Doane, and Dick Ringer (eds.) 1992. *Old English and New*, New York: Garland.

Hall, Stuart 1991. "The local and the global: globalization and ethnicity," in King (ed.), 19–39.

Halliday, M. A. K., and Ruqaiya Hasan 1976. *Cohesion in English*, London: Longman.

Hancock, Ian 1986. "On the classification of Afro-Seminole Creole," in Montgomery and Bailey (eds.), 85–101.

Hardcastle, Valerie Gray (ed.) 2000. *Where Biology Meets Psychology: Philosophical Essays*, Cambridge, MA: MIT Press.

Hawkins, Opal 1982. "Southern linguistic variation as revealed through overseers' letters, 1829–1858," University of North Carolina dissertation.

Hazen, Kirk 2000. *Identity and Ethnicity in the Rural South: A Sociolinguistic View Through Past and Present* be, Publication of the American Dialect Society 83, Tuscaloosa: University of Alabama Press.

Heath, Shirley Brice 1983. *Ways with Words: Language, Life, and Work in Communities and Classrooms*, Cambridge University Press.

Hempl, George 1896. "Grease and greasy," *Dialect Notes* 1: 438–44.

Hendrickson, Robert 1986. *American Talk*, New York: Viking.

1993. *Whistlin' Dixie: A Dictionary of Southern Expressions*, New York: Facts on File.

Herman, Lewis Helmar 1947. *Manual of American Dialects*, Chicago: Ziff-Davis.

Hickey, Raymond (ed.) forthcoming. *Transported Dialects: The Legacy of Non-Standard Colonial English*, Cambridge University Press.

Hill, Benjamin H. 1909–13. "The stars and stripes," in Watson (ed.), 176–80.

Hill, Jane H. 1999. "Styling locally, styling globally: what does it mean?," *Journal of Sociolinguistics* 3.4: 542–56.

Holloway, Charles E. 1997. *Dialect Death: The Case of Brule Spanish*, Amsterdam: Benjamins.

Holm, John 1984. "Variability of the copula in Black English and its creole kin," *American Speech* 59: 291–309.

1991. "The Atlantic Creoles and the language of the ex-slave recordings," in Bailey, Maynor and Cukor-Avila (eds.), 231–48.

Holm, John A. with Alison W. Shilling 1982. *Dictionary of Bahamian English*, Cold Spring, NY: Lexik House.

Holt, Grace Sims 1972. "'Inversion' in Black communication," in Kochman (ed.), 152–9.

Hopper, Paul J. and Elizabeth Closs Traugott 1993. *Grammaticalization*, Cambridge University Press.

Houston, Susan 1969. "A sociolinguistic consideration of the Black English of children in Northern Florida," *Language* 45: 599–607.

1970. "Competence and performance in child Black English," *Language Sciences* 12: 9–14.

1972. "Child Black English: the school register," *Linguistics* 90: 20–34.

An Index by Region, Usage, and Etymology to the Dictionary of American Regional English, vols. 1 and 2, 1993. Publication of the American Dialect Society 77, Tuscaloosa: University of Alabama Press.

Ives, Sumner 1971. "A theory of literary dialect," in Williamson and Burke (eds.), 145–77.

Jahr, Ernst Håkon (ed.) 1998. *Language Change Advances in Historical Sociolinguistics*, Berlin: Mouton de Gruyter.

Jefferson, Gail 1974. "Error correction as an interactional resource," *Language in Society* 3: 181–99.

Jensen, Arthur 1969. "How much can we boost IQ and scholastic achievement?," *Harvard Educational Review*, no. 39.

Johnson, Ellen 1996. *Lexical Change and Variation in the Southeastern United States*, Tuscaloosa: University of Alabama Press.

Johnson, Guy 1930. *Folk Culture on St. Helena Island, South Carolina*, Chapel Hill: University of North Carolina Press.

Johnstone, Barbara 1990a. *Stories, Community, and Place: Narratives from Middle America*, Bloomington: Indiana University Press.

  1990b. "Variation in discourse: Midwestern narrative style," *American Speech* 63: 195–214.

  1992. "Violence and civility in discourse: uses of mitigation by rural southern white men," *SECOL Review* 16: 1–19.

  1994. "'You gone have to learn to talk right': linguistic deference and regional dialect in Harry Crews's *Body*," in Bernstein (ed.), 278–95.

  1995. "Sociolinguistic resources, individual identities and the public speech styles of Texas women," *Journal of Linguistic Anthropology* 5: 1–20.

  1996. *The Linguistic Individual: Self-Expression in Language and Linguistics*, Oxford University Press.

  1998. "'Sounding country' in urbanizing Texas: private speech in public discourse," *Michigan Discussions in Anthropology* 13: 153–64.

  1999. "Uses of Southern speech by contemporary Texas women," *Journal of Sociolinguistics*, special issue: *Styling the Other*, ed. Ben Rampton, 3: 505–22.

  2000. "Representing American speech," *American Speech* 75: 390–2.

  forthcoming. "Place, globalization, and linguistic variation," in Fought (ed.).

Johnstone, Barbara and Judith Mattson Bean 1997. "Self-expression and linguistic variation," *Language in Society* 26: 221–46.

Jones-Jackson, Patricia 1983. "Some persistent linguistic features of contemporary Gullah," *Journal of Black Studies* 13: 289–303.

  1986. "On the status of Gullah on the Sea Islands," in Montgomery and Bailey (eds.), 63–72.

Joyner, Charles 1984. *Down by the Riverside: A South Carolina Slave Community*, Chicago: University of Illinois Press.

Kallen, Jeffrey L. 1989. "Tense and aspect categories in Irish English," *English World-Wide* 10: 1–39.

Kautzsch, Alexander 2002. *The Historical Evolution of Earlier African American English: An Empirical Comparison of Early Sources*, Berlin: Mouton de Gruyter.

Kerswill, Paul 1994. *Dialects Converging: Rural Speech in Urban Norway*, Oxford: Clarendon Press.

Kerswill, Paul and Ann Williams 2000. "Creating a new town koine: children and language in Milton Keynes," *Language in Society* 29: 65–115.

King, Anthony D. (ed.) 1991. *Culture, Globalization, and the World-System*, Basingstoke, UK: MacMillan.

Klemola, Juhani, Merja Kytö, and Matti Rissanen (eds.) 1996. *Speech Past and Present: Studies in English Dialectology in Memory of Ossi Ihalainen*, Frankfurt: Lang.

Klingler, Tom 1997. "Colonial society and the development of Louisiana Creole," in Bernstein, Nunnally, and Sabino (eds.), 140–51.

Kochman, Thomas 1981. *Black and White Styles in Conflict*, University of Chicago Press.

  (ed.) 1972. *Rappin' and Stylin' Out*, Urbana: University of Illinois Press.

Krapp, George Philip 1924. "The English of the Negro," *The American Mercury* 2: 190–5.

Kretzschmar, William 1996. "Quantitative areal analysis of dialect features," *Language Variation and Change* 8: 13–39.

Kretzschmar, William A., Virginia G. McDavid, Theodore K. Lerud and Ellen Johnson 1994. *Handbook of the Linguistic Atlas of the Middle and South Atlantic States*, University of Chicago Press.

Krueger, Misty 2001. "The progress of perfective *done* in the American South," paper presented at the Southeastern Conference on Linguistics (SECOL), Knoxville, TN.

Kulikoff, Allan 1986. *Tobacco and Slaves: The Development of Southern Cultures in the Chesapeake, 1680–1800*, Chapel Hill: University of North Carolina Press.

1991. "Colonial economy," in Foner and Garraty (eds.), 201–3.

Kurath, Hans 1928. "The origin of the dialectal differences in spoken American English," *Modern Philology* 25: 385–95.

1949. *A Word Geography of the Eastern United States*, Ann Arbor: University of Michigan Press.

1964. "British sources of selected features of American pronunciation: problems and methods," in Abercrombie et al. (eds.), 146–55.

1968. "Contributions of British folk speech to American pronunciation," in Ellis (ed.), 129–34.

1970. "English sources of some American regional words and verb forms," *American Speech* 45: 60–8.

1972. "Relics of English folk speech in American English," in Davis (ed.), 367–75.

Kurath, Hans, et al. 1939–43. *The Linguistic Atlas of New England*, Providence: Brown University.

Kurath, Hans and Raven I. McDavid, Jr. 1961. *The Pronunciation of English in the Atlantic States*, Ann Arbor: University of Michigan Press.

Kytö, Merja 1993. "Third-person present singular verb inflection in Early British and American English," *Language Variation and Change* 5: 113–39.

Labov, William 1963. "The social motivation of a sound change," *Word* 19: 273–309.

1966. *The Social Stratification of English in New York City*, Washington, DC: Center for Applied Linguistics.

1969. "The logic of non-standard English," in Alatis (ed.), 1–44.

1972a. *Language in the Inner City: Studies in the Black English Vernacular*, Philadelphia: University of Pennsylvania Press.

1972b. *Sociolinguistic Patterns*, Philadelphia: University of Pennsylvania Press.

1982. "Objectivity and commitment in linguistic science: the case of the black English trial in Ann Arbor," *Language in Society* 11: 165–202.

1986. "Sources of inherent variation in the speech process," in Perkell and Klatt (eds.), 402–25.

1987. "Are Black and White vernaculars diverging?," papers from the NWAV–XIV panel discussion, *American Speech* 62: 5–12.

1991. "The three dialects of English," in Eckert (ed.), 1–44.

1994. *Principles of Linguistic Change*, vol. 1: *Internal Factors*, Oxford: Blackwell.

1998. "Co-existent systems in AAVE," in Mufwene, Rickford, Bailey, and Baugh (eds.), 110–53.

2001. *Principles of Linguistic Change*, vol. 2: *Social Factors*, Oxford: Blackwell.

(ed.) 1980. *Locating Language in Time and Space*, New York: Academic.

Labov, William and Sharon Ash 1997. "Understanding Birmingham," in Bernstein, Nunnally, and Sabino (eds.), 508–73.

Labov, William, Sharon Ash, and Charles Boberg 1999. "The first continental map of North American phonology," poster presented at the New Ways of Analyzing Variation in Language (NWAV) Conference, Toronto.
    forthcoming. *Atlas of North American English*, Berlin: Mouton de Gruyter.

Labov, William, Paul Cohen, Clarence Robins, and John Lewis 1968. *A Study of the Non-Standard English of Negro and Puerto Rican Speakers in New York City*, Cooperative Research Project #3288. Washington: Office of Education, Department of Health, Education, and Welfare.

Labov, William and Wendall A. Harris 1986. "Defacto segregration of Black and White vernaculars," in Sankoff (ed.), 1–24.

Labov, William, and Joshua Waletzky 1997. "Narrative analysis: oral versions of personal experience," *Journal of Narrative Life and History*, special issue: *Oral Versions of Personal Experience: Three Decades of Narrative Analysis*, Guest Editor, Michael G. W. Bamberg, 7: 3–38.

Labov, William, Malcah Yaeger, Richard Steiner 1972. *A Quantitative Study of Sound Change in Progress*, Philadelphia: US Regional Survey.

LAGS. *Linguistic Atlas of the Gulf States* 1986–92. Lee Pederson (ed.) 7 vols. Athens: University of Georgia Press.

Lambert, K. Sage 1995. "The r-ful truth of the matter: an analysis of the constriction of /r/ in Mississippi and Louisiana," University of Memphis master's thesis.

Lanehart, Sonja (ed.) 2001. *Historical and Sociocultural Contexts of African American Vernacular English*, Amsterdam: Benjamins.

Larson, Susan 1999. *The Booklover's Guide to New Orleans*, Baton Rouge: Louisiana State University Press.

Lass, Roger 1990. "How to do things with junk: exaptation in language evolution," *Journal of Linguistics* 26: 79–102.
    1992. "Phonology and morphology," in Blake (ed.), 23–155.
    (ed.). 1999. *The Cambridge History of the English Language*, vol. 3: *1476–1776*, Cambridge University Press.

Leas, Susan E. 1981. "The Emory collection of the Louisiana workbooks," *LAGS Working Papers*, 1st series, no. 3. Microfiche 1181.

Levey, Kelli 1991. "Veteran trustee Bryan bids farewell to board," *Bryan-College Station Eagle*, 8 May, 1A, 9A.

Levine, Lawrence 1978. *Black Culture and Black Consciousness: Afro-American Folk Thought from Slavery Through Freedom*, Oxford University Press.

Lipski, John M. 1990. *The Language of the Isleños: Vestigial Spanish in Louisiana*, Baton Rouge: Louisiana State University Press.
    1993. "*Y'all* in American English," *English World-Wide* 14: 23–56.

Little, Greta D. and Michael Montgomery (eds.) 1994. *Centennial Usage Studies*, Publication of the American Dialect Society 78, Tuscaloosa: University of Alabama Press.

Locklear, Hayes Alan, Walt Wolfram, Natalie Schilling-Estes, and Clare Dannenberg 1999. *A Dialect Dictionary of Lumbee English*, Raleigh: North Carolina Language and Life Project.

Loman, Bengt 1967. *Conversations in a Negro American Dialect*, Washington, DC: Center for Applied Linguistics.

Malin, Helen Rahm 1972. "A questionnaire of lexical items used by New Orleans English speakers," University of New Orleans master's thesis.

Marckwardt, Albert H. 1958. *American English*, Oxford University Press.

Mardispeak 2000. Mardi Gras unmasked. http://www.mardigrasunmasked.com/mardispeak.htm

Martin, Jennifer and Ed Martin 1993. *Speaking Louisiana: A Cajun Dictionary*, Prairieville, Louisiana: Louisiana Gifts.

Martin, Stefan and Walt Wolfram 1998. "The sentence in African-American vernacular English," in Mufwene, Rickford, Bailey, and Baugh (eds.), 11–36.

Mason, Bobbie Anne 1993. "Terms of office," *The New Yorker*, 26 July, 90.

Mathews, Mitford McLeod (ed.) 1931. *The Beginnings of American English: Essays and Comments*, University of Chicago Press.

Matthews, Bunny 1978. *F'sure: Actual Dialog Heard on the Streets of New Orleans*, New Orleans: Neetof.

Maynor, Natalie 1988. "Written records of spoken language: how reliable are they?," in Thomas (ed.), 109–19.

    1996. "The pronoun y'all," *Journal of English Linguistics* 24: 288–94.

    2000. "Battle of the pronouns: y'all versus you-guys," *American Speech* 75: 416–18.

McArthur, Tom (ed.) 1992. *The Oxford Companion to the English Language*, Oxford University Press.

McDavid, Raven I., Jr. 1948. "Postvocalic /-r/ in South Carolina: a social analysis," *American Speech* 23: 194–203.

    1955. "The position of the Charleston dialect," *Publication of the American Dialect Society* 23: 35–49.

    1958. "The dialects of American English," in Francis W. Nelson (ed.), *The Structure of American English*, New York: Ronald, ch. 9.

    1967. "Needed research in southern dialects," in Thompson (ed.), 113–24.

McDavid, Raven I., Jr. and Virginia G. McDavid 1951. "The relationship of the speech of American Negroes to the speech of whites," *American Speech* 26: 3–27.

McDavid, Virginia G. 1998. "Educational and gender-related differences in the use of verb forms in the South Atlantic States," in Montgomery and Nunnally (eds.), 201–15.

McKern, Sharon 1979. *Redneck Mothers, Good Ol' Girls, and Other Southern Belles*, New York: Viking.

McLemore, Cynthia A. 1991. "The pragmatic interpretation of English intonation: sorority speech," University of Texas at Austin dissertation.

McLeod-Porter, Delma 1992. "Guardian of linguistic tradition: a case study of a Southern lady," paper presented at the South Central Modern Language Association, Memphis, TN.

McMillan, James and Michael B. Montgomery 1989. *Annotated Bibliography of Southern American English*, Tuscaloosa: University of Alabama Press.

McNair-Dupree, Lisa 2002. "Mill villagers and farmers: dialect and economics in a small southern town," University of Chicago dissertation.

McPherson, James M. 1991. "Civil War: causes and results," in Foner and Garraty (eds.), 182–5.

McWhiney, Grady 1988. *Cracker Culture: Celtic Ways in the Old South*, Tuscaloosa: University of Alabama Press.

Medeiros, Regina del Negri 1982. "American Brazilian English," *American Speech* 57: 150–2.

Melançon, Megan 2000. "The sociolinguistic situation of Creoles in southern Louisiana: identity, characteristics, attitudes," Louisiana State University dissertation.

Mesthrie, Rajend (ed.) 2001. *The Concise Encyclopedia of Sociolinguistics*, Oxford: Pergamon.

Mille, Katherine 1990. "A historical analysis of tense-mood-aspect in Gullah Creole: a case of stable variation," University of South Carolina dissertation.

Miller, Michael 1978. "Inflectional morphology in Augusta, Georgia: a sociolinguistic description," University of Chicago dissertation.

  1986. "The greatest blemish: plurals in -*sp*, -*st*, and -*sk*," in Montgomery and Bailey (eds.), 235–53.

Milroy, Lesley 1987. *Language and Social Networks*, 2nd. edn., Cambridge/Oxford: Blackwell.

Mishoe, Margaret, and Michael Montgomery 1994. "The pragmatics of multiple modal variation in North and South Carolina," *American Speech* 69: 1–29.

Mitchell, Margaret 1936. *Gone with the Wind*, New York: MacMillan.

Mitchell, Steve 1976. *How to Speak Southern*, New York: Bantam.

  1980. *More How to Speak Southern*, New York: Bantam.

Mitchell-Kernan, Claudia 1972. "Signifying and marking: two Afro-American speech acts," in Gumperz and Hymes (eds.), 161–79.

Montgomery, Michael [B.] 1979. "A discourse analysis of expository Appalachian English," University of Florida dissertation.

  1980. "Inchoative verbs in East Tennessee English," *SECOL Bulletin* 4: 77–85.

  1989a. "English language," in Wilson and Ferris (eds.), 761–7.

  1989b. "Exploring the roots of Appalachian English," *English World-Wide* 10: 227–78.

  1989c. "A note on *ya'll*," *American Speech* 64: 273–5.

  1991. "The linguistic value of the ex-slave recordings," in Bailey, Maynor and Cukor-Avila (eds.), 173–89.

  1992. "The etymology of y'*all*," in Hall, Doane, and Ringer (eds.), 356–69.

  1993a. "Review article: the Linguistic Atlas of the Gulf States," *American Speech* 68: 263–318.

  1993b. "The Southern accent – alive and well," *Southern Cultures*, inaugural issue: 47–64.

  1993c. "The verb *be* in American Black English: Irish English or what?," paper presented at Language Variety in the South–II (LAVIS–II), Auburn, AL.

  1995. "The koineization of colonial American English," in Phliponneau (ed.), 309–31.

  1996a. "The future of Southern American English," *SECOL Review* 20: 1–24.

  1996b. "Was colonial American English a koine?," in Klemola, Kytö, and Rissanen (eds.), 213–35.

  1997a. "Language variety in the South: a retrospective and assessment," in Bernstein, Nunnally, and Sabino (eds.), 3–20.

  1997b. "Making transatlantic connections between varieties of English: the case of plural verbal -*s*," *Journal of English Linguistics* 25.2: 122–41.

  1998. "Multiple modals in LAGS and LAMSAS," in Montgomery and Nunnally (eds.), 90–122.

1999. "Eighteenth-century Sierra Leone English: another exported variety of African American English," *English World-Wide* 20: 1–34.

2000a. "Inchoative verbs in Appalachian English," paper presented at the Southeastern Conference on Linguistics (SECOL), Oxford, MS.

2000b. "Isolation as a linguistic construct," *Southern Journal of Linguistics* 24: 41–54.

2001. "British and Irish antecedents," in Algeo (ed.), 86–153.

Montgomery, Michael B. and Guy Bailey (eds.) 1986. *Language Variety in the South: Perspectives in Black and White*, Tuscaloosa: University of Alabama Press.

Montgomery, Michael B. and Janet M. Fuller 1996. "What was verbal -s in 19th century African-American English?," in Schneider (ed.), 211–30.

Montgomery, Michael B., Janet M. Fuller and Sharon DeMarse 1993. "The black men has wives and sweet harts [and third person plural -s] Jest like the white men: evidence for verbal -s from written documents on nineteenth-century African-American speech," *Language Variation and Change* 5: 335–57.

Montgomery, Michael B. and Joseph R. Hall forthcoming. *A Dictionary of Smoky Mountain English*, Knoxville: University of Tennessee Press.

Montgomery, Michael B. and Cecil Ataide Melo 1990. "The phonology of the lost cause: the English of the Confederados in Brazil," *English World-Wide* 11: 195–216.

Montgomery, Michael B. and Margaret Mishoe 1999. "'He bes took up with a Yankee girl and moved up North': the verb bes in the Carolinas and its history," *American Speech* 75: 240–81.

Montgomery, Michael B. and Stephen J. Nagle 1993. "Double modals in Scotland and the Southern United States: trans-Atlantic inheritance or independent development?" *Folia Linguistica Historica* 14: 91–107.

Montgomery, Michael B. and Thomas E. Nunnally (eds.) 1998. *From the Gulf States and Beyond: The Legacy of Lee Pederson and LAGS*, Tuscaloosa: University of Alabama Press.

Morgan, John T. 1900. "Speech to Congress on the gold question," *Atlanta Constitution*, 16 Feb., 5.

Morgan, Marcyliena (ed.) 1994. *Language and the Social Construction of Identity in Creole Situations*, Los Angeles: Center for Afro-American Studies.

Morrison, Estelle Rees 1928. "'You all' again," *American Speech* 4: 54–5.

Mufwene, Salikoko S. 1991. "Is Gullah decreolizing? A comparison of a speech sample of the 1930's with a speech sample of the 1980's," in Bailey, Maynor, and Cukor-Avila (eds.), 213–30.

1993. "Introduction," in Mufwene (ed.), 1–31.

1994. "On decreolization: the case of Gullah," in Morgan (ed.), 63–99.

1996a. "The development of American Englishes: some questions from a creole genesis perspective," in Schneider (ed.), 231–63.

1996b. "The founder principle in creole genesis," *Diachronica* 13: 83–134.

1998. "The structure of the noun phrase in African-American vernacular English," in Mufwene, Rickford, Bailey, and Baugh (eds.), 69–81.

1999. "North American varieties of English as byproducts of population contacts," in Wheeler (ed.), 15–37.

2000a. "Population contacts and the evolution of English," *The European English Messenger* 9: 9–15.

2000b. "Some sociohistorical inferences about the development of African-American English," in Poplack (ed.), 233–63.

2001a. "African-American English," in Algeo (ed.), 291–324.

2001b. *The Ecology of Language Evolution*, Cambridge University Press.

(ed.) 1993. *Africanisms in Afro-American Language Varieties*, Athens: University of Georgia Press.

Mufwene, Salikoko S., John R. Rickford, Guy Bailey, and John Baugh (eds.) 1998. *African-American English: Structure, History and Use*, London: Routledge.

Mustanoja, Tauno F. 1960. *A Middle English Syntax. Part I. Parts of Speech*, Mémoires de la Société Néophilologique de Helsinki, XXIII. Helsinki: Société Néophilologique.

Myhill, John 1995. "The use of features of present-day AAVE in the ex-slave recordings," *American Speech* 70: 115–47.

Myhill, John and Wendell A. Harris 1986. "The use of the verbal -*s* inflection in BEV," in Sankoff (ed.), 25–31.

Nagle, Stephen J. 1993. "Double modals in Early English," in Aertsen and Jeffers (eds.), 363–70.

N'awlins food! 2000. New Orleans restaurants.com
http://www.neworleansrestaurants.com/glossary.html

Nevalainen, Terttu and Helena Raumolin-Brunberg 2000. "The third-person singular -(e)s and -(e)th revisited: the morphophonemic hypothesis," in Dalton-Puffer and Ritt (eds.), 235–48.

(eds.) 1996. *Sociolinguistics and Language History: Studies Based on the Corpus of Early English Correspondence*, Amsterdam: Rodopi.

Nichols, Patricia 1983. "Black and white speaking in the rural South: differences in the pronominal system," *American Speech* 58: 201–15.

1986. "Prepositions in Black and White English of coastal South Carolina," in Montgomery and Bailey (eds.), 73–84.

Niedzielski, Nancy 1997. "The effect of social information on the phonetic perception of sociolinguistic variables (American dialects)," University of California, Santa Barbara, dissertation.

Nix, Ruth 1980. "Linguistic variation in the speech of Wilmington, North Carolina," Duke University dissertation.

O'Cain, Raymond K. 1972. "A social dialect survey of Charleston, South Carolina," University of Chicago dissertation.

Ogura, Mieko and William S-Y. Wang 1996. "Snowball effect in lexical diffusion: the development of -s in the third person singular present indicative in English," in Britton (ed.), 119–42.

Orr, Elinor 1987. *Twice as Less: Black English and the Performance of Black Students in Mathematics and Science*, New York: Norton.

Orton, Harold, et al. 1962–71. *Survey of English Dialects: The Basic Materials*, 4 vols. in 3 parts, Leeds, UK: E. J. Arnold and Son.

Orton, Harold, Stewart Sanderson and John Widdowson 1978. *The Linguistic Atlas of England*, London: Croom Helm.

Palmer, Frank Robert 1990. *Modality and the English Modals*, New York: Longman.

Paparone, Sharon C. and Janet Fuller 1993. "Mid-19th century African-American Speech," paper presented at Language Variety in the South–II (LAVIS–II), Auburn, AL.

Patton, Douglas W. K. 1999. "*Y'all* in America," *Southern Living*, March, 210.

Payne, Arvilla 1980. "Factors controlling the acquisition of the Philadelphia dialect by out-of-state children," in Labov (ed.), 143–78.

Pederson, Lee 1983. *East Tennessee Folk Speech*, Frankfurt: Lang.

2001. "Dialects," in Algeo (ed.), 253–90.

Pederson, Lee, Susan Leas McDaniel, Guy Bailey, and Marvin Bassett (eds.) 1986. *Linguistic Atlas of the Gulf states*, vol.1: *Handbook for the Linguistic Atlas of the Gulf States*, Athens: University of Georgia Press.

Pederson, Lee, et al. (eds.) 1986–92. *Linguistic Atlas of the Gulf States*, 7 vols., Athens: University of Georgia Press.

Percy, Carol 1991. "Variation between *-(e)th* and *-(e)s* spellings of the third person singular present indicative: Captain James Cook's 'Endeavour' Journal 1768–1771," *Neuphilologische Mitteilungen* 92: 351–8.

Perkell, Joseph S. and Dennis H. Klatt (eds.) 1986. *Invariance and Variability in Speech Processes*, Hillsdale, NJ: Lawrence Erlbaum.

Perkins, Edwin J. 1988. *The Economy of Colonial America*, 2nd. edn., New York: Columbia University Press.

Perkins, T. W. 1931. " 'You all' again," *American Speech* 6: 304–5.

Perritt, Margaret Floyd 1943. "The Louisiana 'R,'" *Southern Speech Journal* 9: 102–6.

Phliponneau, Catherine (ed.) 1995. *Sociolinguistic Studies and Language Planning: Proceedings of the XVIth Annual Meeting of the Atlantic Provinces Linguistic Association*, Moncton: NB: Centre de Recherche en Linguistique Appliquée.

Picone, Michael D. 1994. "Cajun language and culture Q&A," *Newsletter of the American Dialect Society* 26: 9–10.

2001. "Surviving French in Louisiana outside of Acadiana," paper presented at the annual meeting of the American Dialect Society, Washington, DC.

Pitts, Walter 1981. "Beyond hypercorrection: the use of emphatic *-z* in BEV," *Chicago Linguistic Society* 17: 303–10.

Polanyi, Livia 1985. *Telling the American Story: A Structural and Cultural Analysis of Conversational Storytelling*, Norwood, NJ: Ablex.

Poplack, Shana 1999. "Verbal *-s* variability in the African American Diaspora: African Nova Scotian and Samaná English," paper presented at the Tenth International Conference on Methods in Dialectology, St. Johns, Newfoundland.

(ed.) 2000. *The English History of African American English*, Oxford: Blackwell.

Poplack, Shana and David Sankoff 1987. "The Philadelphia story in the Spanish Caribbean," *American Speech* 62: 291–314.

Poplack, Shana and Sali Tagliamonte 1989. "There's no tense like the present: verbal *-s* inflection in Early Black English," *Language Variation and Change* 1: 47–84; and revised in Bailey, Maynor, and Cukor-Avila (eds.), 275–324.

1991. "African-American English in the diaspora: evidence from old line Nova Scotians," *Language Variation and Change* 3: 301–39.

1994. "*-S* or nothing: marking the plural in the African-American diaspora," *American Speech* 69: 227–59.

2001. *African American English in the Diaspora: Tense and Aspect*, Oxford: Blackwell.

Preston, Dennis R. 1989. *Perceptual Dialectology*, Dordrecht, Netherlands: Foris.

1996. "Where the worst English is spoken," in Schneider (ed.), 297–360.

1997. "The South: the touchstone," in Bernstein, Nunnally, and Sabino (eds.), 311–51.

1999. *Handbook of Perceptual Dialectology*, vol. 1, Amsterdam: Benjamins.

(ed.). 1993. *American Dialect Research*, Amsterdam: Benjamins.

Primer, Sylvester 1888. "Charleston provincialisms," *American Journal of Philology* 9: 198–213.

Prioli, Carmine 1998. *Hope for a Good Season: The Ca'e Bankers of Harkers Island*, Asheboro, NC: The Down Home Press.

Rampton, Ben 1995. *Crossing: Language and Ethnicity Among Adolescents*, London: Longman.

(ed.) 1999. *Styling the Other*, special issue of *Journal of Sociolinguistics* 3: 421–556.

Randolph, Vance, and George P. Wilson 1953. *Down in the Holler: A Gallery of Ozark Folkspeech*, Norman: University of Oklahoma Press.

Raumolin-Brunberg, Helena 1991. *The Noun Phrase in Early Sixteenth-Century English: A Study Based on Sir Thomas More's Writings*, Mémoires de la Société Néophilologique de Helsinki, 50.

Rawick, George P. (ed.) 1972. *The American Slave: A Composite Autobiography*, Contributions in Afro-American and African Studies, 19 vols., Westport, CT: Greenwood.

(ed.) 1977. *The American Slave: A Composite Autobiography*, supplement, series 1, 12 vols., Westport, CT: Greenwood.

(ed.) 1979. *The American Slave: A Composite Autobiography*, supplement, series 2, 10 vols., Westport, CT: Greenwood.

Read, William A. 1909. "The vowel system of the southern United States," *Englische Studien* 41: 70–8.

1911. "Some variant pronunciations in the new South," *Dialect Notes* 3: 497–536.

Reed, John Shelton and Dale Volberg Reed 1996. *1001 Things Everyone Should Know About the South*, New York: Doubleday.

Reed, Judy 1991. "Evolution of the loss of /h/ before /w/ word initially in Texas," University of Houston master's thesis.

Reinecke, George 1951. "New Orleans pronunciation among school children and educated adults," Tulane University master's thesis.

Reissman, Catherine Kohler 1988. "Worlds of difference: contrasting experience in marriage and narrative style," in Todd and Fisher (eds.), 151–73.

Richardson, Gina 1984. "Can *y'all* function as a singular pronoun in Southern dialect?" *American Speech* 59: 51–9.

Rickford, John R. 1974. "The insights of the mesolect," in DeCamp and Hancock (eds.), 92–117.

1975. "Carrying the new wave into syntax: the case of Black English BIN," in Fasold and Shuy (eds.), 162–83.

1977. "The question of prior creolization in Black English," in Valdman (ed.), 199–221.

1986a. "Social contact and linguistic diffusion: Hiberno-English and New World Black English," *Language* 52: 245–90.

1986b. "Some principles in the study of Black and White speech in the South," in Montgomery and Bailey (eds.), 38–62.

1987a. "Are Black and White vernaculars diverging?" papers from the NWAV–XIV panel discussion, *American Speech* 62: 55–62.

1987b. *Dimensions of a Creole Continuum. History, Texts, and Linguistic Analysis of Guyanese Creole*, Stanford University Press.

1992. "Grammatical variation and divergence in vernacular black English," in Gerritsen and Stein (eds.), 175–200.

1998. "Prior creolization of AAVE? Sociohistorical and textual evidence from the 17th and 18th centuries," *Journal of Sociolinguistics* 1: 315–36.

1998. "The creole origins of African-American Vernacular English: evidence from copula absence," in Mufwene, Rickford, Bailey, and Baugh (eds.), 154–200.

1999. *African American Vernacular English*, Malden and Oxford: Blackwell.

Rickford, John R. and Christine Théberge Rafal 1996. "Preterite *had*+V-*ed* in the narratives of African-American preadolescents," *American Speech* 71: 227–54.

Rickford, John R. and Russell J. Rickford 2000. *Spoken Soul: The Story of Black English*, New York: Wiley.

Rissanen, Matti 1999. "Syntax," in Lass (ed.), 187–331.

Romaine, Suzanne 2001. "Contact with other languages," in Algeo (ed.), 154–83.

Ross, Stephen M. 1989. *Fiction's Inexhaustible Voice: Speech and Writing in Faulkner*, Athens: University of Georgia Press.

Rubin, L. D., Jr. (ed.) 1980. *The American South: Portrait of a Culture*, Baton Rouge: Louisiana State University Press.

Rubrecht, August 1971. "Regional phonological variants in Louisiana speech," University of Florida dissertation.

1977 [1971]. "*DARE* in Louisiana," in Shores and Hines (eds.), 45–59.

Russo, Michael F. 1995. *Yats in Movieland*, Mahomet, Illinois: Mayhaven Publishing.

Rydén, M. and S. Brorström 1987. *The Be/Have Variation with Intransitives in English*, Stockholm: Almqvist and Wiksell.

Sabban, Annette 1984. "Investigations into the syntax of Hebridean English," *Scottish Language* 3: 5–32.

Sack, Robert D. 1988. "The consumer's world: place as context," *Annals of the Association of American Geographers* 78: 642–64.

Sacks, Harvey, Emanuel A. Schegloff, and Gail Jefferson 1974. "A simplest systematics for the organization of turntaking for conversation," *Language* 50: 696–735.

Sankoff, David (ed.) 1986. *Diversity and Diachrony*, Amsterdam: Benjamins.

Schendl, Herbert 1996. "The 3rd plural present indicative in Early Modern English – variation and linguistic contact," in Britton (ed.), 143–60.

2000. "The third person present plural in Shakespeare's First Folio: a case of interaction of morphology and syntax?," in Dalton-Puffer and Ritt (eds.), 263–76.

Schieffelin, Bambi B., Kathryn A. Woolard, and Paul V. Kroskrity (eds.) 1998. *Language Ideologies: Practice and Theory*, Oxford University Press.

Schiffrin, Deborah 1981. "Tense variation in narrative," *Language* 57: 45–62.

1987. *Discourse Markers*, Cambridge University Press.

Schilling-Estes, Natalie 1997. "Accommodation versus concentration: dialect death in two post-insular island communities," *American Speech* 72: 12–32.

2000a. "Exploring morphological change: the *was/weren't* pattern in Smith Island English," paper presented at the New Ways of Analyzing Variation Conference (NWAV) 29, East Lansing, MI.

2000b. "Investigating intra-ethnic differentiation: /ay/ in Lumbee Native American English," *Language Variation and Change* 12: 141–74.

Schilling-Estes, Natalie and Walt Wolfram 1994. "Convergent explanation and alternative regularization patterns: *were/weren't* leveling in a vernacular English variety," *Language Variation and Change* 6: 273–302.

1999. "Alternative models of dialect death: dissipation vs. concentration," *Language* 75: 486–521.

Schneider, Edgar W. 1982. "On the history of Black English in the USA: some new evidence," *English World-Wide* 3.1: 18–46.

1983a. "The diachronic development of the Black English perfective auxiliary phrase," *Journal of English Linguistics* 16: 55–64.

1983b. "The origin of verbal -s in Black English," *American Speech* 58: 99–113.

1989. *American Earlier Black English: Morphological and Syntactic Variables*, Tuscaloosa: University of Alabama Press.

1995. "Black–White language contact through the centuries: diachronic aspects of linguistic convergence or divergence in the United States of America," in Fisiak (ed.), 237–52.

1998. "The Chattahoochee river: a linguistic boundary?," in Montgomery and Nunnally (eds.), 123–46.

2001. "Investigating variation and change in written documents," in Chambers, Trudgill, and Schilling-Estes (eds.), 67–96.

forthcoming. "The English dialect heritage of the Southern United States," in Hickey (ed.).

(ed.) 1996. *Focus on the USA*, Amsterdam: Benjamins.

(ed.) 1997. *Englishes Around the World*, vol. 1: *General Studies, British Isles, North America: Studies in Honour of Manfred Gorlach*, Amsterdam: Benjamins.

Schneider, Edgar W. and Michael Montgomery 2001. "On the trail of early nonstandard grammar: an electronic corpus of Southern U.S. antebellum overseers' letters," *American Speech* 76: 388–410.

Schremp, Mary Bemi 1995. "The distribution of [wi] in the American South," University of Memphis master's thesis.

Scott, Ann Martin 1992. *Cajun Vernacular English: Informal English in French Louisiana*, special issue of *Louisiana English Journal*.

Shores, David L. 2000. *Tangier Island: People, Place, and Talk*, Newark: University of Delaware Press.

Shores, David L. and Carole P. Hines (eds.) 1977. *Papers in Language Variation: SAMLA-ADS Collection*, Tuscaloosa: University of Alabama Press.

Simpkins, Karen L. 1969. "Terminology used in selected local settings," University of North Carolina, Chapel Hill, master's thesis.

Singler, John Victor 1991. "Liberian settler English and the ex-slave recordings: a comparative study," in Bailey, Maynor and Cukor-Avila (eds.), 249–74.

1998. "What's not new in AAVE," *American Speech* 73: 227–56.

1999. "Passing verbal -s from Northern British vernacular to the Liberian settler English of Sinoe: transfer interrupted!," paper presented at the Tenth International Conference on Methods in Dialectology, St. Johns, Newfoundland.

Sledd, James 1966. "Breaking, umlaut, and the southern drawl," *Language* 42: 18–41.

Smith, M. A. Sharwood 1999. *Mood and Modality*. http://www.let.uu.nl/~slr/gram4/. Published online 2 April.

Sommer, Elizabeth 1986. "Variation in Southern urban English," in Bailey and Montgomery (eds.), 180–201.

Sothern, James M. 1977. *Cajun Dictionary: A Collection of Some Commonly Used Words and Phrases by the People of Southern Louisiana*, 2nd. edn., Houma, LA: MarketShare Enterprises.

Spears, Arthur K. 1988. "Black American English," in Cole (ed.), 96–113.

1998. "African-American language use: ideology and so-called obscenity," in Mufwene, Rickford, Bailey, and Baugh (eds.), 226–50.

Spears, James E. 1974. "Southern folk greetings and responses," *Mississippi Folklore Register* 8: 218–20.

Spencer, Nancy 1975. "Singular y'*all*," *American Speech* 4: 54–5.

Sutcliffe, David 1998. "Gone with the wind? Evidence for 19th century African American speech," *Links and Letters* 5: 127–45.

Steeg, Clarence L. Ver 1975. *Origins of a Southern Mosaic*, Athens: University of Georgia Press.

Stein, Dieter 1985. "Discourse markers in Early Modern English," in Eaton, Fischer, Koopman, and van der Leek (eds.), 283–302.

1987. "At the crossroads of philology, linguistics and semiotics: notes on the replacement of th by s in the third person singular in English," *English Studies* 68: 406–32.

Stevens, Liz 1996. "It's the drawl, y'all," *Fort Worth Star Telegram*, May 25, E1, 8.

Stewart, William 1967. "Sociolinguistic factors in the history of American Negro dialects," *Florida Foreign Language Reporter* 5: 1–4.

Summerlin, Nan Jo Corbitt 1972. "A dialect study: affective parameters in the deletion and substitution of consonants in the deep South," Florida State University dissertation.

Taggert, Chuck 2000. "Yat-speak: a lexicon of New Orleans terminology and speech," http://www.gumbopages.com/yatspeak.html

Tagliamonte, Sali 1997. "Obsolescence in the English perfect? Evidence from Samaná English," *American Speech* 72: 33–68.

1999. "Verbal -*s* in 20th century Southwest England: the case of Devon," paper presented at the Tenth International Conference on Methods in Dialectology, St. Johns, Newfoundland.

Tagliamonte, Sali and Shana Poplack 1988. "How Black English *PAST* got to the present: evidence from Samaná," *Language in Society* 17: 513–33.

Tagliamonte, Sali and Jennifer Smith 1998. "Roots of English in the African American diaspora," *Links and Letters* 5: 147–65.

Tannen, Deborah 1981. "New York Jewish conversational style," *International Journal of the Sociology of Language* 30: 133–49.

1984. *Conversational Style: Analyzing Talk Among Friends*, Norwood, NJ: Ablex.

(ed.) 1988. *Coherence in Spoken and Written Discourse*, Norwood, NJ: Ablex.

Tate, Thad W. 1965. *The Negro in Eighteenth-Century Williamsburg*, Williamsburg, VA: The Colonial Williamsburg Foundation.

Thernstrom, Stephen 1980. *Harvard Encyclopedia of American Ethnic Groups*, Cambridge, MA: Harvard University Press.

Thomas, Allan R. (ed.) 1988. *Methods in Dialectology*, Philadelphia: Multilingual Matters.

Thomas, Erik R. 1997. "A rural/metropolitan split in the speech of Texas Anglos," *Language Variation and Change* 9: 309–32.

2001. *An Acoustic Analysis of Vowel Variation in New World English*, Publication of the American Dialect Society 85, Durham: Duke University Press.

Thomas, Erik R. and Guy Bailey 1998. "Parallels between vowel subsystems of African American Vernacular English and Caribbean Anglophone Creoles," *Journal of Pidgin and Creole Languages* 13: 267–96.

Thomas, Hugh 1998. *The Slave Trade*, New York: Simon and Schuster.

Thompson, Edgar T. (ed.) 1967. *Perspectives on the South: Agenda for Research*, Durham, NC: Duke University Press.

Tillery, Jan and Guy Bailey 2001. "Urbanization and the development of Southern American English," paper presented at the Southeastern Conference on Linguistics (SECOL) LXIV, Knoxville, TN.

Tillery, Jan, Tom Wikle, and Guy Bailey 2000. "The nationalization of a southernism," *Journal of English Linguistics* 28: 280–94.

Tindall, George B. 1980. "The resurgence of Southern identity," in Rubin, Jr. (ed.), 161–8.

Titon, Jeff Todd 1988. *Powerhouse for God: Speech, Chant, and Song in an Appalachian Baptist Church*, Austin: University of Texas Press.

Todd, Alexandra. D. and Sue Fisher (eds.) 1988, *Gender and Discourse: The Power of Talk*, Norwood, NJ: Ablex.

Toole, John Kennedy 1980. *Confederacy of Dunces*, Baton Rouge: Louisiana State University Press.

Torbert, Benjamin 2001. "Tracing Native American language history through consonant cluster reduction: the case of Lumbee English," *American Speech* 76: 361–88.

Traugott, Elizabeth Closs 1972. *History of English Syntax: A Transformational Approach to the History of English Sentence Structure*, New York: Holt, Rinehart and Winston.

Trudgill, Peter 1972. "Sex, covert prestige and linguistic change in the urban British English of Norwich," *Language in Society* 1: 179–95.

1990. *The Dialects of England*. Oxford and Cambridge, MA: Blackwell.

Trudgill, Peter, Elizabeth Gordon, and Gillian Lewis 1998. "New dialect formation and southern hemisphere English: the New Zealand short front vowels," *Journal of Sociolinguistics* 2: 35–51.

Turner, Lorenzo Dow 1949. *Africanisms in the Gullah Dialect*, University of Chicago Press.

Valdman, Albert (ed.) 1977. *Pidgin and Creole Linguistics*, Bloomington: Indiana University Press.

(ed.) 1997. *French and Creole in Louisiana*, New York: Plenum.

Vaughn-Cooke, Faye 1986. "Lexical diffusion: evidence from a decreolizing variety of Black English," in Montgomery and Bailey (eds.), 111–30.

1987. "Are Black and White vernaculars diverging?," papers from the NWAV–XIV panel discussion, *American Speech* 62: 12–32.

Viereck, Wolfgang 1988. "Invariant *be* in an unnoticed source of American early Black English," *American Speech* 63: 291–303.

1995. "Verbal -s inflection in 'early' American Black English," in Fisiak (ed.), 315–26.

1998. "African American English: verbal -*s* and *be2* in Hyatt's earlier and later corpus," in Jahr (ed.), 245–59.

Virgets, Ronnie 1997. *Say, Cap!: The New Orleans Views of Ronnie Virgets*, New Orleans: Arthur Harley Enterprises.

Visser, F. Th. 1963–73. *An Historical Syntax of the English Language*, 3 vols., Leiden: Brill.

Von Schneidemesser, Luanne 1999. *An Index by Region, Usage, and Etymology to the Dictionary of American Regional English*, vol. 3, Publication of the American Dialect Society 82, Durham, North Carolina: Duke University Press.

Vowles, Guy R. 1944. "A few observations on Southern 'you-all,'" *American Speech* 19: 146–7.

Wareing, John 2000. "The regulation and organisation of the trade in indentured servants for the American Colonies in London, 1645–1718," University of London dissertation.

Watson, Thomas E. (ed.) 1909–13. *History of Southern Oratory*, Richmond, VA: The Southern Historical Publication Society.

Weldon, Tracey 1998. "Exploring the AAVE-Gullah connection: a comparative study of copula variability," Ohio State University dissertation.

Wells, John 1982. *Accents of English*, vol. 3: *Beyond the British Isles*, Cambridge University Press.

Wentworth, Harold 1944. *American Dialect Dictionary*, New York: Crowell.

Wheeler, Rebecca (ed.) 1999.*The Workings of Language: From Prescriptions to Perspectives*, Westport, MA: Greenwood Publishing Group.

Williamson, Juanita V. and Virginia M. Burke (eds.) 1971. *A Various Language: Perspectives on American Dialects*, New York: Holt, Rinehart and Winston.

Wilson, Charles and William Ferris (eds.) 1989. *Encyclopedia of Southern Culture*, Chapel Hill: University of North Carolina Press.

Wilson, Martha Lynn 1973. "A vocabulary study of St. Tammany Parish using the New Orleans questionnaire," University of New Orleans master's thesis.

Wimsatt, William C. 2000. "Generativity, entrenchment, evolution, and innateness," in Hardcastle (ed.), 139–79.

Winford, Donald 1998. "On the origins of African American Vernacular English: a creolist perspective. Part II: Linguistic features," *Diachronica* 15.1: 99–154.

Wise, Claude Merton 1933. "A specimen of Louisiana French-English, or 'Cajan' dialect in transcription," *American Speech* 8: 63–4.

  1945. "The dialect atlas of Louisiana – a report of progress," *Studies in Linguistics* 3: 37–42.

Wolf, George, Michele Bocquillon, Debbie De La Houssaye, Phyllis Krzyzek, Clifton Meynard, and Lisbeth Philip 1996. "Pronouncing French names in New Orleans," *Language in Society* 25: 407–26.

Wolfram, Walt 1969. *A Sociolinguistic Description of Detroit Negro Speech*, Washington, DC: Center for Applied Linguistics.

  1971. "Black–White speech differences revisited," in Wolfram and Clark (eds.), 139–61.

  1973. "Review of *Black English* by J. L. Dillard," *Language* 49: 670–9.

  1974. "The relationship of white southern speech to Vernacular Black English," *Language* 50: 498–527.

  1987. "Are Black and White vernaculars diverging?," papers from the NWAV–XIV panel discussion, *American Speech* 62: 40–8.

  1991. *Dialects and American English*. Englewood Cliffs, NJ: Prentice Hall.

  forthcoming. "The sociolinguistic construction of remnant dialects," in Fought (ed.).

Wolfram, Walt and Donna Christian 1976. *Appalachian Speech*, Arlington: Center for Applied Linguistics.

Wolfram, Walt and Clare Dannenberg 1999. "Dialect identity in a tri-ethnic context: the case of Lumbee American Indian English," *English World-Wide* 20: 179–216.

Wolfram, Walt and Ralph Fasold 1974. *The Study of Social Dialects in American English*, Englewood Cliffs, NJ: Prentice-Hall.

Wolfram, Walt, Kirk Hazen and Natalie Schilling-Estes 1999. *Dialect Change and Maintenance on the Outer Banks*, Publication of the American Dialect Society 80, Tuscaloosa: University of Alabama Press.

Wolfram, Walt and Natalie Schilling-Estes 1995. "Moribund dialects and the endangerment canon: the case of the Ocracoke brogue," *Language* 71: 696–721.

  1996. "Dialect change and maintenance in a post-insular island community," in Schneider (ed.), 101–48.

1997. *Hoi Toide on the Outer Banks: The Story of the Ocracoke Brogue*, Chapel Hill: University of North Carolina Press.

1998. *American English: Dialects and Variation*, Malden and Oxford: Blackwell.

forthcoming. "Remnant dialects in the Coastal United States," in Hickey (ed.).

Wolfram, Walt and Jason Sellers 1999. "Ethnolinguistic marking of past *be* in Lumbee Vernacular English," *Journal of English Linguistics* 27: 94–114.

Wolfram, Walt, Erik R. Thomas and Elaine W. Green 2000. "The regional context of earlier African-American speech: reconstructing the development of African American Vernacular English," *Language in Society* 29: 315–55.

Wolfram, Walt and Erik R. Thomas 2002. *The Development of African American English: Evidence from an Isolated Community*, Oxford: Blackwell.

Wolfram, Walt and Nona H. Clarke (eds.) 1971. *Black-White Speech Relationships*, Washington, DC: Center for Applied Linguistics.

Wolfson, Nessa 1979. "The conversational historical present alternation," *Language* 55: 168–82.

Wood, Peter H. 1974. *Black Majority: Negroes in Colonial South Carolina from 1670 through the Stono Rebellion*, New York: Knopf.

Wright, Joseph 1898–1905. *The English Dialect Dictionary*, London: Frowde.

Wright, Laura 1995. "Syntactic structure of witnesses' narratives from the sixteenth-century court minute books of the royal hospitals of Bridewell and Bedlam," *Neuphilologische Mitteilungen* 96.1: 93–105.

2000. "On the construction of some Early Modern English courtroom narratives," in Di Martino and Lima (eds.), 79–102.

2001. "Third person singular present tense -*s*, -*th* and zero, 1575–1648," *American Speech* 76: 236–58.

forthcoming a. "Depositions of sixteenth- and seventeenth-century Londoners deported to Virginia and the Bermudas: third-person-singular present-tense markers," in Hickey (ed.).

forthcoming b. "Third-person-plural present-tense markers in London prisoners' depositions, 1562–1623".

Yeager, Malcah 1975. "Speaking style: some phonetic realizations and their significance," *Penn Working Papers* I.1.

Zeigler, Mary 1997. "Ain no such word: a dictionary history of 'fixin to,'" paper presented at the Southeastern Conference on Linguistics (SECOL), Charlotte, NC.

1998. "The grammaticalization of 'fixin to,'" paper presented at the Southeastern Conference on Linguistics (SECOL), Lafayette, LA.

Index

a+verb+*ing* 2, 59, 60, 61
AAVE (African-American Vernacular English)
    2, 3, 11, 12, 19, 32, 38, 42, 43, 47, 49, 52,
    53, 55, 58, 60, 61, 62, 64, 65, 66, 67, 68,
    69, 70, 72, 76, 78, 82, 83, 84, 85, 86, 87,
    88, 89, 92, 93, 94, 95, 98, 99, 102, 103,
    105, 111, 117, 118, 123, 141
Abbott, Shirley 190, 204
Abel, James W. 176
Abney, Lisa 86
Abrahams, Roger D. 191
Acadians 175, 187
acceptability (of linguistic forms) 111, 201
Africa, East 6
Africa, West 2, 37, 43, 52, 62, 63, 83
African-American Vernacular English (AAVE)
    (*see* AAVE)
African Americans
    discourse styles of 191
African stratum 2
age 21, 24, 60, 84, 86, 100, 108, 112, 116, 129,
    130, 131, 132, 133, 137, 138, 177, 186
agreement 85, 97, 98
ain't 29, 93, 107, 117, 118, 151, 156, 194
Alabama 7, 53, 70, 107, 111, 112, 115, 121, 126,
    127, 128, 129, 131, 137, 138, 139, 174
    Cumberlands central highlands 7
    sand hills and pine flats 7
    wire grass piney woods 7
Algeo, John 1, 2, 6, 20, 76
Algonquian 12
Allen, Harold B. 146
Alvarez, Louis 180
American White Southern English (AWSE)
    (*see* AWSE)
Americanization 175
Amerindian 12, 13

analogical leveling 146
Anglicist position 83
Anniston, AL 53, 129, 131, 132, 133, 136, 137,
    138
Anshen, Frank 104
Appalachian English 10, 18, 32, 59, 63, 74, 75,
    76, 78, 117, 118, 141, 149
Appalachian region 10, 13, 16, 20, 53, 62, 121,
    198
apparent time 22, 88, 95, 112, 164, 166
a-prefixing 117, 146, 165, 166
archival records 17, 22, 33
archive(s) 2, 22, 31, 36, 37, 39, 44, 49, 53, 177
Arends, Jacques 18
Arkansas 111, 115, 121, 168, 190, 198
Arkansas Ozarks western highlands 7
Arkansas River basin 7
Ash, Sharon 126, 127, 128, 129, 137
Atchafalaya River basin 7
Atherton, Lewis 104
Atlantic, South 16
attitudes 17, 173, 190, 199, 202
Atwood, E. Bagby 83, 111, 176
Auber-Gex, Madeline 181
AuCoin, Michelle 79, 81
AWSE (American White Southern English) 64,
    65, 67, 68, 69, 70, 78
Axley, Lowry 109
Aycock, S. Campbell 109
Ayers, Edward L. 104, 171, 172

Babington, Mima 176
back shift 135, 136
Bahamian Creole 110
Bailey, Beryl Loftman 83, 110
Bailey, Guy 2, 4, 17, 21, 22, 25, 26, 33, 34, 39,
    42, 48, 53, 58, 60, 63, 65, 81, 82, 83, 84,

Bailey, Guy (*cont.*)
    85, 86, 87, 88, 92, 93, 95, 97, 99, 103, 104,
    105, 107, 108, 109, 111, 112, 116, 121, 122,
    123, 124, 127, 128, 139, 152, 159, 166, 168,
    172, 200, 202, 206
Bailey, Richard W. 181
Bailyn, Bernard 9, 73, 74, 75, 76
Baranowski, Maciej 127, 129, 130, 136, 137,
    138, 139
Barber, Charles 51
Bassett, Marvin 42, 93
Baugh, John 83, 84
Bauman, Richard 199
be
    habitual 38, 86, 92, 93, 106, 117, 118
    invariant 12, 38, 42, 60, 61, 85, 86, 93
    perfective 92, 146, 147
    plural indicative 38, 39, 42, 60, 61
    subjunctive 60
be done 92, 105
been (remote time) 117
bes 117, 149
be+V+ing 60, 93, 99
Bean, Judith Mattson 116, 162, 164, 200
Bereiter, Carl 104
Berlin, Ira 69, 72, 79
Bernstein, Cynthia 3, 10, 17, 19, 26, 29, 53,
    106, 113, 118, 122
Blanton, Mackie 180, 181
Boberg, Charles 127, 128
Bocquillon, Michele 181 (*see* Wolf)
Bodnar, John 70
Body 193, 195
Boertien, Harmon S. 110
Boorstin, Daniel J. 13
Boston 10, 107, 114
Boyle, Robert 14
Braden, Waldo W. 196
Brasch, Ila Wales 81, 123
Brasch, Walter Milton 66, 123
Brasil/Americana community 26
breaking (of vowels) 123, 135, 138, 139
Brewer, Jeutonne P. 93
brickhouse Indian 154
Bridewell 36, 37, 38, 39, 40, 43, 44, 47, 49, 50,
    53, 54, 55, 56, 58, 61, 62, 63
Britain 9, 13, 15, 27, 29, 33, 50, 74, 110, 159
Britain, David 148
British English 3, 18, 20, 27, 29, 30, 68, 69, 71,
    73, 110
British Isles 6, 13, 15, 68, 71, 73, 146, 147, 148,
    149, 151

Britons 13
Brooks, Cleanth 21, 27
Brorström, S. 147
Brown, Penelope 190, 192
Brown, Vivian 160, 164
Bucholtz, Mary 207
Burkett, Eva M. 106, 190
Burling, Robbins 84
Butters, Ronald R. 12, 29, 86, 109, 110,
    111

Cajun (Acadian) English 5, 176, 177, 178, 179,
    180
    glossary 183
    Grip the Rat 176
    identity 177
Cajun French 175, 177
Cajun motto 174
Cajun Renaissance 177, 178
call and response 198
Caribbean 67, 68, 73, 83
Caribbean creole(s) 70, 85, 110
Caribbean features 137
Carolinas 198
Carver, Craig M. 137
Cassidy, Frederic G. 12, 15, 79, 110, 114, 122,
    154
Cavalier myth 9
Chafe, Wallace 194
Charleston, SC 123, 126, 127, 128, 129, 130,
    131, 137, 138, 139, 169
Chaudenson, Robert 69
Cheramie, Deany-Marie 177
Chesapeake 66, 67, 70, 71, 73, 80, 149, 155
Chesapeake Bay 4, 122, 144, 148, 149, 152, 154,
    155, 158
Cheshire, Jenny 146, 148
Chinese 12
Ching, Marvin K. L. 115, 116, 192, 195
chi-square 32
choice in Southern American English 107, 110,
    162
Christian, Donna 111, 118, 144
Christie, Pauline 110
Chtareva, Anguelina 114
Civil War 9, 19, 21, 22, 24, 26, 33, 34, 87, 104,
    160, 162, 172, 196, 197, 200, 204
Clark, Thomas D. 104
Clarke, Sandra 78
class 2, 9, 25, 60, 65, 70, 73, 84, 111, 112, 131,
    132, 135, 138, 180,
    lower 11, 111, 181, 191

middle 11, 84, 106, 111, 126, 131, 137, 138, 181, 191
   upper 11, 106, 111, 112, 132, 133, 135, 136, 138, 139
   working 9, 47, 53, 92, 106, 112, 126, 131, 132, 133, 135, 136, 138, 191, 198
Clements, W. M. 198
coastal communities 73, 106
Coastal Southern 123
Cobb, James C. 171
Coca-Cola 14, 15
Cohen, Paul (see Labov et al. 1968) 1, 84, 93, 94, 111
Coleman, Kenneth 66
Coles, Felice A. 192
colloquial usage 22
colonial lag 1, 20
colonies 9, 10, 13, 64, 66, 67, 68, 69, 70, 71, 73, 74, 75, 76, 78
colonization 66, 74, 75, 78
conditional syntax 5, 193, 194
Confederacy 19, 24, 181, 200
consonant cluster reduction 152
constricted /r/ 164
copula 29, 32, 83, 95
copula, zero 92
Corcoran, Chris 67
corpus 1, 18, 30, 31, 33, 38, 43, 95
cotton 11, 14, 20, 63, 65, 66, 67, 69, 70, 72, 73, 87, 169, 170
court(s) 2, 36, 37, 38, 39, 40, 41, 42, 43, 44, 45, 47, 48, 50, 52, 58, 61, 62, 63, 185, 186, 187
counterfactual *liketa* 29, 53
Cox, Kevin R. 206
creole(s) 2, 3, 11, 18, 37, 43, 49, 56, 58, 59, 60, 63, 65, 66, 67, 68, 70, 72, 78, 83, 84, 85, 86, 110, 145, 175, 177, 180, 183, 185, 188
Creole 11, 18, 110, 174, 177, 181
Creole hypothesis 83
Crews, Harry 193, 194, 195
Cukor-Avila, Patricia 3, 19, 43, 49, 82, 86, 87, 88, 93, 95, 97, 99, 101, 103, 104, 105
culture 1, 2, 4, 5, 12, 18, 20, 26, 34, 67, 83, 87, 111, 119, 139, 144, 168, 170, 171, 173, 174, 175, 180, 196, 201, 206
Cunningham, Irma Aloyce Ewing 110, 118
Cutler, Cecelia A. 207

Danes 12
Dannenberg, Clare 138, 144, 149, 154

DARE (*Dictionary of American Regional English*) 10, 15, 53, 114, 122, 168, 169, 174, 176, 177, 179, 182, 183
database 38, 40, 141, 175
Davies, Catherine 192
Davis, Lawrence M. 21
Dayton, Elizabeth 92
D'Costa, Jean 18
De La Houssaye, Debbie 181 (see Wolf)
decreolization 83, 84
Delaware 10, 111, 124
deletion 56, 86, 89
Delta 7, 122
DeMarse, Sharon 17, 32, 62, 86, 93, 95
Denmark 6
descendants 10, 62, 64, 65, 67, 69, 72, 73, 175
Deutsch, Martin 104
development(s) 2, 4, 8, 11, 12, 21, 22, 26, 29, 34, 57, 66, 68, 72, 74, 75, 76, 77, 78, 85, 93, 101, 110, 112, 139, 142, 144, 145, 147, 148, 149, 152, 157, 159, 162, 168, 170, 171, 172, 177, 206
Di Paolo, Marianna 110, 111, 112, 113, 114
diachronic 8, 21, 22, 31, 33, 84, 85, 112
diachrony/history 17
dialect enclave 4, 141, 142, 151, 152
dialect geography 21, 82, 83, 84, 137, 138
dialect, regional 8, 13, 21, 26, 77, 78, 121, 122, 155, 157, 159, 180, 183, 200
dialect, social 3, 106, 123,
diaspora 86
Dictionary of American Regional English (*DARE*) see DARE
Dillard, J. L. 74, 83
dingbatter 154
diphthongization 4, 122, 138, 139
direct transmission 27, 29, 30
discourse style 190, 191, 195, 205, 206
divergence hypothesis 65, 85, 86, 104
done 29, 92, 117
   perfective 29, 33, 160, 161, 162
Dorrill, George T. 3, 19, 119, 123, 182, 190
double modals 10, 26, 29, 109, 110, 111, 112, 113, 114
double negatives 107
Douglas, Connie Woodruff 181
drawl 19, 26, 34, 64, 120, 123, 124, 203, 204
Dube, Nanjo 118, 144
Dubois, Sylvie 175, 177, 179
Dunlap, Howard G. 104
Dutch 11, 12, 49, 63

Early Modern English 2, 8, 20, 37, 38, 42, 44, 51, 53, 55, 60, 61, 62, 63
Eble, Connie 5, 173, 177
eighteenth century 11, 14, 58, 59, 60, 64, 66, 67, 69, 72, 74, 75, 76, 77, 78
Eliason, Norman E. 22
Elizabeth I, Queen 15, 20
ellick 154
Elliott, Colleen Morse 24, 25
Ellis, Michael 26
enclave dialect 4, 142, 143, 144, 145, 146, 147, 148, 149, 151, 152, 153, 154, 155, 157
enclave speech community 144
endangered dialect 141
Engelmann, Siegfried 104
England 9, 10, 14, 20, 27, 110, 126, 139, 147, 152
English Civil War 9
English core of Southern American English 2, 9
English, Early Modern 2, 8, 20, 37, 38, 42, 44, 51, 53, 55, 60, 61, 62, 63
English, Middle 38, 48, 49, 55, 57, 61, 62, 63, 110
English, Old 15, 44, 51, 61, 63
Entrikin, J. Nicholas 206
environment of Southern American English 13
Erikson, Frederick 191
Etter-Lewis, Gwendolyn 191
Eurasia 6
Europeans 12, 64, 65, 67, 69, 70, 72, 73, 174
European-American 68, 71, 72, 149, 191
evidentiality 194
exaptation 52, 61
ex-slaves' narratives 52, 57, 85

falsetto 64, 191
family metaphor for language 9
family resemblance 76
Fasold, Ralph W. 62, 84, 93, 94, 106
Feagin, Crawford 4, 42, 47, 49, 53, 54, 59, 64, 84, 92, 110, 111, 112, 122, 123, 124, 126, 129, 132, 139, 140, 168, 191
Fennell, Barbara A. 29, 110, 111
Fetscher, Margaret Elisabeth 104
field hands 11, 87
fieldwork 21, 82, 86, 88, 120, 121, 173, 175, 176, 177
Filppula, Markku 95
Finns 12
Fischer, David Hackett 9, 10, 69, 73, 75, 147

Fischer, Olga 47, 51, 55, 62, 63
fixin' to 34, 116
Florida 7, 104, 111, 115, 121, 128, 190
folk speech 83, 97
food terms 179
foreigner 154
forms of address/address forms 191, 192, 193, 194, 196
founder effect 142, 147, 149, 157
founder period 70, 72
founder population 69, 71, 73, 77
founder principle 66, 67, 77, 78
fourteenth century 15, 43
French 5, 8, 12, 15, 43, 45, 47, 49, 80, 174, 175, 176, 177, 178, 181, 183, 186, 187, 188
Fridland, Valerie 126, 127, 128, 129, 130, 131, 136, 137, 138, 139
front shift 130, 131, 135, 136, 139
Fuller, Janet M. 17, 32, 62, 86, 93, 95, 178
fusion 108

Gantt, Amy 144
Garber, Aubrey 114
gender 25, 116, 132, 177
general American 12, 148
genesis 18, 22
genitive 29, 51, 61
geographic 143
George, Donald 176
Georgia 7, 10, 11, 14, 53, 66, 68, 70, 83, 104, 107, 111, 115, 120, 121, 124, 126, 145, 193, 198
    Blue Ridge eastern highlands 7
    wire grass piney woods 7
Germanic languages 15
Germanic, West 8
German(s) 13, 80, 110, 174, 175
Germany 6, 69, 71
Giles, Howard 201
globalization 206
Goffman, Erving 114, 204
Gordon, Elizabeth 18, 34, (*see* Trudgill et al. 1998) 139
grammar 3, 8, 14, 19, 27, 29, 34, 84, 86, 87, 88, 92, 93, 94, 102, 117, 157, 177, 190, 191
Grammatical Investigation of Texas Speech (GRITS) 112, 113, 166
grammaticalization 3, 108, 109
Graves, Richard Layton 104
Great Rift Valley 6
Greek 8
Green, Elaine W. 144

greetings 109, 191, 192, 205
Grip the Rat 176
GRITS (Grammatical Investigation of Texas
    Speech) 112, 113, 166
grits 178
Gulf Coastal Southern 7
Gulf Plains Interior Southern 7
Gullah 11, 65, 66, 67, 68, 70, 72, 73, 76, 78, 84,
    110, 137, 145
Gumperz, John J. 191, 200

habitual *be* 92, 106, 118
had+past 93, 99, 105
Haley, Kenneth 207
Hall, Joan Houston 12, 15, 114
Hall, Joseph R. 141, 145, 154
Hall, Stuart 206
Halliday, M. A. K. 190, 205
Hancock, Ian F. 84
Harkers Island 156
Harris, Wendall A. 85, 93, 94
Hasan, Ruqaiya 190, 205
Hawaiian 12
Hawkins, Opal 85
Hazen, Kirk 118, 144
Heath, Shirley Brice 191, 198, 199
Hempl, George 124
Hendrickson, Robert 114
heredity 1, 2, 9
Herman, Lewis Helmar 106
Hill, Benjamin H. 197
Hill, Jane H. 206
historic present 47
historical isolation 142, 144
historical records 22
historical stages 21
history 3, 6, 7, 8, 10, 14, 16, 17, 18, 19, 20, 24,
    37, 38, 56, 58, 64, 65, 66, 67, 68, 70, 73,
    82, 84, 86, 120, 129, 144, 159, 166, 168,
    169, 171, 174, 191, 199, 200
Holloway, Charles E. 174
Holm, John A. 37, 52, 63, 83, 110
Holt, Grace Sims 156
Hopper, Paul J. 108
Horvath, Barbara 177, 179
house servants 11, 67
Houston, Susan 104
hypothesis 15, 27, 33, 83, 86, 180

identity 3, 5, 7, 8, 18, 21, 99, 101, 116, 131, 143,
    144, 157, 171, 173, 174, 177, 179, 180, 181,
    183, 192, 201, 206

idiolect 8, 39, 42, 60, 63
idiom(s) 112, 114
idiomatic expressions 34
immigrant(s) 9, 10, 13, 15, 69, 71, 74, 75, 77,
    87, 147, 175
inceptives 162
indentured servants 9, 11, 66, 67, 70, 71, 72, 73
India 71
indicative 38, 39, 42, 43, 45, 46, 47, 49, 50, 60,
    61, 62
indirectness 5, 191, 193, 200
Indo-European 6
inflectional typological structure 8
informants 21, 22, 40, 47, 53, 83, 92, 108, 121,
    122, 160, 161, 162, 164, 166, 177
Inland South 16, 126, 128, 129, 130, 131, 136
innovation 2, 4, 15, 21, 29, 30, 34, 53, 58, 86,
    122, 159, 168, 170
innovative 2, 4, 83, 84, 88, 92, 93, 99, 164, 166,
    171
interdental fricatives 151
interview(s) 3, 82, 83, 88, 111, 112, 115, 120,
    121, 123, 126, 129, 130, 131, 133, 137, 138,
    176, 177, 180, 192, 200, 201
intonation 191, 192, 195, 204
intragroup variation 99
intrusive /r/ 34, 121
invariant *be* 12, 38, 42, 60, 61, 85, 86, 93
Ireland 10, 20, 69, 71, 110
Irish 2, 10, 11, 20, 50, 63, 71, 73, 74, 75, 108,
    110, 117, 146, 147, 149, 152, 175
irregular verb(s) 94, 117, 146
isolating typological structure 8
isolation 62, 75, 142, 144
Italian(s) 13, 174, 175, 186
Italic 8
Ives, Sumner 26

/j/ retention 34
/j/ deletion 34
Jamaican Creole 18, 110
Jamestown, Virginia 9, 36
Japanese 13
Jefferson, Gail 205
Jensen, Arthur 104
Jews 13, 190
Jim Crow laws 65, 66, 67, 72
jimmy 155
Johnson, Ellen 172
Johnson, Guy 65
Johnstone, Barbara 5, 144, 173, 180, 189, 191,
    193, 195, 200, 202, 203, 204, 206

Jones-Jackson, Patricia 84
Joyner, Charles 67
juvember 154

Kallen, Jeffrey L. 147
Katz, Irwin 104
Kay Elemetrics Computerized Speech
      Laboratory 129, 130
Kentucky 7, 10, 111, 128
   eastern highlands 7
Kerswill, Paul 139
kin(folk) 155
Kochman, Thomas 191
koiné, koinéization 3, 64, 72, 74, 75, 76, 77, 78,
      139, 148
Kolker, Andrew 180
Krapp, George Philip 65
Kretzschmar, William 21, 76, 77, 83
Kroskrity, Paul V. 199
Krueger, Misty 160, 164
Krzyzek, Phyllis 181 (*see* Wolf)
Kulikoff, Allan 66, 67, 71
Kurath, Hans 20, 21, 65, 73, 77, 83, 105, 120,
      121, 124, 130, 146, 176
Kytö, Merja 62

laborers 67, 69, 70, 73
Labov, William 4, 38, 47, 60, 65, 78, 83, 84,
      85, 86, 92, 93, 94, 106, 111, 122, 126,
      127, 128, 129, 130, 131, 132, 136, 137,
      139, 140, 191, 199
laggin' 155
LAGS (Linguistic Atlas of the Gulf States)
      21, 92, 105, 108, 111, 112, 115, 116,
      121, 160, 162, 164, 166, 174, 176, 177,
      179, 183
Lalla, Barbara 18
Lambert, K. Sage 164
LAMSAS (Linguistic Atlas of the Middle and
      South Atlantic States) 21, 82, 83, 111, 120,
      121, 123, 160, 163
LANE (Linguistic Atlas of New England) 1,
      105, 120, 121
Lanehart, Sonja 19
language ideology 199
language variation and change 18, 146
langue 2, 6, 7
Larson, Susan 181
Lass, Roger 38, 39, 43, 48, 49, 50, 57, 58,
      61
Latin 8
Lavoisier, Antoine 14

Leas, Susan E. 176
legal papers 22
Lerud, Theodore K. (*see* Kretzschmar et al.
      1994) 21, 83,
letters 17, 31, 38, 43, 62, 75, 85, 95, 168
Levey, Kelli 189
Levine, Lawrence 171
Levinson, Stephen C. 190, 192
Lewis, Gillian (*see* Trudgill et al. 1998) 139
Lewis, John (*see* Labov et al. 1968) 1, 84, 93, 94,
      111
lexicon 154, 155, 157
lexis 8
liketa 2, 29, 53, 55, 60, 61, 165, 166
Linguistic Atlas of England (LAE) 1, 27
Linguistic Atlas of the Gulf States (LAGS) *see*
      LAGS
Linguistic Atlas of the Middle and South
      Atlantic States (LAMSAS) *see* LAMSAS
Linguistic Atlas of New England (LANE) *see*
      LANE
Lipski, John M. 109, 174
literary dialect 26, 27, 109
literature 26, 62, 66, 67, 68, 78, 86, 142, 196
Little, Greta D. 118
Locklear, Hayes Alan 154
Loman, Bengt 84
Louisiana French 5, 12, 175
Louisiana piney woods 7
Lower Mississippi River basin 7
Lower South 20, 117, 121, 122
Lumbee(s) 144, 147, 148, 149, 152, 153, 154

ma'am 192, 193
Mair, Andrew 206
Malin, Helen Rahm 181, 182, 184
manuscript sources 22, 63
Marckwardt, Albert H. 20,
Martin, Ed 177, 178
Martin, Jennifer 177, 178, 183
Martin, Stefan 55
Maryland 83, 111, 120, 127, 144
mash 155
Mason and Dixon line 19
Mason, Bobbie Anne 190
Mathews, Mitford McLeod 13
Matthews, Bunny 180
Maynor, Natalie 65, 85, 86, 92, 93, 95, 97, 104,
      107, 108, 109
McDavid, Raven I., Jr. 21, 83, 92, 117, 120,
      121, 123, 124, 130
McDavid, Virginia G. 57, 83, 92

McKern, Sharon 196
McLemore, Cynthia A. 195
McLeod-Porter, Delma 200, 201, 202
McMillan, James B. 1, 17, 118, 119, 172, 174, 191
McNair-Dupree, Lisa 65
McPherson, James M. 66
McWhiney, Grady 190, 196
Medeiros, Regina del Negri 26
meehonkey 154
Melançon, Megan 175
Melo, Cecil Ataide 26
Memphis 114, 126, 127, 128, 129, 130, 131, 136, 137, 138, 139
metaphor 2, 6, 7, 8, 9, 53, 154, 155, 200
metapopulation 76, 77, 78
methodology 69, 74, 76
metropole 69, 74, 76
metropolitanization 171
Meynard, Clifton 181 (*see* Wolf)
Mid-Atlantic 141, 142, 144, 146, 147, 149
Midland American English 2, 8
midwestern United States 146
might could 3, 10, 29, 106, 109, 110, 111, 112, 113, 114, 115, 118
Mille, Katherine 65
Miller, Michael 84, 123, 124
Milroy, Lesley 143
Mishoe, Margaret 110, 111, 113, 114, 149
Mississippi 7, 70, 85, 107, 111, 121, 122, 137, 164, 174, 175, 178, 179, 184, 185, 186, 188
Mississippi piney woods 7
Missouri 7, 111, 128
Missouri Ozarks western highlands 7
Mitchell, Margaret 189, 204
Mitchell, Steve 106
Mitchell-Kernan, Claudia 191
modal auxiliaries 3, 109, 110
modality 113
modals
    deontic 113
    double 3, 10, 26, 29, 109, 110, 111, 112, 113, 114
    dynamic 113
    epistemic 113
    multiple 3, 93, 109, 112
    triple 110
mommuck 155
monophthongization 71, 130, 139, 179
monophthongization of /ay/ 26, 34, 71, 123, 128, 130, 168, 178, 200, 204

Montgomery, Michael [B.] 1, 3, 5, 9, 10, 15, 16, 17, 18, 22, 26, 27, 29, 30, 31, 32, 33, 50, 56, 62, 63, 64, 74, 75, 76, 77, 78, 82, 83, 84, 86, 93, 95, 106, 108, 109, 110, 111, 112, 113, 114, 116, 118, 119, 120, 121, 123, 124, 128, 141, 142, 145, 147, 149, 154, 159, 172, 173, 174, 191, 206
mood 40, 43, 44, 61, 62
Moore, Francis 13
Morgan, John T. 197
morphology 16, 25, 27, 29, 34, 52, 85, 118, 123
Morrison, Estelle Rees 109
mountain(s) 20, 69, 107, 122, 143, 144, 149, 154, 190, 199
mountainous areas 20, 106
Moxley, Louise Armstrong 24, 25
Mufwene, Salikoko S. 2, 11, 19, 52, 55, 63, 64, 65, 66, 67, 68, 69, 71, 72, 75, 76, 77, 78, 79, 81, 84, 86, 142, 147
mulatto(es) 66, 67
multiple modals 3, 93, 109, 112
Mustanoja, Tauno F. 44, 59
Myhill, John 85, 92, 93, 94, 98

Nagle, Stephen J. 29, 110
narrative(s) 5, 36, 39, 40, 47, 52, 57, 85, 105, 191, 198, 199
narratives, ex-slaves' 52, 57, 85
negative concord 146
Negroes 13
Netherlands 6, 175
Nevalainen, Terttu 38, 43, 62
New England 69, 72, 73, 77, 78, 120, 123, 146
New Orleans 5, 137, 169, 175, 176, 177, 179, 180, 181, 182, 185, 186, 187, 188, 192
    glossary 182, 183, 184, 185, 186, 187, 188
    identity 180, 181
    phonology 180, 182
    websites 182
    Yatspeak 181, 182
New South(ern) 34
New World 1, 12, 36, 51, 68, 71, 110
New York 10, 130, 180, 182
Newfoundland vernacular English 78
Nichols, Johanna 194
Nichols, Patricia 84, 194
Niedzielski, Nancy 137
nineteenth century 2, 3, 4, 14, 18, 21, 22, 25, 26, 31, 32, 33, 34, 48, 53, 64, 65, 66, 67, 68, 70, 72, 75, 78, 83, 85, 93, 95, 152, 159, 160, 164, 166, 168, 169, 170, 175, 190, 196
Nix, Ruth 84

non-rhoticism 64, 72
non-standard 11, 15, 18, 25, 29, 31, 65, 71, 73, 80
norms 99, 102, 124, 131, 143
Norse 8
North Carolina 4, 15, 20, 22, 83, 104, 107, 120, 122, 126, 127, 128, 138, 140, 144, 148, 151, 152, 154, 156
northern concord rule 1, 31
NP/PRO constraint 50, 95, 97, 101
Nunnally, Thomas 17, 118

O'Cain, Raymond K. 84, 123
Ocracoke 154, 155
offglides 163, 164, 168
Ogura, Mieko 62
Old French 15
Old South 1, 24, 34
on the swamp 154
oratorical style 191, 197, 198
oratory 5, 190, 191, 196, 197, 198
ordering of back shift 136
ordering of front shift 136
origins of Southern American English 1, 6, 8, 9, 13, 19, 33, 159
Orr, Elinor 104
Orton, Harold 27, 149
ought 110, 194
oughta 110, 182
Outer Banks 4, 20, 122, 126, 144, 149, 151, 152, 154, 155, 156, 158
over the left 156
overseers 18, 22, 30, 31, 33, 66, 85, 95, 168

Palmer, Frank Robert 113
Paparone, Sharon C. 86
parole 2, 7
Patton, Douglas W. K. 107
Payne, Arvilla 138
Pederson, Lee 7, 17, 21, 57, 108, 115, 116, 121, 164
peeler 155
pen/pin merger 19, 22, 26, 34, 123, 124, 160
Pennsylvania 10, 111, 114, 121, 122, 124, 130
Pepsi-Cola 15
perception 35, 59, 60, 122, 142, 173, 180
Percy, Carol 62
perfective *be* 92, 146, 147
perfective *done* 29, 33, 160, 161, 162
performance 173, 180, 197, 204
peripheral vowels 128, 135
Perkins, Edwin J. 66, 67

Perkins, T. W. 109
person/number 85, 95, 97, 98
    first 92, 102
    second 19, 92, 107, 109, 149
    third 15, 32, 37, 42, 43, 47, 48, 49, 51, 60, 61, 62, 85, 92, 94, 95, 102, 110, 117, 147
Philip, Lisbeth 181 (*see* Wolf)
phonological features 3, 4, 27, 120, 153, 168, 177, 200
Phonological Survey of Texas (PST) 162, 166
phonology 3, 4, 8, 16, 27, 34, 85, 119, 120, 121, 122, 123, 124, 125, 137, 139, 157, 161, 176, 191, 206
Picone, Michael D. 175
Piedmont 7, 20, 69, 121, 198
Piedmont Interior Southern 7
pin/pen merger 19, 26, 34, 123, 160
Pitts, Walter 93
Pittsburgh 107
plantation 11, 14, 18, 20, 22, 30, 31, 34, 36, 62, 65, 66, 67, 69, 70, 73, 83, 87, 170, 199, 204
PLOTNIK 129, 140
plural verbal *-s* 48, 92, 166
Polanyi, Livia 191
politeness 5, 109, 114, 190, 191, 192, 193, 194, 195, 196, 205
Polynesian 12
Poplack, Shana 62, 65, 86, 93, 94, 141
Portuguese 13, 26
possessive 51, 61, 109
    -n 118
    -s 51, 61, 109, 118
    double-marked 51, 61
    zero 37, 52, 53, 60, 61, 118
    his and *her* 61
postvocalic /r/ 77, 85, 121, 122, 123, 152, 164, 200
Powesland, Peter F. 201
prescriptive grammarians 58
prestige forms 1, 131
Preston, Dennis R. 17, 107, 173
preterits 57, 58, 60, 61, 92, 165, 166
    come 165, 166
    dove 166
Priestley, Joseph 14
Primer, Sylvester 130
principle of dialect exclusion 157
principle of generalization 146, 157
principle of localized identity 157
principle of regionalization 157
principle of regularization 146, 157
principle of selective language change 147, 157

principle of social marginalization 146, 157
principle of vernacular dialect congruity 146,
    157
Prioli, Carmine 156
pronoun(s) 15, 32, 50, 95, 107, 118, 147, 149,
    178
    first 204
    plural 29, 107
    relative 55, 56, 60, 61, 92, 118
    second 19, 26, 29, 34, 107, 109, 149
    singular 107
    third 32, 50, 51
pronoun reference system 107
pronunciation 12, 15, 19, 25, 26, 27, 120, 121,
    122, 124, 151, 152, 163, 164, 166, 174, 177,
    178, 179, 180, 181, 182, 207
Proto-Germanic 6, 8
Proto-Human 6
Proto-Indo-European 6
proximity constraint 50, 74, 75
PST (Phonological Survey of Texas) 162,
    166
Puritan Commonwealth 9

quamish 155
questionnaire(s) 22, 24, 120, 122, 160, 162, 172,
    181, 192

/r/ 128
/r/-constriction 164
r-ful 164
r-lessness 26, 34, 64, 152, 200
Rafal, Christine Théberge 86, 105
Rampton, Ben 203, 205, 206
Randolph, Vance 111
Raumolin-Brunberg, Helena 38, 43, 51, 62
Rawick, George P. 85, 104
Read, William A. 120
real time 88, 99, 102
Reconstruction 21, 34
Red River basin 7
Reed, Dale Volberg 106
Reed, John Shelton 106
Reed, Judy 161, 162, 164, 172
regularized past tense 146, 148
Reinecke, George 180, 181
Reissman, Catherine Kohler 191
relative pronouns 55, 56, 60, 61, 92, 118
relic areas 122
representative government 1
retention(s) 18, 20, 21, 26, 34, 151
retentionist assumption 21

retentionist hypothesis 27
rice 11, 65, 66, 67, 68, 73, 179, 182, 183, 184,
    185, 186
Richardson, Gina 109
Rickford, John R. 18, 60, 65, 79, 83, 84, 86, 93,
    94, 104, 105, 110, 152
Rickford, Russell J. 65, 79, 104
Rissanen, Matti 45, 47, 51, 55, 59, 62
Robins, Clarence (*see* Labov et al. 1968) 1, 84,
    93, 94, 111
Romaine, Suzanne 12
Ross, Garry 53, 86, 172
Ross, Stephen M. 190, 196, 197, 198
Rubrecht, August 176
rule generalization 146
rural 3, 9, 19, 34, 42, 47, 60, 62, 65, 82, 87, 92,
    95, 98, 99, 100, 101, 107, 116, 117, 131,
    132, 133, 135, 136, 138, 139, 146, 148, 154,
    159, 170, 171, 172, 200, 202
Russian(s) 13, 154
Russian rat 154
Russo, Michael F. 181
Rydén, M. 147

-*s* verb ending 26, 32, 34, 39, 42, 43, 44, 46, 47,
    48, 49, 50, 51, 61, 62, 85, 92, 93, 94, 95,
    97, 98, 99, 100, 101, 102, 104, 117, 159,
    165, 166
Sabban, Annette 147
Sabino, Robin 17, 118
Sack, Robert D. 206
Sacks, Harvey 205
SAE (Southern American English) 82, 119,
    120, 121, 122, 123, 124, 159, 160, 161, 162,
    164, 166, 168, 169, 170, 171, 172
Sand, Lori 103, 166, 172
Sanderson, Stewart 149
Sankoff, David 86, 141
Scandinavians 13
Schegloff, Emanuel A. 205
Schendl, Herbert 48
Schieffelin, Bambi B. 199
Schiffrin, Deborah 85, 190, 205
Schilling-Estes, Natalie 3, 38, 47, 52, 53, 55, 58,
    59, 107, 117, 127, 138, 141, 142, 143, 144,
    146, 148, 154, 155, 156, 158
Schneider, Edgar W. 2, 4, 17, 18, 20, 22, 27, 29,
    30, 31, 33, 43, 52, 55, 57, 59, 62, 65, 86,
    95, 109, 159, 168
Schremp, Mary Bemi 163, 164
Schweppe, Jacob 14
Scotland 10, 20, 29, 30, 110

Scots 3, 10, 32, 51, 62, 110, 117, 147
Scots-Irish 2, 10, 11, 20, 50, 63, 75, 108, 110,
     117, 147, 149
Scots-Irish stratum of Southern American
     English 2, 10
Scott, Ann Martin 177
Scottish 10, 29, 110
Scottish English 110, 149
second-person pronoun (*see* pronoun, second)
segregation 3, 62, 64, 65, 66, 67, 68, 69, 70, 72,
     73, 78
Sellers, Jason 148
semantic inversion 156
seventeenth century 14, 38, 43, 44, 52, 59, 67,
     68, 70, 71, 147, 155
Shakespeare 2, 17, 20, 53, 54, 55
Shakespearean English 159
Shilling, Alison 110
Shores, David L. 149, 154, 156, 158
Simpkins, Karen L. 192
Singler, John Victor 52, 92, 93
singular *-th* 42, 43, 44, 47, 48, 50, 51, 61, 62
sir 192, 193, 196
sixteenth century 15, 38, 48, 55
slave(s) 9, 11, 19, 24, 25, 31, 52, 56, 57, 63, 66,
     67, 69, 70, 72, 73, 85, 92, 95, 98, 109, 174,
     200, 204
slave traders 11
slavery 11, 19, 66, 69, 200, 204
Slavs 13
Sledd, James 124, 138,
small town 138, 139, 170, 202
Smith Island 148, 154, 156
Smith, Clyde 26, 86
Smith, Jennifer 86
Smith, M. A. Sharwood 113
Smoky Mountains 20, 144, 149, 154
social factors 20, 106, 116
     socioeconomic 65, 66, 68, 70, 75, 84, 106,
          123, 176
     sociohistorical 2, 3, 64, 68, 78, 83, 87, 102,
          177
     sociospatial 4, 143, 146
     sociolinguistic principle(s) 4, 145, 146
SOD (Survey of Oklahoma Dialects) 1, 162, 164
soft drinks 14, 15
Sommer, Elizabeth 62
Sothern, James M. 177, 178, 183
sound change(s) 21, 85, 128
South Carolina 11, 66, 67, 68, 70, 72, 82, 83,
     107, 111, 120, 121, 123, 126, 129, 130, 140,
     145, 149, 178

South Midland 7, 16, 121, 123
southern
     discourse 191, 203, 204, 205, 206
     drawl 19, 26, 64, 120, 123, 124, 203, 204
     vernacular 2, 93
Southern American English (SAE) 1, 2, 6, 7, 8,
     9, 10, 11, 13, 15, 82, 110, 117, 118, 119,
     159, 174
southern belle 204
Southern Focus Poll 107, 108
Southern Plantation Overseers' Corpus
     (SPOC) 1, 30, 31, 32, 33
Southern Shift 4, 126, 128, 130, 131, 168
Southern White Vernacular English (SWVE) 3,
     42, 82
Southerners 5, 15, 21, 26, 42, 64, 68, 73, 106,
     107, 108, 109, 110, 112, 113, 114, 129, 168,
     169, 170, 172, 174, 189, 190, 191, 192, 193,
     196, 199, 200, 202, 204, 205, 206
     characterizations of 189, 190
Spaniards 13
Spanish 107, 174
Spears, Arthur K. 70
Spears, James E. 192
speech act(s) 157, 190
speech community 4, 26, 85, 101, 141, 144, 158,
     173
Spencer, Nancy 109
SPOC / Southern Plantation Overseers'
     Corpus 1, 30, 31, 32, 33
sprag 155
Springville, TX 87, 88, 89, 92, 93, 94, 95, 98,
     99, 100, 101, 102, 105
status 67, 71, 72, 98, 115, 116, 137, 141, 143,
     146, 151, 152, 154, 157, 175
Steeg, Clarence L. Ver 66
Stein, Dieter 62
Steiner, Richard 85, 126, 128, 137
stereotype(s) 18, 20, 141, 160, 168, 174, 189,
     205
Stevens, Liz 203
Stewart, William 83
stigma 18, 111, 112
strippin' hole 155
style 5, 38, 75, 93, 94, 123, 137, 171, 189, 190,
     191, 192, 195, 196, 197, 198, 199, 200, 201,
     204, 205, 206, 207
subject–type constraint 1, 74
subject–verb concord 26, 74, 75, 76
subjunctive 38, 40, 42, 43, 44, 46, 47, 48, 60, 61,
     62
subvarieties of Southern American English 7, 8

Summerlin, Nan Jo Corbitt 104
Survey of English Dialects (SED) 27
Survey of Oklahoma Dialects (SOD) 1, 162, 164
Sutcliffe, David 81
swamp Indian 154
Swiss 13
SWVE (Southern White Vernacular English) 3,
    42, 43, 47, 59, 60, 62, 82, 84, 86, 87, 88,
    89, 92, 93, 95, 102, 103, 105
syllabic /r/ 164, 166
Synchronic 8, 63, 84
syntactic features 106, 117
syntax 5, 16, 25, 55, 85, 113, 118, 123, 193, 194

Taggert, Chuck 180, 182
Tagliamonte, Sali 62, 65, 86, 93, 94, 95, 141,
    147
talking backwards 156
Tangier Island 154, 156
Tannen, Deborah 190
target language 69, 71
Tarheel Talk 22
Tate, Thad W. 67, 71
Telsur 127, 129, 130, 137
Tennessee 7, 10, 22, 24, 70, 109, 111, 116, 121,
    122, 128, 129, 130, 160, 162, 168, 172,
    195
  central highlands 7
  Civil War Veterans' Questionnaires 22, 24,
    160, 162, 172
  eastern highlands 7
Texas 3, 20, 58, 84, 85, 87, 111, 112, 115, 122,
    126, 127, 128, 129, 138, 139, 162, 166, 168,
    172, 189, 191, 195, 196, 199, 200, 201, 202,
    204, 206
  east 111, 122, 201
  Inland 128
  pine flats 7
Thernstrom, Stephen 10
they-constraint 48, 50, 51, 60
third person
  singular 32, 110
  plural 32, 51
  zero 1, 61
  -*s* (*see* -*s* verb ending)
  -*th* 42, 43, 44, 47, 48, 49, 50, 51, 61, 62
Thomas, Erik [R.] 65, 81, 86, 104, 127, 128,
    129, 138, 139, 144, 148, 152, 168
Thomas, Hugh 66, 72
Tillery, Jan 4, 53, 103, 107, 108, 109, 111, 159,
    166, 172
Tindall, George B. 204

Titon, Jeff Todd 198
tobacco 9, 11, 14, 20, 65, 66, 67, 69, 70, 72, 73
token 155
token(s) 40, 99, 130, 157, 164
Toole, John Kennedy 181
topographical term 13
Torbert, Benjamin 152
Traditional Southern 34, 195
Traugott, Elizabeth Closs 108, 110
tree metaphor for language 8, 9
Trudgill, Peter 131, 139, 146, 148
Turner, Lorenzo Dow 67
twentieth century 4, 19, 22, 24, 34, 65, 93, 95,
    121, 166, 170, 171, 175, 176

Ulster 10, 11, 51, 62, 110, 147
Ulster Scots/Scots-Irish 51, 62, 110, 147
Uncle Remus Stories 27
United Kingdom 68, 69
upper class (*see* class, upper)
upper-class speakers 138
Upper South 10, 20, 75, 121
urban 34, 47, 65, 84, 86, 87, 94, 95, 98, 99, 100,
    101, 116, 121, 122, 129, 130, 131, 132, 133,
    135, 136, 139, 169, 170, 172, 175, 191, 202
urbanization 4, 19, 34, 159, 169, 170, 171
Urheimat 6

Valdman, Albert 175
Vaughn-Cooke, Faye 86
verbal -*s* (*see* -*s* verb ending)
vernacular(s) 2, 3, 11, 18, 22, 60, 64, 65, 67, 68,
    70, 71, 72, 73, 76, 77, 78, 82, 83, 84, 85,
    86, 87, 88, 92, 93, 94, 101, 102, 103, 117,
    118, 141, 146, 148, 149, 151, 158, 181,
    201
veteran(s) 1, 22, 24, 25, 160, 162, 172
Viereck, Wolfgang 66
Virgets, Ronnie 180, 181
Virginia 9, 10, 12, 20, 36, 41, 42, 43, 46, 52, 53,
    58, 66, 70, 72, 83, 111, 117, 120, 121, 128,
    144, 168, 198
Virginia colony 9, 10, 36, 37
Virginia eastern highlands 7
Visser, F. Th. 47, 110
vittles 155
vocabulary 8, 10, 12, 15, 19, 25, 27, 120, 137,
    154, 155, 174, 179, 180, 181, 182, 191
Von Schneidemesser, Luanne 179
vowel shifts/shifting 4, 78, 124, 126, 127, 128,
    129, 130, 131, 136, 137, 138, 139
Vowles, Guy R. 109

Waletzky, Joshua 199
Wang, William S-Y. 62
Ward, Martha 180
Wareing, John 62
Weldon, Tracey 140
Wells, John 27
Wentworth, Harold 110, 114
weren't regularization 148, 149
West African creole 2, 37
West Indian creole(s) 1, 68
Widdowson, John 149
Wikle, Tom 103, 107, 108, 109, 166, 172
will/would deletion 86
Williams, Ann 139
Wilson, George P. 111
Wilson, Martha Lynn 181
Wimsatt, William C. 77
Winford, Donald 62
Wise, Claude Merton 176, 178
Wolf, George 181
Wolfram, Walt 3, 4, 38, 47, 52, 53, 55, 58, 59,
   83, 84, 86, 93, 104, 106, 107, 111, 117, 118,
   127, 138, 141, 142, 143, 144, 146, 147, 148,
   149, 152, 154, 155, 157, 158, 180
Wolfson, Nessa 85
women 37, 44, 46, 53, 66, 106, 107, 109, 111,
   115, 129, 130, 131, 133, 135, 136, 190,
   191, 193, 195, 198, 199, 200, 204, 205

Wood, Peter H. 66, 67, 72
Woolard, Kathryn A. 199
working-class speakers (*see* class, working)
World War II 87, 88, 89, 93, 102, 105, 121,
   160, 162, 163, 164, 166, 168, 170, 172,
   176
Wright, Joseph 110
Wright, Laura 2, 29, 36, 37, 40, 43, 44, 47, 48,
   50, 61, 62

y'all 19, 26, 29, 34, 107, 108, 109, 149, 200, 202,
   203
yall 3, 106, 107, 108, 109, 115, 118, 166
yall's 109
Yaeger [-Dror], Malcah 126, 128, 137
Yat 180, 181, 182
Yazoo River basin 7
Yeah You Rite 180, 181
you guys 107, 108
you(uns) 107, 108
you-all 107, 108, 109
young 'uns 155
yourn 118, 149
youse 29, 107

Zeigler, Mary 115
zero copula 83, 92
zero plural 25